Zones of Proletarian Development

Mastaneh Shah-Shuja

OPENMUTE

London, 2008

Published, POD (print on demand) design and production by
OpenMute <openmute.org>, Simon Worthington and Laura Oldenbourg

ISBN: 978-1-906496-06-7 pbk

1. Political Science-History & Theory - Radical Thought
2. Psychology-Social Psychology
3. Social Science-Sociology - Social Theory

Mastaneh Shah-Shuja welcomes comments and criticisms.
You can contact her at m.shahshuja@yahoo.com

Printed by Lightning Source UK Ltd.

Contents

Introduction

'Capitalism is dying and if it has its way,
it will take all of us down with it'.

Introduction

A beginning is the time for taking the most delicate care that the balances are correct. This every sister of the Bene Gesserit knows.

- Frank Herbert, *Dune*, 1968: 13.

Of all writings I love only that which is written with blood ... It is not an easy thing to understand unfamiliar blood: I hate the reading idler.

-Friedrich Nietzsche, *Thus Spoke Zarathustra*, 1883/1969: 67

C apitalism is dying and if it has its way, it will take all of us down with it. Paraphrasing the *Toad of Nazareth*[1] it declares with all the venom its decaying corpse can muster, 'Vengeance is mine; I will repay, saith [Capital]' (Jesus, *The Bible*, circa 30 A.D., The Epistle of Paul to the Romans, xii, 19).

My book is a *study-extension* of the class struggle aimed at the abolition of the capitalist Leviathan through a worldwide proletarian social revolution. Bourgeois social sciences study in order to control and regulate or at best to 'explain'. They simu-

---

1   The phrase is borrowed from one of the most famous graffiti-slogans of the May 1968 Paris events, 'Down with the Toad of Nazareth', which jostled for attention on the walls of Paris with other expressions of atheism such as, 'How can you think freely in the shadow of a chapel?' and the unforgettable 'We want a place to piss, not a place to pray' (Knabb, 1999).

late objectivity by distancing themselves from the subject of study. Study-extension, by contrast, sets itself the task of extending and intensifying the class struggle through reflecting upon past and present conflict and proposing an alternative course of action. The researcher in this case is herself the subject of study since she is not apart from the social movement under investigation. Study-extension resurrects *critique* as practical activity. Critique was posited by Left-Hegelians, Marx and Karl Korsch in contradistinction to mere *criticism*.[2] Critique undermines capitalism by encouraging a total negation of all contemporary social relations whereas criticism, by concentrating on a few superficial symptoms of capitalism, ends up strengthening it in the long term.

My study-extension is born out of a mixture of hatred and hope. Hatred for the ruling classes of the world (whether Bush, Blair, Hussein, Hitler, Lenin, Khomeini, Ahmadi-Nezhad, Castro, Chavez, Annan, Gandhi, Mandela or their numerous faceless lackeys) and hope that a world without capital and capitalists is (more than ever) possible. In reformulating a *praxis* capable of self-reflexively overcoming class society, I have had few accomplices to help me along the way. The usual suspects come to mind: Mazdak, Karl Marx, Karl Korsch, Anton Pannekoek, Paul Mattick, Sylvia Pankhurst, Guy Debord, Paul Cardan, Rosa Luxemburg, Leopoldina Fortunati, Loren Goldner, John Holloway and Harry Cleaver.

However, the sad truth is that contemporary literature regarding proletarian movements is a poor shadow of previous illustrious periods of struggle. An exhaustive trawl through the social sciences yields precious few useful conceptual handles on the complex problems facing an emergent 'anti-capitalist movement'. Some of the better ones deserve a mention: in the field of social psychology (Billig, 1978; Drury and Reicher, 1999; Gergen and Gergen, 1997; Reicher, 2001; Drury, Reicher and Stott, 2003), in critical psychology (Parker, 2007), in social movement studies (Rosenfeld, 1997; Sellman, 1999), in sociology (Useem, 1985; Tilly, 2004), in political philosophy (Holloway, 2002; Hardt and Negri, 2004), in history (Perlman, 1983; Arshinov, 1987; Linebaugh, 1991; Tompsett, 2000; Rediker, 2004), in race and border studies (Mitropoulos, 2006), in anthropology (Taussig, 1980; Graeber, 2005), in politics (Aufheben, 2004; Goldner, 2005; Mentinis, 2006), in political economy (Caffentzis and Federici, 1982; Cleaver, 2000; Harvie, 2005) and in cultural studies (Home, 1988; Negrin, 1993; Slater, 2001, Shukaitis and Graeber, 2007).

The fact that these few gems are hidden beneath layers of antiquated cobweb makes the quest even more frustrating. It seems atavistic ideas masquerading in new postmodern linguistic attire (cf. Baudrillard, 1994; Žižek, 2001), modernist dogmas camouflaged as *radical common sense* (cf. Callinicos, 1990), rickety academic banalities (cf. Chomsky, 1994) and the temper tantrums of the spoiled children of the bour-

---

2   Korsch (1971: 65) writes, '*Critique* is to be understood not in a merely idealistic sense but as a materialistic critique'. It is to go to the root of the problem by demonstrating the objective and subjective dimensions of *being* and *becoming*.

geoisie (cf. Klein, 2002) are all jostling for the right to be the storytellers of the class struggle. The act of storytelling confers power on the storyteller, after all (Ellyatt, 2002; Parker, 2005). Storytelling gradually becomes a form of ownership of the social movement which allows the owner to dismiss criticism (Dowling, 2005: 205).

And so, this is *my* story of the class struggle- a tale that requires terminological precision and clarity. It is, for example, essential to posit a working definition of 'class' before I can discuss class struggle. I am here heavily indebted to a definition put forward by Melancholic Troglodytes (2003a). A shortened version follows,

> Since class is, amongst other things, a dialectical relationship between a thing and a process, it stands to reason that both qualitative and quantitative methods of research should be employed for its understanding ... class is both a result of capitalism and a tool for understanding and changing the present state of affairs- a *tool-and-result* ... Class is best perceived as a concept with three 'levels': At the most *abstract*, it is a set of social relations. At the *intermediary* level, class finds an institutional expression ... at the *concrete* level class represents the real flesh and bone individuals who make up and reproduce the abstract social relations ... To complicate matters each of these three levels (abstract, intermediary, concrete) has both an *objective* and a *subjective* aspect to it ... These three levels and their objective-subjective dimensions must be followed through the *production-circulation-reproduction* cycle in order for both the exploitative and power relations involved to be exposed (Melancholic Troglodytes, 2003a: 196).

Having become increasingly disenchanted with the current state of affairs in the abovementioned disciplines as well as the lack of innovation within the proletarian *underground* press, I felt compelled to seek alternative ways of study-extending the class struggle.

Vygotsky, Vološinov, Bakhtin and proponents of Activity Theory may seem an odd place to begin the reconstruction of an alternative praxis. After all, it could be justifiably argued that none of these individuals (or schools of thought) warrants the designation, 'revolutionary'. Vygotsky's politics could be perceived as an off-shoot of Leninism and he was certainly unaware of the capitalist nature of the USSR[3.] Vološinov's contribution has been minimal and posited at an unnecessarily high level of abstraction. Bakhtin was at the end, perhaps, no more than a liberal mystic. Leontiev rarely transcended the limitations of Leninist-Stalinism and contemporary Activity Theory seems to be obsessed with making capitalist structures more efficient

---

3   The suppression of Vygotsky's thought during the reign of Stalin, his more nuanced understanding of the limitations of the USSR compared to some of his Stalinist contemporaries, as well as superficial similarities between his concepts and Trotsky's notion of 'uneven development' and 'permanent revolution' suggest he was fortunate to die of tuberculosis when he did. Had he survived his disease, all Vygotsky had to look forward to would have been a show trial. Worse still he could have survived the regime by making compromises as did a number of his colleagues. (On the capitalist nature of the USSR the best reference remains Fernandez, 1997).

whilst adapting individuals to capitalist domination (cf. Engeström, 1995; Holzman, 2001; Hong and Engeström, 2004).

And yet the amalgamation of these writers, once encased in a sound historical materialist epistemology, transmutes into an approach commensurate with the aim of turning the world upside down. Why should this be? Well, for one thing, Vygotsky, Vološinov, Bakhtin and Activity Theorists seem to intuitively cover up each others' shortcomings, as if embarrassed by their fellow-travellers' lack of insight into certain fields of investigation. Thus Vygotsky covers up for Bakhtin's lack of knowledge regarding development and learning; Bakhtin returns the compliment in relation to Vygotsky's rather anaemic conceptualisation of the *social*; and contemporary Activity Theorists cement both Vygotsky and Bakhtin by providing a framework of analysis for various political and economic imperatives. Moreover, all these approaches have a richness about their textual and conceptual tool-making kits which makes them productive theory-generators across a multiplicity of disciplines.

As I progressed with my study, it became abundantly clear that most thinkers (be they bourgeois or petty-bourgeois) are not enamoured of proletarian crowds. Ironically this is also true of many *Leftist* ideologues (i.e., a derogatory term used to describe those occupying *the extreme left wing of capital*). Le Bon (1895) may represent a 'right-wing' thinker hateful of crowds[4] and the positivist Comte may have 'regarded revolutionary periods of society as analogous to disease in the human body' (Korsch, 1971: 33), but Durkheim's views on the susceptibility of crowds to 'collective effervescence' have arguably been just as important in delegitimising rioting from a 'left-wing' perspective (Mac Ginty, 2004: 860).

The many-headed hydra and its numerous detractors!

Thinkers described as 'folksy populists' such as Mark Twain were no better. Twain used his wicked sense of humour at the expense of his own country-folk, 'Consider the intelligence of the average American. Then consider the fact that half of them

---

4   Gustave Le Bon's work influenced the likes of Goebbels, Mussolini and Hitler. Le Bon reduced crowd behaviour to intra-individual events and ignored social conflict (Reicher and Potter, 1985: 168). The French elite of his period were suffering a loss of confidence following defeat in the Franco-Prussian war (1870-1871) and the Paris Commune (1871) and the rise of working class unrest. This was the historical context of Le Bon's disparaging of crowds.

aren't even that smart' (Twain quoted in Graeber, 2005: 5).

Proletarian crowds perched forever on the threshold of mobility and excitability (from where the term *mob* originates), have always terrified the authorities. This is as true of those in power as aspirants to the throne. The Roman Empire mobilised itself against the Spartacus rebellion (73-71 B.C.), whilst the Islamic Empire had to struggle against the Zott (820-833 A.D.) and the Zanj (868-883 A.D.). The Persian Empire found in the Mazdakis (5th century A.D. revolutionaries) a formidable adversary and the British Empire had almost as much trouble domesticating internal opponents such as Diggers and Ranters (17th century A.D.) as it faced in the colonies (Hill, 1972).[5] In *The Many-Headed Hydra*, Linebaugh and Rediker narrate how 'mobs' in America initiated an unprecedented imperial crisis in the 18th century,

> Mobs were crucial to the effective protests against the Stamp Act, the Townshend Revenue Act, the increased power of the British customs service, the Quartering Act, the Tea Act, the 'Intolerable Acts', and therefore in the revolutionary rupture itself (Linebaugh and Rediker, 2001: 137).

What distinguished these American events was that, perhaps, for the first time in modern times the practical activity of the maritime working class was translated into political discourse. The movement's main theoretician was a Sam Adams. Adams used the Knowles Riot to formulate a new 'ideology of resistance, in which the natural rights of man were used for the first time to justify mob activity'[6] (Linebaugh and Rediker, 1993: 135). In more recent times, we have witnessed mechanisms of recuperation, channelling, containment, surveillance and intimidation in order to keep the mob, and its articulators, at bay. As a corollary to oppression, the bourgeoisie has set its lackeys the task of mystifying crowd behaviour in order to ensure its own continued *hegemony*. Hegemony is not mere domination or leadership as understood by Mao Tse-Tung and Lenin but more commonly used in its Gramscian sense. Initially Gramsci used

---

5 The *Zott* were Indians enslaved by the Islamic Empire and brought to the marshlands of the Tigris to work the land (Kenrick, 2004: 21). The *Zanj* were also slaves (probably from Zanzibar) who were joined by Iranians, Turks, and Slavs in a seminal struggle against the Islamic Empire (Popovic, 1999; Melancholic Troglodytes, 2002). The Mazdakis are known as the first 'successful' communist movement in the world since they managed to abolish private property for a while before the ruling classes of the day rallied against them, massacring thousands as punishment (Perlman, 1983). The Diggers and Ranters were, respectively, the 'Marxist' and 'Anarchist' wings of the English communist movement in the 17th century.

6 Today we would find this terminology arcane. 'Rights' have been exposed as either illusory or exchangeable commodities miserly sold to 'citizens' by an increasingly draconian state that unilaterally rewrites the 'social contract' according to its whims (Marx, 1984). Perhaps Howard Zinn's (2003: 60) take on Samuel Adams is more accurate than Linebaugh's. Zinn believes individuals like Samuel Adams were members of the Boston ruling class who were 'excluded from the ruling circles close to England'. Adams and others called the 'mob' into action and 'shaped its behaviour' (Zinn, 2003: 60). His sympathy for mobs therefore had definite limits as future events demonstrated.

the word to refer to the system of alliances which the working class must create to overthrow the bourgeois state and to serve as the social basis of the workers' state ... [but later] he goes beyond this use of term ... to apply it to the way the bourgeoisie establishes and maintains its rule (Bottomore *et al.*, 1988: 201).

The bourgeoisie goes beyond the use of mere organised force and exerts a moral and intellectual leadership in order to achieve a mixture of coercion and consent to ensure hegemony. It operates by shaping 'the cognitive and affective structures through which people perceive and evaluate reality ...' (Mentinis, 2006: 32). Here is one such early flunky, Edward Alsworth Ross, pontificating most scholarly about a subject that clearly puts the fear of Jesus into his pretty little civilised soul,

> There is no question that, taken herdwise, people are less sane and sensible than they are dispersed ... In the fugitive, structureless crowd there can be no debate ... The crowd self is *credulous* ... the crowd self is *irrational* ... the crowd self shows *simplicity*. Like children and savages, it cannot embrace in a single judgment several factors and details ... Finally, the crowd self is immoral ... it is safe to conclude that amorphous, heterogeneous gatherings are morally and intellectually below the average of their members (Ross, 1919: 47).

My book aims to oppose such drivel by demonstrating that *radical* proletarian crowds could be an ideal 'zone of proximal development' (i.e., dialectical learning zone) for participants. Proletarian crowds (and examples would include carnivals, May Day celebrations, riots, meetings, demonstrations and strikes) that manage to overcome the bourgeois within themselves, succeed in creating an autonomous zone where 'the free development of each is the condition for the free development of all' (Marx, 1847-48/1986: 105).

My approach assumes a connected, unitary subject matter that is temporarily separated into three dimensions (the intra-psychological, inter-psychological and extra-psychological) for the sake of analysis. At the risk of oversimplification, it could be stated that Vygotskian psychology tends to foreground the intra- and inter-psychological aspects of the investigation; Bakhtinian psychology is extremely helpful in tracing the inter-psychological dynamics of crowds, whilst Activity Theory (AT) is most fruitful at the extra-psychological dimension, such as cultural and economic factors. The trick, of course, is to ensure analysis runs through all three dimensions, crisscrossing artificial boundaries and enriching itself in the process. Given the constraints of time, space and resources, this option may not always be readily available.

Thus my first case-study (May Day celebrations in London between 1999 and 2003) relies heavily on Vygotsky (with the occasional nod to Bakhtin). It argues these celebrations represent Vygotskian *zones of proximal development* where different factions of the proletariat learn from each other and develop a radical consciousness in the process of joint activity. The second study (Iranian football riots) is, by and large, a Bakhtinian reading of events (with the occasional helping hand from Vygotsky). These emancipatory riots were characterised by excess, grotesquerie, sexual transgressions, profanity, dialogic interaction and a carnivalesque mode of social being. I suggest these empowering riots signify a seminal turning point in the politics and culture of the region. The third study (a comparative study of the anti-poll tax rebellion and the February 2003 anti-war march in London) is based almost exclusively on AT. By looking at the organisation and structure of the events, I argue that the violence associated with the anti-poll tax riot may have concealed a conservative core at the heart of the campaign whereas the seemingly innocuous anti-war march represents a real rupture with previous political consensus in Britain.

At the end of each chapter I explore the limitations of employing a single-strand approach to social movements. It is only during my last case-study (the problem of revolutionary proletarian organisations) that I attempt a systematic integration of Vygotsky and Bakhtin with AT in an effort to capture the complex three-dimensionality of the subject. In so doing, I have been mindful 'that the subject matter of social psychology is historically contingent' (Gergen and Gergen, 1997: 99). More specifically, it is necessary to study social history in order to 'achieve a better understanding of the variations in social behaviour we humans experience' (Moghaddam, 1997: 200).

What would, for example, a social historical analysis of our times contribute to our understanding of emergent subjectivities, crowd behaviour and 'social movements'? Breaking with both bourgeois and orthodox Marxist traditions of analysis, we could briefly and provisionally state the changes in the following terms.

Capitalism is mutating on various fronts simultaneously, hence the breakneck speed of change as transformation in one modality feeds into another. The three registers[7] I would like to flag at this point could be classified as the 'intensive', 'extensive' and 'ideological' aspects of capitalism. The 'intensive' changes involve the restructuring of labour power and a greater flexibility in modes of surplus value extraction. The 'extensive' register includes a new wave of 'enclosures' and 'primitive capital accumulation' which is linked to 'globalisation'. Finally, the 'ideological' register has seen the emergence of a new brand of neo-liberalism in Anglo-Saxon countries which, at the risk of sounding pretentious, I would like to call 'roll-out-neo-liberal-fascism'. I will discuss these three registers in more detail below:

1. The 'intensive' transformations present perhaps the most novel changes we have witnessed for decades. Now that USSR and Eastern European forms of capitalism,

---

7   Of course, there are more than three registers that need to be analysed. I have ignored 'institutional', and 'technological' changes for the sake of brevity.

what Debord (1987: 64) called 'backward' capitalism, and what could be more rigorously described as societies belonging to the *early* phase of the *formal* domination of capital, specialising in the extraction of *absolute* surplus value from the proletariat (Melancholic Troglodytes, 2001), have come a cropper (cf. Fernandez, 1997), the journalistically inane euphemism, 'globalisation', has come to stand for an intensification of the class struggle.[8] Globalisation at the 'intensive' register is about making *all* labour productive of value[9] (cf. Harvie, 2005: 133).

In fact, 21st century capitalism is gradually moving towards a juncture where the two usual modes of domination over the proletariat, what Marx (1867/1979) called *formal* and *real* phases of domination, will be supplemented by another. I have called this new phase, the *surreal* phase of domination. What is interesting about this emerging phase is that it consists of (not two but) four methods of surplus value extraction thus giving both capital and labour more flexibility.

I believe the two common forms of surplus value extraction (*formal* and *real*) are gradually becoming sandwiched between two more- provisionally named the *pre-formal* and *post-real* methods of extraction. The 'pre-formal' mode represents a vicious return of all those methods of surplus value extraction that were deemed outdated, such as large-scale slavery, child labor, forced prostitution, 'criminal' subsistence, illegal refugee labor and prison-work. They are now, needless to say, not quite as they were in the past since they are resurfacing within established capitalist norms. Twenty-first century slavery, for instance, has both similarities and differences with slavery in the ancient and feudal worlds.[10] At a global scale, the overall effect of 'pre-formal' methods of extraction will be largely social/psychological rather than economic.

The 'post-real' mode of extraction, by contrast, will be completely original, and will involve the application of the latest computing, cyber, genetic and bio-technologies to labour power. Alongside *material* commodities, proletarians will come to produce more and more *immaterial* (Negri, 1992; Fortunati, 2007) as well as *hyper-material* (Melancholic Troglodytes, 2003) labour. In the process, the very *essence* of labour power will undergo a metamorphosis and due to its substantial production of surplus value, the 'post-real' mode of extraction may

---

8   By 'proletariat' I am simply referring to the class that produces (directly as well as indirectly) the wealth of this world and is everywhere subjected to exploitation and oppression by capitalism.

9   Harvie (2005: 160) has recently argued, '... we should understand productive and unproductive labour as *open* categories, as categories of struggle. *All* labour can be *either* productive or unproductive, *or* rather, all labour tends to be *both*. Whether a particular concrete labour activity creates value or not is contingent on class struggle'. Similarly formal and real phases of capital domination are not just diachronic periods but exist side-by-side synchronically. In fact they can only be defined in relation to each other.

10 In an interesting article Tomba (2007) makes similar suggestions. Slavery he argues is not a residue of past epochs but a form that is 'produced and reproduced in the background of the *current* capitalist mode of production' (Tomba, 2007: 34).

come to dominate and shape the interaction within this four-runged matrix.[11, 12] It is the entirety of this four-runged evolving hierarchical matrix (i.e., pre-formal, formal, real, post-real), with all its tensions and potential for joint activity, that I have termed the *surreal* phase of domination. The transition to this new 'surreal' phase of domination will be just as bumpy as the switch from the 'formal' to 'real' phase of domination proved to be. Significantly, this transition may even involve more cataclysmic upheavals since it will probably be compressed into a shorter timespan.

For our purposes, it is necessary to bring out the implications of this new four-runged ladder of exploitation for the formation of new 'subjectivities' and the way it impacts 'new social movements'. It is my argument that collectivities, and perhaps especially those that turn riotous or carnivalesque, (i.e., those that transgress routine) provide a transformative space 'in which subjectivity is unfurled, through the reappropriation of communication and the experience of cooperation, a *transformation in which the material operation of reappropriation is also a moment of self-awareness*' (Negri, 1989: 138).

In what is, by and large, a disappointing collaboration, Guattari and Negri (1990: 18) make a useful analytical distinction between two kinds of struggle in order to better grasp the nature of the new social alliances being forged. The first, they call 'molar antagonisms' by which they mean workplace struggles at the point of production, and the second, 'molecular proliferation', which refers to the osmosis of isolated instances of struggle into the outside world. Demonstrations usually exemplify 'molecular proliferations' where the relations between individuals and collectivities on the one hand, and linguistic signs and material nature, on the other, undergo transformation. Demonstrations provide us with a space conducive to reflexivity. As May (1998: 9) explains, 'In times of crisis, transformations in expected conditions, as well as resistance to existing states of affairs, the capacity to reflect *upon* actions, as opposed to *within* actions, may be enhanced'. Through *reflexive joint activity* the heterogeneity of new subjectivities, which has the potential to be divisive, can become productive.

I am also suggesting that demonstrations and riots will increase during the 21st century because of, a) the return of the 'repressed' (in this context *pre-formal* mode of exploitation) and the persistence of *formal* and *real* modes of domination. These three

---

11 This new postulate has drawn upon, but at the same time superseded, previous articulations of capital's trajectory in Debord's (1987) concept of the *integrated spectacle*, Baudrillard's (1983) *hyper-reality*, Camatte's (1975) notion of *escaped capital*, Negri's (1988) critique of the *social factory* and Vercellone's (2005) usage of the now fashionable term *cognitive capitalism*.

12 I agree with Federici and Caffentzis (2007: 65) on this. They acknowledge how important it is to identify the leading forms of capitalist accumulation. However, they go on to explain that 'capitalist accumulation has thrived precisely through its capacity to simultaneously organize development and underdevelopment, waged and un-waged labor, production at the highest levels of technological know-how and production at the lowest levels'. Thus my emphasis on understanding the intermix of pre-formal, formal, real, post-real modes of extraction within the surreal phase of accumulation.

modes are suffused with collective proletarian resistance; b) the *post-real* method of exploitation will be resisted by a highly skilled but discontented section of the proletariat that is not shackled by reactionary institutions of mediation such as trade unions; and c) the increasing heterogeneity of proletarians from this four-runged matrix will result in more volatile interactions.

Since no 'permanent' autonomous organisation has been devised to articulate their protests, it is safe to assume that the more rapid translation of 'molar antagonisms' into 'molecular proliferations' will be carried out during and around the arena of demonstrations, strikes, riots and carnivals for the foreseeable future.

2. The 'extensive' register must account for the ambiguous term 'globalisation' as well as reformulating the primitive process of capital accumulation and the enclosure movements that have been unleashed by the most recent wave of 'globalisation'. In a formulation superior to the common journalistic usage of the term, Charles Tilly (2004: 98) suggests 'globalisation' is occurring whenever 'a distinctive set of social connections and practices expands from a regional to a transcontinental scale'. According to this definition humanity has experienced three waves of globalisation since 1500. Tilly (2004: 99-100) again,

> The first [wave of globalisation] arrived around 1500. It resulted from the rapidly spreading influence of Europe, growth of the Ottoman Empire, and parallel expansions of Chinese and Arab merchants into the Indian Ocean and the Pacific ... We can place the second major post-1500 wave of globalisation approximately at 1850-1914 ... During this period, international trade and capital flows reached unmatched heights, especially across the Atlantic ... Massive movement of labor, goods, and capital made prices of trade goods more uniform across the world ... Migration, trade, and capital flows slowed between the two world wars. But as Europe and Asia recovered from World War II, a third post-1500 surge of globalisation began ... Post-1945 globalisation featured such high-tech industries as electronics and pharmaceuticals.

What Tilly does not underscore with conviction is the exploitative and violent nature of this phenomenon. Contemporary 'globalisation', for instance, is predicated upon the asymmetrical relations existing both *between* and *within* nation-states. *Between* nation-states one finds the more 'advanced' national capitalists extracting surplus value and raw material from 'foreign' workers in an accelerated cycle of exploitation. Those nation-states enjoying a mostly 'relative' surplus value extraction process, for instance, can augment their wealth through a more sophisticated labour process as well as military, technological and communication superiority at the expense of less 'advanced' states which overwhelmingly produce 'absolute' surplus value.[13] *Within*

---

13 A prime example of this would be the way in which Israel (a predominantly relative surplus value

nation-states, highly concentrated urban centres and financial nodes are changing the landscape of rural agriculture through commodification and proletarianistaion (Lewontin, 1998: 4). Mariarosa Dalla Costa is a useful corrective to Tilly's rather detached perspective on globalisation,

> ... *from the human viewpoint, capitalist development has always been unsustainable* since it has assumed from the start, and continues to assume, extermination and hunger for an increasingly large part of humanity. [This process] is founded on a class relationship and must continually refound this relationship at a global level ... (Dalla Costa, 2005: 176).

The 'extensive' dimension of capitalist change is intertwined with the 'new enclosure movement' which since the 1970s has kick-started a new wave of primitive capital accumulation. As the Midnight Notes Collective (1992: 318) has pointed out,

> The Enclosures ... are not a one time process exhausted at the dawn of capitalism. They are a regular return on the path of accumulation and a structural component of class struggle ... Enclosure is one process that unifies proletarians throughout capital's history, for despite our differences we all have entered capitalism through the same door: the loss of our land and of the right attached to it, whether this loss has taken place in Front Mill, England, in southern Italy, in the Andes, on the Niger Delta, or in the Lower East Side of New York City.

So Enclosures, or the separation of labourers from any means of production in order to turn them into wage-slaves, is a process not just having happened in the past, but is continuing to this day (de Angelis, 1999). Here is where agreement amongst the *Midnight Notes* autonomists and the group around the journal *The Commoner* (the two major journals debating this issue) ends. For some (Bonefeld, 2002) there is little or no distinction between accumulation and primitive accumulation. De Angelis (2001) tries to avoid this conclusion through a more nuanced positioning, whilst Zarembka (2002) draws a sharp distinction between them.

I find these discussions ultimately unsatisfactory and would propose an alternative classification to avoid confusion. It is possible, I believe, to make a distinction between three kinds of primitive capital accumulation. The first we could call *classic primitive accumulation* which refers to the historical process of land grab, violent removal of peasants from their farmlands and their transformation into wage-slaves, as described by Marx based on his detailed study of English capitalism. The second process is the replaying of this classical model in other countries following a time lag. Let

---

production society) has managed to limit Palestinian capitalism to mostly absolute surplus value production (for a discussion of how this superiority relates to the vital issue of water usage, see, Melancholic Troglodytes, 2003).

us refer to it as *displaced primitive accumulation*. For instance, the process of primitive accumulation in Russia, India, USA, Japan and Iran consisted of many similarities with the English model but also contrasts (e.g., the state played a more prominent role in Russia, India and Iran whilst USA's path involved not so much a transition from feudalism to capitalism but the introduction of capitalist relations from the outside and the destruction of Native American communities). The third category of primitive accumulation occurs when, following labour restructuring or a successful resistance mounted by the proletariat or a switch from formal to real domination of capital or the introduction of new technology or the destruction of a mass of productive forces following war/natural disaster or the discovery of precious raw material,[14] a particular enterprise or sector of economy has to restart accumulation from scratch. This third category we could call *primitive accumulation revisited*.

The 'extensive' dimension of change is, therefore, not just about acquiring new territories or expanding spatially. As Chris Burman (2004: 741) has suggested it could be about revisiting old sites of exploitation,

> It is not just the case that capital must expand into new geographical territories to thwart crisis; it is just as cogent a response to crisis to return to original sites in search of layers of social life that were left suspended ...

The increasing interrelatedness of the three forms of primitive accumulation discussed has led to a considerable increase in labour migration and the intermingling of proletarians from different backgrounds. It has also created confusion and chaos every time primitive accumulation has merged into accumulation proper. This volatile mix is key to understanding the specific crisis that led to the partial marginalisation of Keynesianism in favour of neo-liberalism and then the transmutation of the latter into what I have rather awkwardly called 'roll-out-neo-liberal-fascism'. As with the 'intensive' registers of subjectivity discussed above, this increased 'extensive' interrelatedness could also be either a source of strength or tension, depending on circumstances.

3. Finally, having discussed the 'intensive' and 'extensive' registers, we come to the 'ideological' transformations that are occurring right under our nose. The foregoing discussion suggests capitalism has entered a more 'flexible' period of development where it will need to keep its ideological options open. Conversely, we could add that whenever a traumatic, crisis-ridden transformation is on the cards, capitalism reverts to a more 'authoritarian' ideology. Taken these two markers together (*flexibility* and *authoritarianism*) certain subtle changes occurring within 'neo-liberalism' become discernible.

---

14 A terrifying example of 'capital accumulation revisited' would be the way US capitalism, having militarily defeated Native Americans and having enclosed them into reservations (Brown, 1974), is now returning to what was considered 'barren' land in order to explore for uranium ores and dump the waste by-products on Native American land (Churchill, 1992: 24-25).

Peck and Tickell (2002) have divided neo-liberalism into two periods. The first which was prevalent in the 1980s they term 'roll-back neoliberalism' which is characterised by a 'pattern of deregulation and dismantlement (e.g., of state-financed welfare, education, and health services and environment protection)' (cited in Routledge, 2004: 1). This was the phase during which neo-liberalism was struggling against the 'industrial proletariat' and 'multiculturalism'. It was the era of Reagan and Thatcher. Once victory was assured against these two enemies, neo-liberalism's assault gathered pace and entered a new phase. Peck and Tickell suggest the 'roll-back' form of neo-liberalism is now shifting toward a 'roll-out' neoliberalism, which they define as,

> an aggressive intervention by governments around issues such as crime, policing, welfare reform, and urban surveillance with the purpose of disciplining and containing those marginalised or dispossessed by the neoliberalisation of the 1980s (Routledge, 2004: 1).

This description characterises the Bush regime. Two caveats are in order. First, in my view both phases of neo-liberalism have been attacks on the *entire* proletariat and not just 'marginalised' sections within the class, as Routledge suggests. Second, the notion of the demise of the state form in favour of transnational corporations (Hardt and Negri, 2000) is looking more and more mythical everyday. Harvie (2005: 150) lists some of the reasons for the continued indispensability of the state for capital formation,

> If we think of individual nation states competing in order to attract and retain private capital within their borders ... then the organisation and 'efficiency' of state labour, along with the quantity and 'quality' of the unwaged reproductive labour of mothers and others, are as important parameters within this competition as are the tax regimes, juridical framework and level of infrastructure.

Furthermore, as powerful states in the 'West' shed certain layers of bureaucratic control, new areas of social life become hostage to their whim. Two parallel and overlapping processes are creating analytic confusion. First, in most powerful societies we are witnessing the strengthening of the *executive* branch of the state at the expense of the judiciary and legislative as well as the citizenry. So a recomposition of the state apparatus should not be taken for loss of sovereignty. Second, there *is* a real tendency for less powerful states to lose independence and sovereignty to both transnational corporations and more powerful states.

However, even these two caveats do not fully grasp the peculiarly *ideological* dimension of bourgeois ideas dominant today, especially in the USA and Britain. For that, I feel, we need to look more closely at the political ideas of two individuals, namely, Leo Strauss and H. G. Wells.[15]

Recently the influence of Leo Strauss (1899-1973) on the most important figures within the Bush administration has become clearer. This is the culmination of a Straussian *putsch* that began at least as early as the mid 1980s during Reagan's presidency.[16] Born in Germany, Strauss would eventually move to the States and become a US citizen. He believed that 'premodern philosophy is *better* than modern philosophy' [emphasis in original] (Jahn, 2000: 1). In fact, he was fiercely anti-modern and contemptuous of the weaknesses of US liberalism which reminded him of similar frailties within the Weimar Republic. As Barker (2005) has pointed out:

> Decadence, the nagging psychic fear of it and the accompanying metaphors of softness and disease, is a language both of various fundamentalisms, and more significantly, of empires and their elites, however vestigial they might be.

The *egalitarianism* and *multiculturalism* Strauss associated with liberalism were responsible for the diminishing of creativity, heroism, authority and elitism. He was also opposed to '20th century relativism, scientism, historicism and nihilism' (Wikipedia, 2004: 1). He believed in universal principles that transcend historicity and sought to discover these in the texts of ancient philosophers. In a manoeuvre similar to mystics, he suggests that ancient texts contain both an esoteric hidden knowledge only accessible to the *elite* and an exoteric shell only fit for the consumption of the vulgar masses (Wikipedia, 2004: 1).

As Jim Lobe (2004: 2) makes clear, 'Strauss [had] few qualms about using deception in politics, he saw it as a necessity'. One gets the impression his art of persuasion was devoid of the philosophical nuances of Plato and the humanistic virtuosity of Machiavelli. Strauss argued for a much greater role for religion in the public sphere. Some Straussians such as Irving Kristol have gone as far as denouncing the Founding Fathers of the American Republic for 'separating the church from the state' (Lobe, 2004: 2). Religion is used even by those Straussians who do not believe in it to manipulate and pacify the masses. Strauss thought of religion as a 'pious fraud' (Cabrejas, 2003: 20). He believed external threats are necessary in order to ensure the stability of

---

15 In their latest book, *Multitude*, Hardt and Negri suggest Samuel Huntingdon is the most significant *Geheimrat* (secret advisor to sovereign) of recent times. Huntingdon believed US 'democracy' was in danger from organised labor and 'newly activated social groups, such as women and African Americans' (Hardt and Negri, 2004: 33). Democracy, he believed, 'must be tempered with authority' (Hardt and Negri, 2004: 33). I take on board Hardt and Negri's flagging of Huntingdon's reactionary credentials. However, I still feel Leo Strauss and H. G. Wells represent closer approximations of where the Anglo-Saxon elite have been heading.

16 This is not to ignore previous similar attempts at monopolising levers of power in the USA. James Burnham (a one-time leftist), for instance, turned to a group of thinkers popular in fascist Italy in order to buttress his managerial analysis. These were Gaetano Mosca, Robert Michels and Vilfredo Pareto (Barbrook, 2005). Thus he was able to make his ideas palatable for the US elite. In fact, many US Trotskyites began drifting rightward, first crystallising as a right wing faction in the Democratic Party (supporting the Vietnam War) and later transforming into neo-conservatives (supporting the two Gulf Wars).

a political order (Lobe, 2004: 2). When there was no viable threat, one should be man-ufactured. Rumsfeld and Cheney were in the business of manufacturing evidence of a USSR threat as early as thirty years ago- lies that went against CIA assessment (Bark-er, 2005). Paul Wolfowitz and Abram Shulsky (responsible for 'finding' evidence to justify the war in Iraq) are self-proclaimed followers of Strauss (Drury, 2007: 62). In addition to religious propaganda a mythic patriotism is constructed in order to en-hance internal coherency. Accordingly, it is perpetual war that provides the state with the greatest measure of stability not peace. Straussians during the Reagan era man-aged to fuse the two wings of the Republican Party – one wing consisted of elites in favour of minimal state intervention in market mechanisms and the other wing was rooted in 19th century 'populism' (Bronner, The Guardian, 31 August 2007). The ideo-logical commonalities with the earlier doctrine of Manifest Destiny 'which helped fuel westward expansion and was invoked to justify the wars against Mexico and many Native American nations', is self evident (Cabrejas, 2003: 21).

Despite being a Jew who had to flee Nazi Germany, Strauss is on record as be-ing sympathetic to fascist ideology. In fact, he settled for fascism in opposition to Nazism. In a letter to Löwith in 1933 he wrote,

> Just because Germany has turned to the right and has expelled us [Jews] it simply does not follow that the principles of the right are therefore to be rejected. To the contrary, only on the basis of principles of the right - fascist, authoritarian, imperial - is it possible in a dignified manner, without the ridiculous and pitiful appeal to 'the inalienable right of man' to protest against this mean nonentity [i.e., the Nazi Party] (Xenos, 2004: 3).

Political policy makers influenced by Leo Strauss have been the primary force behind George W. Bush's presidency. As well as Wolfowitz and Shulsky these included Donald Rumsfeld, Dick Cheney, Allan Bloom, Harry Jaffa, and Francis Fukuyama. Even some of

their political *rhetoric* (meant in the negative sense of manipulation) is borrowed from Strauss: terms such as 'regime change', 'good versus evil', 'terror' and 'tyranny' (Xenos, 2004: 8-9). If Strauss's influence has been well docu-mented by researchers and journalists in recent years, another (perhaps less direct) historical inspiration has gone mostly unnoticed.

H. G. Wells was a 'political animal'. Dur-ing his adult life, he searched for the perfect ideology to buttress his beloved capitalism. What needs to be born in mind is that he re-mained faithful to liberalism throughout his political life even though he was extremely sceptical regarding liberalism's ability to deliver the goods. The Wellsian liberal utopia, with its renunciation of parliamentarianism and individualism, was a far cry from the conventional understanding of liberalism (Coupland, 2000: 543).[17]

His liberalism should be compared with Winston Churchill's convictions. In fact the two were friends who first met in 1902 and kept in touch until Wells died in 1946 (The Independent, 27 November 2006). In 1908 Wells supported Churchill's election campaign for the parliament. Churchill, an avid sci-fi reader, borrowed phrases from Wells's novels- terms such as 'the gathering storm' to describe the rise of Nazi Germany. He also borrowed ideas from Wells's *Anticipations*, 'a book of predictions about the future calling for the establishment of a scientifically organised New Republic' (The Independent, 27 November 2006). Finally, the two admirers shared a belief in eugenics and the desirability of the political unification of 'the English-speaking states' (ibid.).

According to Coupland, Wells switched from Liberals to the Labour movement in December 1932. However, his call in the *Daily Herald* for a world 'revolution' evoked 'very little response' (Coupland, 2000: 545). This was a 'revolution' without the proletariat,

> If ... we lose the delusive comfort of belief in that magic giant, the Proletariat, who will dictate, arrange, restore and create, ... we clear the way for the recognition of an elite of intelligent ... people ... (Wells, 1905/2003).

When the Fabian connection failed to satisfy Wells, he switched his attention to the Bolsheviks. He even had sit downs with Lenin and Stalin. However, his intention to synthesise liberalism with Bolshevism also came to nothing. At this stage, he was still an anti-fascist although prepared to concede a minor role for fascist forces in his world 'revolutionary' movement. By 1933, however, he was warming up to Mussolini's version of fascism,

> The intellectual content of fascism was limited, nationalist and romantic, its methods, especially in its opening phases, were violent and dreadful; but at least it insisted upon discipline and public service for its members ... Fascism indeed was not an altogether bad thing; it was a bad good thing; and Mussolini had left his mark on history (Wells, 1933/2002: 106).

In association with his newly found respect for the authoritarian aspects of fascism Wells's anti-Semitism was also manifest by this time in, for instance, his description of the 'Communist' Party as 'that band of Russian Jews' (Coupland, 2000: 550). He also

---

17 Samuel Huntingdon was arguing in the 1960s that *democracy* (by which he meant parliamentary democracy) 'is only one way of constituting authority; and it is not necessarily a universally applicable one' (Huntingdon, quoted in Barker, 2005). As a leading member of the American Enterprise Institute, Huntingdon too has combined a call for military adventurism abroad (e.g., his long-term enthusiasm for the invasion of Iraq) with Malthusian population control of *undesirables* at home (Barker, 2005). Barker describes the American Enterprise Institute ('these armchair Spartans') as 'a fascistic version of what is decadence'. The designation, 'fascistic', is not intended as hyperbole by Barker.

believed that 'the prevention of *congenital invalids* and certain anti-social types from breeding' had a role to play in his scientific utopia (Partington, 2003: 74). He floated the idea of voluntary sterilisation for slum-dwellers whom he blamed for 'a large amount of vice, disease, defect and pauperism' (quoted in Partington, 2003: 77). As he learned more about eugenics, however, he moderated his views on the subject of sterilisation and ultimately rejected Galton and genetic engineering altogether (Partington, 2003: 80).

However, politically he was still infatuated with Fascism in the 1930s. So having tried the Liberal Party, the Labour movement and the Bolsheviks as possible political partners, Wells finally decided to give his allegiance to Fascism. As Coupland makes clear,

> It was thus fascism which, of all extant political movements of the 1930s, came closest to the 'aggressive order of religiously devoted men and women who will try out and establish and impose a new pattern of living upon our race', which Wells appealed for in the final line of *The Shape of Things to Come* (Coupland, 2000: 551).

Lenin with H.G. Wells, Moscow,
6 October, 1920

Wells was absolutely convinced (as I am sure Blair and Bush are) that 'he hates fascism; he is horror-struck as any liberal at its brutality, its barbarism, its philistinism, its illogicality and its narrow nationalism, but he puts all the blame on the last quality; if it was only international it wouldn't be so bad' (Gorer, 1935: 199). Wells having drawn from a myriad of sources including the Jesuits, Puritans, 'Communists', and Fascists attempted to turn liberalism from a woolly soft doctrine into a disciplined and militaristic outfit. In *The Shape of Things to Come* (1933/2002) and *The Holy Terror* (1939/2001) Fascist iconography and characters began to populate Wells's work. Wells alluded to the 'various arms, the infantry, air forces, shock troops into which its militant members would be organised' (Coupland, 2000: 545). In real life, Wells became friends with Oswald Mosley for a while before an acrimonious falling out (due to both personal and political factors).

Concomitant to his concept of 'Liberal Fascism' was Wells's notion of the 'open conspiracy', which found expression in *What Are We To Do With Our Lives?* (1931/2002). Wells's notion of the 'open conspiracy' was 'an intellectual élite movement which would in time develop into a world religion' (Coupland, 2000: 543). There was nothing hidden or under-handed about this conspiracy, since Wells was convinced the most effective conspiracy is an 'open' one. Members of the Wellsian élite 'owed allegiance only to the dictates of Wellsian *common sense*' (Coupland, 2000: 544), and not to 'charismatic leaders'. The 'open conspiracy' then was a 'cultural movement', which would finally 'swallow up the entire population of the world and become the new human community'. Its practitioners were the 'few thousand' media and state leaders who would mould public opinion (Wells, quoted in Coupland, 2000: 544).

The irony of our times is that constructs such as 'Liberal Fascism'[18] and the 'open conspiracy' which might have been dismissed as the febrile convulsions of a deluded 'amateur' politician in the 1930s have become accurate descriptions of the ideological forces representative of the most powerful elements within contemporary capitalism (i.e., the Anglo-Saxon bourgeoisie). The Bush-Blair-Brown axis deploys a 'roll-out-neo-liberal-fascism' as a politico-cultural adjunct to its military adventurism. It conspires to invade 'sovereign' countries 'openly'. More significantly for social movements and anti-capitalist forces, 'roll-out-neo-liberal-fascism' uses its unequal confrontation with *backward* (meaning less adept at accumulating capital) capitalists such as Saddam Hussein, Ahmadi-Nezhad and Osama Bin Laden as cover for suppressing the proletariat at 'home'. The curtailment of 'rights' in 'Western' countries has precious little to do with the so called fight against terrorism and everything to do with our leaders' intent to shift the balance of class forces in their own favour, in anticipation of future crises.

In summary: the introduction has set out to explain some of the reasons for my disappointment with most previous investigations into social movements (further criticisms will be furnished throughout the book). Vygotsky, Bakhtin and Activity Theory will act as our lodestar for an alternative model of 'study-extending' the social movement. I have posited a new phase of capitalist development, entitled the 'surreal phase of capital domination' characterised by four methods of surplus value extraction (i.e., the pre-formal, formal, real, and post-real). If capitalism succeeds in regenerating it-

18 I have retained Wells's original amalgamation although it would be more accurate to call this contemporary phenomenon *fascistic liberalism*. After all we are dealing with a basically liberal philosophy which has garnered fascistic elements in order to make itself more competitive and not a liberal fascism.

self, then these four methods of surplus value extraction will catalyse the new 'enclosure' movement. These attacks have been spear-headed by a more draconian form of neo-liberalism from the US-UK axis in the form of 'roll-out-neo-liberal-fascism' inspired by Leo Strauss and H. G. Wells. This doctrine is likely to remain in ascendancy for the period of restructuring heralded by 'globalisation', even if its main cheerleaders, Bush, Rumsfeld and Blair have reached the end of their political careers. However, the fight-back that has already begun will manifest itself increasingly in factories, workplaces, neighbourhoods and on the streets. In chapter 1 below, I will describe my investigative approach. In chapters 2-5, I will study some of the significant moments in the 'anti-capitalist movement'.

Epistemology, Methodology and Method

'One of the main reasons revolutionaries have failed to say much of significance in recent times is their inattentiveness to matters methodological'.

Chapter one:

Epistemology, Methodology and Method

There are problems that one cannot approach flying, but have to be approached on foot, limping and ... in these cases it is no shame to limp. But he who only sees the limping is methodologically blind. For it would not be difficult to show that Hegel is an idealist, the crows proclaim it from the house-tops; it needed genius to see in his system an idealism that stood materialism on its head, that is, to sever the methodological truth (dialectics) from the factual lies, to see that Hegel, limping, was approaching the truth.

- L. S. Vygotsky, The Historical Meaning of the Crisis In Psychology, 1927/1987, Ch. 7.

One of the main reasons revolutionaries have failed to say much of significance in recent times is their inattentiveness to matters methodological. Too often impressionistic accounts are lazily constructed as a poor substitute for rigorous investigation. To remedy this shortcoming, I have spent a great deal of time laying a foundation which I hope will be employed by future researchers in similar context.

I have followed Sandra Harding (1987, cited in Henwood and Pidgeon, 1994: 228) in making a distinction between epistemological positions ('assumptions about the bases or possibilities for knowledge'), methodology ('a theoretical analysis defining a research problem and how research should proceed'), and methods ('research strategy or technique adopted'). As it becomes clear, there is a great deal in Harding that I find useful and one or two things I disagree with.

My epistemology is based on a materialist conception of history. My methodology will employ Vygotskian psychology, Bakhtinian psychology and Activity Theory. Finally, I will discuss my methods which consist of Ethnography, Participation Action Research (PAR) and Discourse Analysis (DA). The remainder of the chapter dwells on problems of reflexivity, standpoint and writing style. I consider this chapter crucial for my subsequent arguments but the impatient reader may read the subsequent chapters before coming back to this chapter.

1.1 EPISTEMOLOGY

The epistemological complications of *study-extending* social movements are immense. As a bare minimum, one has to start by 'ascending from the abstract to the concrete', where the concrete is defined as 'a convergence of many [social, historical and psychological] determinations ... and thus a unity of diversities' (Marx, 1857/1974). From a psychological perspective, Hayes (1996: 161) reminds us that, 'substantial social changes have taken place whenever there is a shift from abstract individuality to concrete individuality'.[19] This does not mean, however, that one has to look for an explanation of human behaviour in the human mind, as Kant did (Sohn-Rethel, 1978: 17). Rather the aim is to map the dialectics of a socialised individuality and collectivity.

A historical materialist epistemology must include a rejection of dualistic models of the relation between consciousness and being. Marx put it succinctly in the *Economic and Philosophical Manuscripts of 1844*, 'Thought and being are indeed [epistemologically] *distinct*, but they are also in unity with each other' (quoted in Jakubowski, 1976: 15). 'Epistemology' in this perspective is not purely contemplative as Hegel insisted, but has a transformational function (Jakubowski, 1976: 19).

If we also concur with Marx in viewing 'the material [as] the sensuously real, something whose reality does not exist only in consciousness', then we would have no difficulty in making the next conceptual jump and grasp the significance of 'revolutionary-practical-critical' activity as (human) social being, as the subject-object of knowledge. This subject-object of 'study-extension' manifests itself on many planes simultaneously. For instance, on the level of what Marx called *superstructure*, it can further be sub-divided into political, legal and cultural superstructure as distinct from ideological superstructure. 'The former represent the form in which class struggle occurs; the latter is the form in which men [sic] become conscious of these struggles' (Jakubowski, 1976: 50). The strength of the bourgeoisie in the past has been to keep these elements isolated.

It is my contention that the recent spate of anti-capitalist demonstrations, embedded as they are in a flowing 'zone of proximal development' (zoped), are beginning to challenge the artificial barriers between the political, economic, legal and cultural forms of the struggle by foregrounding the *social* dimension. This is the only definition of '*social* movements' worth contemplating. So, in effect, what we are witnessing is the 'unification in opposition' of the *base* (pre-formal, formal, real, post-real surplus value extraction), the *structure* (Fordism, post-Fordism), and the *superstructure* (political, legal, cultural, ideological).[20]

---

19 One of the abiding contradictions of capitalism is that what we call personal life is not personal at all, but administrated by capital and the state. Much of individuality today remains non-autonomous, what Marx called 'abstract individuality' (Hayes, 1996: 161).

20 The base-structure-superstructure metaphor is considered by contemporary scholars to be atavistic. Pity! If their reading of Marx was thorough they would not deny themselves this useful conceptual tool of analysis.

What seems to be catalysing this 'unity in opposition' is the break-up of both the *social* and *technical* divisions of labour (Rubin, 1982: 14) at precisely the moment when productive forces are rising faster than ever. This trend is in its infancy, it represents itself erratically and unevenly. Nevertheless, it is an increasingly prominent feature of this phase of capitalism. The separation of mental from physical labour,

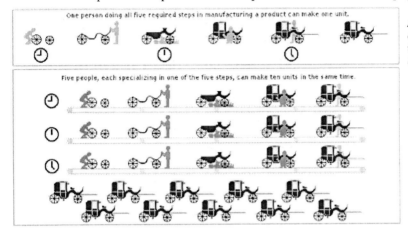

A pictorial depiction of the Division of Labour

which according to Sohn-Rethel (1978: 88) became possible first in ancient Egypt and ancient Greece because of the evolution of coined money, and is the real source of a *false consciousness* which believes itself to be independent of material factors has turned a corner.

Proletarian collectivities are the perfect arena for negating this trend, turning quantitative growth in the struggles of different strata of the proletariat into a qualitative new type of struggle. The revolution, lest we forget, is a moment in evolution. It is the performative aspect of the 'zone of *proletarian development*' (ZPD) to negate money, wage-slavery, the state and spatio-temporal abstractions such as god and nationalism that transforms them into developmental zones. Different sections of the proletariat are forced into confronting capital first as a class 'in itself', and when the consciousness of this becomes widespread, into a class 'for itself'. Vygotsky, employing Hegelian terms, agreed that a person has to transform an ability 'in itself' into an ability 'for him/herself'.[21]

As German critical psychologists have pointed out, we should be trying to work out the implications of the fundamental, generalised societal mediatedness of individual human action (Tolman, 1994: 95). More precisely,

---

For a successful attempt at updating the metaphor see Melancholic Troglodytes (1999).

21 However, this text will assume that the preferred unit of analysis of such a multi-dimensional matrix cannot be the inadequate formulation of 'word-meaning' (as put forward by Vygotsky) but the more embracing concept of 'tool-mediated, goal-directed action' as postulated by Zinchenko (1985: 95-96).

societal mediatedness ... consists of a dynamic relation among at least three factors: the historically determined, overall societal structure; the position that individuals may assume within the structure ... and the immediate life circumstances or situation of the individual.

This is another way of restating our original distinction between intra-, inter- and extra-psychological registers of social movements. To neglect any of these registers leads to an inadequate formulation of the class struggle. Furthermore, Holzkamp explains that the actions of subjects are not arbitrary or indeterminate 'since the subject, from his/her standpoint, has grounds for executing one particular action and no other, and the comprehensibility of his/her actions for others lies precisely in their groundedness'[22] (Holzkamp, 1992: 199).

In a similar vein, Harding's feminist *standpoint* theory also tries to use women's experience as a basis for generating knowledge. Here 'knowledge is understood as a system of practice as opposed to a system of representation' (Piatelli and Leckenby, 2003: 1). By re-orientating herself, Harding is asking what we can see from this alternative practice rather than from the perspective of dominant bourgeois representation. She answers her own question by suggesting that starting from the standpoint of the subjugated 'leads not to an [absolute] objective truth but to a less false, less partial, less distorted view' (Piatelli and Leckenby, 2003: 2). It does not require too much imagination in order to extend Harding's arguments to the proletariat (both male and female). At other times, Harding goes further and suggests that women by virtue of being subjugated and also by virtue of occupying *different* social locations have become 'knowing subjects' whose understating of the world is 'superior' (Harding, 1991: pp. 48 and 74). Alison Jaggar (2004: 57) has put it succinctly,

> The standpoint of the oppressed is not just different from that of the ruling class; it is also *epistemologically advantageous*. It provides the basis for a view of reality that is *more impartial than that of the ruling class and also more comprehensive*. It is more impartial because it comes closer to representing the interests of society as a whole; whereas the standpoint of the ruling class reflects the interests only of one section of the population, the standpoint of the oppressed represents the interests of the totality in that historical period. Moreover, whereas the condition of the oppressed groups is visible only dimly to the ruling class, *the oppressed are able to see more clearly the rules as well as the rulers and the relation between them. Thus, the standpoint of the oppressed includes and is able to explain the standpoint of the ruling class.*

All this sounds very familiar since feminist standpoint theory is partially based on Lukács's (admittedly error-prone) earlier arguments put forward in 1923 (cf. Lukács, 1990: 149-222). There both the structural position of the proletariat in the social order

---

22 Holzkamp goes on to explain, '... it needs to be made clear that this mediational level of subjective grounds for action does not imply that every action is grounded and therefore also comprehensible' (1992: 199-200). For one thing, there is the perennial problem of false consciousness, which creates incomprehension, and for another there are real, irreconcilable limits to intersubjective communicability.

and the specific forms of exploitation and oppression it was subjected to, were believed to provide it with a unique standpoint for understanding the world. This understanding or consciousness was in terms of flux and process. More specifically, critical consciousness perceives the contradictions of society (a task beyond the bourgeoisie) and proposes ideas for emancipation.

Carl Ratner's work can also be read as supportive of Harding's standpoint theory. From a slightly different viewpoint, Ratner (1971: 107) explains why personal awareness can be 'achieved through working to realise the possibilities of a situation rather than by attempting to maintain the status quo'. He also makes the valid point that 'the more one works to bring the future about, the clearer he [sic] can know the world and the better he can know himself. Conversely, the more one is confined to the present, the less he can know it and the less developed can his self-awareness be' (Ratner, 1971: 107).[23] So transformational epistemology depends on harnessing the dialectics of *being* and *becoming*.

However, here a further complication creeps in since Fredric Jameson has claimed that 'the disintegrating boundaries between the present and the future means that it is no longer possible to even imagine the future, and that we have therefore lost the capacity to think in utopian terms' (Wolmark, 1995: 13-14). The fact that culture seems to increasingly lack a sense of history (Jameson, 1990) has disrupted spatial and temporal relations, undermining them by transmitting information more or less instantaneously. In other words, our age has foregrounded being at the expense of becoming.

Jameson's concerns are valid but overstated. Genuine strikes, demonstrations, carnivals and riots could be perceived as a *reappropriation of both time and space by imposing playtime and spatial transgression on boundaries*, in the process exposing the fixed temporal-spatial binary as a construct. This act of reappropriation permits the reanimation of the dialectics of being and becoming. Protesters have this in common with prison convicts who also posit 'carnivalesque time' in conscious opposition to 'official linear time'.

Throughout the book, I have assumed that the inner contradictions of proletarian collectivities are 'the principles of its self-movement and ... the form in which the development is cast' (Il'enkov, 1977: 330). 'A dialectical interpretation of human development', writes Riegel (1976: 696),

---

23 In a more recent article Ratner (1999: 7-31) has proposed an integrated model of cultural psychology based on three schools of thought: the Symbolic approach (exemplified by the likes of Geertz, Shweder, Lutz, etc.); the Individualistic approach (Valsiner, Voestermans, etc.); and, Activity Theory (Leontiev, Zinchenko, etc.). This model is very similar to the approach taken up by the present work in that I too deploy Activity Theory and insist on a three-level model (socio-economic, cultural, psychological) for analysing consciousness development. However, whilst I agree with Ratner's choice of Activity Theory, I cannot see what is to be gained by integrating Symbolic and Individualistic approaches to my outlook. So instead of Symbolic studies I have opted for a Bakhtinian cultural investigation and likewise in place of the inherently flawed doctrine of individualistic (cultural) psychology, I have foregrounded Vygotsky's contributions. This approach is, I believe, an improvement on Ratner's.

... does not emphasise the plateaus at which equilibrium or balance is achieved. Development is rather seen as consisting in continuing changes along several dimensions of progression at the same time. Critical changes occur whenever two sequences are in conflict ...

In an epistemology based on historical materialism, the researcher is sensitive to dialectical possibilities. Time and again 'new qualitative forms of activity emerge as a solution to the contradictions of the preceding form. This in turn takes place in the form of *invisible breakthrough* innovations from below' (CHAT, 1998: 11). How else, for example, can we understand the proletarian assault on (bourgeois) cats during the Great Cat Massacre in the late 1730s France (Darnton, 1988), if not as a symbolic solution to the widening

That will show the bosses!

contradictions between apprentice and master? Or the advent of 'flying pickets' by miners caught between a belligerent state-bourgeoisie and reactionary union bureaucrats? Or the emergence of new vocabulary in order to encapsulate changing times?

1.2 METHODOLOGY

Let us remind ourselves that Harding describes *methodology* as 'a theoretical analysis defining a research problem and how research should proceed' (Harding, 1987, quoted in Henwood and Pidgeon, 1994: 228). My 'research problem' has been defined according to the tenets of Vygotskian psychology, Bakhtinian psychology and Activity Theory. Chapters 2-5 demonstrate in practice how these theories shape my research. In this chapter, therefore, it is only necessary to provide the reader with a brief outline of these three methodologies.

Vygotsky's approach always emphasised the dialectical linkage between *process* and *product*. His rejection of IQ testing, for instance, was premised on the need to trace the process of *intelligent activity* instead of a partial and biased snapshot of cognitive ability. We need to remind ourselves of Vygotsky's debt to Hegel and Marx[24], since neo-Vygotskian psychology in its Anglo-Saxon version is, by and large, 'grounded in the British empiricist philosophy and French Cartesian

---

24 Gillen (2000: 187) demonstrates how 'the early translators and editors of Vygotsky cut out references to Marxism, presumably under the influence of the McCarthy-inspired *great red scare* in the USA ... and Kozulin [an early translator] cut out reference to Marx, Engels, Plekhanov and so on but preserved references to literary figures'.

dualism [and perhaps, we should add, North American pragmatism]' (Elham-moumi, 2002: 95) [my addition].

Veresov (1996: 7) has perceptively noted that for Vygotsky, consciousness was not the 'structure of human behaviour' but the entity *that organises this structure*. Moreover, it is the unity of perception, thinking, speech and action which constitutes the central subject matter of any analysis of the origin of uniquely human forms of behaviour (Vygotsky, 1978). His views on consciousness coalesced partly as a reaction against behaviourism and Gestalt psychology. In contradistinction to these conventions, Vygotsky believed

> If consciousness is taken as the subject of study, then its explanation must be sought in some other dimension of reality [otherwise explanation becomes tautological] (Lindblom and Ziemke, 2003: 81).

By emphasising the significance of 'word-meaning' (something that admittedly I have distanced myself from), Vygotsky underlined the importance of the generalised reflection of reality (a notion I have no difficulties with, so long as it is properly distinguished from the metaphysical kind of reality mentioned above). It also allowed him to outline an ontogenetic progression from 'unorganised heaps' to 'complexes' and then (via 'pseudo-concepts') to 'concepts'. This progression of generalisation was the starting point for his notion of development. The distinction by Vygotsky between *word* and *sense* allowed him to further refine the analysis of consciousness as the analysis 'of the dynamic unity of meaning and sense' (Veresov, 1996: 13). By 'word' he meant the long-term, stable, dictionary meaning of the term and 'sense' refers to the personal interpretation of the term.

Here we must underline that throughout the book Vygotsky's distinction between 'internal' and 'external' has been used sparingly. If 'all mental processes are quasi-social' (Vygotsky, 1978) then Veresov is right in pointing out that, 'the problem of external and internal is related to the problem of the location or the modes of existence of these processes, but not as their essential matter' (Veresov, 1996: 14). In other words, there are not two systems but only one system. If a distinction is made from time to time, it is merely a temporary spacing out for analytical purposes. Therefore, it is too simple to say as Vygotsky sometimes did that external stimuli and ideas become 'internalised'. At other times he was more circumspect. For instance, Vygotsky stipulated the relationship between 'schizophrenia' and 'primitive man' in the following terms,

> And just as it is not admissible to make a genetic comparison of thought as it occurs in dreams with thought as it occurs in primitive man or spiders, simply because such forms of thought are all below the stage of conceptual thought, neither has one the right to assume that the thought of the patient with schizophrenia im-

mediately drops into the abyss of millions of years, or needs for its understanding analogies with the spider, which does not recognise its prey after the prey has been removed from the web and placed in the nest (Vygotsky, 1997b: 317).

Although the language may seem a tad archaic to present-day readers, the basic conceptual approach is sound enough. Alternatively, we could look at Vygotsky's critique of fascism (1997c) as further proof of his methodological superiority over some of his contemporaries regarding racial issues. He identifies Spranger, Ach and Jaensch as the harbingers of a fascist psychology. It is obvious Vygotsky considers fascism contemptible. He has difficulty throughout the text in taking its intellectual stalwarts seriously. 'To try and counter Jaensch's views in any meaningful way', says Vygotsky, 'would amount to the same thing as trying to disprove mad ravings by using logical arguments' (Vygotsky, 1997c: 333). Later on, however, he does trace accurately the true origins of fascist psychology,

> Essentially, Jaensch's system is built on the same methodological foundations as all the rest of bourgeois psychology. It represents an integration of idealism and mechanism, similar to that typological integration which Jaensch would like to see in the unification of the German philosopher with the peasant (Vygotsky, 1997c: 334).

Despite such insights, Vygotsky was a product of his times and there remains a number of issues with his own methodology. For instance, R. van der Veer and J. Valsiner (1994a: 317) are basically correct in saying that when investigating cooperation, Vygotsky, did not have the primacy of equal collaborators in mind. Rather, Vygotsky considered the asymmetric relationship in the cooperation between the developing child and his/her elders to be the norm. Scribner points out the insufficiency of focusing on the 'child history' and proposes instead the notion of 'life history' (Scribner, 1985: 140). This is an improvement on the restricted focus of Vygotsky and much current developmental psychology. Likewise, Cathrine Hasse (2001: 206) following Scribner (1985) has argued,

> Much of Vygotsky's theoretical thinking can be applied to adults as well - not only in the ontogenetic or the phylogenetic sense (and Vygotsky concerned himself with both aspects), but also as relevant theories analysing everyday interactions between socially interacting adults.

This is especially the case if we remind ourselves that for Vygotsky the 'zone of proximal development' (zoped) was specifically observable in situations of interplay between pre-scientific and scientific worldviews. As Stephen T. Kerr (1997: 2) has argued,

> ... in later Western discussions and interpretations, this focus ... came to be submerged under a general image of the interplay between adult and childish conceptions as aids to development.

In other words, the pre-scientific and scientific distinction does not neatly map onto the child-adult distinction. Both adults and children employ both pre-scientific and scientific notions but in different ratios and linked into a different matrix of higher mental functions. Children use more 'complex' types of thinking; adults employ more 'conceptual' types of thinking and there may very well be qualitatively different intellectual processes at work amongst these two groups (Vygotsky, 1997b: 314). The essential point worth remembering is that both similarities and differences between adults and children need to be flagged when discussing development. As it will become obvious in chapters 2-5, many of Vygotsky's shortcomings can be overcome through the application of Bakhtinian conceptual tools. A précis of Bakhtin's methodological completion of Vygotsky will be presented at this stage.

Bakhtin's use of *utterance* as 'the real unit of communication' focuses on contextualised, mediated action. According to Morris (1994) 'utterance' is,

> any unit of language, from a single word to an entire 'text'... [an utterance is] the locus of encounter between my self-consciousness, my mind and the world with all its socio-historical meaning; the utterance is always an answer to a previous utterance, and always expects an answer in the future (Morris, 1994: 251).

Most contemporary researchers find Bakhtin's *utterance* to be an improvement on Vygotsky's unit of analysis- *word meaning*. As Clark and Holquist (1984: 10) have noted, for Bakhtin constancy and uniqueness in language enter into contact and struggle within the utterance. The study of free-flowing utterance requires a new methodology, which Bakhtin called 'translinguistics'. Translinguistics refers to the study of the life of the word before it has become reified in separate disciplines and overlaps with what we would today call 'pragmatics' or 'discourse' (Sherzer, 1987, cited in Wertsch, 1991: 51). An utterance is associated at the very least with two voices, the *addresser* (the person doing the speaking) and the *addressee* (the person the utterance is directed at). In fact, there is usually more than two voices. 'The utterance', as Bakhtin (1986: 102) put it, 'is filled with *dialogic overtones'*. Words and thoughts, according to Bakhtin, always enter into dialogue with the other.

Bakhtin then charted the relationship between the unique speech event (utterance) and categories or types of speech event (or languages). He made a further distinction between *national* languages (i.e., the traditional linguistic unities with systematic grammar and semantics like English) and *social* languages (i.e., social dialects, characteristic group behaviour, professional jargons, etc.). Bakhtin was able to study both national and social languages, something considered untenable by structuralist followers of Ferdinand de Saussure (1959) who emphasised the study of *langue* (the system of linguistic codes abstracted from concrete events) at the expense of *parole* (the random aspects of communication). Bakhtin saw patterns of organisation where structuralist linguists only saw accident and randomness. He believed individual speakers do not 'have the kind of freedom *parole* assumes they have' (Holquist, 1986: xvi). This process of creating unique utterances within a social language was governed by a special type of dailogicality called 'ventriloquation', roughly defined as one voice speaking *through* another. As Bakhtin put it,

> The word in language is half someone else's. It becomes 'one's own' only when the speaker populates it with his own intentions, his own accent ... Prior to this moment of appropriation, the word does not exist in a neutral and impersonal language ... but rather it exists in other people's mouths, in other people's concrete contexts, serving other people's intentions ... (Bakhtin, 1981: 293-294).

This quote brings us to another thorny issue. The question, 'Who owns meaning?' Structuralists have traditionally responded to this question by advocating that meaning is owned by certain speakers and post-structuralists usually claim that no one owns meaning. Bakhtin, grounding himself in the concept of dailogicality, maintained an intermediate position (Wertsch, 1991: 68). Accordingly, speakers 'rent' meaning (Bakhtin in Holquist, 1981: 164). In other words,

> I can mean what I say, but only *indirectly*, at a second remove, in the words I take and give back to the community according to the protocols it establishes. My voice can mean, but only with others: at times in chorus, but at the best of times in a dialogue (Bakhtin, quoted in Holquist, 1981: 165).

Bakhtin's methodology will become clearer in chapter 3, where I use his ideas to analyse a series of football riots in Iran. Now I would like to set out briefly the principles of Activity Theory as the third, and final, methodology employed in the book.

In the 'West', Activity Theory emerged in many ways as a reaction against the 'fixation with the processing of information' that cognitive psychology became hostage to in the 1970s (Martin *et al.*, 1995b: 1). This was ironic since cognitive psychology itself surfaced partly as a reaction against behaviourism's rejection of the 'subjective'. However, the limitations of cognitive psychology were to manifest themselves in the 1980s and 1990s in partial critiques by those who felt the 'messy, real-life factors that influence cognitive functioning' are not taken account of by 'tidy laboratory' investigations (Hirst and Manier, 1995: 93).

Paralleling Bakhtin's critique of Saussure's fixation with *langue*, Activity Theory became critical of cognitive psychology's obsession with 'understanding the fixed, general characteristics of human information processing system- the cognitive 'machine'- rather than on the way people use the system' (Hirst and Manier, 1995: 94). In other words, once it became clear that 'the original goal of cognitive psychology to understand meaning was subverted by computational metaphors' (Martin *et al.*, 1995b: 8), Russian Activity Theory became an attractive option for those researchers interested in real-life events. As Rogoff *et al.* (1995: 126) have argued,

> Sociocultural perspectives assert that individual developmental processes are inherently involved with the actual activities in which people engage with others in cultural practices and institutions, and that variation is inherent to human functioning.

All forms of sociocultural psychology (or for our purposes Activity Theory) share certain assumptions. For instance, activity is assumed to be a unit of analysis. So the emphasis of the investigation tends to be on the way people engage in joint-activity, work with and extend cultural tools inherited from previous generations to solve problems (Rogoff *et al.*, 1995: 127). *Joint-activity*, as the crucial unit of analysis, compliments Vygotsky's *word meaning* and Bakhtin's *utterance*. Moreover,

> The sociocultural approach does not assume generality, but seeks to understand both similarities and variation according to the processes involved as people participate in cultural practices (Rogoff *et al.*, 1995: 128).

Following Vygotsky (1978), contemporary Activity Theory is not interested in examining products or human attributes separate from their development. Rather, as mentioned above, it focuses on the dialectics of product and process. Likewise, there is an attempt to investigate problems multi-dimensionally. The intra-, inter- and extra-psychological dimensions of research in the present work find an echo in Rogoff *et al.* (1995: 129) who suggest,

> ... the examination of individual, interpersonal, and community developmental processes involves different planes of observation, with any one plane being the topic of focus but with the others necessarily observed in the background.

Rogoff *et al.* (1995: 130) make a further point worthy of consideration regarding the cultural-historical nature of the research endeavour. According to them,

> Researchers can gain an understanding of their research endeavour and of the phenomena studied by examining their own roles in the inquiry and those of institutions in which the inquiry occurs.

An interesting example of this self-inquiry is the 'anti-capitalism' special issue of the *Annual Review of Critical Psychology* (Melancholic Troglodytes, 2003), where the editors have subjected the contributors and themselves to a (semi-serious) political 'interrogation'. A questionnaire at the beginning and a discussion section at the end of each article queries issues around social class, political affiliations and the psychological tensions arising from a 'joint-activity' such as the production of a scholarly journal.

1.3   METHODS

We now have a better understanding of our epistemology and methodology. In this section, I will briefly justify the three chosen *methods* ('research strategy or technique adopted') of investigation. These are: Ethnography, Participation Action Research (PAR), and Discourse Analysis (DA). All three methods were employed to some extent in every one of the case studies under investigation. As it becomes clear, none of these methods could be called problem-free. However, in the same way that Vygotsky, Bakhtin and Activity Theory combine well collectively, the three strands of qualitative methods I have used (Ethnography, PAR and DA) seem to cover up each others' inadequacies.

1.3.1   Ethnography

Ian Parker's (2005: 28) warnings about the origins of ethnography are quite ominous,

> Ethnography is sometimes characterised as a fairly innocent practice of 'hanging around' an organisation or community and 'making something of it' (e.g., Bowers, 1996). However, the history of ethnography is the history of observation, interference and control, intertwined with the history of colonialism; for the ruling of others was much more efficient when it was possible to understand better local 'natives' perceptions of the colonising powers (Clifford and Marcus, 1986).

Any radical ethnography worth engaging in, therefore, must be cautious of every representation of a 'community', whether it comes from the outside or is generated by members of the 'community' itself (Parker, 2005: 28). This type of research is a long-term commitment. Laura Nader (1993: 7) has argued, 'ethnography entails deep immersion and is seldom accomplished in short periods of time ... it is a feat of empathy and analysis'. To investigate the class struggle the researcher has to be an active participant in the social movement that negates capital. An ethnographic study has to place the researcher, the topic, and the sense-making process within an interactive framework (Altheide and Johnson, 1994: 485-486).

Mindful of the above limitations, I will use defamiliarisation as a way of bringing out the opposition between 'common sense' and subversive sub-cultures operating at the periphery of capital's media empire (Morrow and Brown, 1994). This approach will also lay bare the power relations involved *within* and *between* collectivities. These two ideas (defamiliarisation and power relations) are perhaps the two key ideas in ethnography. Parker (2005: 29) reminds us,

> ... although the researcher's initial encounters with a new life-world may be confusing, they need to beware of the transformation of the strangeness into familiarity. A community or sub-culture that they do not know will always very rapidly turn into something they think they know all too well, and so what is potentially interesting about the work starts to evaporate. The writing of a diary account through the course of the research should aim to keep alive the process of *defamiliarisation* (cf. Bennett 1979) ... [Moreover as researchers] get drawn into the particular language of a life-world they may lose sight of how that language is organised around patterns of *power*. It is worth keeping in mind that language always operates in the service of power, as feminist studies of the privilege given to men by the English language have shown ...

Poorly designed ethnographic studies suffer from certain other biases that need to be highlighted lest we inadvertently contribute to their re-production. For example, the fact that most ethnographic studies are conducted during 'peace' times,[25] when societal tension is contained, creates a built-in tendency to represent 'minorities' as victims. It also foregrounds differences between 'minorities' at the expense of what unites them into a 'majority'- their interest in overcoming capital.[26] In attempting to 'give a voice' to 'minorities', an ethnographic study could have the unfortunate side-effect of cementing the internal division within that 'community' by strengthening the status of 'community leaders'. The very notion of community is usually presented as unproblematic by most ethnographers. I, on the other hand, have replaced community with the more accurate term 'milieu' in most places. Where I have retained it, 'community' has been used in inverted commas since I assume, following Marx, that 'primitive community' was destroyed with the advent of classes and states, and that the true supercession of capital can only come about if a re-emergent community (*Gemeinwesen*) succeeds in abolishing capitalist society. In the *Economic and Philosophical Manuscripts* (1844/1984) Marx explained that the community cannot be opposed to the individual.

---

25 One of the few exceptions to this trend is Woofitt's (1993) study of violent clashes between punk rockers and the police. But then to reduce these incidents to examples of constructing/defending 'group identities', as Woofitt does, is to ignore the complex social dynamics of the phenomenon.

26 Today the proletariat constitutes the overwhelming majority section of society (everywhere) and yet if current psychological, sociological and historical research is to be taken seriously, the proletariat is only a small and diminishing segment of the population. Concepts such as 'race', 'ethnicity', 'gender', 'sexual orientation' and 'nationality' are usually misused in order to obscure essential features of the history of the working class. It is the working class (as employed or unemployed, male or female, black or white, homosexual or heterosexual, foreign or native, able or disable) that is the subject-object of my study and not the emasculated caricature favoured by most social scientists.

According to this definition there is no such thing as a community under capitalism, be it a 'European community', a 'mining community' or a *Ethnographic scuba-diving is not 'giving voice' to the fishes!*
'gay community'. These are examples of *false* communities even if one finds more solidarity and communication amongst its members than the rest of 'society'. However, the zone of proletarian development (ZPD) is capable of creating pockets of autonomy where the bourgeois rules of society are temporarily suspended in favour of a 'proto-community'. Demonstrations, strikes, carnivals and riots could be examples of this tendency.

Bearing in mind all these concerns, we may suggest that ethnography only becomes radical when it is part of 'a multimethod form of research' (Bannister *et al.,* 1994: 36). It is possible to combine a variety of data gathering techniques and to check construct validity from different angles, including participation research, interviews, observation, and discourse analysis. Demonstrations, strikes, carnivals and riots are sites of study-extension dealing with ineffable truths, unutterable partly because they are between meaning and action. For this reason, following Altheide and Johnson (1994: 492-493), they are acknowledged as the realm of 'tacit knowledge'. They

may even include 'deep structures from the *emotional* memory of past generations' (Altheide and Johnson, 1994: 492). Let me quote them once more to underline this vital approach,

> ... [in such research] the key issue is not to capture the informant's voice, but to
> elucidate the experience that is implicated by the subjects in the context of their
> activities as they perform them, and as they are understood by the ethnographer
> ... Tacit knowledge includes what actors know, take for granted, and leave unex-
> plicated in specific situations ... tacit knowledge may also include deep structures
> from the emotional memory of past generations (Altheide and Johnson, 1994: 492).

Any analysis that treats the subject matter as *merely* ethnographic or discursive or
textual overlooks the subtle and significant role of tacit knowledge.

1.3.2 Participation Action Research (PAR)

It is usually claimed that the origins of 'action research' lie in the humanist traditions
of Kurt Lewin and his attempt to blend theory, research and action (Pancer, 1997: 152-
153). Jiménez-Domínguez (1996: 223) suggests, however, that 'we have to recognise
the Anglo-Saxon origin of Participation Action Research, as well as its relationship
with Protestant methods of indoctrination ...'. Ironically, in 'Catholic Latin America'
followers of liberation theology indulge in a form of PAR and in the process enhance
the influence of religious ideas amongst the proletariat as well as cementing the authority of 'community leaders' such as priests and shamans (Parker, 2005: 99).

Lewin has also been criticised for adhering too uncritically to various tenets of
American liberalism and 'democratic social engineering' (cf. van Elteren, 1992: 52).
However, at his best and under the influence of his friend Karl Korsch, Lewin made a
genuine contribution to social psychology. In the 1930s, his psychological social psychology (PSP) was enhanced by Korsch's sociological social psychology (SSP) and although there was no lasting legacy from this collaboration, some of their ideas
predated Gergen's turn toward history by four decades (van Elteren, 1992).

Although mindful of some of Lewin's dubious historical baggage, I believe I
have taken sufficient precautions by (a) using a de-colonised version of Participation
Action Research, (b) relegating PAR to a method of research rather than methodology
thus minimising any ill effect, and (c) using PAR as 'prefigurative political practice'
(Parker, 2005: 95).

These amendments allowed me to minimise any inherent problem with traditional PAR and employ more recent versions of PAR in my efforts to study-extend
proletarian collectivities. Elliott's definition, for instance, is an acceptable updated version of
Lewin's approach, '[action research] is the study of a social situation with a view to improv-
ing the quality of action within it' (Elliot quoted in Banister *et al.*, 1994: 110). A stronger

definition would describe 'prefigurative' action research as 'the relationship between action research and the creation of alternatives to the existing social order' (Kagan and Burton, 2000: 73). Furthermore, the 'model of prefigurative action research provides a framework for keeping the micro, meso and macro actions and theories focused and connected' (Kagan and Burton, 2000: 84). According to Kagan and Burton (2000: 76),

> Action research suggests that the best way to understand something is to try to change it- but in the case of prefigurative action research, that understanding is itself part of a 'higher order' change project, sometimes reduced in its ambition, and sometimes suppressed, but an essential part of any critical project that goes beyond 'merely interpreting' the world …

A demonstration, a strike or a riot, especially one that requires solidarity and collective problem solving on the part of the participants in order to resist state oppression, is very similar to the experimental construct known as 'the jigsaw group technique'. This is a technique pioneered by Aronson and Gonzalez (1988: 301) with groups of school children where,

> … [they] are organised into small, multi-ethnic and multi-racial learning groups. Each member of the group is assigned one portion of the day's lesson, which he or she must teach to the rest of the group. Thus each group member must rely on the other group members to learn all the material.

Mistaken identities at the Paris Commune, 1871

A working class demonstration, composed as it is of a heterogeneous kaleidoscope of proletarian sub-cultures with different experiences and competencies, relies on a similar collective learning process to solve the problems class struggle sets it. An ideal

44

participation action research makes participants cognizant of the different pieces of the jigsaw and establishes the preconditions for solving the puzzle. The technique can be potentially 'empowering', so long as we understand the term to mean a form of enabling where 'research facilitates things to happen without setting the agenda or guiding the activities of co-researchers' (Parker, 2005: 98). I say 'potentially' since there are other types of 'empowering' which appear under certain conditions and these invariably lead to anti-working class practices. There is, according to Parker (2005: 97), 'empowering as the task of the *vanguard* where an elite appoints itself the champion of the oppressed. There is also 'empowering as *helping* where an institution embarks on charitable work, such as contemporary Non-Governmental Organisations (NGOs). We will have occasion to look at the reactionary nature of such 'empowering' practices in later chapters.

1.3.3 Discourse Analysis

> POLONIUS: What do you read, my lord?
> HAMLET: Words, words, words.
> …
> POLONIUS: (Aside) Though this be madness,
> Yet there is method in't.
> - Shakespeare, Hamlet: Prince of Denmark, Act II, Scene II.

Parker (1992: 5) provides a useful starting definition of discourse as 'a system of statements which constructs an object'. Even when a hermeneutic style of inquiry is used, '[discourse analysis remains] a type of hermeneutics which does not attempt to trace the meanings to an author' (Parker, 1992: 5). Discourses reproduce institutions and power relations and have definite ideological effects. Parker (2005: 68) again,

> Patterns of discourse in capitalist society hold in place chains of demeaning images of human beings divided from each other on the basis of different categories (of class and race, for example). These images are repeated across the many kinds of text we encounter each day … so that we live them out and come to believe them to be true … these images also require certain kinds of relationships between people, the social bonds that confirm to participants that this is the way the world is … Discourse working in this kind of way is the stuff of ideology, and so *'discourse' is the organisation of language into certain kinds of social bond.* [Emphasis in original]

The text is part of the machinery of desire. Actors are enticed into the scene of the play (say the annual Cenotaph commemorations in Britain), as players with power 'but not in command of the apparatus of power' (Parker, 1992: 5). Nikander (1995: 6) has summarised some of the features common to all forms of discursive analysis. I will present these features in relation to the leaflet reproduced as Appendix 1:

1) Discursive approaches see language as an active site for the continuing negotiation of various meanings and not as a window to an individual's mental state or cognitive processes. The uses and effects of language are foregrounded at the expense of the hidden meaning. The leaflet in Appendix 1 (*Mindful Thuggery and the Spectacularisation of Drama)* exemplifies this contestation by addressing its arguments to those workers who may hold conflicting ideas. In a sense, it is asking the rest of the working class to respond to its criticisms. It also displays a high level of self-reflexively with regard to its own construction as a 'committed' textual analysis.

2) Discursive analysts usually choose a dyad or some other relational group as their unit of analysis. Appendix 1 obviously chooses a rather larger group as its subject matter- the *proletariat.* However, it knowingly brings to attention the unity in opposition of its constituent parts by looking at the interaction of different sections of the demonstration, their general as well as specific interests.

3) Discursive approaches 'are often reluctant to present their analysis as the final truth or as the only possible reading of the data' (Nikander, 1995: 6). At first sight it seems that our leaflet does not meet this condition. After all, everything about the leaflet connotes monologic certainty if not downright dogmatism. At a first reading, it also smacks of patriarchal tendencies. The 'macho' discourse that permeates the leaflet at times conceals the emotive aspirations of solidarity and egalitarianism that informs it. However, a deeper familiarity with this many-sided sub-literature suggests that although revolutionaries consider certain principles beyond negotiation, the text is open. In fact, it actively seeks criticism and completion. The uncompromising discursive style including its 'machismo' reveals itself, on closer examination, to be nothing but a deliberate pose- an admittedly significant strategic pose.

If the above are features common to all forms of discourse analysis, then the following key ideas are usually associated with more radical forms of discourse analysis. Parker (2005: 68-69) mentions four key ideas. The first is the concept of *multivoicedness* of language (Bakhtin, 1981) which pays attention to contradictions and variability instead of hiding them. Multivoicedness is a particular form of *polyphony*, which Bakhtin discovered in some novels including Dostoevsky's work. In

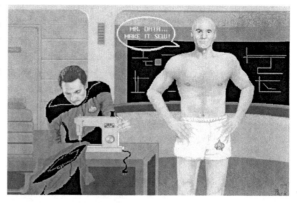

The multi-layered complexities of discourse

multi-voiced novels, the authors' and heroes' discourses interact on equal terms. Multivoicedness differs from *heteroglassia*, which refers to the clash of antagonistic social forces, especially the conflict between official and unofficial discourses within the same language (Morris, 1994: 249).

The second idea is the focus on *semiotics* (Barthes, 1973) which foregrounds the 'way we put language together in discussions and other kinds of text … and how we are put together … by language' (Parker, 2005: 69). The third idea is that of *resistance*, which shows how oppression and exploitation is legitimised (cf. Drury, 2003) sometimes by the banal ways certain repertoires, images and categories are flagged in everyday discourse (Billig, 1995). The fourth idea in discourse is the *chain of words and images* that organise language into certain kinds of social bond. Here it becomes essential to include a historical analysis of the discursive practice under investigation. I have attempted to incorporate all of these ideas in my book. However, it needs to be remembered that as with ethnography and PAR, discourse analysis too has its problems.

Some of the most biting criticisms of discourse analysis have emerged not from the positivist and empiricist traditions but, ironically, from within the ranks of discourse analysts themselves.[27] In a scathing attack on the limitations of the method, Parker and Burman (1993) cite numerous obstacles, some of which are pertinent to the current study. One major problem with discourse analysis is that 'it is sometimes difficult to determine that *different* discourses are at work' (Parker and Burman, 1993: 156). In our example (Appendix 1), the deliberate meshing of 'scholarly', 'radical', 'Shakespearian' and 'vulgar' discourses initially correspond to the rational, rhetorical, poetic, and carnivalesque aspects of communication. However, once the correspondence is established, the authors take great pleasure in undermining these constructs. Charting this meandering discursive road was at times problematic. A further problem relates to discourse analysis's tendency for *reification*. Reification has been defined as,

> The act of transforming human properties, relation and actions into properties, relations and actions of man-produced things which have become independent … of man and govern his life. Also transformation of human beings into thing-like beings which do not behave in a human way but according to the laws of the thing-world (Bottomore et al., 1988: 411).

---

27 Derek Hook is another critical psychologist who has made telling criticisms of Parker's use of discourse analysis. Accordingly, Parker by concentrating too much on discourse as text omits issue related to power, institutions and history. These criticisms may be true of the early Parker (1992). Discourse should be understood as activity, as 'event' (Hook, 2001) and not merely as a text. In later works (Parker, 2005) these problems are overcome. By employing discourse analysis as a method rather than methodology or epistemology and by using PAR and ethnography alongside DA, I have chosen an approach which should be immune to Hook's criticisms.

I have tried to overcome this problem by not treating the leaflet as an abstract and autonomous system of meaning. After all, it was produced at a specific socio-economic junction by a group of proletarians in what used to be called the 'West'. To generalise either its findings or the discursive method by which it was analysed to other settings would be a mistake. One further criticism of discourse analysis is relevant to the task at hand. Holzman (1996: 136) writes,

> Even before the emergence of discourse analysis, the tendency among philosophers, linguists, and psychologists interested in language has been to ignore emotive language, focusing instead on cognitive language (a practice, no doubt, which is a product and perpetuation of an overly masculine view of what language is and is of scientific value).

In other words, discourse analysis's over-emphasis on cognitive as opposed to emotive language should be overcome lest it skews our findings. Thankfully, this is less of a problem today than in years gone by.

I.4 REFLEXIVITY

Parker (2005: 19) has described *reflexivity* as 'a way of working with subjectivity in such a way that we are able to break out of the self-referential circle that characterises most academic work'. This is a useful starting point so long as we are mindful that reflexivity must also 'work with objectivity'.

The three layered model offered earlier is the framework for this kind of reflexive investigation. Reflexivity then becomes a way of attending to historical social relations, institutional locations and personal aspects of research. These three levels contain both a subjective and an objective dimension. This form of reflexivity does not psychologise the phenomenon under investigation nor does it reduce the account to a personal journey.

Cultural-historical psychology emphasises remembering as a collective process and not an isolated cognitive act by individuals. Instead of using a personal diary, for example, I have employed a myriad of personal accounts to provide a comprehensive account of May Day celebrations, football riots, anti-poll tax and anti-war demonstrations. In synthesising these accounts, I have been at pains to point out that some are posited by bourgeois commentators (e.g., various politicians' account of the 'desecration' of Churchill's statue falls in this category), others by leftist activists (e.g., most of the accounts appearing on IndyMedia, Schnews and PGA websites), and finally, those accounts that I feel most comfortable with (e.g., descriptions of events by fellow revolutionaries).

Reflexivity, therefore, does not treat the 'self' as the alpha and omega of analysis. Instead, it problematises the very notion of 'selfhood' by locating it within a cultural-historical psychology. It even suggests that 'self-identity' may be nothing more than a distorted and emasculated form of subjectivity. In other words, a limited and limiting 'self-identity' emerges since subjectivity cannot find expression within a col-

Cultural-historical psychology emphasises remembering as a collective process and not an isolated cognitive act ...

lectivity. The kinds of social ruptures described in the following pages become vital precisely because they provide the space for the expression of subjectivity within collectivity and thus the possibility of superseding 'identity' (cf. Holloway, 2002). The working class 'identities' discussed throughout the book are never treated as fixed and ahistorical. Rather they are viewed as a site of contradictions. Once these contradictions are resolved, 'identity' evolves. *Occasionally, the evolving identities attain the level of autonomous subjectivity.*

In view of the preceding arguments, how could a reflexive account of my research deal with the historical, institutional and personal levels of experience? At the historical level of analysis, I live in a capitalist world where my sole possession is an exchangeable labour power with a precarious market value. As a wage-slave I have produced surplus value in a number of occupations ranging from assembly-line factory work to teaching to building and decorating. I have been employed in the catering industry as both a cleaner and a sandwich-maker and in the film industry as a sub-titler, lighting-woman and sound recorder. This trajectory has provided ample experience with both the *formal* and *real* phases of capitalist development. What I lack in this regard is experience of *pre-formal* and *post-real* exploitation. My subjectivity and the various 'self-identities' I have donned and discarded along the way are shaped, although not determined, by this journey.

My criss-crossing of cultural boundaries has been equally enriching. I was born in what sociologists refer to as a 'developing' society within a cultural tradition steeped in Mithraic, Zoroastrian, Yazidi and Islamic beliefs. My early rejection of both religion and nationalism at the age of thirteen was a tremendous impetus for my further development. It also enabled me to take full advantage of my new cultural environment when at the age of fifteen I travelled to Britain for the purpose of 'educational improvement'. My initial experience with a British school was both exhilarating and frustrating since there was still at that stage a language barrier. Gradually I became as comfortable in my new British environment as I once were in my previous Afghani-Iraqi culture. Extended stays in Iran and Russia have also played a significant role in extending my horizons. I have employed the term *transcultural proletarian* to describe my current position. A person born and bred in one culture, who becomes immersed in another and as a result of constant and deliberate juxtaposing of these conflicting worldviews, ultimately supersedes all (official) cultures.

Finally, I was fully aware my work was addressing different groups of people. First, there are all those leftist individuals/organisations who may find my subject matter interesting but cannot possibly agree with my political interpretations. Second, various networks of radicals and revolutionaries who have participated (knowingly or inadvertently) in this joint-investigation. Third, various 'specialists' who may be interested in only parts of the work related to their own investigations. Fourth, the unknown *other* in the shape of proletarians who have never come across my work before. I was very mindful of these tensions as I was writing the book. It is, of course, unrealistic to expect a favourable reception within all these readerships. Nevertheless my unwarranted eternal optimism compels me to '[realistically] demand the impossible'!

I.5 STANDPOINT

There exist two interrelated issues that interest me regarding *standpoint*. The first concerns some of the claims made on behalf of standpoint theory (Harding, 1987; Hartsock, 1997). Is it valid to suggest that being located in an exploited, oppressed or disadvantaged group somehow confers moral or political authority upon members of that group? And secondly, does it always make good research sense to clarify the standpoint of the researcher to the reader?

Regarding the first question, there are a number of contradictory positions held by advocates of standpoint epistemologies. All agree, however, on basic tenets. As Ellis and Fopp (2001: 2) make clear,

> Although standpoint epistemologies argue that all knowledge is socially located, they maintain that knowledge gained from social locations outside or marginal to the socially dominant views challenge the discourses and practices which legitimate the subjugation and marginalisation of others.

So far, this is uncontroversial stuff since I presume even most members of the ruling class consider 'marginalised' knowledge to be in conflict with hegemonic knowledge. Standpoint's critique of 'Western' rationalism pushes its adherents to further argue that the experience and activities of certain 'marginal' or 'oppressed' groups provide a less partial and distorted account (Harding, 1991: 268), or an enlarged understanding (Harding, 1993: 24). The rejection of rationalism is grounded on the marginalised group's activity and practice. The bourgeois fragmentation of knowledge into 'fact' and 'value', or 'is' and 'ought' further underscores the need for treating the claims of rationality with caution.

It is noteworthy that some advocates of standpoint epistemology still possess faith in Enlightenment notions such as reason, rationality and progress (cf. Harding, 1991). Whether this represents genuine affection or a strategic pose is a moot point. Its implications inevitably lead to a certain moralism creeping into analysis. Now the marginalised group is fetishized as a magical site of knowledge production whose practice is more 'moral' than others. This 'moral superiority' may be concealed in terms of women's special relationship with nature and nurturing or the proletariat's 'dignity of labour'. In either case, it is an argument fraught with danger and perhaps unnecessary danger at that since there is no need to legitimise the marginalised group's activities through recourse to morality. The proletariat, for instance, fights against wage slavery not because of some moral imperative but because it is in its interest to do so.

In any case, *morality* as a separate sphere of human activity should itself be subjected to critique since it is both a tool and result of class society. Its role as a *tool* for launching crusades is becoming more explicit as capitalism's crisis deepens. This is evident in the almost constant reliance on propagandistic mini-crusades around asylum seekers, drug users, terrorists, paedophiles and Romanies/Gypsies. Morality is also a *result* of class differentiation since it first emerged in response to the separation of community into classes and private and public spheres. Morality is the glue keeping these spheres together. The proletariat does not need to base its cause on morality. We can leave such musings to the self-righteous.

My position throughout the book is to assume that groups that occupy a number of localities along the surplus value producing ladder and contain cultural/sexual diversity and move dynamically between various subjectivities are probably in possession of superior standpoint. Their multi-perspective epistemology permits them to understand their activities and the impact of their activities on society. This, however, does not confer any moral authority on their practices nor is it by itself guarantor of political success.

The second question posed at the beginning of this section related to the usefulness of clarifying the researcher's standpoint to the reader. Some claim readers do not need to know the position of the researcher for the research to be effective and radical (e.g., Gegenstandpunkt, 2003). There is *some* truth in this but only some. Ironically, if there is any validity to this position, it is not based on the arguments put forwarded by the Gegenstandpunkt group. I need to unpack this issue further below.

THE LADDER OF FORTUNE.

As can be discerned from the preceding sections, I have deemed it essential to clarify my *general* politics and personal developmental trajectory at the beginning of the book and at various seminal junctions throughout. For instance, the reader needs to be aware of my hostility toward religion prior to the chapter on Bakhtinian football riots (chapter 3), if s/he is to comprehend both the content and style of delivery. Likewise, it is necessary for the reader to be mindful of my antagonism toward both Leninism and Anarchism if the chapters on Mayday celebrations (chapter 2) and proletarian organisations (chapter 5) are to make any sense. However, is it absolutely essential for the reader to be cognisant of the myriad of 'ultra-left' communist, libertarian Marxist, autonomist, anarcho-communist, feminist-Marxist and situationist groupings that impacted my political thinking throughout the 1980s and 1990s? I would reply in the negative. A detailed exposition of these meanderings would be of interest to only a handful of readers and may even get in the way of the 'main message'.

An altogether more sensible approach was taken by the editors of the third issue of the *Annual Review of Critical Psychology* (2003), which I have already alluded to above. There a brief and open-ended questionnaire begins each text and an interrogative debate brings it to an end. The open-ended questionnaire deals with the class composition and political development of the authors. They are general conceptual handles which orient the reader toward certain pertinent issue usually concealed by choice or academic convention. Once these signposts are firmly planted, the reader can choose to follow or ignore them. I have followed a similar path.

The arguments presented by Gegenstandpunkt (2003) in favour of not clarifying the researcher's position, however, smack of a desire to maintain the myth of 'objectivity'. Gegenstandpunkt suggest 'the recourse to *standpoint* leads to the substitution of a clear logic of argumentation by emotional appeals' (Parker, 2005: 25). Similarly, they are wary of turning the political into personal issues because this may lead to the assumption that only personal issues are worth discussing. These are weak objections. In contradistinction, I would contend that arguments should be based on the dialectical urge to synthesise logic and emotions (as well as the political and the personal). To summarise, I believe it is usually worthwhile to make explicit the researcher's general standpoint without going into too much detail, thus leaving enough room for the reader to fill in the gaps as they see fit.

1.6 WRITING STYLE

A number of currents and thinkers have shaped the writing style of the book. Chief amongst these factors has been the need to critique previous political discourses around social movements and to contribute towards the creation of an alternative vocabulary. The alternative discourse relies on dislodging and altering existing utterances and/or inventing new ones. I have relied mostly on the former approach since I feel inventing new terms and discursive practices ought to be more of a collective endeavour.

In order to dislodge and alter existing discourses a number of thinkers and techniques were employed. These include,

> **Vygotsky:** Vygotsky (1978) reminds us to be mindful of both the *meaning* of terms and their *sense*. Meaning refers to stable, long term, dictionary definition of terms whilst sense refers to the personal nuance with which the term is imbued. I have dislodged common political discourse by providing the reader with alternative meaning and sense. The term 'class', for example, is given a very strict meaning which lasts throughout the book but at seminal points I have relaxed or deliberately undermined this novel meaning by offering a variety of senses. I have done this in order to provide the reader with ample opportunity to either oppose my categories or complete my thought process should they wish to do so. This is an argument familiar to post-structuralist and deconstructionists through the works of Susan Sontag and Michael Ryan on metaphor. Sontag (1990) sensitises us to the misuse of metaphors, especially the way conditions such as cancer and AIDS are inflic-

ted with military connotations. Ryan (1989), on the other hand, discusses how metaphors when used critically can underpin marginalised ideas dismissed by orthodoxy.

Leontiev: Leontiev (1981) underlines the fact that playing with the meaning and sense of words is not sufficient unless one also knows the *motivation* behind each term. Terms such as 'internationalism', 'socialism' and 'communism', for instance, have been employed by numerous political factions for substantially different purposes. By tracing the genealogy of such terms, it becomes possible to decide whether they can be refreshed or are best discarded in favour of new ones. In my work, for example, the terms 'internationalism' and 'socialism' are discarded as mystifying and reactionary whilst 'communism', once properly distinguished from bolshevism, is retained as the expression of proletarian social movement fighting capitalism.

Brecht: There is a great deal in Brecht that is reactionary. Brecht's insistence on objective viewing was, for example, based on behaviourist psychology. He also falsely 'assumed that the exercise of a critical attitude inevitably leads to the truth' (Lovell, 1982: 66). However, his notion of *Verfremdung* (translated as distanciation or estrangement or alienating) is still a useful tool for defamiliarising ideas so long as it does not lead us into reaffirming the Kantian split between objective and subjective dimensions of experience. It should be underlined that Brechtian distanciation is best thought of as an evolving process of defamiliarisation and not as a mere technique. My use of phrases such as 'leftism as the left wing of capital' is a prime example of distanciation. My rejection of 'Atheism' as yet another form of religiosity is another. In both cases, distanciation is intended to pave the way for an alternative

concept to emerge. Thus 'proletarian atheism' gradually comes to replace 'mechanical atheism' and a re-accentuated 'communism' takes the place of the discredited 'leftism'. This is in keeping with Sandra Harding's use of Brecht to shock, 'incite, discomfit and provoke' (Harding, 1991: xi). As Lyon and Conway (1995: 1) have explained, 'Harding asks us to read her, incited

54

and provoked, but ultimately to be able to use her work as a catalyst for … navigating between, the empiricist and the relativist positions and then finally for designing libratory social relations'.

Debord: Two ideas from Debord and the Situationists in general have been employed. The first is the notion of *detournement*, which stands for the 'integration of present and past artistic production into a superior construction' (cf. Knabb, 1989: 45). Many of the images are detourned in order to use existing bourgeois concepts in a rearranged and reassembled manner to undermine reactionary ideas. Detournement goes beyond mere negation (e.g., Duchamp's drawing of a moustache on the Mona Lisa) by negating the negation. The second defining imperative is Debord's desire to do away with the audience's passive consumption of a text/film. Although the Situationists over-emphasised the notion of passive consumption (mistaking quiet contemplation for passive consumption), there is a difference between dialogic texts that actively seek criticism, completion or even total rejection and those that monologically restrict the readers' response. I found Bakhtin's notion of *carnivalesque* very useful in fusing a sense of humorous playfulness and proletarian excess into my detourned ideas. Bakhtin allows us to move from 'high culture' to 'low culture' and back again in the process questioning both.

Detournement goes beyond mere negation (e.g., Duchamp's drawing of a moustache on the Mona Lisa) by negating the negation.

Chapter two:
Vygotskian May Days

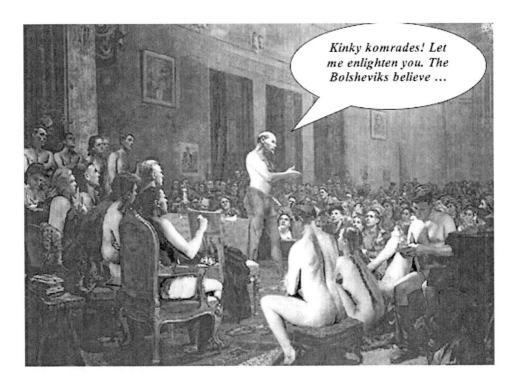

Not a Zone of Proletarian Development!

C h a p t e r   t w o :

Vygotskian May Days

*The concept of a historically based psycho-
logy is misunderstood by most who study
child development. For them to study
something historically means ... to study
some past event. They naively imagine an
insurmountable barrier between historic
study and the study of present-day behavioural forms.* To study something historically means to study it in the process of
change; *that is the dialectical method's basic demand.*

- Vygotsky, 1978: 64-65.

This chapter investigates May Day celebrations in London between 1999 and 2003 from a Vygotskian perspective. It argues that a 'zone of proximal development' (zoped) could be conceived as a social activity where individuality and collectivity are synthesised. Collaborative learning takes place within the zoped through the mediation of tools and with the aid of various strategies. A particular instance of this zone of *proximal* development (zoped) is the zone of *proletarian* development (ZPD). The chapter begins with a thumbnail history of the origins of May Day, followed by a précis of May Day activities as resurrected by radicals between 1999 and 2003.

It then introduces Vygotskian concepts useful for a study-extension of May Day. The chapter goes on to reformulate Vygotsky's 'zone of proximal development'[28] (zoped) in terms of Bakhtin's notion of 'carnivalesque'. Next, Vygotsky's methodological limitations are discussed. The chapter ends by discussing the relevance of Vygotsky to May Day celebrations.

2.1 THUMBNAIL HISTORICAL ORIGINS OF MAY

Peter Linebaugh's (1986) approach to May Day has proved productive for analysing the history of May Day. He traces its history along the 'green' and 'red'[29] dimensions. His slightly embellished definitions are also interesting,

> Green is a relationship to the earth and what grows therefrom. Red is a relationship to other people and the blood spilt there among. Green designates life with only necessary labor; Red designates death with surplus labor. Green is natural appropriation; Red is social expropriation. Green is husbandry and nurturance; Red is proletarianization and prostitution. Green is useful activity; Red is useless toil. Green is creation of desire; Red is class struggle. May Day is both (Linebaugh, 1986: 1).

The 'green' and 'red' categories represent a *politico-philosophical* distinction. I have added a *temporal* distinction between 'ancient' and 'modern' examples of May Day. There has been sufficient qualitative change between people's relationship to Nature and each other over the centuries to warrant such a move (cf. Lafargue, 1883/2000; Kovel, 1991; Zerzan, 1988). In ancient times, we related to Nature and the ruling class from a position of weakness. Today, increasingly, we are restating the relationship with our bosses from a position of strength and our bond with Nature dialectically. Below, I briefly look at these four permutations. Later, I will look at the conscious revival of these four strands of May Day by contemporary rebels.

2.1.1 The Ancient Green

Linebaugh suggests that the Green 'origins of May Day is to be found in the Woodland Epoch of History'. Its appeal seems to have been universal,

> The Greeks had their sacred groves, the Druids their oak worship, the Romans

---

28 According to Nissen *et al.* (1999: 419) Vygotsky adopted the term 'zone of proximal development' from city planning.

29 I include in the 'red' dimension not only autonomists, libertarian communists, anarchist and radicals of other hues but also, to some extent, the Leninists who have had an impact on the evolution of May Day (albeit a negative one, in my view). To deny that Leninists have been involved in organising May Day celebrations seems to be wishful thinking. The Leninist contribution represents the zone of bourgeois development (ZBP) within May Day zones of proletarian development.

their games in honour of Floralia. In Scotland the herdsmen formed circles and danced around fires. The Celts lit bonfires in hilltops to honour their god, Beltane. In the Tyrol people let their dogs bark and made music with pots and pans. In Scandinavia fires were lit and the witches came out (Linebaugh, 1986: 3).

· A·GARLAND·FOR·MAY·DAY·1895·

Why is Nature always feminine?

The battle over the length and content of May Day celebrations was fierce with the ruling classes attempting to both sanitise and curb the festivities. Linebaugh continues (1986: 4),

> The farmers, workers, and child-bearers (labourers) of the Middle Ages had hundreds of holy days which preserved the May Green, despite the attack on peasants and witches. Despite the complexities, whether May Day was celebrated by sacred or profane rituals, by pagan or Christian, by magic or not, by straights or gays, by gentle or calloused hands, it was always a celebration of all that is free and life-giving in the world. That is the Green side of the story.

2.1.2 The Ancient Red

The burning of witches was both an attack on women as well as a social offensive against the lower classes. Joan of Arc who was burned as a witch in May 1431 made the judges' task simpler through her candour. She told the judge,

> There is a tree that they call 'The Ladies Tree'- others call it 'The Fairies Tree'. It is a beautiful tree, from which comes the Maypole. I have sometimes been to play with the young girls to make garlands for Our Lady of Domremy. Often I have heard the old folk say that the fairies haunt this tree... (Quoted in Linebaugh, 1986: 3).

In addition to the charge of heresy, Joan of Arc was also accused of dressing as a man. Her 'religion' was animistic and promoted both men and women as shamans, hence its threat to a patriarchal institution such as the Church[30].

The repression, which began with the European witch-hunts, was extended to the slave trade and with the advent of capitalism, to the urban proletariat. In 1550 the British Parliament passed a law demanding the destruction of Maypoles and in 1644 the Puritans in England abolished May Day altogether.

---

30 Admittedly, this is but one interpretation of Joan of Arc. She is also revered by some as a Christian icon.

2.1.3 The Modern Green

With the intensification of religious repression the

> ... ancient charaders of May were transformed into an outlaw community, Maid Marions and Little Johns ... Merry Mount became a refuge for Indians, the discontented, gay people, runaway servants, and what the governor called the 'scum of the countrie' [sic] (Linebaugh, 1986: 5).

The May sports were from the 17th century onwards called the 'Robin Hood Games'. With the development of large-scale capitalist production in the cities, chimney sweeps and dairymaids became involved in the fight back. According to Linebaugh (1986: 6), 'the sweeps dressed up as women on May Day, or put on aristocratic periwigs ... Milk maids [got] the dairymen to distribute their milk-yield freely'. In the 19th century 'we may see Green themes in Mozambique where the workers lamented the absence of beer, or in Germany where three hundred witches rampaged through Hamburg' (Linebaugh, 1986: 11).

2.1.4 The Modern Red

In Britain, the Diggers and Ranters fought the repressions as effectively as possible given the limitations of their movement. The Ranters, in particular, understood very well the carnivalesque aspect of their struggle against encroaching capital relationships. The bosses' attack gathered pace throughout the 19th century and became consciously intertwined with the imposition of wage-slavery and discipline.

In America waves of immigrants entered urban centres after the Civil War. Linebaugh (1986: 8) recounts how 'in 1885 the Chicago police used Gatling guns against workers who protested the closing of the beer gardens', and how 'in the Bread Riots of 1872 the police clubbed hungry people in a tunnel under the river'. The local police, unable to deal with proletarian resistance, were trained by the

Is martyrdom part of May Day celebrations?

Pinkerton Detective Agency in the art of surveillance and anti-riot tactics.

From May 1, 1886 the celebrations were linked to the demand for the eight-hour day. Three days later, an unknown hand threw a stick of dynamite at a demonstration at Haymarket and all hell broke loose. When the dust settled, four radicals were found guilty at a show trial and hanged. Lucy Parsons, a widow of one of the hanged men went to England 'and encouraged English workers to make May Day an international holiday for shortening the hours of work' (Linebaugh, 1986: 9). There have been recent attempts to abolish May Day.

> Strikes were a regular feature of May 1st, until 1978, when the Labour Gov't declared the day a Bank Holiday. Attempts to wipe out the history of May Day have been common. The US has attempted to re-name May Day as Americanism Day, as well as Loyalty Day. Thatcher wanted to rename it Trafalgar Day! Hey, why not Thatcher Day!?! (urban75 bulletin board, 14 April 2000).

The four strands of May Day celebrations are usually kept apart by counter-revolution. It is to the credit of radicals resident in London that they were treated as part of a whole. It is to a brief account of their contribution that we now turn.

2.2 THE RESURRECTION OF MAY DAY IN BRITAIN (1999-2003)

> What's not destroy'd by Time's devouring hand?
> Where's Troy, and where's the May-pole in the Strand?
>
> - Reverend James Bramston (1694?-1744)

In 1999 British radicals made a conscious effort to revive the revolutionary traditions of May Day, which they rightly viewed as having been recuperated[31] by the official 'labour movement' (i.e., the Labour Party and the Trade Union Council).

In this process of revival, radicals set about uniting the Green and Red as well as the ancient and modern dimensions of May Day disconnected decades earlier. It is noteworthy how a small group of activists could establish the preconditions for collaborative activity and how these joint activities led to collective development. These May Day actions are 'zones of proximal development' (Vygotsky, 1978: 84) where *intersubjectivity* between participants permits the smooth transfer of responsibility and ensures 'knowledge consolidation' (Stone, 1998: 15). Minimally, *intersubjectivity* has been defined as,

> Individuals come to a task, problem, or conversation with their own subjective ways of making sense of it. If they then discuss their differing viewpoints, shared understanding may be attained ... In the course of communication, par-

---

31 *Recuperation* is not to be confused with mere co-option. Recuperation is the bourgeois act of turning a radical critique in the form of a text, idea, aesthetic or action into its opposite. The recuperated object, idea or activity then bolsters bourgeois relations and creates profit for the system. The commodification of Surrealist and Dadaist works would be an example of recuperation.

ticipants arrive at some mutually agreed-upon, or intersubjective, understanding (Tudge, 1992: 1365).

Admittedly, this is still a rather cognitivist take on intersubjectivity which both over-emphasises the rational aspects of the relationship and ignores that individuals' subjectivities are social even prior to coming together in group settings. Moreover, we should remember that intersubjectivity also involves the 'spiritual' dimension of col-

In Zurich May Day protesters travel in style.

lectivity, more suitably discussed in terms of 'solidarity' and 'comradeship'. The cognitivist bias of this definition also ignores Wertsch's demonstration that effective communication comes about through *partial* rather than complete intersubjectivity (Wertsch, 1980).

Perhaps a better take on *intersubjectivity* would be that of Maiers and Tolman (1996: 105) who define it, 'not as mere contemplation or self-reflection but as effective agency, which is achieved only in cooperation with others, that is, in societal, historical relations'. Once this crucial precondition is met, a special type of learning can take place. Engeström (1999: 2 and 5) refers to it as cycles of 'expansive learning',

a historically new type of learning which emerges as practitioners struggle through developmental transformations in their activity systems, moving across zones of proximal development ... the expansive cycle begins with individual subjects questioning the accepted practice, and it gradually expands into a collective movement or institutions ... At the same time, the cycle produces new theoretical concepts -theoretically grasped practice-concrete in systemic richness and multiplicity of manifestations.

Expansive learning does not run away from actually existing conflicts, disagreements, tensions and antagonisms but actively uses them in 'a process of learning through self-organisation from below' (Engeström, 1996: 168). For instance, disagreements routinely break out amongst protesters about violent and peaceful methods of protest. One such standoff became well known enough to reach the pages of newspapers,

> Divisions have emerged among the protesters, too. Peter Cadogan, who helped or-
> ganise the 1968 anti-Vietnam war protest in London, criticised the 'Wombles' - the
> self-styled leaders of May Day Monopoly, who plan to wear padded boiler suits to
> protect them from police batons ... 'The enemy is not the police', he said. 'If we
> misidentify the enemy we shall be the agents of our own defeat' ... He broke with
> the organisers when they refused to identify any aims beyond anti-capitalism, and
> they in turn have called him a 'splitter' ... Cadogan said this weekend: 'The lead-
> ership want sheep-like solidarity, and they are condemning anyone who doesn't
> fall into line' (The Observer, 22 April 2001).

Such exchanges have become better informed and less dogmatic in recent years fol-lowing death and detention meted out to protesters from Genoa to London. They have become part of our 'expansive learning'. For instance, in analysing the role of the 'Black Bloc' and its connections to violent attacks on property during the Genoa protest, the anarchist journal *Thrall* makes the following observations,

> ... an unholy alliance of capitalist media, politicians, relief agencies, debt cam-
> paigners and even rock 'stars'[32] are blaming anarchists for 'violence' ... [in this re-
> gard] a distinction needs to be made between violence against the private property
> of capitalist exploiters and against human beings. Violence against property is un-
> derstandable, but violence against human beings is nearly always unjustifiable, ex-
> cept in legitimate cases of self-defence ... [and regarding the Black Bloc] it is a
> mistake to claim that anarchism equals the Black Bloc ... it is a widely known fact
> that much of the violence in Genoa was committed by police provocateurs as well
> as fascist groups who infiltrated the Black Bloc ... (Thrall, 2001).

I do not know whether the Black Bloc was infiltrated by fascist and police pro-vocateurs or not. For me the significance of the above analysis lies in its calm, assured manner and its genuine desire to confront problems within the movement. The fact that the Black Bloc's tactics (including anonymity and black masks) makes them an easy target for infiltration was one of the most salient lessons that came out of the dis-cussions following Genoa. From a Communist perspective, Melancholic Troglodytes who criticised the media's depiction of 'violence' as a 'de-contextualised metaphysical entity' reached a similar conclusion,

---

32 This is four years before Sir Bob Geldof's denunciation of rioters at Gleneagles (Scotland) as 'idiots' and 'losers' (BBC TV News, 5/07/2005).

... *violence* was posited as a de-contextualised metaphysical entity, so that the media could equate the subversive *violence* directed against private property and the state, with the reactionary attacks of [German Nazis] on blacks and asylum seekers. The *dictatorship of the proletariat* can be 'violent' or 'peaceful', it can be 'silent' or 'deafening', it can be expressed 'individually' or 'collectively', with a 'frown' or a 'smile'. But it must always be out in the open, for all to see, debate and critique (Melancholic Troglodytes, appendix 1).

The following paragraphs are brief accounts of the May Day events that took place in London between 1999 and 2003. The whole process of preparing, executing and analysing these celebrations should be considered as an example of 'expansive learning'.

2.2.1 May Day on the Tube (1999)
On 1 May 1999,

> several hundred people gather at the Tower of London. In smaller groups they descend underground, on to the Tube ... On board decorations go up ... balloons are released, slogans displayed, games set out, music played, food given away and signs erected declaring the line under joint worker/passenger control ... a leaflet is distributed, mimicking in style that of London Underground (LU) ... setting out the case against privatisation, showing how strikes are good for workers and commuters alike, and linking this to a demand for a free transport system and to the need for a new world (Black Flag, 1999: 1).

The underground was chosen as the site of action because there was already a bitter struggle between tube workers and management of London Underground. The action was intended to show solidarity with tube workers 'with the potential to unite all proletarian Londoners' (Black Flag, 1999: 1). There were homemade placards declaring 'we love the Tube Strikers' seen in London. Large numbers of police officers met the protesters. The police stopped the train. Most of the passengers left the train and the train was then allowed to proceed to its destination station without stopping on the way.

Many 'protesters' turned up expecting to be 'entertained'- a problem that becomes more acute in the following years. Once on the train, only a few of the protesters engaged the passengers in a debate. Despite these shortcomings, The Black Flag (1999: 2) article concludes,

> In the main, the action was a success. A large number of people attended. The decorations were brilliant, the food good (although not enough people brought any), the atmosphere was light hearted and the leaflet was great. So far, there has only been limited feedback from tube workers, but there have been requests for further information and a number of positive comments. The leaflet has also become sought after.

After such an action, however, we have the opportunity to reflect upon it with the benefit of hindsight, and to draw what lessons we can for the future.

The Black Monolith demands to be the centre of attention!

2.2.2 Festival of Anti-Capitalist Ideas and Action (2000)

This four-day festival involved,

> a Critical Mass cycle ride in central London and a revolutionary history walk of the East End. The highlight of the latter was the surreal sight of a group of revolutionaries standing outside the former Match Girl strike factory, which is now Yuppie flats, in the pouring rain surrounded by cops! (Ourmayday website, 2003).

We will discuss later how these historical walks act as external aids for social memory as described by Vygotsky (1978). During the four-day festival around 2,000 people attended various workshops. On May Day itself,

> Parliament Square was transformed by Guerilla gardening … The enduring image was of the statue of mass murderer Churchill dressed in a green turf mohican and the desecration of the cenotaph (Ourmayday website, 2003).

Borrowing sentiments from the English Diggers and Ranters as well as the more recent example of the US Wobblies, the protesters tied a banner across the treasury building declaring, 'the earth is a common treasury for all'. They also engaged in gardening outside

Parliament Square. This simple action exposed the private nature of 'public' space as well as its nationalistic underpinnings (see also Chan and Sharma, 2007 for an alternative version of *commoning*). The guerilla gardening action was made easier due to police incompetence,

> The police had swamped the one acre field with water the previous night in an attempt to discourage people from sitting around, but this only made the turf easier for the guerrilla gardeners to 'relocate' on to the road (urban75 bulletin board, 2 May 2000).

May Day 2000 also saw a mini-riot at Trafalgar Square. One of the leaflets produced immediately after the event (Melancholic Troglodytes, 2000, Appendix 1) has already been

alluded to. A strange mix of narrative, analysis, Shakespearean quotes and gutter vulgarity, the leaflet inspired the present investigation into May Day celebrations as zones of proximal development. After the demonstration William Hague the ex-Tory leader 'challenged Mr Blair to back a call by Steve Norris, the Conservative candidate for London mayor, to ban May Day demonstrations next year' (The Guardian, 3 May, 2000).

Altering the psycho-geography of Parliament Square

2.2.3 Monopoly May Day (2001)

A monopoly board game theme was designed for May Day 2001. As the game guide put it, 'the game of monopoly is one of accumulation, making it perfect for our times' (Our May Day website, 2003). This is how the Guardian reported it,

> Activists have dubbed this year's demonstration 'May Day Monopoly' after the property-buying board game. Last week organisers distributed a game guide on the internet, identifying targets on the famous Monopoly streets. Although none of these is in the City, police believe the demonstrators are unlikely to turn down the chance to hit at the heart of British capitalism (The Guardian, Sunday April 8, 2001).

About 5,000 anti-capitalists turned out to play May Day Monopoly despite threats by the media, police, Blair and Mayor Livingstone. The media is well accustomed to terrorising would-be demonstrators. For instance, the police through the media threatened to shoot demonstrators with rubber bullets,

The police believe the event will attract a hard core of activists still on the wanted list from last year's May Day demonstration, which brought chaos to Parliament Square, Whitehall and Trafalgar Square. Over the coming weeks they will make fresh appeals to the public to identify rioters from photos taken last year, and hope to seize the ringleaders when they arrive in London (The Guardian, Sunday April 8, 2001).

The actions carried out on the day were varied and geographically dispersed enough to make the task of the authorities difficult. These included,

A picket of Coutts bank for the abolition of money, a demonstration outside HMP Pentonville, and, for the finale, a party against consumerism in that metropolis of shopping, Oxford Street (Ourmayday website, 2003).

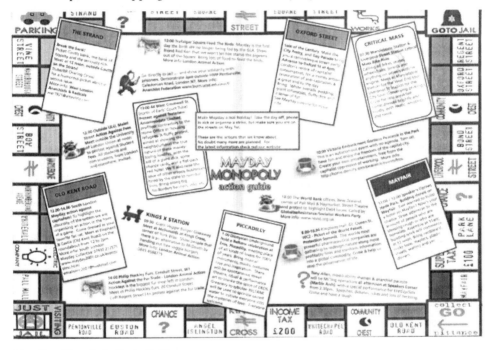

May Day Monopoly Game Guide

In general, people seemed more aware of counter-revolutionary tactics employed by the Trotskyite front group Globalise Resistance who marched some sections of the protesters (but not as many as they wanted to) into Oxford Circus. Learning from past encounters, the demonstrators also employed various decoys to confuse the police. Even having prior knowledge of this tactic does not help the authorities since its flexibility and speed of action can take them by surprise,

Although London's financial district is not included on the Monopoly board, City police sources said previous experience of anti-capitalist demonstrations showed that targets identified in advance by the organisers often turned out to be decoys (The Observer, 22 April, 2001)

Another leaflet (reproduced as Appendix 2, ironically entitled, *The Glorious Proletarian Siege of Oxford Street: a Revisionist Misinterpretation of the May Day 2001 Debacle!*) by Melancholic Troglodytes sets out to analyse the reasons for the state's success in cordoning off thousands of protesters in Oxford Street. Using quotes from Sun Tzu's *The Art of War*, the leaflet makes comparisons with past struggles including the First Gulf War, the anti-poll tax rebellion and 'the 1990 Brixton Prison' demonstration (which was attacked by mounted police and driven off the roads). The use of Sun Tzu's *The Art of War* is highly ironic, since the leaflet warns against being 'militarised'. Echoing H. G. Wells's notion of 'open conspiracy', the leaflet explicitly discusses how revolutionaries can out-manoeuvre the media and use legal counsellors without losing the initiative.

2.2.4 Sex Workers' May Day (2002)

Protesters were determined to avoid being cordoned off by the police as they were in 2001. Consequently, they 'split into several large groups, on bicycles and on foot, and began walking in a seemingly pointless circle' (The Guardian, 2 May 2002).

The day consisted of a number of smaller workshops, including *psycho-geographic* tours of strategic nodes of power in central London, culminating in a demonstration/carnival in Soho, organised chiefly by the Sex Workers' Collective. As described by the Situationists, 'psychogeography is the study of the specific effects of the geographical environment, consciously organised or not, on the emotions and behaviour of individuals' (Knabb, 1989: 45). Psycho-geography opposes bourgeois disciplines dealing with the effects of environment on individuals such as Behavioural Geography, Time-and-Motion studies, Ethology, Industrial Sociology and Games Theory.

Old Compton Road was chosen as the location for this symbolic action. Months earlier, a member of the neo-fascist British National Party had blown up a pub on Old Compton Road as part of his campaign against gays, Blacks and Asians.[33] This action coincided with demonstrations by sex workers in India and Bangladesh,

---

33 The perpetrator was portrayed by the state as a 'deranged loner' and not connected to the BNP. This is in dire contrast to the subtle ways in which the same state has stigmatised the 'Muslim community' in Britain for the actions of Al-Qaeda. Here the very 'normalcy' of the terrorists is being used to tarnish the entire sub-population from which they came.

In India nearly 3,000 sex workers carried torches through the streets of Calcutta in a May Day parade to demand legal status and social security. Sex workers from neighbouring Bangladesh and Nepal, two key suppliers of prostitutes to Indian brothels, also took part (The Guardian, 1 May 2002).

In France May Day was turned into a 1 million strong demonstration against Le Pen's National Front, displaying the flexibility of May Day as a platform for a variety of causes to converge and strengthen each other.

The French interior ministry and media reports have put the numbers on the streets at close to 900,000 across at least 70 cities in the country but this does not take into account the 200,000 people already massed in Paris for a demonstration later today. It is the biggest protest in France since the student demonstrations of 1968 ... The rallies came after the far rightwing leader held a much smaller demonstration in Paris to honour Joan of Arc, who his National Front party has adopted as its heroine (The Guardian, 1 May 2002).

The co-option of Joan of Arc from a rebel to a pillar of the establishment is an interesting phenomenon in relation to Linebaugh's earlier discussion of her role as a witch-warrior. Meanwhile in Britain there was a detectable shift in the attitude of trade union leaders. Previously both them and the police had sought to separate TUC rank-and-file from anti-capitalist protesters. One way of doing this was to organise a numerically smaller (and therefore manageable) trade union march. However, on this occasion trade union leaders employed a slightly different tactic for harbouring division and competition between these two factions of the proletariat. The manoeuvre was accompanied by a predictable depoliticisation of May Day,

> ... the trade union movement sought to reclaim May Day after two years in which it has become the preserve of the emergent anti-globalisation movement ... Last year just 500 people attended the TUC march in London, but yesterday more than 5,000 people joined a march to Trafalgar Square which brought together a wide range of different groups, from traditional unions to international radical organisations (The Guardian, 2 May 2002).

So whilst the police and media isolated the most militant section of the crowd, trade union leaders were working overtime to reclaim May Day for official Labourism.

2.2.5 The one that time forgot! Or at least tried to! (2003)

The police had absorbed a valuable lesson from past Critical-Mass bike demos and 20 police officers on fancy bikes chaperoned the protesters. Some 'fluffy' protesters used the occasion to discuss bike issues with the boys in blue. Most had enough sense to avoid unnecessary chitchat. A protest outside the arms manufacturers, Lockheed Martin, was organised for the afternoon. The police tried to kettle-in the demonstrators as in previous years but many broke free and joined the main march before the cordon was tightened. There were minor scuffles but few arrests. Around 3,000 attended the well organised trade union march which ended at Trafalgar Square before breaking up peacefully. According to the Guardian (1 May 2003),

> Animal rights activists targeted shops selling fur, with about 30 protesters gathering outside Dolce and Gabbana and another 15 or so outside Hockley's fur shop.

The protests intended against the City of London organised for the next day failed to materialise, due largely to apathy. Some protesters moaned about lack of interest and low turn-outs. Some wondered if May Day celebrations had become unfashionable. This is a problem that torpedoes next year's (2004) celebrations. In fact, a handful of organisers were so dismayed by the response to planning and preparatory meetings for the May Day 2004 events that they declared 'May Day cancelled' (Anonymous, 2004). Although the leaflet was lambasted as arrogant by many radicals who could not fathom how any group can cancel May Day unilaterally (not even in jest!), it nonetheless made a number of salient points worthy of attention. Whilst criticising the 'scattergun' approach of many activists (e.g., Reclaim the Streets) and the 'insipid' creeping culture of leftist Johnny-come-latelies (i.e., Leninists), it also criticises Communists and Anarchists for not overcoming the theory-practice divide. It goes on to discuss how the 9/11 events, the war in the Middle East and 'embedded police forward intelligence and surveillance and preemptive tactics' have largely worn down the radicals (Anonymous, 2004: 3).

As far as I am concerned, May Day lost its appeal as a zone of proximal development around 2003 and the 2004 picnic at Hyde Park was a confirmation of this negative trend. Whether this trend is easily reversible or not remains to be seen. According to a recent leaflet circulated in London and on the Net, things have deteriorated further with the advent of Euro-May Days and Pan-European organising in general. I quote from *Why is organising on a 'Europe-wide' basis such a bad idea?* (2005),

> At various meetings arranged to help mobilise against the G8 summit, the idea of creating European Networks has been presented ... Whereas some may see 'European-wide' links as being a healthy way of breaking out of the limits of the nation, for us the real key to internationalism lies in its universalism. We suggest that the abandonment of 'Europe-wide' organising is necessary to allow a more egalitarian way of organising which does not privilege the 'European', whether understood in terms of culture, race or region (West Essex Zapatista, 2005).

The fact that such basic lessons of class struggle have to be stated time and again is indicative of dogged resistance by a core of middle class reactionary activists who seek to monopolise the 'anti-capitalist pulpit' for their own agenda.

2.3 VYGOTSKY AND MAY DAY DEMONSTRATIONS

> A problem must arise that cannot be solved otherwise than through the formation of new concepts.
>
> -Vygotsky, 1987b: 55.

2.3.1 Concepts reformulated

The 'zone of proximal development' (zoped) is the distance between what a child can do on his/her own and what he/she can do with the aid of a teacher or able peer. Or at least this was Vygotsky's original take on the concept as described in chapter 6 of *Mind in Society* (Vygotsky, 1978). Here the emphasis was on the potential to go beyond IQ testing and embrace a more dynamic concept of intellectual development. Later, in chapter 6 of *Thinking and Speech* (1987c) the 'emphasis falls more heavily on instruction' (Wells, 1999). In any case, we must endeavour to move beyond Vygotsky's definition(s), for his normative predilections could be quite reactionary at times.

In this task, we face an immediate obstacle. After all, it has been argued that the projection of developmental findings from adult-child interactions onto the terrain of cultural psychology has a whiff of racism about it, something Vygotsky himself was partially guilty of (Speaker, Jr., 1999: 4). I feel it would be impossible to exonerate Vygotsky completely of this charge by pointing out the worst aspects of cross-cultural studies inspired by him were in fact carried out by his disciples such as A. R. Luria.[34]

Parallel to the rejection of interpreting developmental studies cross-culturally, there has been a move in recent years amongst neo-Vygotskians toward the studying of adult-adult relations. In conjunction with these reinterpretations, co-constructionist perspectives have placed emphasis on the active role of adult and child learning and

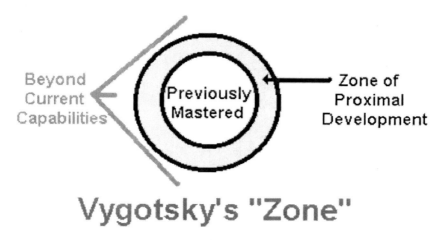

Vygotsky's "Zone"

A simplistic and outmoded notion of zoped.

in so doing have further restored the symmetry of this relationship. Hasse (2001: 208) has 'proposed adding something to Vygotsky's model, namely that the teacher himself [sic] also has an actual and a potential developmental zone'.

The zoped is, after all, a way of describing and engaging in joint activity not a disposition, trait, skill or ability. Unfortunately many pragmatic interpretations of Vygotsky focus on 'skill transmission of discrete bits of knowledge via social interaction from the knower to the learner' (Kinginger, 2002: 245). These interpretations are in harmony with a utilitarian/Taylorist view of education as transmission of quantifiable information commodities.[35]

---

34 In fact the Anglo-Americanisation of Vygotsky has privileged adult-child educational dyads as the ideal subject of Vygotskian intervention: 'It is interesting to note that nowadays countless investigators of mother-child dialogues and joint problem solving (with their emphasis on the steering role of the more experienced other in an intimate setting) feel obliged to refer to Vygotsky, although in fact Vygotsky never discussed these situations and instead focused more upon culture as providing tools for thinking' (van der Veer and Valsiner, 1994b :6).
Regarding cross-cultural interpretations, Blunden (2001: 5) reminds us that for Vygotsky the 'raw sense power' of city-rural dwellers as well as able-disable individuals to be roughly the same: '... according to Vygotsky, ... the raw power of all our senses is near to identical with those people who live in the tribal way, close to Nature, and the hearing of blind people is in fact no more acute than that of sighted people'.

35 For a seminal discussion of the influence of utilitarian ethics (via the sensationalist philosophy of the 18th

Hasse, on the other hand, sees the zoped as always relational and connected to activity systems. She has also convincingly reinterpreted the notion of *creativity* from an individualistic perspective to a relational one: 'Apart from being a relation between a mentor and an apprentice, creativity can be seen as a meeting between an individual and a wider activity system' (Hasse, 2001: 200). This approach does not deny individual creativity. It merely points out that to be 'considered creative, creative persons have to be recognized as such from the social movement' (Hasse, 2001: 216).

So gradually, we are moving from Vygotsky's (alleged) favourite relationship in the form of a dyad to wider collectivities and re-accentuating notions such as development and creativity accordingly- a move away from cognitive interpretations of the zoped toward an activity-based understanding of the concept. Regarding this form of group activity Shotter (1995: 1) has noted how 'other human beings can *call* us, so to speak, into (what for us) is a new practice, into a new activity, into new ways of making links and connections between things that we have not done before'. During demonstrations in response to 'the circumstances they create, we spontaneously come to do what we have never done before … [afterwards] they can point to us what it is we are already doing spontaneously, and cause us to attend to its details and features' (Shotter, 1995: 5).

… *we spontaneously come to do what we have never done before …*

The way I have interpreted the zoped underlines what Super and Harkness, (1986, quoted in Cole and Wertsch, 1996: 4) have aptly referred to as a 'developmental niche' for the newcomer. The zoped is 'simultaneously a socio-physical location, a cultural medium, and an interpretive framework' (Cole and Wertsch, 1996: 5). Shotter is further helpful because he emphasises the heterogeneous nature of our culture, 'and the fact that so-called primitive, mytho-poetic forms of thought and action [Vico] co-exist with modern, more rational forms- indeed, the two mutually support each other' (Shotter, 1996: 1). Social and cultural psychologies have historically been unable to deal with such complex networks of associations.

In an attempt to unite Vygotsky's zoped with psychotherapeutic notions, Leiman (2001: 315) has had to conduct a manoeuvre similar to my investigation, i.e.,

---

century French philosopher Condillac) on pedagogy in England, see Nikolas Rose (1985: 19).

change some of the features of zoped in order to make it more amenable to adult-adult relations. He notes that achieving problem solving skills for children may be hampered by limits to cognitive ability[36] but for clients overcoming problems may be hindered due to psychological pain.

This is certainly true of learning/re-learning about revolutionary ideas, a process involving the ditching of old certainties in favour of positions in constant flux. One can understand how this process leads to a certain conservatism amongst *most* Leninists and *many* Anarchists, Left-Communists, Autonomists and Situationists. In extreme cases this conservatism may even result in a 'fundamentalist' outlook.[37]

Leiman also observes how clients sometimes advance along various 'stages' of development more than one level at a time, something rarely seen in children. This is also true of dialectical moments of revolutionary insight, moments of insight that are at the same time points of rupture from the conservative self. This multi-stage developmental jump is also a feature of some post-event discussions especially during long-term campaigns.

The Trafalgar Square Defendants Campaign, for instance, was set up to support people arrested after one of the most severe riots in British history, the anti-poll tax riot of 1990. The role of such long-term campaigns, apart from providing psychological support and solidarity to defendants, involves a close engagement with four groups/institutions: the defendants themselves (who may or may not wish to 'politicise' their defence); the families of the defendants (who may or may not be supportive of their relatives' political actions but are in either case an intrinsic part of the campaign); the lawyers, organisations such as Amnesty International and local MPs (who again may or may not be politically sympathetic to the defendants' cause but could be gently persuaded to use their 'good offices' for the benefit of the defendants); and finally, hostile groups such as the police, Crown Prosecution Services and the media (whose lies and distortions must be exposed at every turn).

Close involvement with the vicissitudes of such campaigns may result in advancement along various *stages* of development more than one level at a time. Leiman also notes that the nature of therapeutic assistance is altered in adult-adult interactions. Here therapists familiarise the client,

> with the art of self-observation and self-reflection, mostly by providing a variety of useful semiotic tools, such as redescriptions, clarifications and confrontations, focusing of joint at-

---

36 A further difficulty with the concept of problem solving is that it is an essentially *reactive form of learning* (Engeström, 1987: 14). Learning is defined in a restrictive manner without the opportunity for the learner to alter the context of the learning experience.

37 By 'fundamentalism' here I am referring to an outlook with three features: 1) an extreme 'conservatism' which sets itself against experimentation and originality; 2) a reverence for precedence and the 'word' which comes to dominate *praxis*; and 3) a certain moralising and self-righteous attitude which prejudges all and sundry since it considers its lofty principles superior to the uninitiated. 'Fundamentalism' does not have to be religious. 'Secular' doctrines such as contemporary Anarchism, Leninism, Left-Communism, Libertarian Communism, Autonomism and Situationism all have their fundamentalist versions vying with each other in the realm of imbecility.

tention, elaboration, and interpretation. In some therapies, the client is encouraged to explore alternative viewpoints or even to try alternative action forms … (Leiman, 2001: 315).

The above quote is a remarkably accurate description of how more knowledgeable revolutionaries assist less knowledgeable ones through a series of unofficial rehearsals, redescriptions and reinterpretations of events, especially during periods when state persecution reaches new heights.

Another reformulation that needs underscoring is the use of terms such as 'internal' and 'external'. Throughout this text, these terms are employed as a loose conceptualisation. As Erica Burman (1994: 33) has rightly observed, '… there is no easy separation between internal and external, and the exhibition of … behaviour must be regarded as both reactive and interactive'. Moreover, in order to overcome dualistic interpretations, various researchers have tried to revive (and update) Vygotsky's dialectical notions. For instance, P. van Geert (1994: 350) emphasises the 'notion of mutual or reciprocal causality' and Valsiner (1994) underpins bidirectionality in the person-environment relationship. In 1999, Wells proposed a dialectical approach to learning in the zoped and has extended learning and development across the life span (see Chak, 2001: 385).

Understandably, the *meaning, sense* and *boundaries* of zoped have undergone reformulation since Vygotsky's times.[38] Some of the most insightful commentary on zoped, commentary directly relevant to viewing the zoped as moments of social metamorphosis, comes from Newman and Holzman (1993a). The zoped, they contend,

is where and how human beings totally transform our circumstances (making something new); it is the location of human (revolutionary) activity. The zoped, then, is simultaneously the production of revolutionary activity and the environment which makes revolutionary activity possible (Newman and Holzman, 1993b: 29).

Therefore, the zoped is not just a space. It is also an activity. The zoped is the creation of an environment or an engagement where emotions, philosophy and consciousness can develop. Vygotsky was clear that the exclusion of consciousness from psychology would lead to either behaviourism or idealism,

… what is most important is that the exclusion of consciousness from the domain of scientific psychology to a considerable extent preserves all the dualism and spiritualism of former subjective psychology (Vygotsky, 1999: 4).

The study of consciousness aims to supersede such dualism. Ratner (2000), for instance, explains how the segregation of personal life from public life was the institu-

---

38 I will discuss these terms more fully below. Briefly, *meaning* refers to the stable, dictionary definition of a term; *sense* refers to the constantly altering personal significations of a term; and *boundaries* refer to the upper and lower limits within a zoped.

tionalised foundation for the general dismissal of emotions as irrational, impulsive, personal, and primitive. This is precisely the reason why there is a concerted attempt to suppress emotions in *most* cultural activities associated with ruling class hegemony (such as the Cenotaph commemorations and western funerals in general).[39] Ratner also looks at the connection between *consciousness* and *sociality*. First, he makes a distinction between 'genuine sociality' which 'is a profound interpenetration of individuals such that each is a formative influence on the other', and lesser forms of sociality which include 'primitive communication, modelling, and stimulating of sequential behaviours' (Ratner, 1991: 28-29). Then he demonstrates the interdependence of this 'genuine sociality' and consciousness,

> Sociality generates consciousness in two complementary ways: (a) Sociality acts as a goal (or 'final cause' in Aristotle's terminology), the realisation of which spurs consciousness to develop. In this case, consciousness extends itself *in order* to accomplish the social goal. (b) Sociality also acts as an established *force* (or, 'efficient cause' in Aristotle's terminology) on consciousness. Here, consciousness develops *because* of existing social influences. The distinction between the two is not always plain because they typically operate jointly.

The last sentence is important. I do not believe it is essential for participants in a demonstration to be aware of the exact nature of sociality (i.e. whether it is working as a 'final cause' or an 'efficient cause'). But this 'genuine sociality' is a prerequisite for dialectical consciousness; the kind of consciousness that breaks down false compartmentalisation, such as the private-public or emotion-intellect binaries. Some demonstrations break down the split between private and public and in so doing challenge the interpretation of emotions as irrational as well as subverting bourgeois morality which requires for its perpetuation a strict regimentation between the private and public spheres of living. And here is where Vygotsky's notion of *learning leading development* finds a focus, for 'creating a philosophical environment involves, in Vygotskian terms, *relating to people as ahead of themselves*' (Ratner, 1991: 136, emphasis added). This is the exact opposite of bourgeois *common sense*. Positivist science sets up experimental situations to describe and control alienated life. The Vygotskian enterprise creates zones of proximal development 'in order to transform alienated reality' (Newman and Holzman, 1993a: 29).

Let us stay with Newman and Holzman's contribution to this area a bit further because I feel they have more to offer. They make a distinction between the 'Zone of Bourgeois Development' (ZBD) and the 'Zone of Proletarian Development' (ZPD). The ZBD refers to the creation of 'European-style universities', which at a particular

---

39 Western Fascist and Islamic gatherings on the contrary do not suppress emotions. They merely manage emotions by pushing them onto the terrain of *emotionalism*, where the spectators are manipulated by a mixture of spectacle and rhetoric (see chapter three of present work for more on this issue).

historical junction required an urban-based research-educational community. It allowed the bourgeoisie to pursue its research and educational agenda with a modicum of freedom from the church and the nobility. The evolution of the ZBD is 'inseparable from the philosophical hegemony of believing and thinking (more generally, cognitive acts) and the closely related ... hegemony of perception' (Newman and Holzman, 1993a: 91). The ZPD is emerging partly under its own impetus and partly as a reaction against the ZBD.

This connection is so strong that although we know our zones of proletarian development have to be qualitatively different from its bourgeois predecessors, yet we find them indelibly marked by some of the same 'eurocentric, patriarchal [and] cognitive-visual biases' (Newman and Holzman, 1993a: 91). It is the ability of the historically emergent 'zone of *proletarian* development' (ZPD) to negate money, wage-slavery, the state and spatio-temporal abstractions (such as God and nation) that transforms it into *performative* Vygotskian zones of proximal development. The performative aspects of actions undermines *imposed* 'identities' and as a result different sections of the proletariat come to confront capital first as a class 'in itself', and when the consciousness of this becomes dialectically generalised, into a class 'for itself'.[40] In chapter 5, I will clarify this distinction between ZBD and ZPD in order to posit an alternative mode of proletarian organising.

2.3.2 Collaborative learning, scaffolding and group zones

All the learning that goes on/in/during the zoped is *social* in nature even when expressed in individualistic terms. Most of this learning also happens to be explicitly *collaborative*. Forman and Cazden (1985: 329) suggest, 'collaboration requires a mutual task in which the partners work together to produce something that neither could have produced alone'. Barfurth (1995: 2) cites emergency situations as examples of genuine collaboration, 'Something happens (an earthquake, a bus accident) and total strangers work together to provide help, establish priorities, plan for the next move, organise others, etc.' Here is a concrete example from May Day 2001,

> As mentioned above, the huge, unchecked crowd that streamed through Soho had every opportunity to trash and destroy. McD's [McDonald's] went untouched and lone nutter riot cops were left to their own devices ... This wasn't an out-of-control mob. This was a party on the move. Outwitting and outmanoeuvring the Met's [Metropolitan Police's] finest at

---

40 This is a problematic distinction if understood in a strict Hegelian sense. Hegel adopted a child-centred metaphor for demonstrating the difference between 'being in-itself' and 'for-itself'. He writes, 'the man [sic], in himself, is the child. And what the child has to do is to rise out of this abstract and undeveloped *in-himself* and become *for-himself* what he is at first only *in-himself*- a free and reasonable being' (Hegel, Shorter Logic, s. 124 n, quoted in Blunden, 1997: 4).

every turn. The decisions were made on-the-fly and we didn't need nannying ... Those were our streets. Several times the crowd turned away from using narrow streets and alley-ways that could have resulted in horrendous injuries. This was done without panic and showed that we can make our own decisions, look after our own interests, even in high-pressured situations (urban75 bulletin board, 6 May 2001).

The learning experienced in such circumstances is a bottom-up process where the more able protesters facilitate, rather than direct, problem solving and the consolidation of knowledge. As already mentioned a great deal of Vygotsky's research concentrates on adult-child relations. It is the intention of my work to demonstrate that most of his concepts, once properly reformulated, can provide us with even greater insight into adult-adult relations. Vygotsky was, I believe, acutely aware that dialectical development is a life-span process that does not come to an abrupt stop at adolescence. Conceptual thinking, for instance, was not considered by Vygotsky to be a fully developed form in adults, 'The transitional, pseudoconceptual form of thought is not confined to the child's thinking; we too resort to it very often in our daily lives' (Vygotsky quoted in Speaker, Jr., 1999: 3). 'Egalitarian' settings allow all to participate in decision-making as co-constructors of meaning, goals and approach, and in the process feel empowered.

It could be objected that this collaborative model may very well be true of idealised demonstrations consisting of 'equals', when one would expect to find 'genuine sociality' (Ratner, 1991) at its peak. However, not all learning is necessarily collaborative. Pea (1994: 286) provides an insightful reflection when he argues, 'not all learning feels or probably is collaborative; it is sometimes competitive or coercive in nature'. Anyone who has been subjected to the persistent newspaper peddling of various *left wing* (i.e., representatives of the leftwing of capital) gangs of 'soul-kidnappers' on a 'political' march would readily attest to this. This is the kind of negative 'empowerment' organised from above by vanguardists that Ian Parker (2005: 97) criticises in his discussion of Participation Action Research (cf. chapter one). The 'narcissism of minor differences' (Freud, 1929-1930) between various leftists sects can be quite stomach-churning at times. Yet, even this nauseating parody of political activity is not devoid of 'pedagogical' credentials, as comparing the reactionary positions of leftist organisations is an excellent barometer of the class struggle.

A more congenial example of collaborative learning is provided courtesy of two paramedics caught up in New Orleans in the aftermath of hurricane Katrina (Bradshaw and Slonsky, 2005). The attitude of politicians, media, police and the National Guard had created a completely anti-working class atmosphere. The survivors of Katrina were treated as 'insurgents', especially if they were 'black'. On more than one occasion, Bradshaw and Slonsky were forced off highways and shelters at gunpoint. The military saw 'mob' and 'rioters' in every congregation of survivors (Bradshaw, and Slonsky, 2005: 4). They were even deliberately lied to by officials in order to get them moving away from the police station. Their food and transport were 'commandeered' by the army. Yet, despite so many problems once the two most important necessities -food and water- were secured, 'cooperation, community, and creativity flowered. [A group of survivors] organised a clean up and hung garbage bags from the rebar poles. [They] made beds from wood pallets and cardboard. [They] designated a storm drain as the bathroom ... [they] even organised a food recycling system ...' (Bradshaw and Slonsky, 2005: 3).

During collaborative learning, certain supportive strategies are employed to solve problems. Following Wood, Bruner and Ross (1976) we refer to these strategies

May Day 2000, Trafalgar Square, London. Collaborative learning or teenage tantrums? Em, tricky one that!

as 'scaffolding'.[41] Scaffolding promotes instructional exchange and allows the process of other-regulation to become self-regulating. Many studies (e.g., Day and Cordon, 1993) have shown that scaffolding results in not only faster learning but learning that

41 Neither Vygotsky nor Luria used the term 'scaffolding'. If Wood, *et al.* (1976) were the first to employ the term, then Cazden (1979) was the first to explicitly link the scaffolding metaphor to Vygotsky's zoped. I do not wish to adhere to this metaphor too literally since its structuralist imperatives are problematic. In addition, it encourages focusing on quantitative rather than qualitative changes in development and concerns have been raised over its applicability to large groups (see Stone, 1998). Furthermore, Griffin and Cole (1984: 47) have expressed concern that scaffolding 'leaves open questions of children's creativity'. It may even restrict children's development. I share most of these concerns. However, for our purposes the scaffolding metaphor does describe adequately a certain kind of learning that takes place amongst radical circles, hence its inclusion here.

lasts over time. People's 'grasp of the world is *teased along* by others who are *already there*' (Lock, 2000: 108). Not every individual has to rediscover the links between every event afresh. They can be 'set up' to find them by the actions and words of others (Lock, 2000: 108).

When experienced protesters demonstrate ways to evade roadblocks, tree-evictions and arrests or minimise the adverse effects of gas canisters and police baton charges, the instructional exchange is rapidly absorbed by less experienced members of the crowd and it becomes part of the protesters' repertoire of resistance. The May Day 2000 Festival of Anti-Capitalist Ideas and Actions included many workshops with the stated aim of transferring knowledge to less experienced protesters. Not all of these workshops could be described as examples of scaffolding but some certainly fit the bill. Additionally, demonstrators learning from previous experience have become quite adept at neutralising surveillance cameras. For instance, during the J18 demonstration (June 1999 anti-capitalist demonstration that turned riotous), a number of activists carrying a ladder and putting bags over the lenses covered security cameras, thus diminishing the state's ability to spy on demonstrations (Vidal and Hopkins, The Guardian, 27 May 2000). However, the action was not entirely successful since 'in what appeared to be a calculated snub to the protesters, City of London police paraded pictures of suspects after the J18 protest - on its website' (BBC News, 26 November 1999).

Scaffolding does not have to be about completing a specific task. It could just as readily be about conceptualising the task and a proper sequence of steps towards its accomplishment (Stone, 1998: 3). As Kermani and Brenner (2000: 2) have observed 'successful scaffolding requires establishing *intersubjectivity*, or a shared understanding of the task'. Here intersubjectivity does not merely refer to a shared feeling but more significantly to *shared presuppositional knowledge between collaborators* (Lock, 2000: 117). Within proletarian collectivities, a more elaborate referential domain, for instance a complex shared set of ideas and principles for intervening in the class struggle, usually allows for greater intersubjectivity.

Crowd scaffolding can be roughly divided into 'egalitarian directiveness' (favoured by non-hierarchal protesters who employ it sparingly and briefly) and 'intrusive intervention' (favoured by party-builders and Leninist organisers, who employ it in order to construct a permanent power base and recruit new apprentices). It is the argument of the present work that what Bakhtin called 'dialogic interaction', and an aspect of it Basil Bernstein referred to as 'elaborated communication code' (Lock, 2000: 117), is a vital ingredient in establishing and maintaining intersubjectivity and egalitarian directiveness. These are the building blocks of successful actions. Conversely 'monologic discourse' and what Bernstein termed a 'restricted communication code' undermine intersubjectivity and pave the way for 'intrusive intervention'. The way people communicate with each other, in other words, is a good indication of how they will end up working with each other.

Kermani and Brenner (2000: 4) underscore the Vygotskian finding that '... the more structured, difficult, and novel a specific task is for the child, the more likely it is for the mother to adopt a directive role'. This is sadly in line with the patronising and elitist attitude of party builders (mostly Leninist but also increasingly Anarchist organisers), who insist on a regimented and top-down course of learning for less experienced demonstrators who are, more often than not, treated as children. This is particularly evident when novel situations are encountered. Faced with novel situations, the party-builder, armed with a lifetime experience of disciplining proletarians rushes in to offer 'advice' and 'guidance'. A quite nauseating example of this practice was witnessed during the late 1980s and early 1990s in Britain during May Day demonstrations when Turkish, Kurdish and Iranian leftists (mostly Maoists and Stalinists of various shades), would vie for recruits and power during set rituals. Music, bands and marching in unison were used in order to gain control of the march and direct the course of events. There are, of course, counter-examples when music and bands are used to energise people on the march and even act as decoy. For instance, during May Day 2001, some protesters broke through police lines,

> Helped by the beating of samba drums, a non-violent push was made and many made it into the clear to join those in Soho. The Samba Band knew that although they had the opportunity to escape themselves, they would be better placed for the benefit of those locked in to stay (urban75 bulletin board, 6 May 2001).

I am arguing that music can have a radicalising or negative effect on joint-activity and learning, depending on circumstances. I shall return to this crucial use/misuse of music during demonstrations in chapter 3 on Bakhtinian football rioting.

Continuing with the different types of scaffolding strategy, the 'egalitarian' radical, mindful of the counter-productive nature of 'intrusive intervention', is wary of becoming entangled in an asymmetrical relationship.[42] Since many instances of crowd dynamics, such as riots, are not conducive to 'egalitarian directiveness', historically there has been a tendency for 'party-builders' to usurp 'leadership' at these crucial turning points and try to manipulate the crowds according to preconceived political agendas. More recently, however, proletarian crowds have shown signs of resisting

---

42 Asymmetrical relations are disparaged for a variety of reasons. In the case of intra-group relationships, it is considered 'counter-revolutionary' and wrong to impose on less experienced activists. In the case of inter-group dynamics with governmental organisations such as the police, it is deemed a tactical mistake to engage in any sort of relationship. After all, the knowledge of security forces and the police regarding British revolutionaries is limited precisely because attempts by them to set up meetings have been rebuffed time and again. Contrasting this sensible distanciation with the ghastly spectacle of Leninist leaders chumming up to the state (e.g., Stop the War Coalition, a front for the Socialist Workers' Party and their religious chums) is instructive. This coalition is desperate to ingratiate itself with the highest echelons of the ruling class. In return for scraps from the bosses' table, Stop the War Coalition is required to police anti-war demonstrations.

such 'intrusive interventions'. Failure of 'leftist' organisations to 'lead' the Brixton riots of 1981, the Great poll-tax riots of 1990, the Los Angeles riots of 1992 or the Iranian football riots of 2001 are prominent instances of this gradual turning of the tide. (A more comprehensive list of autonomous proletarian activities which resist 'intrusive intervention' can be found on the excellent Libertarian Communism website http://libcom.org/). Likewise, many have wised up to the mindless teenage violence of 'anarchist fundamentalists', who are naïve enough to think they can take on the police on a military terrain,

> We all marched down the road accompanied by the Riot Police, we then seem to get taken into an alley, near the oval tube, where one marcher thought it would be funny to jump on someone's car. He did not last very long as he was pulled down and given a few words of wisdom from quite a few protesters (<u>urban75 bulletin board</u>, 2 May 2000, Craig Rhodes).

In reality the varying and complex nature of political activities, tend to shape the scaffolding strategies employed in unforeseen ways. For instance, when the activity is goal-oriented (say preventing tree-eviction by determined bailiffs and security guards backed up by police), scaffolding maybe characterised by detailed planning and consequently has a tendency to result in 'intrusive intervention'. This approach could be favoured by the most laid-back non-hierarchical anarchist and in some occasions may very well be warranted if the goal is to be achieved. Alternatively, the most control-freakish Leninist may feel content to use 'egalitarian directiveness' in the form of support and encouragement for scaffolding strategies during instances of playful demonstrations or debate. In other words, the choice of scaffolding strategy is not quite as black and white as one would suspect.

What seems to be of great importance is the *sensitivity* displayed by participants in a zoped to the moving nature of the learning space. Feuerstein has suggested concerning Mediated Learning Experience (MLE) that what 'explains the individual's development of cognitive modifiability, does not depend on the content embodied in the culture but on the quality of the interaction between mediators and learners' (Feuerstein, 1991, quoted in Tzuriel and Kaufman, 1999: 362). For instance, most actions by a certain section of the proletariat, especially those aiming to disrupt the production-circulation-consumption cycle, seem to inconvenience another section of the proletariat. The May Day 2002 Critical Mass go-slow mass bike ride in London (Camberwell Green) was calculated to create traffic gridlocks. There was also a genuine attempt made by the cyclists to connect to fellow car driving proletarians through leaflets and impromptu discussion, in order to 'win them over'. The media described this attempt at communication as a failure,

> The cyclists blew whistles and air horns, handed out leaflets to bemused pedestrians, and encouraged drivers to ditch their cars. No one took them up on it (The Guardian, Sarah Left, 1 May 2002).

However, this smug narrative only relates half the story. Although no one 'ditched' their cars, a connection was established with many car owners who understood and at least partially agreed with the protesters' critique of the car industry.[43] What was significant on this occasion was the 'quality of the interaction between mediators and learners' and not necessarily the content or winning of arguments. This produced a partial sensitivity to the moving nature of the zoped by both voluntary and forced participants of the go-slow procession.

Kermani and Brenner (2000: 19) demonstrate how changes in scaffolding strategies amongst groups of North American and Iranian-American mothers,

> showed that these mothers were highly sensitive to the children's verbal cues and signals in performing, and that they were able to respond promptly and appropriately to child-initiated activities and behaviours. The more skilled the child was in performing the task independently, the less frequently the mother provided guidance. Here, the mother appeared to follow a *moving* zone of proximal development [emphasis added].

Kermani and Brenner (2000: 21) also suggest that,

> [i]n many unfamiliar, demanding or non-standard tasks or learning/teaching situations, the non-directive teaching style is simply not explicit or focused enough to ensure the child's understanding.

So, for example, North American mothers who usually prefer non-directive methods of instruction (e.g. explanations, verbal hint, verbal prompt, etc.), resort to more directive methods (e.g., modelling, correction, physical control, etc), when the task becomes too difficult. Kermani and Brenner (2000: 24) conclude by noting that,

---

43 We must not get carried away with this temporary break out of harmony. There is, in general, a great deal of animosity between London cyclists and car/bus drivers. A self-proclaimed 'activist journalist' naively assumes, 'Critical Mass always gets lots of support from bus drivers, who must also have a distaste for suited businessmen driving into town, on their own, in their petrol-guzzling cars' (The Guardian, 1 May 2003, Gideon Burrows). Having *once* attempted cycling within London (thankfully my bike was soon stolen by a kind-hearted soul depriving me of the necessity to repeat the experience), and having also been financially desperate enough to apply for a bus driving position (thankfully I failed the driving test- my braking was not hard enough!), I can say with the assurance of a consummate fence-jumper that most bus drivers consider nudging cyclists gently out of the way as one of the perks of the job! It is, therefore, to the credit of Critical Mass cyclists who continually explain their actions to car drivers.

cultural variations in scaffolding patterns [North American mothers preferring non-directive and Iranian-American mothers employing more directive methods] should not be judged as problematic, but rather be appreciated as an enrichment of the interactional patterns available for use in school instruction.

Likewise, the more varied the cultural background of demonstrators or strikers in a particular dispute the more heterogeneous the methods of scaffolding they can draw upon for solving problems. A historical example of this is the proliferation of new scaffolding techniques in the North American proletarian movement at the turn of the twentieth century, in particular within the Wobblies (International Workers of the World) movement, with the infusion of Italian, German and Afro-Caribbean workers to the ranks of white native US workers.[44]

A more strictly Vygotskian example of this learning process is provided by Strickland and Holzman (1989: 385). Describing the teaching methods employed at the Barbara Taylor School in New York, they demonstrate how working class children from African-American, Caribbean, Puerto Rican and Dominican background are assisted to 'develop ways of relating collectively to minimise discriminatory behaviours and attitudes' connected to racism, sexism, classism, heterosexism and so on. Crucially emotions are not 'off-limits' as with orthodox schooling but encouraged to be expressed alongside intellectuality. Conflict is not ignored but used to bring out 'private' emotional problems into the public domain. Strickland and Holzman (1989: 389) claim,

> Very young children appear to handle the conflictedness of society with relative ease. It is only with later socialisation that they learn to avoid conflict and to cover over to attempt to resolve it. Conflict, however, is a social reality of contemporary life. Learning to live conflictedly puts one in greater coherency with actual social conditions and is potentially empowering.

Within a ZPD, people take collective responsibility for the learning and development of one another's friends and comrades. This is achieved through breaking the leader-led paradigm and using one's emotions as well as intellect to 'grow'. Dialogic communication plays a vital role here. During the 2001 May Day celebrations, thousands were trapped by the police in Parliament Square. Negotiations began between the police and representatives from Reclaim The Streets (RTS). Significantly, these negotiations were relayed to people in the Square,

> One of the PA systems, which earlier had been used for speeches and smaller discussions (as well as some acoustic music), was now used to discuss the situation. Throughout the discussions an RTS guerrilla gardener relayed the negotiating pos-

---

44 These historical examples of 'scaffolding' allow us to supersede the 'neo-liberal' interpretations of zoped where everyone is encouraged to participate and share the floor 'but they are not authorized to question what they are accomplishing and why' (Kinginger, 2002: 255). These 'neo-liberal' interpretations are in harmony with the needs of 'the new Fast Capitalism' with its emphasis on 'distributive communication' and 'flexible' workers.

itions between the public assembly and the police. The assembly eventually decided to leave the square en masse together, and to leave immediately, after the police had proposed people could leave, but that they would have to wait for at least another half hour ... With the samba band playing the crowd moved directly towards the police lines. After a short while with no movement the crowd made a push to get through the police line, but failed. While there was some pushing and shoving the crowd remained calm and defiant. Still dancing with the samba band they made another attempt to push through, and this time succeeded with the police line dissolving as people began to pour down Millbank cheering and clapping (urban75 bulletin board, 2 May 2001).

To summarise this section: the learning that takes place within a ZPD is collaborative most of the time but I have also suggested it could display competitive or coercive characteristics at times. Scaffolding strategies are of two main varieties, *egalitarian directiveness* and *intrusive intervention*. Both are usually at work in most circumstances but in varying ratios. I also showed that the *sensitivity* of participants to the moving nature of the ZPD and the *heterogeneity* of the participants themselves are crucial factors in the establishment of a genuine developmental zone.

2.3.3 Group zones and the horizontal dimension of learning

We should push the boundaries of our speculations further. Beyond determining each person's individual zone of proximal development, and perhaps even beyond surmising the precise region within this zone (upper limit, midpoint or lower limit) where different scaffolding strategies may yield varying results (Kermani and Brenner, 2000), we may also posit the notion of a *group zone* (cf. John-Steiner and Tatter, 1983; Donato, 1988; Aljaafreh and Lantolf, 1994; and Nyikos and Hashimoto, 1997).

These writers suggest that alongside the individual zoped there may also exist 'a zone of potential growth for the group as a whole, at a point where each individual's zone intersects and is expanded as a result of the collaborative interaction' (Nyikos and Hashimoto, 1997: 507). This group zone may allow 'exponential growth due to the social mediation allowed by multiple discussions, points of view, and creative problem solving' (Nyikos and Hashimoto, 1997: 507). What these writers are describing is akin to those rare revolutionary moments of insight that occur when tremendous changes are about to happen.

Previously we observed how crucial intersubjectivity is to this process of 'exponential growth'. Nyikos and Hashimoto (1997: 508) have shown how intersubjectivity is helped by, amongst other factors, 'cognitive apprenticeship'. This is a notion similar to scaffolding, characterised by reflective thinking. However, in cognitive apprenticeship the participants are encouraged, to move between the roles of knower and learner to stimulate use of multiple perspectives which, in turn, stimulate different types of cognitive activities in order to expand their perspectives (Nyikos and Hashimoto, 1997: 508).

Thus during cognitive apprenticeship (unlike scaffolding), it is never forgotten that the 'educator himself [sic] needs educating' (Marx, 1845/1984: 423). In an ideal situation of cognitive apprenticeship, 'the apprentice continues to build personal empowerment through increasing participation in communities of practice' (Nyikos and Hashimoto, 1997: 508). Having looked at learning in a variety of circumstances ranging from Mexican Yucatec midwives to American meatcutters and alcoholic anonymous, Lave and Wenger (1991) 'point out that in all their examples there is very little observable teaching but a lot of well-motivated and effective learning' (quoted in Daniels, 1996: 162). Moreover, Bruner (1965: 1013) has observed among tribal people,

> One virtually never sees an instance of 'teaching' taking place outside the situation where the behaviour to be learned is relevant. Nobody 'teaches' in our prepared sense of the word. There is nothing like school, nothing like 'lessons'… [In such societies] it is almost impossible to separate what one does from what one knows.[45]

In a zoped, participants gradually move from peripheral tasks to core tasks, harnessing various skills along the way.[46] This approach, it seems to me, is far closer to the actuality of interactions within radical movements where, once formal 'equality' is established within the group, it becomes possible for each person to take transitory responsibility as 'knower' and once her task of 'imparting knowledge' is completed slide seamlessly back into the role of the 'learner'. Working class Sunday schools have *occasionally* operated in this manner providing a supportive social nexus for learning without creating specialists and experts. This is one way in which the 'zone of proletarian development' differs from the 'zone of bourgeois development' (Newman and Holzman, 1993a: 91). For instance, when the police

---

45 I do not wish to fetishize 'tribal learning'. To suggest that people have to be limited in what they know according to their activities intolerably reduces our field of knowledge and de-legitimises learning that can take place by observing and studying other peoples' activities. However, it is true that the linking of 'knowing' and 'doing' has a tremendous impact on learning and could act as spur to a superior mode of comprehension. It is also worth noting that there have been conscious proletarian attempts to ape bourgeois schooling. 'Sunday schools' and the more contemporary US-style 'teach-ins' are examples. The limitations of such efforts are beyond the scope of the present study.

46 We have to be mindful of using terms such as 'skill acquisition'. Burman justifiably writes, '… research preoccupation with tracing skilled performance mirrors the societal value placed on productive aspects of labour, while the negative, maladaptive features of infant action are screened out … The cognitive model of the infant as problem solver mirrors that of the assembly worker, with research privileging those activities and products which will enhance performance' (1994: 33). Vygotskian psychology (especially in its Anglo-American reincarnation) is tainted by cognitivist assumptions. For me 'development' is not necessarily linear or natural or inevitable or even inherently beneficial. It may involve acquiring problem solving skills, but it also requires emotional change. We should not fetishize any of these 'qualities'.

cordoned off protesters in Oxford Circus and Holles Street during May Day 2001, some fought back by trying to break through locked up stores,

> Two protesters [admittedly very drunk protesters], who climbed on to a balcony of the John Lewis building in Holles Street, Oxford Circus, rip two CCTV cameras from their mounts [in the process almost getting fried] and pass them down to the crowd. They also strip metal segments and pass them into the crowd where people appear to be trying to smash John Lewis windows (S. Left *et al.*, The Guardian, 1 May 2001) [comments added].

Others, whilst appreciating the entertainment value of such stunts were talking about turning the street into a 'learning zone' and debating issues of concern. Bad weather and lack of space prevented this idea being taken up but the proposal will remain in the collective 'memory banks' of protesters for future reference. Zinchenko (1983-84: 78) has pointed out how memorising goes beyond its 'mechanical' variety when it is embedded within a meaningful activity. It is, therefore, important to emphasise the need for an autonomous social space where people can engage in meaningful learning and memorising in relation to their activity-object. Collins (1999a: 12) has rightly argued the development of an unofficial ideology 'requires the creation and maintenance of a social space, free from the immediate surveillance of dominant groups, in which subordinate groups can come together with a degree of mutuality and trust'. However, even bourgeois space can be appropriated by proletarians. A year later in Melbourne, Australia the cordoning tactic was turned against the state when,

> a few hundred protesters used wire mesh to erect a makeshift 'detention centre' around the department of immigration offices. A small protest was held in Brisbane against the asylum seeker detention centres (The Guardian, 1 May 2002).

Learning, let us remember, does not take place merely within the zoped but also *between* various zones of proximal development. In manufacturing workplaces, the apprentice worker learns from the 'master' through a vertical relationship characterised by a discourse of 'stages' and 'levels' of skill. As Engeström (2001: 1) has noted,

> Such a vertical image assumes a uniform, singular model of what counts as 'expert' in a given field. However, the world of work is increasingly organised in ways that require horizontal movement and boundary crossing.

Thus, the spiral model of expansive learning needs to be complemented with movement along the horizontal dimension. It is the contemporary activists' belonging to a series of groups/organisations (e.g. an individual may attend anti-war groups, a local 'black awareness' group and a 'mad pride' group, etc.) that allows 'boundary-crossing' to become productive for both the individual and the activity systems s/he attends. The individuals engage in what Engeström calls *negotiated knotworking*. Such negotiated knotworking 'requires learning in dialogue across organisational boundaries' (Engeström, 2001: 7).

This boundary-crossing is evident in working class attempts to overcome racial difference. Lamont and Aksartova (2002) interviewed 150 workers from France and the USA about notions of equality with regard to race. Some of the interviewees were white and some were black. Whilst the four groups used a variety of cultural repertoires to argue for equality between the races most of the blacks (whether US blacks or African-French blacks) drew 'on a much wider range of evidence to demonstrate their belonging to the community of humankind' (Lamont and Aksartova, 2002: 17). They achieved this not by basing themselves on the bourgeois notion of 'identity' but by engaging in knotworking at the boundary. Their

Unless I am very much mistaken we are in for a long, arduous day!

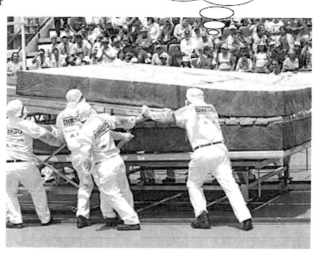

need to go beyond racial stereotypes and cross artificial boundaries within the working class was an 'inclusive thinking and acting' based on class interests rather than lofty intellectual constructs such as 'multiculturalism'.

Of course, small-scale innovative learning such as the knotworking example just cited can take place within each activity system without this leading to expansive learning which then transforms the group. For instance, some protesters noticed from the amount and frequency of sandwiches reaching the police during the May Day 2001 demonstration that their officers had planned for a long, arduous day. However, this piece of information was quite useless since most protesters were already entrapped within solid cordons.

For expansive learning to occur, it seems necessary for radicals from a number of anti-capitalist activity systems to engage in collective negotiated knotworking and for peripheral participants of the 'community' to 'have broad access to different parts of the activity and eventually proceed to full participation in core tasks' (Hung, 2002: 130). It seems from the evidence of Lamont and Aksartova (2002) that it is also very useful to have as wide a repertoire of cultural and political arguments to draw upon. Finally, it seems essential for 'the tools and structures of the community of practice' to be transparent, so that 'their inner workings can become available for the learner's inspection' (Hung, 2002: 130). The lack of transparency is one of the major contributory factors leading to alienation, apathy and non-participation. Significantly, this lack of transparency is observable in both top-down Leninist structures as well as tyrannical 'unstructured' anarchist organisations.

Yet despite these stringent preconditions, expansive learning occurs frequently. One recent example relates to British 'radicals' in the 1990s when a number of single issue campaigns 'merged' after protracted informal negotiated knotworking to form wider activity systems with broader anti-capitalist agendas. Another example would be the coming together of various local/national anti-globalisation groups and the regular knotworking that occurs between them prior to major demonstrations. A third example would be the emergence of grass-root media groups which try to foreground the movement's viewpoint,

> Key to the protesters' strategy of circumventing the mainstream media is a proliferation of new grassroots media organisations that are supportive of the movement. One of the most striking things about the mass incarceration at Oxford Circus on May Day was the number of people carrying cameras, both stills and video. Much of the material will appear on websites such as Squall, Schnews and Indymedia, which show video and carry reports sympathetic to the protest. Protesters claim that journalists from these alternative news sources are excluded from police briefings (The Guardian, 7 May 2001).

Engeström (2001: 19) argues that those boundary-crossing actions that involve new concept formation tend to be more successful in achieving expansive learning. A shared temporary plan/proposal seems to be very useful in focusing actions towards expansive learning.

In summary: I have argued that crowd psychology should look at group zones of proximal development rather than individual ones. Both the development within and between such groups should be mapped out. This calls for understanding 'spiral' as well as 'horizontal' learning. Once an autonomous social space is established, strategies such as *cognitive apprenticeship* and *negotiated knotworking* catalyse expansive learning. Organisational transparency, a wide repertoire of rhetorical devices and the ability to form new concepts then become vital for the continued success of expansive learning.

2.3.4 Slogans and chanting as 'private' Speech

At first sight, the slogans and chanting that accompany demonstrations, seem to fall exclusively within the domain of social (i.e., intersubjective) speech. And indeed one of their functions is to provide an unmediated mode of communication between proletarians away from the distorting apparatus of the media.[47] Public chanting is a performance with its own distinct value (Graeber, 2005: 48).

However, I would like to suggest that they might also be viewed as forms of 'private' speech, mediating between 'social' and 'inner' speech. And if they can be justifiably brought under the rubric of 'private' speech then what Vygotsky said about the dialectical notion of completion is also applicable to (at least some) slogans and chants: 'Thought is restructured as it is transformed into speech. It is not expressed but completed in the word' (Vygotsky, 1987b: 251).

As Laura E. Berk makes clear not every major psychologist was attuned to the complexities of 'private' speech. The behaviourist John Watson, for instance, 'viewed it simply as inappropriate verbal behaviour that gradually ends as parents and teachers pressure children to stop muttering and talking out loud' (Berk, 1986: 1).

Jean Piaget too failed to grasp the significance of private speech, which he called 'egocentric speech'. He considered it symptomatic of immaturity and self-centredness and devoid of social purpose. By contrast, Vygotsky saw private speech as social communication with self and essential for the integration of language with thought and the controlling of action. Vygotsky says in *Thought and Language* (1962, Chapter 2),

> The earliest speech of the child is ... essentially social ... At a certain age the social speech of the child is quite sharply divided into private and communicative speech ... [Private] speech emerges when the child transfers social, collaborative forms of behaviour to the sphere of inner-personal psychic functions ... [Private] speech, splintered off from general social speech, in time leads to inner speech, which serves both autistic and logical thinking ... the true direction of the development of thinking is not from the individual to the socialised, but from the social to the individual.

This explains why 'private speech is more frequent when children play together in large groups rather than alone, with one child or with an adult' (Berk, 1986: 3). There is also as Vygotsky (1987c: 259–260) pointed out a close relationship between 'private speech' and 'inner speech',

---

47 Holzman (1996: 135) explains how bourgeois communication differs from collective proletarian meaning making: 'The dominant discourse style of contemporary culture is equally meta-physical, anti-activistic; common conversation in everyday life is interpretative and essentially competitive. The total adult communicative environment is not conducive to creating jointly new meanings. People take turn *expressing* their thoughts, identifying with what someone else says, and trying to figure out its deeper meaning and significance. The completive, activistic discourse modality that is jointly created in the linguistic zoped of early childhood is nearly universally practiced, but it is rare after childhood and even, for many, difficult to imagine'. To follow this, a quote from Marx (1857/1974: 111) is pertinent, 'A man [sic] cannot become a child again, or he becomes childish. But does he not find joy in the child's naïveté, and must he himself not strive to reproduce its truth at a higher stage?'

the function of [private] speech is closely related to the function of inner speech. It is not an accompaniment of the child's activity. It is an independent melody or function that facilitates intellectual orientation, conscious awareness, the overcoming of difficulties and impediments, and imagination and thinking. It is speech for oneself.

Vygotsky relied on Kohlberg's experiments to support his theories. Kohlberg had discovered that 'the most sociable and popular children used private speech the most, a finding in line with Vygotsky's belief that such speech originates in and is stimulated by early social experience' (Berk, 1986: 2). A second set of evidence was provided in the 1970s by (mostly) Russian psychologists who demonstrated how private speech helps bring behaviour under the control of 'internal' thinking. Later still Berk discovered,

that the kind of egocentric communication Piaget had described made up less than 1 percent of the children's language ... [It was also confirmed] ... that the most socially advanced preschool children talked to themselves the most, and that such speech was more frequent when children played together in large groups rather than alone, with one child or with an adult (Berk, 1986: 3-4).

Berk also shows when children are working on new problems and trying to push the upper limit of their competencies, they need 'learning environments that permit them to be verbally active while solving problems and completing tasks' (Berk, 1986: 4). Anecdotal confirmation of these findings is provided in descriptions of crowd psychology. For instance, there is less frequent and less imaginative chanting at football grounds with low crowds. Likewise, verbally active demonstrations provide greater opportunities for the crowd to overcome potential problems, such as police roadblocks.

Therefore, private speech has both an inter-personal and an intra-personal dimension (Ahmed, 1998). With regard to demonstrations, I think a case could be made for viewing placards, slogans, stickers, fly-posters and graffiti as forms of extra-personal speech as well. By extra-personal speech I mean communication directed at the absent 'other' (in this case all those proletarians who are not directly experiencing the demonstration but viewing it through the distorted prism of the media- the slogan, 'workers of the world, unite!' would be a good example). So, once again the three dimensions of analysis (the intra-psychological, inter-psychological and extra-psychological) have to be assessed simultaneously if we are to appreciate the entire functionality of private speech.

A concrete example would be useful here. Contrasting the limited slogans raised during the Iranian revolution of 1979 with the complex and imaginative slogans/graffiti during the May 1968 demonstrations in France illustrates the point neatly. There is a world of difference between the repetitive, monotonous chants against the Shah (e.g., 'Death to the Shah!', 'Death to Savak [security services]!') and the Situationists inspired poetry-cum-slogans that adorned the walls and placards of Paris in the hot summer of 1968 (e.g., 'Beneath the cobblestones, the beach!', or 'Quick, comrades! The old world is behind you' or 'Boredom is counter-revolutionary'). Signs used in joint activities, joint observation and joint-reflection (whether they are chants, slogans, placards or whatever) can only become mental tools for independent self-reflection if they are created organically within a ZPD and expressive of a 'collective will'. Otherwise, their ossified nature becomes rapidly apparent to all.

The 'Chant Laureate' campaign run by Barclaycard, the sponsors of the English Premiership Football League, is an excellent example of the authorities' attempt to recuperate terrace chanting and turn it into a safe and domesticated competition. As can

Chant recuperation

be seen in the reproduction, this campaign aims to discover the 'Byron of Blackburn, the Wordsworth of Wolverhampton or the Eminem of Elland Road'. The inducement is a £10,000 bursary courtesy of Barclaycard. The traditional 'hooligan' battle cry of 'Come and have a go if you think you're *hard* enough!' is turned into the lame 'Come and have a go if you think you're *good* enough', in a PR stunt which smacks of desperation. Even a 'Hotline' is set up for the benefit of would be Chant Laureates! The campaign has been running for months (appearing in every issue of Tottenham Hotspurs' Official Matchday Programme, as well as other clubs) with, as far as anecdotal evidence suggests, very little enthusiasm from football fans.

Private speech does not merely find expression on football terraces. John-Steiner (1992) has increased our understanding of adult private speech by identifying three main contexts where it can occur: *thinking aloud speech, embedded private speech*, and *self-regulatory utterances*. In addition, the form this private speech can take could be of the spoken as well as the written variety. A few examples will illustrate the distinction.

Political discussions are replete with examples of *thinking aloud speech*. Where sensitivity to the others' need to engage in thinking aloud is prevalent, radicals can complete thought processes by thinking aloud. This verbal exploration increases in magnitude as unfamiliar or challenging problems are faced. Following the death of an activist (Carlo Giuliani) at the huge Genoa anti-capitalist demonstration of 2001, the unfamiliarity of the situation witnessed a flurry of thinking aloud utterances amongst radicals regarding the best way to respond to state repression.[48]

Embedded private speech 'refers to utterances that occur in public performance settings, e.g., public lectures' (Ahmed, 1998: 4). For this to occur there usually has to be a disturbance of some kind or another- heckling or public criticism or alternatively the speaker may be under emotional strain. The speaker's well-rehearsed talk then veers off into unexpected territory. Emotions become entangled with intellect. Inside a zoped utterances of this kind catalyse learning and development. Laura L. Sullivan (2005: 351-352) describes a poignant scene when she was bullied by authoritarian leftists (including the chairperson) at a preparatory meeting for the European Social Forum UK. Her original speech was interrupted a number of times leading to embedded private speech, which helped her perceive the bureaucratic problems she was entangled in with clarity. As Vygotsky pointed out,

> The simplest utterance, far from reflecting a constant rigid correspondence between sound and meaning, is really a process. Verbal expressions cannot emerge fully formed, but must develop gradually (Vygotsky, 1987b: 222).

What is significant about this last example is that learning occurred within a hostile and competitive environment unlike the more typical benign setting favoured by Vygotsky. As Ivanchenko (2002: 2) has argued 'any development process consists not only of growth and complication but of loss and decline as well'. Most 'westerners', especially bourgeois westerners, are greatly fearful of 'anger's potential to disrupt social relationships' which is why over the years they have developed various mechanisms for 'immediately [dissipating] anger in order to ensure continuous amicable relation' (Ratner, 1991: 78). In this case, the mechanisms of

Anti-graffiti squad in Tehran (apologies for the picture quality. My hand was shaking at the time!)

anger management failed and the result was dialectical development.

Finally, *self-regulatory private speech* occurs frequently in public political meetings

---

48 There is another interesting point worth mentioning here. Some researchers have made an analogy between the actual-potential level of development within a zoped and the familiarity-novelty continuum (van Geert, 1998). In other words, if a demand or problem is too novel it is likely to create confusion and frustration in people. This seems to be a factor in Genoa where the unfamiliarity of the circumstances led some British activists to feel despondent and frustrated.

involving non-native speakers or inexperienced speakers who need to self-direct utterances in order to express themselves with more clarity. For example, 'I don't know what you call it in English … ah, self-valorisation', or 'what do you call them? Ah, wildcat strikes'.

Having classified these three main forms of adult private speech, John-Steiner (1992: 292) makes a further distinction between *spoken* and *written* private speech. In relation to our investigation, chanting would fall into the spoken private speech category whilst placards or graffiti are examples of written private speech. The latter John-Steiner calls 'inner speech writing' or 'telegrams to the self'. These condensed forms of writing may seem obscure and cryptic at times but they provide invaluable clues into the individual creativity of protesters.

Again, one should make a distinction between creative placards made individually by demonstrators and mass-produced placards that are handed out by leftist organisations as part of their market-branding exercise. Genuine creativity is a function of ability to gain control over life activities. 'Vygotsky emphasised that genuine creativity does not precede or lie beyond socialisation, it is the *result* of socialisation and therefore depends upon the kind of socialisation one receives'[49] (Ratner, 1991: 181). Creativity flourishes where demonstrators possess social knowledge and manage to turn that social knowledge into social control over their surroundings and activities.

Following from Vygotsky's work on art (Vygotsky, 1930/1971), I argue that May Day celebrations, by dragging demonstrators into a topsy-turvy world, help to unite the intellectual and emotional aspects of imagination. The dancing, singing, theatre, chanting and graffiti of May Day help create what the formalist Sklovsky called *defamiliarisation* (cf. Brecht's *Verfremdungseffekt*), a distance which enhances the sensitivity and replaces the perception of life. Sigel (1993: 143) is another researcher who proposes that distancing strategy allows one to seek alternatives or to reconstruct past experiences. 'This [distancing strategy] also includes … absurdities, nonsense, and parody' (Linqvist, 2003: 248). Here is Vygotsky writing on children's rhymes,

> Only recently was it noticed that certain absurdities or amusing nonsense which can be found in nursery rhymes by inverting the most commonplace events play a tremendously important role in child art (Vygotsky, 1930/1971: 258).

Vygotsky believed that, 'compared to other emotional reactions, aesthetic emotion results in delayed action … Art releases aspects that are not expressed in everyday life' (Linqvist, 2003: 248). In other words, the performative actions on May Day celebrations enable us to experience things that we would not otherwise experience, 'art is the organisation of our future behaviour' (Vygotsky, 1930/1971: 253). Significantly, in a break with romantic notions of children's imagination, Vygotsky believed that since

---

49 By *socialisation* I am not referring to mindless conformity to societal norms but the kind of voluntary and reflective socialisation that produces a creative individual consciousness. Vygotsky wrote that 'all cultural development has three stages: development in itself, for others, and for oneself' (Vygotsky, 1989: 56).

'the creative activity is directly dependent upon the individual's experiences, and the extent and degree of these experiences', the imagination of the child tends to be poorer than adults (Vygotsky quoted in Linqvist, 2003: 249).

In summary, this section has called for investigating slogans, graffiti and placards as examples of 'private speech'. In the process, researchers can also differentiate between *creative* and *mechanical* forms of imagination employed in the construction of such 'private speech'.

2.3.5 Performance, play, masks and gestures

Street masks

One of the detrimental modes of behaviour, which reinforces isolation and hinders solidarity during a demonstration, is the self-disciplining of our emotions that we have been conditioned into. Goffman (1972, quoted in Kuzmics, 1991: 1) has described how self-control is 'a precondition for successful interaction' in a bourgeois world and how this self-control is related to *embarrassment*.[50] Goffman argues that 'the participants in a social encounter expect certain competences', for instance, the ability to suppress emotional reactions, the ability to move from informal privacy to the public sphere without confusion, and the ability to control one's facial and auditory expressions. 'If', however, 'there are any discrepancies between claim and reality then this activates feelings of shame and embarrassment' (Goffman quoted in Kuzmics, 1991: 3).

The masks we wear to hide our embarrassment during dealings in a bourgeois world find their historical antecedents in courtly behaviour and etiquette where one's 'honour' and 'prestige' depended on other people's opinion of oneself. In fact, Elias (1983) has gone as far as 'describing the civilising process in the West as the continuous advance of the threshold of shame and embarrassment' (Elias, 1983, quoted in Kuzmics, 1991: 9). A process that, according to Elias, began in the 13th century has

---

50 I do not wish to convey the impression that 'self-control' is totally negative. As Ratner has explained, it may be a vital element in the development of consciousness: 'Another aspect of consciousness that is causally and teleologically fostered by tool use is self-control and the ability to postpone immediate need-satisfaction' (Ratner, 1991: 52). Presumably, what this suggests is that there is a gulf separating imposed 'self-control', the kind fostered on the individual by society which Goffman critiques in relation to embarrassment and the voluntary form of 'self-control' essential for achieving an individual/collective goal.

now been extended to proletarians (especially younger ones) regarding how to be-have in bourgeois society. As Malcolm Pines (2002: 16) has observed,

> This affects the correct way to deal, for example, with libidinal energy, eating, dis-posal of waste matter from the body, cleanliness and hygiene- every aspect of how to behave so as to obtain recognition and favours from their masters.

The dynamics of this phenomenon may be externally imposed initially, but gradually self-constraint becomes the primary aspect of the process. The kind of embarrassment related to shyness, a feeling of bashfulness in social situations, creates an impasse. In fact, it results in a form of robot-like acting, alienated be-haviour of a coerced conformity (Newman and Holzman, 1993a: 118). This 'Par-sonian doll-like acting' (Nissen *et al.*, 1999: 419) is behaviour under conditions that cannot be altered.

One method of overcoming this obstacle is through *performance,* which is 'activity changing its conditions during its course' (Nissen *et al.,* 1999: 420). Street theatres performed by recent May Day celebrants posit the possibility of linking play with the zoped. Vygotsky (quoted in van der Veer and Valsiner, 1994a: 345) was fully cognisant of this linkage,

> play also creates the zone of proximal development of the child. In play the child is always behaving beyond his [sic] age, above his usual everyday behaviour; in play he is, as it were, a head above himself. Play contains in a concentrated form, as in the focus of a magnifying glass, all developmental tendencies ...

Vygotsky believed the defining characteristic of play to be the 'creation of an imagin-ary situation', which is linked to the presence of rules.[51] Alternatively, he referred to 'imagination [as] play without action' (Vygotsky, 1978: 93). In fact, he expressed this relationship developmentally, 'The development from games with an overt imaginary situation and covert rules to games with an overt imaginary situation outlines the evolution of children's play' (quoted in Newman and Holzman, 1993a: 97). Could this also be true of adult political activities during carnivalesque bouts of serious-play? Vygotsky certainly thought so. He talks about 'deliberate representations of fantasy' when projecting 'utopian constructions' (Vygotsky, 1987c: 346). Here, creative imagin-ation[52] is a directed form of activity towards a goal.

Let us remember that Vygotsky also argues that *'play gives a child a new form of desire.* It teaches him [sic] to desire by relating his desires to a fictitious *I,* to his role

---

51 Vygotsky was against making pleasure the defining characteristic of play. As he put it, 'pleasure cannot be the defining characteristic of play' (Vygotsky, 1978) because it can be experienced outside a play situation and not all playful activity is necessarily pleasurable.

52 Vygotsky writes, 'Fundamental to *creative* imagination is the production of new images, images that have never existed in consciousness or in past experience' (Vygotsky, 1987a: 340).

in the game and its rules' (Vygotsky, 1978: 100). Imagination, conceptual thinking and role taking are an important part of adult development as well as children (West, 2001: 62). The existence of restraints and the spontaneous urge to break the rules of the game exist in dialectical tension and in such circumstances, play mediates the learning that takes place. Vygotsky made further claims for play, '... a child's greatest achievements are possible in play, achievements that tomorrow will become [her] basic level of action ...' (Vygotsky, 1978: 100). In fact, he suggested that the sphere of pretence play is where 'children aspire to and practise skills[53] they are not yet allowed to demonstrate in the arena of adult life' (Gillen, 2000: 173-174). So ironically, children could demonstrate more mature behaviour in play. As West (2001: 62) argues,

> Children develop and practice self-regulation skills in play that they had not yet learned. An example of this is the child who may have trouble standing in line without fidgeting, but when asked to play a person who is unconscious and waiting to be rescued by a fireman, this child may be able to lay quietly for quite some time.

Adults use their imagination to create roles and situations, which can point the way to possible alternatives. According to West (2001: 63), such playful activities may prefigure what Morson calls 'sideshadowing', the realisation that 'things could have been different from the way they were, there were real alternatives to the present we know, and the future admits of various paths' (G. Morson, 1994, quoted in West, 2001: 63). This

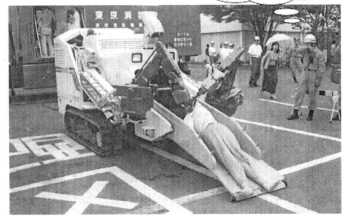

... when asked to play a person who is unconscious and waiting to be rescued by a fireman ...

ability to imagine and talk about *possible* rather than *actual* circumstances, the utopian element within communism so to speak, has become easier to conceive as 'our linguistic abilities increase' (Shotter, 1993: 93).[54]

---

53 'Skills' for Vygotsky and Activity Theorists is not defined in terms of a particular set of actions. Rather it is a more general ability to understand the functioning of a system and its related inner mechanisms. Skilful demonstrators/protesters are therefore those who can think flexibly in trying to solve problems and contradictions.

54 This statement is in contradiction to Fredric Jameson's (1990) earlier stated claim that as the barriers

Two specific examples of creating imaginary situations in therapy has some pertinence to the way reflexivity is introduced into the process of analysis and decision making undertaken by radicals before and after political events. The first is known as 'the miracle question' (de Shazer, 1991) and refers to an imaginary situation when the cause of the problem is miraculously solved. The 'patient' is then asked about its implications, 'How would you know [the problem is solved]? What would be different? … What would your spouse notice?' (de Shazer, 1991: 113).

This therapeutic technique has a real counterpart in political activity. Part of radical activity has traditionally involved the creation of utopian situations in dreams, art works, speeches and discussions, which has imagined a world beyond the dictatorship of time, space, value and authority. How would 'transgressors' be dealt with in a post-revolutionary world? Will there be 'laws', 'criminals' and 'punishment' as we know them today? After all, if money is abolished, maybe crime will be too. How will the abolition of wage-slavery and commodity fetishism effect people's relations with each other? What is important in these imaginary situations is not the attainment of definitive answers but the process of co-creating a post-capitalist world human community. The play activity permits the development of new forms of desires. It allows us to be better than ourselves. The Situationists, foremost amongst others, understood how this surplus of desires could become a force for revolutionary change.

The second therapeutic question favoured by play-therapists is more specific and is referred to as the 'hypothetical event question' (Freedman and Combs, 1996). An example relevant to our subject matter would be 'What would you do if you are arrested on the demo?' or 'What would you do if the police use force?', or 'How should we react if challenged by reactionaries such as fascists or religious fundamentalists on an anti-war march?', or 'What would you do after coming out on strike?'

These questions aid the creation of an imaginary scenario where participants within a ZPD could actively reflect and expand on the debate without feeling pressure to enact preconceived roles and positions. Additionally, it allows participants to gaze internally at their own 'collaboration' in reproducing capitalist relations and become aware of the extent to which commodity fetishism has imposed its warped mindset on all of us.[55] Thus, identity's pretensions of stability and authenticity are ridiculed. Play

---

between present and future registers become blurred, we are losing the ability to envision utopia. I remain undecided as to which proposition is more valid, Jameson's or Shotter's. It is, of course, conceivable that both are correct. Jameson may be right in suggesting that imagining the future is becoming more problematic in general and Shotter may be right in suggesting our increased linguistic and performative skills are acting as counterbalancing factors.

55 An excellent new book on the Zapatistas makes similar points. Mentinis (2006: 168) argues, '… in the case of the Zapatistas protection from the enemy does not constitute the primary reason for masking'. There are other more pertinent reasons, for instance, '… Fear and anxiety can be overcome by becoming *los sin rostro* ('those without faces') … It is after they have transcended the limits of the individual self and have become a revolutionary unity that a sense of freedom starts growing among them … It is now that they can challenge not only the *bad government* but also their own *secret*' (Mentinis, 2006: 171-172). By their own 'secret', Mentinis is referring to everything that is problematic in Maya culture and the Zapatistas

and performance allows us to be against-and-beyond fixed categories and identities. As John Holloway has rightly pointed out, 'We do not struggle *as* working class, we struggle *against* being working class, against being classified. Our struggle is not the struggle of labour: It is the struggle against labour' (Holloway, 2002, 144). Play and performance by demanding and securing the 'right to be lazy' (Lafargue, 1883/2000) and by helping to create imaginative spaces where new possibilities (including the possibility of living without 'identities') are posited, allow individuals to be treated ahead of themselves. In the process, rigid identities are left behind.

During demonstrations gestures come to play an incommensurably important role in communication. This is partly because the division between mental and physical labour has been weakened and partly due to the pragmatic need to find alternative ways of expressing oneself above the background noise of the traffic, chanting, music and police sirens. Again following on from Hegel, Vygotsky (cited in Subbotsky, 1996) postulated the development of gesturing as a three stage process, in which a gesture exists at first 'in itself', then 'for others' and finally 'for itself'. The earliest grasping movements of a child towards a desired object, for instance, are not yet meaningful unless interpreted as such by caregivers. By being mediated through the social environment, gesture 'in itself' has become gesture 'for others' (irrespective of the child's intentions or even awareness of the process). Later still, the gesture may become a tool for self-regulation and only then does the child use it consciously as a gesture 'for itself'.

David McNeill (1999) has taken Vygotsky's work further in this regard. McNeill starts his text by making a distinction between 'emblematic' gestures and 'online' ones. 'Emblematic' gestures are culturally defined, relatively stable, recurrent gestures such as the 'thumps-up' sign for OK' (McNeill, 1999: 78). The other type of gesturing, 'on-line' gestures, are those created by speakers as they speak and not governed by convention. This is another way of saying gestures too have both a meaning and a personal sense. In order to analyse this second variety of gesturing McNeill creates a unit of analysis that can encompass both the utterance and the gesture and calls it 'growth points' (McNeill, 1999: 79). This unit, he claims, retains the essential properties of both linguistic and image categories. Therefore, a growth point is basically a combination of imagery and language information categories. He then goes on to demonstrate the linkage between growth points and the flow of consciousness.

In a complementary investigation, McCafferty (2002: 192) has shown the role played by gestures not only in promoting language learning but also in facilitating positive interaction between people, 'helping to create a sense of shared social, symbolic, physical, and mental space'. In his study, language learners by creating a shared history of signs, scaffolded each other in their efforts to co-construct meaning. McCafferty also points out the intrapersonal self-regulating aspects of gesturing which

---

'communities' that usually go unchallenged.

works concurrently alongside the interpersonal communicative dimension (2002: 197).

One specific aspect of gesturing that is sometimes present in nonverbal interactions is *synchrony* and refers to 'mirroring of rhythm [and] movement, and the meshing of interaction' (Argyle, 1988; 34). In an interesting study McGuire (1980: 125-137) found that,

> An American child, while watching a videotaped version of himself, would mirror his posture and expressions when he agreed with what his screen image was saying but would not do so when he did not agree with his image.

Co-ordination of movement (e.g., punching the air in a clinched salute or shuffling to the tune of a samba band) signals the way people are open to each others' point of view. During demonstrations within a zoped interactional synchrony,

> is attained when the participants come to govern their behaviour in relation to one another in respect to commonly shared frame or joint plan of action. Interactants come to be able to behave together as if they share a common musical score and this can make possible a very high degree of temporal co-ordination between them (Kendon, 1990, quoted in McCafferty, 2002: 200).

It is essential to emphasise this *musical synchrony* emerges spontaneously and not as a top-down directive from Leninist politburos. At its best, such musical synchrony can lead development. Gestures are particularly useful when the *sense* of the discourse is not familiar to one or both communicators. Gestures fill this cultural gap and enhance intersubjectivity.

In summary: this section has shown how play, performance, gestures and imagination can overcome bourgeois embarrassment during demonstrations. In play, people usually behave ahead of themselves. Performance helps us to shed false 'identities' and express our 'subjectivity' within a crowd.

2.4 EXTENDING VYGOTSKY

Reputation is an idle and most false imposition;
oft got without merit and lost without deserving.

- Shakespeare, *Othello*, Act II, Scene III.

2.4.1 The First of the Mohicans: Carnivalesque as zoped

One of the most startling manifestations of the carnivalesque sense of proletarian humour in recent times occurred during the May Day 2000 demonstration at Parliament Square when a *detourned* version of Winston Churchill 'provided the festivities with a suitable focus of contempt' (cf. Appendix 1). *Detournement* is,

> the integration of present or past artistic production into a superior construction of a milieu. In this sense there can be no situationist painting or music, but only a situationist use of these means. In a more primitive sense, detournement within the old cultural sphere is a method of propaganda, a method which testifies to the wearing out and loss of importance of those spheres (Knabb, 1989: 46).

The disproportionate media assault on the proletarians responsible for beautifying Churchill's statue was an indication of how significant cultural icons still are in underscoring bourgeois hegemony. It was a battle related to Vygotsky's distinction between the *meaning* and *sense* of icons. Vygotsky gave the following example for his meaning-sense distinction. 'Whether we say *the victor of Jena* or *the loser at Waterloo*, we refer to the same person, yet the [sense] of the two phrases differs' (Vygotsky quoted in Veresov, 1996: 9).

After the events, everyone was discussing the same historical figure, Churchill, but the interpretations rapidly coalesced around class polarities. The point is to see words as multidimensional.[56] Chik Collins (1999a: 62) explains it succinctly:

> Meaning is identified as the most stable and fixed of these semantic dimensions – more or less equivalent to the dictionary definition. However the dimension of sense is much more fluid and dynamic. It is that semantic dimension of words which derives from their actual use in living speech. If meaning is abstract and impersonal, sense is distinctly concrete, and often acutely personal.

The meaning-sense polarity is related to the rise of alienation amongst people living in societies based on commodity production. Following on from Hegel, Leontiev (1977: 198) reminds us that this alienation can be observed in both the worker and the bourgeois,

> The hired worker, of course, is aware of the product he [sic] produces; in other words, he is aware of its objective meaning ... at least to the extent required for

---

56 Another example may concretise the distinction between *meaning* and *sense*. Bedny and Karwowski (2004: 128) write, 'This difference between objective meaning and subjective sense is most apparent in social interaction. An example ... A teacher asks a student, "Tell me how long do mice live?" The student responds, "That depends on the cat!" In theory, the student gave the correct answer, since often mice fall prey to cat, and as a result, the length of the mouse's life is determined by when and if it meets a cat. However one has the feeling of a paradox ... The teacher was referring to the biologically determined duration of a mouse's life, while the student was referring to the living conditions imposed by its environment, specifically its encounter with a predator.
Consequently, the same phrase (in this case a question) has several correct interpretations or meanings. That which the subject views as the correct interpretation is the sense of the phrase. Such paradoxes result when a given phrase has different meanings for different subjects. In reality, the sense is made concrete in the context of activity and is often referred to as the contextual sense'.

him to be able to perform his labour functions in a rational way. But this is not the same as the personal meaning [sense] of his labour, which lies in the wages for which he is working … This alienation also manifests itself at the opposite social pole. For the trader in minerals, Marx observes, minerals do not have the *personal meaning* of minerals.

What we observed during and after the May Day 2000 demonstration was slightly more complex. The demonstrators feeling alienated from their environment (with its colossal and awe-inspiring buildings, over-sanitised boulevards, the presence of police, cctv and intrusive journalists), resolved some of the tension by ascribing new meaning and sense to cultural icons, such as Churchill's statue. The environment became, during the act of carnivalisation, a genuine product of their labour. The bourgeoisie rejected this humanisation of Churchill since the stable meaning of Churchill as leader and ideologue was subverted. However (and here is where the difference with the trader of minerals that Marx observed manifests itself), many members of the bourgeoisie (and non-bourgeois members of society contaminated by their ideology) also felt *personally* offended by the Mohicanisation of Churchill's statue. For these individuals, Churchill has both an objective meaning (symbol of bourgeois hegemony) and a personal sense (bravery in the face of overwhelming odds, honour, decency, integrity).

In fact, the only faction of the British bourgeoisie that did not display any personal sense of injury was the bureaucrats responsible for overseeing the

demonstration. They simply did not have the time to reflect on the personal meaning of Churchill for themselves. They had careers to defend, sound bites to dish out. During the predictable buck-passing exercise that took place, these bureaucrats reified Churchill in exactly the same way the trader reifies 'his' minerals. Jack Straw, for example, insisted that the royal parks agency, responsible for Sir Winston Churchill's statue, and English Heritage, which looks after the Cenotaph in Whitehall, had not taken police advice to board them up. However this

version was challenged by Crispin Blunt … who insisted that English Heritage had acted on police advice. In a statement later English Heritage said it had been told that a boarded up Cenotaph might be a 'hiding place for bombs and ammunition'. Police had not provided the extra protection promised (The Guardian, Michael White, Wednesday May 3, 2000).

The strongly worded description of Churchill in the *Mindful Thuggery* leaflet (cf. Appendix 1) is a throwback to the times when he was perceived by the majority of our class as a bigoted reactionary, capable of horrendous acts of carnage. After the death of 3 million proletarians at the Bengal famine of 1943, when Churchill had restricted grain imports as a way of undermining the independence movement, he shrugged off the tragedy with the infamous remark, 'They'll still breed like rabbits' (Reflections on May Day 2000, 2000: 38). Here, after all, was a so-called 'anti-fascist' who in 1939 utters such banality, 'I have always said that if Britain were defeated in war I hoped we should find a Hitler to lead us back to our rightful place among the nations' (Reflections on May Day 2000, 2000: 38). As if to foreground his Social Darwinist credentials he would write,

> I do not admit that a great wrong has been done to the Red Indians of America or the black people of Australia by the fact a stronger race has come in and taken their place (Reflections on May Day 2000, 2000: 12).

For good measure, he described communists as 'swarms of typhus-bearing vermin'. Churchill is on record as strongly supporting the use of poisonous gas against 'uncivilised tribes' (Reflections on Mayday 2000, 2000: 13). Are we to assume the grandchildren of Welsh miners are the only British proletarians who remember any of this?

What Vygotsky discovered about the relationship between thinking and remembering is crucial here. He believed that, 'for the child, to think means to remember. For the adult, to remember means to think' (Luria, 1987: 370). In other words, in early childhood 'the construction of all other functions reflects a dependence on memory' (Vygotsky, 1987a: 308). Later in life, memory's interfunctional relations change dramatically. Now remembering becomes more based on conceptual thinking. What we find in the case of the Cenotaph ceremony is a special form of selective and imposed remembering that undermines conceptual thinking. It reduces thinking to the recall of a series of cultural markers devoid of historicity. In short, it *infantilises* the proletariat.[57] Ironically, through actions that were deemed 'infantile' and 'childish' by the media, proletarians managed to transform remembering into an active form of thinking about life. The Cenotaph memorial and Churchill's statue can be viewed as external social memory aids. Let us remind ourselves that Vygotsky (1978) defined

> *social memory* as a cognitive process mediated by external aids, be they tools or other individuals. This is the process of creation and elaboration of signs which al-

---

57 Another example of a spectacular ritual being used to shore up nationalism through selective remembering is the case of baseball in the USA. After the Twin Towers bombing there was a concerted effort to use baseball as a 'ritualized vehicle for a belligerent patriotism' (Butterworth, 2005: 107). This 'victimage' ritual, with its quasi-religious overtones and its capacity for a 'nostalgic idealisation of American society' is tailor made for remembering history as a disjointed series of external attacks on the mythical 'American way of life'.

lows an individual to keep track of the past and to reformulate this past in new meaningful representations (Marti *et al.,* 2001: 261).

The ruling class can reify social memory and ensure selective remembering. However, the proletariat is capable of fighting back in this crucial arena. One such example was a pamphlet produced for the 2001 May Day activities, entitled *May Day Monopoly.* This was a tool for learning and sharing knowledge, which suggested activities to co-incide with May Day all around London based on the popular board-game, Monopoly. The introduction explains the choice of the format and style,

> The game of monopoly is one of accumulation, making it perfect for our times. The aim being for each player to make a profit through the sale of a single commodity – land – and to expand their empire. In real life one single commodity generates all profits – our labour power ... Originally invented as The Landlord Game, to expose the parasitic role of landlords, the game was repackaged as Monopoly in the USA at the height of the great depression, as a sop to be sold to those workers who were being laid off and losing their livelihoods, a distraction from the reality of capitalist poverty (The London Mayday Collective, 2001: 3).

The guide then goes on to explain how people can get involved and subvert the game. Various famous landmarks and London streets are flagged in the pamphlet. For instance, the Old Kent Road is described as 'a hotbed of religious and political ideas, the first noted event was that of Wat Tyler who was involved in the poll tax uprising in the 13th century...' (The London Mayday Collective, 2001: 8). On the same page we see a list and description of various symbolic properties, including McDonald's, Tesco, Dixons and B&Q. Tesco, for instance, is described as 'a prominent member of the Freight Transport Association which lobbies for more road building. Encourages intensive monocrop agriculture ... forces third world peasants to grow for exports ...' (The London Mayday Collective, 2001: 8). In addition, there is a 'Don't Go to Jail' section with useful legal advice in case of arrests. The pamphlet ends with a call for a world without money, commodities and wage slavery.

It is important to note that the guide does not act merely as a repository of knowledge. Rather it supports 'the whole process of embodying, processing and transferring of knowledge' (Marti *et al.,* 2001: 264). The guide supports a variety of activities: preparation for the May Day event, the actions performed on the day itself, the ensuing discussion/analysis and future or parallel struggles. Another vital point worth noting is this. According to Vygotsky,

> human memory is generated by a social process. At the beginning of the development, the social memory is the product of knowledge distribution *between the individual and the tools or the other individuals who belong to a certain community*

(and are involved in a specific task). Subsequently the social memory undergoes a process of internalization by which external activities are reconstructed … the knowledge that is acquired through a social process is individualised and can be reused in different contexts (Marti *et al.*, 2001: 271). [Emphasis added]

Now concentrating on the first phase of this process, we underline that social memory is generated as a result of knowledge distribution between the individual and the tools or the other individuals who belong to a certain community. The ruling class generates social memory using tools such as the Cenotaph memorial and statues of its heroes. Its most important tool, of course, is the media. However, these are *tool-for-result* objects that are losing their potency and the individuals belonging to the bourgeois 'community' are also not as persuasive as they once were. By contrast, the proletariat uses tools (such as the Monopoly guide or the internet) in such a way that the toolmakers shape the process of memory embodiment, processing, transfer and consolidation. Here the tools are what Newman and Holzman (1993a: 145) call *tool-and-result*. Moreover, the other individuals that help generate social memory are, in the case of the proletariat, far more varied and knowledgeable than their robotic bourgeois counterparts. All this suggests that in the near future, the proletariat should be able to win struggle after struggle in the arena of social memory interpretation. The balance is *gradually* tilting in favour of the proletariat.

Bow Street Monopoly card

Perhaps it is the 'subconscious' realisation of this subtle shifting of power that explains the venom with which the media attacked the protesters. When, after the May Day 2001 events, the media brandished terms such as 'grotesque' and 'obscene' in describing Churchill's defacement, this was justifiably seen by protesters as a clear declaration of ideological warfare. For these are culturally loaded expressions which celebrate and simultaneously conceal the history of various bourgeois victories. *Obscenity*, for example, has always been the flip side of modernisation in geo-cultural discourse. Modernisation was credited with the power to 'sweep away the filthy and crumbling passageways of old London and open up to light and circulation of traffic, people and goods' (Nead, 1997: 33). The filthy, morally reprehensible proletariat is the obscene which needs to be modernised before entering civil society.

The plethora of leaflets, articles, pamphlets and meetings that were launched to defend, explain, and extend the symbolic attack on Churchill were characterised by a 'kind of Bakhtinian bathos or Brechtian *plumpes Denken* [that swoops] from *Geist* to genitalia, from the oracular to the orificial…' (Eagleton, 1989: 180). Nothing illustrates this style better than the juxtaposition of Shakespearean quotes with the 'gutter' language used to attack Churchill in the *Mindful Thuggery* leaflet (cf. Appendix 1).

Our analysis of the range, novelty and multivoicedness of working class discourse surrounding this event is at odds with the findings of Bernstein (1971, 1972). Bernstein investigated forms of speaking among the working and the middle classes. People from a working class background tended to use what was termed a *restricted* code, characterised by a focus on the concrete aspects of the situation, emotion, clichés and looser syntax. On the other hand, middle class subjects used an *elaborated* code, focusing on abstract aspects of the situation.[58]

Walter, the chinaman who peed on my rug, I can't go give him a bill, so what the fuck are you talking about?

The contrast with both proletarian and bourgeois discursive practice after the May Day 2000 could not be starker. Proletarian discourse (vocal, written and visual) was characterised by a code including inventiveness, multivoicedness and serious-humour. In short, it was an exemplary manifestation of the dialectics of the concrete and abstract (restrictive and elaborated in Bernstein's terms), which helped many think about Churchill and memorials from a fresh perspective. The dialogic interaction is always challenged by history, disagreement and questions. It repositions itself in the light of new events and information.

In contrast, the bourgeois propaganda was a *restrictive* code, which maintained the duality between

What the fuck are you talking about? The chinaman is not the issue here, Dude. I'm talking about drawing a line in the sand, Dude. Across this line, you DO NOT... Also, Dude, chinaman is not the preferred nomenclature. Asian-American, please.

---

58 Bernstein employed a relatively sound interpretation of Vygotsky. Sadly for British education it was the rather problematic interpretations of Vygotsky by James Britton that were taken up instead (Inghilleri, 2002). Britton interpreted the zone of proximal development as a benign and liberal space for enculturation. In the process the significance of class struggle was obscured. Bernstein, on the other hand, emphasised the unequal power relations within the zoped. Bernstein's own research, however, was largely confined to moments of class passivity. My work has foregrounded moments of rupture. This may explain my divergent findings.

concrete and abstract. The concrete analysis remained a banal exercise in naive empiricism (e.g., irrelevant details about the paint used and the police's inability to 'save' the statue from 'desecration'). The abstract was a metaphysical exercise in rhetorical preaching. The whole process was a clear indication of the all-too-slow death agony of a bourgeois class no longer capable of employing discourse for its benefits and an emerging proletarian class that is gradually fostering a new mode of communication.

Some neo-Vygotskians have tended to concentrate too much on the intra-psychological aspects of consciousness. Bakhtin's preference for the inter-psychological register is a useful corrective to this trend. Bakhtin realised that alienation needs to be externalised if it is to survive. At this point, alienation becomes vulnerable to collective rebellion (Emerson, 1996: 134). The solitude of radicals is overcome through carnivalesque communication,

> No Nirvana is possible for a *single* consciousness. A single consciousness is a contradiction in terms … I am conscious of myself and become myself only while revealing myself, through another, and with the help of another … Separation, dissociation and enclosure within the self is the main reason for the loss of one's self. Not that which takes place within, but that which takes place on the *boundary* between one's own and someone else's consciousness, on the *threshold* … To *be* means to *communicate* … To be means to be for another, and through the other, for oneself (Bakhtin, quoted in Emerson, 1996, 135).

The 'desecration' of Churchill's bust is also part of what Bakhtin referred to as *life as authoring*. To understand life, Bakhtin argued, one should approach it as an act of authoring (Clarke and Holquist, 1984: 365). Such authoring could be *behavioural* (for instance a deed), *mental* (for instance a thought or concept) or *communicative* (say a speech or text). Accordingly, the Churchill graffiti displays all three forms of 'life authoring' simultaneously. These 'life authoring' actions were directed toward the 'other' (the dead, the absent, the observers of the demonstration and fellow proletarians involved in similar May Day celebrations throughout the world). 'Life as authoring' emphasises process rather than product. It looks at 'becoming'. 'Life as authoring' adds a new dimension to looking at graffiti and slogans as merely modes of communication. In the last section, I showed how graffiti and slogans could be viewed as forms of 'private speech', which complete a thought process. Here graffiti and slogans play yet another crucial role, that of active inscription and empowerment. Regarding inscription within institutions, Stables (2003: 10) has argued,

> A view of institutions as inscriptions implies that almost any 'mark' made on an institution by an individual is potentially empowering. Thus graffiti might be seen as empowerment via unsolicited inscription.

This explains why graffiti becomes a site of contestation between the powerful and the dis-empowered. The graffiti sprayed on Churchill's statue became, perhaps inadvertently, a political intervention in a debate about nationalism, warfare and racism but it also communicated the ideological vulnerability of the ruling elite to everyone concerned.

To fuse this with Vygotsky's preceding ideas, one could look at authoring as a 'dialectical struggle between socially fixed word *meaning* and idiosyncratic *sense* dependent on specific psychological context' (Kozulin, 1991: 342). Out of such struggles new cultural idioms are forged. If Vygotsky was right in suggesting that 'words expand our consciousness but also limit us as we can only fully experience those things that we have the words for' (Nicholl, 1998: 3), then part of life as authoring is the rejection of old words that have outgrown their usefulness and the creation of new ones. 'Life authorship' may occur within certain inherited cultural constraints but it is forever pushing against boundaries in order to redefine and revitalise our vocabulary. For instance, terms such as 'globalisation' and 'internationalism', which began life as useful descriptions of certain trends, have perhaps become a hindrance to the understanding of class struggle, since the former ignores that capitalism has always been 'global' and the latter assumes the continuing existence of 'nations'.

Was the attack on Churchill's statue an example of what Bakhtin called *ventriloquation*? Was it, in other words, an action that captured people's feelings? Was it an utterance of a collective voice? Probably, not. Most demonstrators, given the chance, would probably have opted for more suitable targets to 'get their massage across'. However, once confronted with a situation not of their choosing, they responded by calmly understanding and then re-pulsing the media assault directed against them. What is vital to remember is that it is possible for the proletariat to recover from a tactical error if it mobilises itself within a ZPD. The ZPD provides us with bouncibility!

To summarise this section, I have attempted to show how a *detourned* image of Churchill forces us to think about the *meaning, sense* and *motivation* behind communication. This thinking is crucial in revitalising proletarian social memory and counteracting bourgeois ideology. My analysis showed that proletarian remembering of the 'desecration' of Churchill's statue was a dialectical process involving concrete and abstract recall. By contrast, bourgeois remembering of the event was *restricted* and devoid of vitality. Finally, I suggested how this graffiti was an example of active inscription and empowerment. Bakhtin was employed to extend Vygotsky here in terms of the former's notion of 'life authoring'.

2.5 LIMITATIONS OF VYGOTSKY

> Do I contradict myself?
> Very well then ... I contradict myself.
> I am large ... I contain multitudes.
>
> -Walt Whitman, 1855/1986: 51.

Vygotskian psychology provides us with a framework for constructing a theory of consciousness, which does not presuppose (or fetishize) equilibrium and consistency. However, the very act of extending Vygotsky has underscored some of his limitations. There is a great deal in Vygotsky that needs to be ditched or at least substantially modified. Many of Vygotsky's problems are traceable to his misjudging of the class struggle of his day. For instance, he does not show any indication of suspecting the USSR of being a capitalist society[59] (For a discussion of the capitalist nature of USSR see Fernandez, 1997). His rather uncritical attitude toward schooling and education is a direct consequence of his mistaken identification of the USSR with communism (or socialism). Kinginger (2002: 243) explains how in the 1930s there was a need to integrate millions of ethnically, culturally and linguistically diverse students into the Bolshevik capitalist Leviathan that was the USSR,

> It was in this context that Vygotsky was brought into the inner circle of revolutionary educational reform led by Lenin's widow, N. K. Krupskaya, to assist in the effort to provide firm scientific foundation, based in part on Dewey's pragmatic epistemology, for the state's programme of education.

Vygotsky was, needless to say, far more critical of concepts such as 'science', 'progress' and 'education' than his Bolshevik taskmasters. In this sense, he was closer to the legacy of Marx than the Engels-Leninist environment he found himself in. However, there is still an unfortunate tendency in Vygotsky to posit the child as in need of formal education and socialisation.[60] This approach, especially amongst neo-Vygotskians, has tended to disenfranchise 'street' knowledge (Burman, 1994: 54).

It may even ignore what Shotter (1997) considers vital, *phronesis,* 'a form of practical knowledge concerned with the know-how of making decisions according to one's social responsibilities'. As Seeger (2001: 43) makes clear, the distinction between *phronesis* and *episteme* is very old. Whilst Aristotle viewed knowledge as episteme (i.e., scientific knowledge, universal, conceptual and abstract), Plato emphasised phronesis (i.e., practical wisdom, particularity, perceptual knowledge and concrete). The emphasis on instrumentalist action by some neo-Vygotskians has exasperated this pro-episteme bias. Vygotsky, it is true, was remarkably uncritical of the educational practices in vogue at the time. His main concern was

---

59 This statement needs qualification. According to Ratner (1991: 172) Vygotsky 'criticised stratification in soviet society as having deleterious effects on the motivation, cognition, and education of lower-class youth. He also condemned authoritarian leadership in the workplace as crippling incentive and creativity in workers'. Whether these basic criticisms would, given time, flourish into a full-fledged critique of USSR as capitalist is a moot point.

60 It is true Vygotsky made certain criticisms of education. For instance, he believed education to be 'the tail behind child development', which was guided not by tomorrow, but by yesterday (cf. Davydov and Zinchenko, 1993: 100). However, in general he confined his criticisms to 'bourgeois' education prior to 1917, not realising that education remained bourgeois under the capitalist rule of the Bolsheviks post 1917.

that education should be 'appropriately in advance of development' (Wells, 1999). However he, by and large, ignored power relations within the zone of proximal development and marginalised forms of knowledge not sanctioned by modernism, such as superstition and magic.

Following on from these initial concerns, we should note that Vygotsky's conception of 'social' is at times rather restrictive. The social is reduced to the dyadic, sometimes the mother-child dyad[61], with all its unstated assumptions about the 'structure of families, about which relationship is the most important for a child, and how the social world is categorised into domestic and the public' (Burman, 1994: 43). Wells (1999) has concluded that to,

> focus exclusively on face-to-face interaction mediated by speech is to seriously limit our understanding of the range of modes of semiotic mediation that play a role in both intrapersonal and interpersonal thinking and problem solving ...

Bakhtin's concept of *collective voice* is, of course, the perfect supplement to Vygotskian face-to-face communication. At other times, the *social* consists for Vygotsky in the 'rules and norms of society', rules and norms that are regarded uncritically (Jaramillo, 1996: 3). James Wertsch (1991: 46) has put it well:

> What is somewhat ironic for someone interested in formulating a Marxist psychology, he made precious little mention of broader historical, institutional, or cultural processes such as class struggle, alienation and the rise of commodity fetishism.

His reliance on the mechanical materialism of Plekhanov and Engels (Vygotsky, 1997a: 176–177) was a genuine problem from which he never fully recovered. This led him, at times, to employ a crude version of the base-superstructure model of development, which is grossly inadequate,

> Nowhere else, according to Plekhanov, does that dependence of consciousness on the way of life manifest itself in a more obvious and direct manner as it does in the life of primitive man (Vygotsky, 1997a: 176).

Vygotsky is almost implying here that for 'primitive man' the relationship between base and superstructure was direct, one-way and deterministic. To underscore the point, he quotes a passage from Engels's *Anti-Dühring* approvingly and concludes with the following sentiment,

---

61 R. van der Veer and J. Valsiner (1994b: 6) write, '... nowadays countless investigators of mother-child dialogues and joint problem solving (with their emphasis on the steering role of the more experienced other in an intimate setting) feel obliged to refer to Vygotsky, although in fact Vygotsky never discussed these situations and instead focused upon culture as providing tools for thinking'. This is a rather dogmatic defence of Vygotsky, which forgets it was initial shortcomings in Vygotsky himself that paved the way for further neo-Vygotskian mistakes.

This is what Engels wrote in 'Anti-Dühring'. We have to proceed from the basic assumption that intellectual production is determined by the form of material production (Vygotsky, 1997a: 177).

Certain other passages in Vygotsky are tainted by a crude cultural determinism, which still finds an occasional echo in the works of contemporary cultural psychologists,

The environment appears in child development, namely in the development of personality and specific human qualities, in the role of the source of development. Hence the environment here plays the role not of the situation of development, but of its source (Vygotsky, quoted in Wertsch and Tulviste, 1996, 68).

Another related problem is Vygotsky's 'intellectualism'. Carl Ratner (1991: 188) is correct when he says,

...Vygotsky's emphasis on the formal linguistic mediation of childhood thinking (and psychological development, in general) apart from children's societal-material intercourse endowed Vygotsky's system of ideas with a certain intellectualism. On many of his writings, linguistic concepts which formed children's cognitive structures were suspended in a world of their own apart from concrete society.

I have criticised Vygotsky's overemphasis on vertical learning, positing the parallel concept of 'contact zone' (Kramsch, 2000) and 'horizontal learning' (Engeström, 2001), which refer to 'important learning and development that takes place as people and ideas from different cultures meet, collide and merge'. With Engeström I would insist 'on working with both dimensions, the horizontal and the vertical, or more generally, the spatial-social and the temporal-historical' (Engeström, 1999: 4). Furthermore, Vygotsky's psychology as promoted today tends to miss individual differences (Blunden, 2001: 17). The solution to this is to attempt to differentiate between (proletarian) *individuality* and (bourgeois) *individualism*. I have also been at pains to distance myself from Vygotsky's uncritical attitude towards rational problem-solving strategies. I would also employ a more extensive definition of psychological tools to include not only speech, works of art, diagrams, maps and conventional signs, but also various modes of artistic and political expression, such as marching, chanting, dancing, drama, play and musical performance.

In line with contemporary researchers in the field of Human-Computer Interaction (HCI), I would argue that a great deal of planning and decision-making regarding political actions is 'characterised by intuition and imagination as the driving force of the process, rather than a rational problem-solving strategy' (Aboulafia *et al.,* 1995: 3). Using the metaphor of the scientifically inclined artist, Johnson Laird (1986: 879) has summarised the reasons for Vygotsky's shortcomings as follows:

He failed to formulate a proper theory of elementary mental processes; he over-looked the role of syntax in language; he proposed a radical discontinuity between evolutionary and cultural processes that is incompatible with anthropological evidence. Vygotsky was an artist trying to construct a scientific psychology in an era when the only language for theories was the vernacular.

As already alluded to, Vygotsky had an unfortunate tendency to demarcate the 'in-ternal' and 'external' registers too strictly, which left him open to the charge of per-petuating the body-mind duality. Lave and Wenger (1991) have criticised this ahistorical approach succinctly,

> ... the historicising of the processes of learning gives the lie to ahistorical views of 'internalisation' as a universal process ... [participation at the core of the learning process] can be neither fully internalised as knowledge structures nor fully extern-alised as instrumental artifacts ... (Lave and Wenger, 1991, quoted in Wells, 1999).

However, once we remind ourselves of another one of Vygotsky's axioms, the notion that 'all mental processes are quasi-social', it becomes obvious that,

> the problem of external and internal is related to the problem of the location or the modes of existence of these processes, but not as their essential matter ... the system is not external or internal, or external and internal, simply because there is no border between [them] ... internalisation is no more than recombination of the elements of this system and appearance of new connections between them (Veresov, 1996: 14).

In other words, *internalisation* is 'an activity of meaning-giving and digestion, not a process of impression in which the individual stays passive' (Wardekker, n.d.: 5). Ac-cording to Wertsch and Tulviste (1996: 63) certain Eurocentric perspectives cloud Vy-gotsky's (and especially Luria's) cross-cultural studies. 'Vygotsky', suggest Wertsch and Tulviste, 'clearly regarded some cultures as inferior to others'. Different problem solving strategies were needlessly placed on a developmental scale with the European cultural tools and forms of mental functioning at the top of a supposed hierarchy. Cole (1985) has demonstrated successfully that most cross-cultural research fails to embed assessment in contexts familiar to subjects. The problem is that Vygotsky and most of his followers did not have a critique of 'progress' and 'rationalism'. Develop-ment is mostly viewed as having an ideal telos. Our understanding of development is somewhat more sophisticated today.

To end this section on a positive note, we could refer to Vygotsky's prediction that capitalism will come full circle and the various artificially created dualities, such as the duality between physical and mental labor, will come to an end. Unlike his con-temporary advocates in the fields of educational and occupational psychology, Vygot-sky desired a supercession of education and work. As he put it,

In this respect the end of the capitalist period presents a striking antithesis to its beginning. If in the beginning the individual was transformed into a fraction, into the executor of a fractional function, into a live extension of the machine, then at the end of it, the very requirements of manufacturing require an all-round developed, flexible person, who would be capable of changing the forms of work, and of organizing the production process and controlling it (Vygotsky, 1997a: 180).

2.6 EXPANSIVE PROLETARIAN LEARNING

Roma locuta est; causa finita est.
Rome has spoken; the case is concluded.

- St. Augustine, Sermons, Book i.

Securus iudicat orbis terrarum.
The verdict of the world is conclusive.

- St Augustine, Contra Epis. Parmen, iii, 24.

Proletarian demonstrations, especially those that supersede the routine, (i.e., those that become revels or riots) are the perfect zone of proximal development. They exemplify the multi-faceted aspects of zoped: as physical space in time; as cultural medium; and, finally, as tool-and result of social activity.

My Vygotskian analysis has shown that demonstrations are concentrated moments of transformation, which reflexively foreground all the contradictory tendencies within society and propose an alternative. In our age, they prefigure the break-up of hollow dichotomies: private-public, subject-object, work-play, mental labor-physical labor, leaders-followers, etc.

No, this is not phatic communion!

They provide a framework for treating individuals 'ahead of themselves'- a learning process that is simultaneously an attempt to change history.

To employ a distinction made by German Critical Psychology, individuals living under capitalism seem to have two alternatives in order to make their actions effective: the first is the *restrictive* mode of action when actions are undertaken 'within the framework of available or conceded conditions'; and, the second is the *generalised* mode of activity when individuals, '... taking the risk of failure and negative sanctions' develop and extend the framework of action (Maiers and Tolman, 1996: 111). Vygotsky seems to us the perfect figure for charting these moments of generalised transgression since he emphasises how the individual changes the zoped as the zone transforms the individual.

At times, the aim of proletarian collectivities is not communication *per se* but what Malinowski (1960) has termed 'phatic communion'- a secular version of the Holy Communion, bringing people together in a circle of companionship. By imposing playtime over official time, zones of proletarian development allow the flourishing of phatic communion. The learning that takes place dialectically integrates the 'everyday' with 'scientific' concepts thus ensuring generalisations. Everyday concepts arise as the result of immediate and concrete experience. They tend to be unsystematic, contextual, reflection on common experience (Estep, Jr., 2002: 148). A 'chair' or 'cat' are examples of everyday concepts. As Luria (1987: 366) has pointed out 'the everyday, practical concept reflects reality, but the system of concealed connections that lie behind that reality may not enter conscious awareness'.

By contrast, scientific concepts are introduced somewhat abstractly into a system of logical categories and oppositions. They tend to be systematic, specialised and de-contextualised. An example of scientific concepts could be the 'class struggle'. The dialectical interaction of everyday and scientific concepts engenders organic learning. However, I have also tried to show that artifacts produced in everyday practical activity could have the character of genuine knowledge and must not be relegated to 'folk' knowledge. Sylvia Scribner (1984: 9-40) has shown that,

> an activity in a work setting that looked dull and routine (i.e., filling orders for milk products by collecting them in a ware-house, and loading them onto delivery trucks), did not mean that workers lacked 'theoretical perspectives' about their work and their activity setting. Actually they were extremely inventive in constructing artifacts, like algorithms, arithmetical procedures and graphical notations, which could help them organise their work. It was remarkable that these inventions mostly did not refer to any form of mathematics or knowledge taught in schools (Seeger, 2001; 42).

I have emphasised that learning is not always 'benign', 'progressive' or 'linear'. Engeström (in press) has underlined learning through the 'destructive rejection of the old' and Pea (1994) has underscored the competitive aspects of development, whilst 'error' has been credited with one of the major contradictory knots that propel development 'forward'. In a study of elementary school children working towards robot construction, Barfurth (1995: 1 and 8) has shown how 'disagreements can be a legitimate source of collaboration [as well as] constructive and productive in the learning process'. During a 5-week period, Barfurth counted 24 substantive disagreements. He concluded that,

> The children were able to discuss, defend, modify and actively seek solutions during disagreements ... The children did more than oppose each other. They attempted to resolve their oppositions ... The opposition during a disagreement was more than negation. The children insisted on explanation and evidence as they

worked on their shared task ... The resolution process of the disagreements included integrating other children's ideas, modifying their own ideas and asking others for clarification and explanation (Barfurth, 1995: 8).

Poddiakov (2001) has taken the notions of disagreement and error further by positing a 'pedagogy of counteraction' against the well-known term, 'pedagogy of cooperation'. His argument is that there is such a thing as *counteraction* to learning which 'is opposite to honest help and cooperation in the course of learning' (Poddiakov, 2001: 4). There are according to Poddiakov two basic kinds of counteraction namely, *unpremeditated* and *premeditated* counteractions. Unpremeditated counteraction is unusually caused by mistakes. Teachers, instructors, experienced peers may make genuine mistakes in the process of teaching. Alternatively, unpremeditated counteraction could be due to some inherent flaw in the educational system, for instance, the hierarchical nature of teaching. An example of premeditated counteraction would be the myth of Prometheus. Zeus who had prevented 'man' from learning how to use fire, cruelly punished Prometheus for disobeying him. Another example closer to our time may be when the media threaten May Day demonstrators in case of rioting or when the police cordon off thousands of demonstrators and force them to endure hours of inactivity and immobility or when websites are shut down prior to mobilisation for a demonstration, hampering communication. Here is a humorous example of media terrorism,

Specialist firearms teams are being drafted in to police this year's [2001] May Day demonstrations in the City of London over fears that rioters armed with samurai swords and machetes will infiltrate the protests (The Observer, 22 April 2001).

Whether development takes place amicably or through substantive disagreement, through cooperation or counteraction, one thing is clear. By suspending commodity relations, demonstrations and strikes have the potential to undermine the tendency toward commodity and money abstraction. Schneider (1974: 110) has posited a linkage between the historical tendency toward abstraction and the degree of social repression under capitalism. Abstraction from use value and sensuousness results in the repression of all useful and sensuous needs. In fact, Alfred Sohn-Rethel (1978) has argued that 'repression' itself is a 'real abstraction' since it occurs outside and without the involvement of consciousness. If Schneider and Sohn-Rethel are right in their assumptions then this explains how desires, needs, sensuousness and drives come to be expressed more freely during moments of rupture, once use-value marginalises exchange value and commodity abstraction.

In summary: it has been the argument of this chapter that, at their best, zones of pro-letarian development are the ideal space for synthesising a fuller socialised individu-ality within community. The synthesis, it has been suggested, fosters the development of a dialectical consciousness. It is consciousness and not intellect that should be the centrepiece of thinking since consciousness is dialogic and the site where intellect meets emotions, whereas intellect is usually monologic and does not fully engage with other areas of thinking. Consciousness is socially acquired, mediated by symbols and interpretive repertoires which can be simple gestures or complex discourses, brought under voluntary self-regulation and exists in a broad and complex network with other functions such as memory and perception. The model offered in this chapter does not imply consciousness, in either an individualised or collective form, is a prerequisite for collective action (cf. Kilgore, 1999). Rather it shows how conscious-ness becomes fused dialectically with genuine social struggles that come to oppose the totality of capitalist relations.

Chapter three:
Iranian Football Riots as Bakhtinian Carnivalesque

'... I hereby deliver myself up body and soul, belly and bowels, to a hundred thousand basketfuls of raving demons ...'

Chapter three:

Iranian Football Riots as Bakhtinian Carnivalesque

... I hereby deliver myself up body and soul, belly and bowels, to a hundred thousand bas-ketfuls of raving demons, if I have lied so much as once throughout this [chapter]. By the same token, may St. Anthony sear you with his erysipelatous fire ... may Mahomet's disease whirl you in epileptic jitters ... may the festers, ulcers and chancres of every puru-lent pox infect, scathe, mangle and rend you, entering your bumgut as tenuously as mercur-alized cow's hair ... and may you vanish into an abyss of brimstone and fire, like Sodom and Gomorrah, if you do not believe implicitly what I am about to relate in the present Chronicles ...

- Rabelais, Book 2, Prologue, quoted in Morris, 1994: 21.

This chapter applies Bakhtin to a weeklong series of Iranian football riots (21-27 October 2001) during the qualifying rounds for the 2002 World Cup. In the first section, the *carnivalesque* and *dialogic* dimensions of rioting are dis-cussed. By re-accentuating Bakhtin's concept of carnival, I will demonstrate its opposition to the concept of *spectacle* (Guy Debord, 1987). Various aspects of the carnival, such as parody, grotesquerie, drinking, eating, sexual contact, excess and hysteria are ex-amined. In the second section, I outline the sequence of events that led to the riots and the dynamics of the forces involved (i.e., the rioters and the police). In the final section, I apply the above-mentioned Bakhtinian concepts to the case study and draw conclusions.

In a world encumbered by an increasingly tyrannical 'roll-out-neo-liberal-fas-cism' hell-bent on colonising every nook and cranny of oppositional creativity, writ-ing from a Bakhtinian perspective has become an enterprise fraught with peril. The mere association of Bakhtin with the proletariat (understood *broadly* as the dispos-sessed and alienated class of wealth producers) is sufficient to awaken the self-ap-pointed ogres of conservatism from their intellectual slumber. Awoken monsters can be very grouchy. Sadly, this confrontation cannot be avoided since Bakhtin is so use-ful for comprehending the social struggle.

The Islamic Republic of Iran is imploding. As a working class atheist, I celebrate this slow death agony with all the joy and euphoria I can muster. I know that the com-

ing social cataclysm in Iran will witness the pro-letariat dancing gleefully on the dung-heap of bourgeois-religious morality. Emma Goldman is alleged to have said, 'If I can't dance, it's not my revolution' (Goldman quoted in Steinem, 1995: 4). We shall gyrate all night long to the memory of Emma (Goldman) and Mazdak, Karl (Marx) and Sylvia (Pankhurst) whilst feasting on a barrel of 'blood wine'. But we shall also take care to remind ourselves that this time round it was different be-cause a genuine social revolution had taken place and not the mere political seizure of power that our Engels-Leninist 'friends' are so fond of. And we shall know that it all began with seven days of carnivalesque football rioting in October 2001 that heralded a rupture in proletarian pessimism.

3.1 BAKHTINIAN TOPOGRAPHY

3.1.1 Carnival re-accentuated

In this section I will describe those Bakhtinian concepts that aid our investigation of proletarian football rioting. I shall begin with a theme that runs through Bakhtin's life and work- the carnival.

Carnival versus spectacle

As Bakhtin has observed, 'Carnival expresses the people's hopes of a happier future, of a more just social and economic order, of a new truth' (Bakhtin, 1973: 269). In con-temporary Iran, this resurgence manifests itself in various forms ranging from the New Year Festival of *Norouz* (literally, 'new day') to the more vociferous football riot.[62] *Carnivalesque*, as a social mode of being and consciousness, has its roots in cul-

---

62 What Stallybrass and White (1986: 14) write about carnivals is relevant to Norouz, 'for long periods [carnival/Norouz] may be a stable and cyclical ritual with no noticeable politically transformative effects but that, given the presence of sharpened political antagonism, it may often act as *catalyst* and *site of actual and symbolic struggle*'.

tural traditions of resistance that predate even the medieval European carnival. I will trace the contours of this remarkable evolution below but I would like the reader to bear in mind throughout that carnivalesque also stands in opposition to what Debord (1987) called the *spectacle* a set of capitalist social relations mediated by the image.

One of a handful of researchers who has noticed this relationship is David M. Boje (2001). He claims that much of global protest is carnivalesque. Indeed the anti-capitalist protesters of Seattle costumed in sea-turtle shells facing the police over-dressed in Darth Vader masks as well as the parodic anti-sweatshop movement have many ideological affinities with Bakhtinian notions of resistance. For Bakhtin the carnival has many attributes. In its purest form, the carnival is a peculiar folk humour that has existed without merging with the official culture of the ruling class. The *spectacle*, on the other hand, can manifest itself as religious procession. Lent in Christianity and Ashura[63] in Islam, exemplify such official ceremonies, which stand opposed to the spirit of carnival. 'In Brueghel's painting of the Battle of Carnival and Lent', writes Michael D. Bristol (1983: 643),

> the personification of carnival rides on a wine barrel instead of a horse, and the combatants brandish cooking utensils instead of weapons ... [After all] the comprehensive rethinking of the social world in terms of common, everyday material and physical experience is central to the process of 'uncrowning'.

The ironic image of Iranian demonstrators, imitating Argentineans, in brandishing kitchen utensils and banging pans during recent street demonstrations is perfectly in tune with this scenario (Kayhan Weekly, p. 1, no. 915, 25 July 2002).

Actually, dad, I think I might be an atheist!

The function of carnival is, however, not restricted to maintaining an 'unsoiled' proletarian culture. As Boje observes, carnival is a theatrics of rant and madness

---

63 *Ashura* is the annual re-enactment of the defeat and murder of the Shi'a Imam Hussein by his Sunni political rivals at Karbala in 680 AD. Hussein was the prophet's grandson and the conflict represents an intra-classist rivalry within the Islamic ruling elite. Although the event is marked by all Muslims it has a special significance for the Shi'a branch of the faith who glory in victimhood. Shi'a mythology falsely represents Ashura as a battle between Good and Evil.

seeking to repair felt separation and alienation (Boje, 2001). The very excess experienced during carnival,

> prepared a new, scientific knowledge of this world which destroyed all alienation; it drew the world closer to man [sic], to his body, permitted him to touch and test every object, examine it from all sides, enter into it, turn it inside out, compare it to every phenomenon (Bakhtin, 1984a: 381).

During the Feast of Fools, for instance, the clergy and nobility were parodied and ridiculed, their belief system subjected to the cruellest of condemnations, but the parody was nearly always a *regenerative* one. Bakhtin was very clear on the conflict between carnival and spectacle, even though he penned his work on carnival many years before Debord's seminal tome on the spectacle,

> Carnival is not a spectacle seen by the people; they live in it, and everyone participates because its very idea embraces all the people. While carnival lasts, there is no other life outside it. During carnival time life is subject only to its laws, that is, the laws of its own freedom (Bakhtin, quoted in Morris, 1994: 198).

In short, carnival participants experience social solidarity and cohesion rather than passive consumption and detachment that are hallmarks of spectacularised ceremonies. This solidarity is connected to what Bakhtin called 'a shared social purview' between the interlocutors in dialogue and permits the disclosure of suppressed thoughts and feelings (Gardiner, 1992: 113).

Carnival historicised

It makes sense to distinguish between three interrelated phenomena: first, the historical or original carnival which we can call the 'classical carnival' (this refers to carnival in its ancient and Middle Ages manifestations); second, the re-enactment of this historical carnival in numerous new, contemporary settings, which we can refer to as 'displaced carnival'; and, thirdly, carnival as a site of contestation which could occur anywhere and at any time following a cycle of struggle or shifting balance of class forces. The last form of carnival we could call, 'carnival revisited'. This categorisation follows closely the distinctions made with regard to primitive capital accumulation in the introduction section.

What needs to be remembered is that within these three forms of carnival, there exists a confrontation between *carnivalesque* as a radical social mode of being and consciousness and the *spectacle*, which is a set of mystified bourgeois social relations mediated by the image. As it becomes clear my investigation into Iranian football riots falls under the second and third abovementioned categories, that of 'displaced carnival' and 'carnival revisited'. The shifting tectonics of Iranian society seems to have created new fault lines where proletarian carnivalesque and Islamic spectacle confront each other in a convoluted social struggle.

Already risking a fatwa from the ayatollahs of Bakhtinology over my association of Bakhtin with proletariat, permit me to irreversibly settle my own fate by linking

Classical carnival   Bakhtin with yet another unfashionable word - the 'D' word. For I believe, Bakhtin who contextualised carnival in its Renaissance settings was also cognisant of its 'Dialectics' of evolution, 'Carnival was the true feast of time, the feast of becoming, change, and renewal. It was hostile to all that was immortalised and completed' (Bakhtin quoted in Sandywell, 1998: 198). This is not to deny that at times 'his understanding of carnival is overly idealised and ahistorical, and that his conception of the people is vague...' (Gardiner, 1992: 182). These ambiguities and the fact that Bakhtin refers to evolution as 'unfinalized' has caused confusion, allowing his postmodernist admirers to deny the existence of antagonism (negation) and synthesis (negation of negation) in his *Weltanschauung*. In general, negativity has been an overlooked element of carnival.

David Gross was one of the first to buck the trend and re-introduce the element of negativity into the carnival. In relation to the European precursors of the carnival, the medieval fairs and the travelling troupes of entertainers, Gross (1978: 128) has postulated the following functions,

> First, they provided popular entertainment and amusement. Second, they offered at least momentary relief from hard work by creating a different kind of space and mood as an antidote to the routines of daily life. And last, but very important, they introduced into a given, fixed world the experience of negativity and otherness.

Scholars of carnival usually emphasise only the first function elicited above. In the case of Iranian football riots the significance of creating zones of proletarian development (ZPD) as well as the introduction of negativity and otherness into an official ideology that frowns upon transgression even more sternly than its European fascist prototypes of the 1930s, cannot be overstated. Gross goes on to chronicle the domestication of the medieval 'pre-carnival', a trend accelerated through cultural fragmentation and specialisation,

> Gradually this essentially medieval phenomenon was institutionalised in three directions: towards the fair, the circus, and the carnival. By being fragmented and formalised in this way, each part lost much of its potential impact and negativity (Gross, 1978: 128).

The fair was the most susceptible to commercialisation and has now become a mercantile and information network for agricultural capitalism. The circus tried to hang on to its craft and artisan-based image since it sees itself as performance art. 'Unlike the fair and circus', Gross continues, 'which were largely *cleaned up* by the 1920s', the carnival has managed to retain elements of subversion (Gross, 1978: 129). A similar division of labor occurred in Iran where pre-carnival types became formalised around, i) Norouz or New Year's celebration (with its distinct pagan undertones); ii) underground 'masques' and 'raves' (comprising of both rich and poor youth); and iii) the tradition of secularised street theatre and the recently acquired penchant for carnavalised demonstrations.

The *grotesque* aspects of carnival manifest themselves in the underground culture of the proletariat specially its *undomesticated* faction (sex-workers, drug addicts, the permanently unemployed, the 'young', etc). The ungovernability of this group has been a constant source of despair for the regime's 'moral police'.

This 'sacrilegious' behaviour finds an echo in both the radical and reactionary strata of Iranian society. Instances of public drinking and sexual liaisons have been reported amongst the younger generation of football rioters, whilst an example of reactionary (sober) profanity was reported recently in the London based *Kayhan* weekly. During Friday prayers, a 'pro-reform' minister of parliament from the central city of Yazd was at first verbally abused and then set upon by supporters of Khamene'i, the traditionalist 'spiritual leader' of the regime (Kayhan Weekly, p 3, no. 915, 25 July 2002). What distinguished this jolly fracas from the customary intra-capitalist conflict over territory and power was the use of prayer-stones as projectiles. The fact that such blasphemy could not even enter the imagination of malcontents previously suggests how far things have shifted.

These examples raise the relationship between carnivalesque and power. One reading of Bakhtin sees carnivalesque as the collective parodic 'centrifugal' forces in opposition to the project of centralisation and bourgeois hegemony. Once *monologism* (a stable, unified, absolutist language) loses its iron grip on the proletariat, *heteroglossia* (conflict between official and unofficial discourses within the same national language or within an utterance) expresses itself publicly and hence more dynamically,

Parallel to his opposition of 'carnival' to 'official' within cultures is another between whole national cultures which are 'self-sufficient' (in the sense of not knowing their otherness to others) and those which are no longer sealed-off and deaf to their polyglot ambience: Bakhtin understands the Renaissance as just such a moment of passages from closed to open across the cultures of Europe (Pechey, 1989:43).

You're ugly! I want the real Mickey Mouse!

State sponsored (domesticated) Iranian 'carnival'

As I said in the last chapter articulating a thought process aids in its process of completion and clarification. Official language tries hard to prevent this articulation. Or to give it a more politico-ideological edge, Vološinov (1987: 89) notes,

> the wider and deeper the breach between the official and unofficial consciousness, the more difficult it becomes for motives of inner speech to turn into outward speech ... wherein they might acquire formulation, clarity, and rigor.

But official culture cannot win for ever. It is precisely this polyglot lava of desire and passion witnessed in riots and demonstrations, heralding an immanent cultural resurgence, which petrifies a mullah-bourgeoisie cognisant of its impending hour of doom. As Bakhtin suggests in *Rabelais*, during the early Renaissance era, people 'built a second world and a second life outside of officialdom, a world in which all medieval people participated more or less' (Bakhtin quoted in Bernard-Donals, 1998: 118).

In fact, Bakhtin goes as far as to suggest that carnivals and feasts came more and more to be associated with *crisis time*, 'moments of death and revival, of change and renewal ... of breaking points in the cycle of nature or in the life of society and man' (Bernard-Donals, 1998: 118). In such intense moments of renewal, the ritualistic aspects of the spectacle are demystified. A religious ritual such as Ashura, for instance, is a highly formalised and rhetorical argument that permits of no alternatives. As Bloch (1989: 42) makes clear,

> Ritual is a kind of tunnel into which one plunges, and where, since there is no possibility of turning either to right or left, the only thing to do is to follow. A genuine proletarian carnival, by contrast, has no script and no end point; it is truly 'unfinalized'.

The 'crisis time' being experienced by Iranian capitalism is analogous to the Renaissance in yet another crucial respect. Gradually a vernacular Farsi (enriched by various ethnic dialects) is superseding the official Arabesque-Farsi monologue of the Muslim elite. This humorous vernacular is now beginning to reach both low and high art, infusing it irreversibility with a proletarian sense of parody and irony. Bakhtin observed how early Christianity condemned laughter and how seriousness was used strategically to prevent criticism of feudal mores,

> An intolerant one-sided tone of seriousness is characteristic of official medieval culture.
> The very contents of medieval ideology- asceticism, sombre providentialism, sin,

atonement, suffering, as well as the character of the feudal regime, with its oppression and intimidation- all these elements determined this tone of icy petrified seriousness (Bakhtin quoted in Morris, 1994: 208).

In this regard, it is noteworthy that the majority of the mullah-bourgeoisie, acutely aware of the need to inject a false, self-deprecating official humour into the body politic welcomed the 'election' of the 'smiling mullah', Khatami, to the office of Presidency in 1997. The intention was to create a partial 'glasnost' where constructive criticism can regenerate 'civil society', which, in turn, would stabilise Muslim political society.[64]

The top-down project of openness and reconstruction failed. The 2001 football riots were one stark manifestation of this failure. The state then turned to the military faction of the regime and recalibrated the ratio of coercion and consent in favour of the former. Proletarian 'violence' forced the regime to retaliate by using tension as a mode of stabilisation and reconstruction. Thus the rise of Ahmadi-Nezhad and his thugs.

In this context, 'violence' is one of the key issues usually downgraded by scholars of carnivalesque.[65] In contradistinction, René Girard emphasises 'mimetic violence' as underlying the carnival rite. Dionysus, he believes, was worshipped by the revellers of Saturnalia as a 'god of homicidal fury' (Girard, 1977: 118). Likewise, as Hilda Hollis (2001: 1) has pointed out, other students of carnival such as the novelist George Elliot acknowledge more readily than Bakhtin 'the threat posed by carnival when it is not simply a textual metaphor. People are killed, maimed and raped during festal fun and freedom'.

Of course Bakhtin readily acknowledged that the crowning of the carnival King 'already contains the idea of immanent decrowning' (Bakhtin, 1984b: 124), but more often than not he views this process as an ambivalent cultural rite devoid of violent class antagonisms. Yet even symbolically 'the Masque of the Furies, called riots' contained an element of aggression. The 'bonfire of vanities' associated with Savonarola's decrowning in Romola, has similarities with the bonfires lighted annually around Norouz, the Persian New Year's celebration. This cleansing Zoroastrian fire of Norouz has taken on explicit anti-Islamic overtones in recent years.[66] Zarathushtra, after all, had sought a god who laughed and

---

64 The fact that a great chunk of the Iranian left sheepishly complied with this counter-revolutionary stratagem speaks volumes for their anti-working class agenda.

65 It is, of course, quite legitimate to argue that the sanitisation of the more violent and malicious dimensions of carnival began with Bakhtin himself. Bernstein (1986: 117) is of the opinion that, 'Bakhtin's love for Rabelais and for what he sees as the redemptive energy of the Saturnalia, at times blinds him to the fact that it is only because Rabelais' novels are manifestly nonmimetic that he is able to assimilate them to anthropological and folkloristic records of actual carnivals, many of which, as recent studies have shown, ended in a violence that proved devastating both to the innocent victims and to the community as a whole'.

66 Whilst amongst exiled Iranians Norouz has become formalised and domesticated, it has regained some of its radical elements for those using it within Iran as an ideological bulwark against Islam. In other words, the same ritual could display spectacularised or carnivalesque tendencies depending on circumstances.

danced joyously. Sadness and gloom he associated with Darkness. As the proletarian group, Melancholic Troglodytes has correctly grasped,

> In the early years of the Islamic 'revolution' the celebration of May Day became an arena of fierce contestation where opposing philosophies of life vied for power- a proletariat expressing the rapture of life with songs, dancing, poetry, debate and games, arrayed against the forces of darkness, parading with the solemnity and discipline of storm-troopers-in-waiting (Melancholic Troglodytes, 1998: 15).

I am mindful of the fact that many instances of violence perpetrated during carnivals have had a reactionary character. Historically, 'part of the festivities of the Roman carnival in-

The Wicker Man

cluded the ritual degradation of Jews, who were forced to participate in races through the streets of the city' (Dentith, 1995: 74). Some forms of *charivari* involved humiliating those who had transgressed sexual 'norms', and the 'farce of Saint Point' was a catholic ritual which 'involved going with some ladies after a party to a prison where Protestants were locked up, freeing them, getting the ladies to chat to them, and then drowning them' (Dentith, 1995: 75). However, it is essential to underline that the carnival (and even more so the carnivalesque) are imbued with features and attributes which makes them more amenable to a subversive undermining of authority rather than the buttressing of hierarchy and 'common sense'. The laughter, mocking, parody, irony, aggression, sexual overtones, dialogic interactions, grotesquerie and heteroglossia dimensions of carnivalesque make it, at least potentially, an emancipatory 'ready-made'.

To summarise: I have argued in this section that an expansive definition of carnivalesque which takes into account its violent, intoxicating and antagonistic class conflicts is essential for understanding recent Iranian football riots. As Bristol (1983: 645) has shown in a different context, 'Festive abuse, competitive events such as footraces, and mock combats in the form of anarchic football matches between whole villages are all part of the general vocabulary of carnivalesque manifestations'. Proletarian force directed at Authority and the Church exposes the enemies' fallibility and its pretensions of perpetuity. As Bakhtin puts it, '[The representatives of old authority and truth] are gloomily serious. They cannot and do not wish to laugh; they strut majestically... and threaten their [foes] with eternal punishment. They do not see themselves in the mirror of time ...' (Bakhtin quoted in Morris, 1994: 225).

3.1.2 Dialogic, utterance and the social dimensions of language

Dialogue within 'concrete utopia'

In an oft-quoted passage, Bakhtin claims,

> To be means to communicate … To be means to be for another, and through the other, for oneself. A person has no internal sovereign territory, he is wholly and always on the boundary; looking inside himself, he looks into the eyes of another or with the eyes of another (Bakhtin, 1984b: 287).

I shall return to this crucial formulation at the end in order to argue it is possible to turn to language, principally through the writings of Bakhtin, Vološinov and Vygotsky, 'without embracing the [postmodernist] linguistic turn' (Collins, 1999a: 6). Additionally, through Marx (1984), Sève (1978) and even Antonin Artaud (1977) it may be possible to conceive of a *socialised individuality* without fetishising an all-embracing (and at times individual-denying) Bakhtinian notion of collectivity (Murasov, 2001).

First, however, I would like to furnish some reasons why a Bakhtinian approach is particularly productive for researchers engaged in the 'once-occurent experiencing' (Bakhtin, 1993) of complex phenomena, such as proletarian riots.

Shotter (in press) warns us that 'something very crucial is lost, when we take the uninvolved, disengaged, mechanistic stance toward people's activities suggested to us in the Cartesian approach'. Investigating riots must, perforce, be done from within an engagement of some kind with the rioters. Moreover, this engagement must be of a relational-responsive kind if the spontaneity of the riot is to be encapsulated. In other words as Shotter writes,

> unnoticed in the background and spontaneously at work in all our communicative relations with each other is what might be called a relational-responsive kind of understanding – a form of understanding much more basic than the representational-referential kind of understanding of which we are, as individuals, consciously aware (Shotter, in press).

Some proletarian riots are 'concrete-utopias' that herald a classless community, precisely because they are intense moments of critical mass during which the separation between intellect and emotions is momentarily superseded. Appropriating Shotter again, we could offer the following description for riotous transgressions,

> For it is in these momentary relational encounters that the influences from many quarters – those from within us, from the past, from our expectations, from the expressions of our listeners, from the rest of our surroundings – can all meet and, in the way in which we responsively interrelate them, we can form a unique responsive answer to them (Shotter, in press).

Not a 'concrete-utopia': self-mutilation and masochism during Ashura

Bakhtin works by 'calling' forth an active responsiveness from us. What makes this active responsiveness possible during a protest is the crowd's ability to decode life collectively by arresting or interrupting,

> the spontaneous, unself-conscious flow of our ongoing activity, to make us notice something fleeting that would have passed us by unnoticed ... [alternatively] by the careful use of selected poetic images, similes, analogies, metaphors, or 'pictures', [Bakhtin and Vološinov] suggest new ways of talking that not only orient us toward sensing otherwise unnoticed distinctions ... but which also suggest new connections and relations with the rest of our proceedings ... (Shotter, in press).

This is one of the functions proletarian slogans and chants should play during demos. They should 'strike' and 'arrest' us, put reality on 'freeze-frame' and then allow us to look at the freeze-frame with fresh eyes. In short, they should provide *revolutionary moments of insight*. We shall investigate examples of this *speech genre* later, but for the time being it would be useful to introduce more Bakhtinian concepts in order to enrich our analysis.

Utterance and Genre

By 'utterance' Bakhtin means 'any unit of language, from a single word to an entire 'text'... [an utterance is] the locus of encounter between my self-consciousness, my mind and the world with all its socio-historical meaning; the utterance is always an answer to a previous utterance, and always expects an answer in the future' (Morris, 1994: 251).

Language has a materiality for Bakhtin not found in Ferdinand de Saussure (1974) and structuralist views of language. Bakhtin emphasised the connection between the signifier and signified rather than their separation (Klages, 2001: 1). He also rejects the Cartesian dichotomy between 'language' and 'speech' and the distinction between synchrony and diachrony (Stewart, 1986: 44). The utterance, like a commodity, 'also includes the congealed *products* or material deposits of past acts of dialogue – the artifacts, practices, common-sense, philosophical doctrines, written texts, and institutions that make up the operative contexts of a living culture' (Sandywell, 1998: 203).

However, Bakhtin also underlines that the dialogic tonalities of these may have become effaced through social amnesia and monologic mystification. The aim of the proletariat, therefore, should be to 'reanimate the voices of the past through an active process of disengagement and self-reflection' (Sandywell, 1998: 203). The freeze-frame opportunity provided by a riot or strike is precisely this synchronic moment of self-reflection before the diachronic fluidity of history once again takes over.

In real life, however, Bakhtin believes that each utterance responds to utterances that have come before it, such that it 'refutes, affirms, supplements, and relies on the others, presupposes them to be known, and somehow takes them into account' (Bakhtin, 1986: 91). According to Collins (1999b: 3), Bakhtin further argued that, 'in the process of interaction between social groups there emerge *relative stable types* of utterances which are associated with particular social contexts of speaking'. Vološinov and Bakhtin called these relative stable types of utterances *speech genres*.

Bakhtin made a distinction between 'primary speech genres' and 'secondary speech genres'. The former refers to everyday talking about the weather or gossip or ordering a round of drinks. Primary genres are flexible and informal. The 'secondary' speech genres are generally more complex and may refer to scientific or political discourse (Morris, 1994: 248). What is significant about periods of social upheaval is the synthesis, which emerges between primary and secondary speech genres, so that political discourse is no longer viewed as alienating. We shall see later how the carnivalesque nature of football riots allows Iranian proletarians to forge a new speech genre, which displays dialogic responsiveness whilst expressing their worldly desires without recourse to obfuscating religious humbug.

In this regard Cheyne and Tarulli's (1999) take on Bakhtin (and Vygotsky) is of crucial relevance in understanding how conflicts in Iran can become riotous so rapidly, taking both the state and demonstrators by surprise. Cheyne and Tarulli argue that some of the most important genres to shape novelistic prose (and remember, for Bakhtin the novel is a privileged genre where the struggle between centrifugal and centripetal forces are played out) are, the *Magistral, Socratic,* and *Menippean* dialogues.

Cheyne and Tarulli (1999) look at these three forms of dialogue in terms of Vygotsky's zone of proximal development. The Magistral dialogue is really not a dialogue in the Bakhtinian sense at all. It resembles more what he called 'official monologism' or what Aristotle referred to as judicial discourse. For our purposes, this can be seen in a bourgeois-Islamic mode of discourse where the first voice (the Magistral voice of the mullah-bourgeois) dominates the second voice (the novitiate proletariat who is usually patronised, sometimes pathologised and treated like a child). 'The maintenance of this asymmetry', write Cheyne and Tarulli (1999: 12), 'requires a third voice, an authoritative and institutional third party upon which the first voice may draw'. In our example, the sacred word of god or the sayings of the prophet Mohammad or, alternatively, his disciple, Imam Khomeini, fulfil this task.

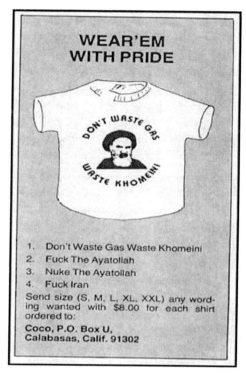

A racist response to the enemies' Magistral voice

The Magistral discussion is premised upon a perceived deficit or an absence of reason and autonomy on the part of the second voice (proletariat). The first (mullah-bourgeoisie) and third (God or Mohammad or Khomeini) 'voices presume to know where the dialogue is heading. Deviations from the proper trajectory are noted and corrections initiated' (Cheyne and Tarulli, 1999: 12). In fact, in Iranian–Islamic jurisprudence workers are routinely infantilised or referred to as objects on a par with domesticated animals, which explains why one of the constant demands of workers in recent demonstrations has been to be treated with 'dignity' (Melancholic Troglodytes, 2006).[67]

---

67 Vološinov (1973: 41) would say, 'each word ... is a little arena for the clash of and criss-crossing of differently oriented social accents'. *Dignity* represents a key term in 'western' history (Berger *et al.*, 1974: 82). My position is that it is a mistake to romanticise it (cf. Holloway, 2002) or dismiss it out of hand as bourgeois (cf. Palinorc, 2003). Like every term, dignity is a site of contestation (Vološinov, 1973), whose *meaning and sense* (Vygotsky, 1978) should be ascertained before judgement is passed. Furthermore, it is essential to discover the *motivation* of the speaker of an utterance as well its location within a genre (i.e., whether it is part of *official* or *unofficial* discourse). Only then can we decide whether a term is being employed in a reactionary or subversive manner. For instance, it seems to me, dignity was used differently during the US Civil Rights movement of the 1960s. Bourgeois blacks (e.g., Martin Luther King) used dignity

The second form of dialogue, the Socratic, 'developed the tradition of a dialogic testing of truth' (Morris, 1994: 188). It is an open-ended dialogue and 'may be turned at any moment against any participant, including the third voice' (Cheyne and Tarulli, 1999: 13). Proletarians using this discourse may subtly modify or re-accentuate the Magistral voice, imbuing utterances with its own 'sense' rather than accepting fixed and monologic dictionary 'meaning'. The Socratic dialogue is forever suspicious of imposed 'consensus', hierarchy and experts. In Aristotelian terminology this form of dialogue corresponds to 'deliberative' discourse and may include political debates and negotiations over wages.

In those societies where the Magistral forms of dominating the proletariat are no longer an option, the aim is to constrain discussion within a Socratic framework. The 'western' bourgeoisie may still dream of the golden age of Magistral monologue when dissent is suppressed indefinitely but realistically it knows that the trade-unionist type of Socratic mediation is the only viable option for maintaining the status quo. In societies such as Iran where Socratic/deliberative discourse is hampered due to re-strictive labor laws, and where corporatism has denied workers legal trade-unionist representation, the riotous Menippean rupture threatens to completely de-legitimatise the first (mullah-bourgeoisie) and third (God/Mohammad/Khomeini) voices. In oth-er words, in societies like Iran where the rulers attempt to impose their hegemony via the Magistral voice alone there comes a time when the proletariat no longer listens. At this junction reformist apologist for the regime scuttle around in a vain attempt to ini-tiate a Socratic dialogue but most people see through this stratagem and nullify it. Menippean discourse then takes over. This goes someway in explaining the radical-ism of the emerging Iranian proletarian movement. As Bakhtin argues,

> ... the most important characteristic of the menippea as a genre is the fact that its bold and unrestrained use of the fantastic and adventure is internally motivated, justified by and devoted to a purely ideational and philosophical end; the creation of extraordinary situations for the provoking and testing of a philosophical idea, a discourse, a truth ... (Bakhtin, 1984b quoted in Morris, 1994: 189).

The ideological affinity between this Bakhtinian notion of creating situations through menippean satire with the Situationist desire to create situations goes beyond the mere semantic. The Situationist International (SI) defined constructed situations as 'a moment of life concretely and deliberately constructed by the collective organisa-

---

as a euphemism for equal opportunities within political society. Other blacks (e.g., Black Panthers) also used dignity in their discourse. For them it amounted to regaining the two-fifth of rights always denied blacks under the law (i.e., equal recognition as full citizens within the realm of civil society). Interestingly, black proletarians also mention their desire for dignity in stories, autobiographies and interviews. However, for them it meant something far more concrete and down to earth: the ability to enter a restaurant, a bar or walk from A to B without being threatened and insulted. This latter demand for dignity is something proletarians from Native America to Palestine can readily identify with.

tion of a unitary ambiance and a game of events' (Knabb, 1989: 45). The transformation of situations brings to 'light forgotten desires and [creates] entirely new ones' (Knabb, 1989: 3). Both Bakhtin and the SI emphasise the role of experimentation. Bakhtin writes,

> In the menippea there appears for the first time what might be called moral-psychological experimentation: a representation of the unusual, abnormal moral and psychic states of man [sic]- insanity of all sorts (the theme of the maniac), split personality, unrestrained daydreaming, unusual dreams, passions bordering on madness, suicides, and so forth (Bakhtin, 1984b quoted in Morris, 1994: 191).

Socratic or Menippean Dialogue?

An instance of this 'madness' is witnessed in the seemingly irrational post-match Iranian demonstrations, where traffic is brought to a stand still by youngsters who neither march in the traditional sense nor raise any demands. In fact, there is no attempt at negotiations - just youngsters screaming 'hysterically' in unison. This 'eccentricity' is a categorical 'refusal to accept the constraints of fixed, pre-given social roles' (Gardiner, 1992: 46). This refusal can be observed in the free and spontaneous combination of fixed attributes. In Bakhtin's words, '[carnival] brings together, unifies, weds, and combines the sacred with the profane, the lofty with the low, the great with the insignificant, the wise and the stupid' (Bakhtin, 1984b: 123).

The Situationists too, through psychogeographic techniques of *dérive* (a technique of transient passage through varied ambiances) and *detournement* (integration of present and past artistic production into a superior construction of a milieu), aimed for a project of unitary urbanism, where the realisation of a mass of desires becomes impossible for the old social order.

This is precisely the impasse the Islamic regime finds itself in. Proletarian desire, demonstrated in underground raves, sexual scandals, excessive intoxication and freedom-seeking acts of transgressions can be neither denied nor satisfied. The flogging of eight national footballers for 'moral transgressions' at an illegal party was met by near universal derision (Kayhan Weekly, p 8, no. 915, 25 July 2002). In fact, Islamic punishments such as hangings, stoning, dismemberment and flogging are coming across the same entrenched proletarian opposition that public hangings in Europe faced in the late 18th century (cf. Foucault, 1977; Linebaugh, 1991). Islamic *thanatocracy* (Peter

Linebaugh's term for a government that rules by the frequent use of the death penalty), has (almost) lost its ability to put the fear of Mohammad in people.

To summarise: It is the power of laughter expressed through menippean satire that is largely responsible for tilting the balance of class power in favour of Iranian proletarians. Cheyne and Tarulli (1999: 15) inform us, 'as the Socratic dialogue evolves into a Menippean dialogue ... the third voice might be mocked, authority turned on its head, flags burned, and leaders burned in effigy (at least)'. Menippean dialogue chimes with what Aristotle called epidictic discourse, which is discourse in praise or blame of someone. The Iranian proletariat, having rejected Magistral/judicial dialogue, and not having recourse to Socratic/deliberative dialogue, are left with Menippean/epidictic dialogue by default. This may begin with a eulogy to soften up the bosses but once the latter proves unresponsiveness to the proletarian charm offensive, things can turn ugly very rapidly with proletarians hurling the obligatory Molotov cocktail at the enemy and in return having degenerate rhetoric thrown back in their face by furious bosses.[68]

Parody, irony, vulgarity, chants, laughter and the thieves' argot

A *multi-voiced* work of art (e.g., a novel by Dostoyevsky) is one where the discourse of the author and heroes interact on equal terms. Parrington (1997: 141) explains parody and its relationship with *multivoicedness* in these terms,

> ... if a speaker repeats the utterances of a well known politician by producing these utterances with a different intonation or in contexts that differ from those in which the original utterances occurred, the parodic effect (be it humour, sarcasm or whatever) derives from the simultaneous presence of two voices ... Parody is only one particular form of multivoicedness.

In other words, parody is supposed to reduce the power of bourgeois discourse to that of proletarians. However, this is not always the case, since there are many forms of parody, not all of them radical.

Recently it has become a matter of considerable urgency to differentiate parodic, ironic and similar styles along class lines. Only a provisional outline of this project

---

68 There is at least one other characteristic that underlines the subversive potential of menippea. It often unites elements of *social utopia* with topical issues and correspondingly it succeeds in synthesizing everyday and political discourse through laughter. Fundamentalists of both rightist (here, Islamic) and leftist (here, Leninist) variety have never comprehended this proletarian dynamic or felt any affinity with it. This explains the Islamic insistence to patronise workers, stigmatising them as sick, immature or deviant or Lenin's normalising predilections once he had managed to establish his gang as the orthodoxy within the Third International. I have in mind here the intellectually flimsy and fatuous infamy known as *Left-Wing Communism: An Infantile Disorder* (1975), which Lenin penned in order to limit the influence of revolutionaries amongst the proletariat.

could be presented here but I would argue that proletarian forms of these discursive styles alone contain the seeds for undermining bourgeois ideology. In contrast to a class analysis, both structuralist and post-structuralist interpretations of Bakhtin severely limit his subversiveness, resulting in an anaemic and anodyne laughter incapable of expressing the true spirit of carnivalesque. After all, the 'laughing truth, expressed in curses and abusive words, [is supposed to] degrade power', not entrench it (Bakhtin quoted in Solomon, 1979: 299). And 'to degrade an object', Bakhtin writes,

> does not imply merely hurling it into the void of nonexistence, into absolute destruction, but to hurl it down to the reproductive lower stratum, the zone in which conception and a new birth take place (Bakhtin, 1984a: 21).

Morris (1994: 200) has argued, 'the carnival is far distant from the negative and formal modern times. Folk humour denies, but it revives and renews at the same time. Bare negation is completely alien to folk culture'. Following from David Gross's discussion of negativity and carnival alluded to above, I would qualify this by suggesting 'bare negation' could go a long way in undermining certain aspects of monologism. Proletarian humour does not necessarily have to be regenerative for it to work. However, it is true that humorous proletarian culture at its best transcends the mere negative in order to 'revive and renew'. Carnival laughter is first of all,

> a festive laughter. Carnival laughter is the laughter of all the people. Second, it is universal in scope; it is directed at all and everyone, including the carnival's participants … third, this laughter is ambivalent: it is gay, triumphant, and at the same time mocking, deriding. It asserts and denies, it buries and revives. Such is the laughter of carnival (Morris, 1994: 200).

There are at least two essential differences between proletarian and bourgeois forms of laughter. The first is an intrinsic distinction related to the separate origin, function and content of class-specific laughter. The second difference relates to the collective and inter-connected quality of the elements constituting laughter within proletarian culture in contrast to their fragmented nature in bourgeois presentations.[69] Discussing the cynicism, indecencies, and the billingsgate in Rabelais' novels Bakhtin warns,

> all these terms are conventional and far from adequate. [They] are not isolated; they are an organic part of the entire system of images and style. They become isolated and specific only for modern literary consciousness (Bakhtin quoted in Morris, 1994: 212).

---

69 This Bakhtinian approach to laughter is at odds with Michael Billig's (2001) belief that all types of laughter have a sadistic origin. In my view, Billig does the proletariat a disservice by his dogmatic generalisations. A more nuanced perspective which is based on a 'solid' understanding of the class struggle theorises a qualitative distinction between the subversive laughter and irony of the proletariat and its bourgeois counterparts.

Such colloquial profanities are a codified form of protest. A few pages earlier Bakhtin asserts, 'medieval laughter is not a subjective, individual and biological consciousness of the interrupted flow of time. It is the social consciousness of all the people' (Bakhtin quoted in Morris, 1994: 210). Laughter contains no didacticism and no preaching,

> The man [sic] who is speaking is one with the crowd; he does not present himself as its opponent, nor does he teach, accuse, or intimidate it. He *laughs* with it. There is not the slightest tone of morose seriousness in his intonation, no fear, piety, or humility (Bakhtin quoted in Morris, 1994: 217).

Just as importantly, it should be remembered, 'laughter liberates not only from external censorship but first of all from the great interior censor' (Bakhtin quoted in Solomon, 1979: 300). Proletarian laughter is a mode of being and consciousness that cannot be reduced to any particular aesthetic form. For instance,

> at the early stages of preclass and prepolitical social order it seems that the serious and the comic aspects of the world and of the deity were equally sacred, equally 'official'… and the funeral ritual [during the early period of the Roman state] was also composed of lamenting (glorifying) and deriding the deceased (Morris, 1994: 197).

Contemporary Iran is perhaps the only battle-hardened society in the world where 'official martyrs' are openly derided and the families of martyrs are insulted and mocked. This is a radical rupture from the officially sanctioned process of fetishisation. It is also a radical rupture from unofficial culture, as it was constituted only a few years ago. The contrast with societies such as Israel and Palestine, where 'martyrs' are still commodified and successfully 'cannibalised' by political society, cannot be starker. It is not just *thanatocracy* (Linebaugh, 1991) that is rapidly being surpassed. *Necrolatry* (idolatry of death and dead people), too, is scorned during riots. As with the medieval marketplace, the

The only good martyr is a dead martyr!

An imaginary celebration of the death of Necrolatry

language employed is often abusive and insulting. During riots, profanities reign in on authorities with the frequency of homemade molotov cocktails. As Bakhtin (1984a: 187) writes,

Abuses, curses, profanities, and improprieties are the unofficial elements of speech. They were and are still [especially so in societies such as Iran] conceived as a breach of the established norms of verbal address... [Comment in brackets added].

To underscore this class distinction let us remind ourselves that some contemporaries of Bakhtin, such as 'Morozov already point to the distinction between conservative and progressive parodies' (Juvan, 1997: 20). Furthermore, 'according to Hutcheon, parody combines two impulses: a normative or conservative one, characterised, according to Bakhtin, as centripetal, and revolutionary one, characterised as centrifugal' (Juvan, 1997: 21). The parody in the hands of 20th century Formalists, for instance, becomes 'a conservative principle in literary history' (Hutcheon, 1984: 36).

What I have suggested here is that bourgeois and revolutionary parodies are both intrinsically distinctive and configured along different lines. One could draw comparisons with the fate of Brechtian *distanciation* and the Situationist concept of *detournement*. Once the embodied dynamism of laughter, parody and irony is reduced to a mere formalistic technique, they lose the ability to reorient us. Recuperation becomes inevitable. Proletarian cross-dressing, for instance, may seem like an outdated form of resistance in 'western' societies, a ritualistic and formulaic pose. In certain circumstances, it could even be viewed as reactionary, cementing stereotypes rather than dislodging them, as with the desperately 'macho' male rugby rite of 'fak-ing' gender bending.

An interesting synthesis of irony and naivety but is it bourgeois or proletarian?

However, the same pose, with a different historical origin, context and social functioning, is capable of dislodging sexual regimes of oppression.

The fact that parody, irony and vulgarity are expressed collectively means that the proletariat is successfully laying claim to public space. Iranian football chanting and the playing of illegal music in gatherings should be seen as an audible challenge to the invasive 'noise' of the Islamic call to prayer and the public recitations of the

Koran.[70] Like the ubiquitous Perry Como elevator-music, Koranic recitation seems always to be hovering at the background, burrowing itself into proletarian psyche, reinforcing a paternalistic-cum-colonising moral order.

In line with the serio-comic tensions of the carnivalesque, the chants and music of the crowd convey both a sense of *irony* and *naivety*. In this synthesis lies one of its revolutionary potential. Friedrich Schlegel defined irony not in a literary or discursive sense, but as a mode of being, in the following terms: 'Irony is the clear consciousness of an infinitely full chaos' (Schlegel quoted in Gross, 1977-78: 167). Life is so complex, argued Schlegel, that no one method or combination of methods can encapsulate its essence. Affinities with postmodernism and academic discourse in general are patently obvious. This form of irony has a kindred spirit in the petty-bourgeois form of Sufism[71], although Sufism, unlike western irony makes no absolute separation between self and the world.

Gross (1977-78: 169) explains, 'almost as soon as [the concept of irony] emerged an anti-ironist mode of thought arose to challenge it'. One of its early adherents Hegel,

> argued that because irony sees the world as fundamentally ambiguous, it tends to condone an attitude of 'irresolution' and 'loss of seriousness', which inevitably leads to escapism and irresponsibility. Furthermore, Hegel contended, the ironic stance is shamelessly elitist. Since the ironist believes the world is too complicated to change, he [sic] feels justified in withdrawing into a 'god-like geniality' (Gross, 1977-78: 169).

One of Hegel's contemporaries, Friedrich Schiller coined the term 'naïve attitude', which meant 'seeing reality as simple and clear-cut once again' (Gross, 1977-78: 171). These two pre-industrial modes of thought, irony and naivety, still hold sway within different sections of the ruling class. Their proletarian counterparts differ both in functioning, content and also the way they fuse with intellect and emotions. Riotous moments of transgressions offer us a glimpse into a post-capitalist community where irony and naivety have been superseded. The point, therefore, is not to take sides with Schlegel's ironist stance or the anti-ironist perspective of Schiller and Hegel, but to synthesise and supersede irony and naivety. The class struggle in Iran has partially gone beyond both Bakhtin and postmodernism's naïve faith in irony as

---

70 It is hard to convey to the casual 'Western' observer how completely devoid of musical inspiration most 'Islamic Fundamentalists' really are. This, of course, is not the case with Islam in its Sufi manifestation but the puritanical branch currently dominating political thought within Islam, which is bereft of music and its accompanying trait of joyful abandonment. As Shakespeare said, 'The man [sic] that hath no music in himself/Nor is not mov'd with concord of sweet sounds/Is fit for treasons, stratagems, and spoils/The motions of his spirit are dull as night/And his affections dark as Erebus/Let no such man be trusted' (Portia in Shakespeare, *Merchant of Venice*, V, I, 1967).

71 Sufism is a mystical and semi-monastic trend within Islam, which emerged between 8th and 10th centuries. According to Tokarev (1989: 377), 'it grew within Shiism, but was also taken up among the Sunnis. Sufism was influenced by the ideas of Mazdaism, perhaps Buddhism and even Neo-Platonism'.

the ideal weapon against authority. I will show below how this emergent language has more commonality with the thieves' and tinkers' argots of bygone ages than at first imagined. It is part of a dynamic process to 'create a new language' (Marx, 1852/2000).

3.1.3 Grotesque bodies and hysterical mobs

The Islamic Republic came to power with the unstated mandate of temporarily reversing capitalist development to its *formal* phase of domination, which entailed the extraction of *absolute* surplus value through 'terroristic' means. The formal phase is now complete and many in this society ache for transition to the *real* phase of domination, with its emphasis on *relative* surplus value extraction, Keynesian macroeconomics, or what is inaccurately termed a 'consumption based economy'. Some hope that cultural openness will bring in its wake a respectful growth rate and economic diversification. The phrase 'civil society' is uttered frequently, sometimes as mantra, sometimes as a code for 'liberalism'. What concerns us here is the *strategy of excess* that is being adopted by both atheistic-proletarian and 'secular'-bourgeois opponents of the clergy as a mechanism for resisting the frugality associated with the formal phase of capital accumulation. It is argued that the two above-mentioned classes utilise *excess* for contrasting reasons, the 'secular'-bourgeoisie, in order to secure and dominate the real phase of domination, and the atheistic proletariat, in order to transcend all forms of capitalist exploitation.

Khomeini the turd,
Ought never to have occurred.
One can only wonder,
At so grotesque a blunder.

Grotesque body as the death of thanatocracy

Grotesquerie as excess

Bataille has characterised this stage of capitalist development 'as an economy of excess reversing Protestant modernity's ascetic emphasis on frugality and self-denial and non-utilitarian expenditure' (Bataille, 2001: 65). Bakhtin (1973: 255) describes 'the people's mass body' as a gigantic, grotesque, excessive, excremental dark matter outside ascetic history,

> It is the people as a whole, but organised *in their way*, the way of the people. It is outside of and contrary to all existing forms of the coercive socioeconomic and political organisation, which is suspended for the time of the festivity.

142

When 'a truck rented by people for the Ethical treatment of animals dumped four tons of cow manure on Pennsylvania Avenue near the world bank HQ' (Boje: 2001: 22), or when copies of the Koran are laced with excrement and urine or when religious icons are juxtaposed with images of shit in surrealist films, the excess of capital's over-production is turned against the ruling class.

Bakhtin talked of *grotesque realism* and the distinction between the *grotesque body* and the *classical body*. 'The essential principle of grotesque realism', Bakhtin writes, 'is degradation', but this degradation is both negative and affirmative (Bakhtin quoted in Dentith, 1995: 67). It lowers all that is high, including spiritual and abstract ideas, but it also regenerates through a 'banquet for all the world'. The grotesque body, aside from being excessive and excremental, is also unfinished, unlike the classical body, which is either complete or close to perfection. 'The grotesque is to be seen', writes Dentith (1995: 80), as the 'expression of that attitude to life which also underlines the carnival, an attitude founded upon the biological con-

Classic Islamic body as performed by cat-walk models

tinuity of the body of the people'. This is a *collective* biological life, in the process of becoming, rather than say the private, subjective grotesque expressed throughout the Romanticist period.

Pam Morris (1994: 205) explains it in these terms: '[the grotesque] body and bodily life have here a cosmic and at the same time an all-people's character; this is not the body and its physiology in the modern sense of the words, because it is not individualised'. The 21st century grotesque as expressed in genuine carnivals has managed to go beyond this formulation, rejecting both the possessive, egotistical notion of (orthodox bourgeois) individualism and its darker Romantic version, in favour of a (proletarian) individuality that seeks and finds synthesis with the bio-historical body of people. The carnivalesque, therefore, does not subsume individuality under a false collectivity. Quite the contrary. Through the creation of a zone of proletarian development (ZPD), the collective bio-historical body comes to protect and promote the 'flowering' individual.

Hysteria as resistance against hierarchy

During October 2001, Iranian football fans would take to the streets after the final whistle and scream *hysterically*. This unsettling tactic has parallels with the British suffragettes' utilisation of madness in the early part of the 20th century as well as the omnipresent madness of medieval carnivals. Although an orthodox political activist may scoff at the lack of articulated, rational consciousness in such protests, a seasoned observer cannot help but be impressed by the *scream*'s ability to withstand recuperation (Holloway, 2002). The scream is interested in neither the Magistral nor the Socratic forms of dialogue with the ruling class.

Yippy! Who says only women can be hysterical?

The hysterical scream as a force for mobility

To the intentional grotesquerie, hysteria and mobility of Iranian football rioters one should add the element of intoxication. The Islamic ban on drinking, initially a dietary method of demarcating Islam from Christianity, has become a genuine site of contestation with proles risking imprisonment, flogging and fines to obtain alcohol.

Earlier I suggested that the scholarly sanitisation of carnival might very well have begun with Bakhtin himself. Mary Roth (1997: 7) concurs,

> When drink appears in Bakhtin's descriptions, it is confined (and distorted) within the phrase 'food and drink' or variants like 'appetite and thirst' and 'excrement and urine'. The phrase 'food and drink' expresses a false symmetry and disrupts social experience even further when the reference is to strong drink …

Emerson and Morson (1987, quoted in Roth, 1997: 8) have charged Bakhtin of 'robbing carnival of its dark potency', and Renate Lachmann (1988-89, quoted in Roth, 1997: 8) claims Bakhtin's carnival allows 'for neither frenzy nor ecstasy'.[72] It is precisely through achieving 'frenzy', at times with the aid of alcohol, that Iranian proletarians have undermined the regime. Imported alcohol plus home-made alcohol and various drug concoctions are consciously taken before demonstrations as catalyst. Those forms of Islam such as Sufism that have had a more tolerant attitude towards 'intoxication' are frowned upon for their flirtations with immorality. The regime's increasingly frenzied attack on ravers, prostitutes, cross-dressers, homosexuals and drug-takers are indicative of a dangerous loss of authority.

Experimentation with drink and sex within zones of proletarian development bene-

---

72 It is conceivable that in our haste to apply a corrective we have been slightly harsh on Bakhtin in this respect. He did, after all, acknowledge the emancipatory potential of alcohol: 'Wine liberates from fear and sanctimoniousness' (Bakhtin quoted in Morris, 1994: 231).

fit from traditional forms of food-sharing. At times of austerity, the offering of food as gift (use-value) is of tremendous importance. In Iran, it is traditional to distribute sweets amongst the crowd during political demonstrations. As Bakhtin (1973: 302) observes, 'The popular image of food and drink are active and triumphant, for they conclude the process of labor and struggle of the social man [sic] against the world'. The material abundance of carnival is in dire contrast to the paternalistic magnanimity of rulers during spectacles such as Ashura or Court entertainment in medieval times. Bristol (1983: 644) notes,

> in Court entertainment and aristocratic pageantry [I would add the Ashura procession] social and economic relations are spiritualised; abundance derives from the correct distribution of authority and deference, and from the recognition of natural superiority. [added]

In a monologic culture the most banal acts of transgression could elicit a ZPD

This is in marked contrast to carnival where abundance results from 'the transformation of everyday work and the consequent renewal of the body' (Bristol, 1983: 644). Morris (1994: 226) makes a significant observation in this respect, 'The sharing of food is also closely associated with free speech and with the defeat of time; festive talk looks towards a utopian future'.

The rhythm of these food and drink binges is related to labor but finds its own frenzied pace during carnivals especially where music provides a catalyst. In Iran, at least, the gyrating rhythms of the crowd convey an ideology that is explicitly anti-capitalist and anti-religious. Mahabir (2002: 17) explains how rhythm can sometimes become 'the cultural signifier of the working classes, and it is therefore seen constantly under siege from the ruling classes, while at the same time appropriated by this class to advance its own ideology'. The most vivid example of this recuperation is the monotonous rhythmic chest beating of Muslim participants of Ashura, signifying the triumph of death over life and propagating eschatological gloom. Perhaps this chest beating, which in its extreme form veers into self-flagellation, should best be described as 'anti-rhythmic rhythm'.

In summary: what profanities, curses, rhythm, intoxication, music, eating, grotesquerie and sexual transgressions point to is the dissolution of the clergy's concept of etiquette. With the demise of etiquette and decorum, hierarchy, fixed social categories and class distinctions are put under collective erasure. 'Conversational immorality'

Let's be friends! (Iran vs. USA, 1998 World Cup)

(Billig's term for deviating from bourgeois turn taking amongst speakers) is no longer experienced as shameful (Billig, in press). Representatives of God on earth are heckled and abused. Carnival's dialogic interactions are 'frank and free, permitting no distance between those who [come] in contact with each other and liberating from norms of etiquette and decency …' (Bakhtin, 1984a: 11). Riots and 'festive time' provide a space for a new form of communication where the proletariat can challenge myths, taboos and beliefs. The marginalised majority regains the centre.

3.2 ANATOMICAL OUTLINE OF THE CASE STUDY

In this section I will focus the analysis on two seminal matches and their immediate aftermaths. The first was a Bahrain-Iran match played on 21 October 2001, which ended with an unexpected 3-1 win for Bahrain. The ensuing riots lasted for two days. The next game was the home leg of the Iran-United Arab Emirates (1-0) match on the 25 October 2001. Again the riots lasted for two days. So the period under investigation is 21-27 October 2001. I chose these two matches as they seemed to be the high points in a longer cycle of football riots. These two riots were, in fact, sandwiched between less significant football upheavals that provide the background for our case studies (e.g., the Republic of Ireland-Iran match of 10 November 2001). The crowds reacted riotously irrespective of the fact that the first match was a defeat whilst the second a victory. The data was collected post hoc from two prominent (and by and large factually reliable) opposition weeklies, *Kayhan* and *Mojahed* respectively. The London based *Kayhan* (Weekly) supports a constitutional monarchy but allows liberals, social democrats and the occasional Leninist to air their views in its pages. *Mojahed* is the newspaper of the *Mojahedin-e Khalq* organisation which began life as a Muslim tendency, shifting leftwards in the 1970s, before returning to its roots. Today they represent more a religious cult rather than a political party in the classic sense (Singleton, 2003). *Mojahedin-e Khalq* are justifiably renowned for their political opportunism and ruthlessness but provide extensive information regarding the riots.

3.2.1 Bahrain vs. Iran (21 October 2001)

This was expected to be a simple walkover. Another appearance in the World Cup beckoned and Iranians were making arrangement to be in Japan and Korea for the summer of 2002. The heavy 3-1 defeat at the hands of Bahrain led to immediate rioting. There were unsubstantiated rumours that players were leaned on by the authorities to lose in order to prevent further carnivals. Alternatively, it was put about that players were kept awake the night before the match by an over-zealous mullah who insisted they pray together. The Head of the Football Federation, Safā'i, had to publicly deny these allegations (Kayhan, P. 14, No. 881, 7 November 2001).

As E. P. Thompson makes clear in the case of 18th century England, rumours had a significant role in generating popular rebellion especially as rulers showed a 'dismissive attitude to these fragmentary and sometimes unreliable snatches of information' (Barker, 2002: 13). In Tehran, hundreds of thousands took part up and down the country and the mood abruptly turned 'political'. The slogans raised became more and more radical as the two-day rioting jamboree progressed. The upheavals in other cities were just as fierce, especially in Tabriz, Kerman, Isfahan, Shiraz, Kerman-shah, Qazvin and Rasht. Friends, families and relatives of the arrested rioters would besiege police stations and demand their release (Mojahed, P. 8, No. 563, 30 October 2001).

In the capital proletarians drew analogies between the defeated Afghani Taleban and Iranian mullahs. The popular chant, 'Death to the Taleban, whether in Kabul or Tehran' and 'Death to the mullahs' was accompanied by the more sanguine, 'Freedom of thought, eternal, eternal'. The defiant 'Cannons, tanks, guns, can't harm us anymore', jostled with the less imaginative, 'Death to despotism, long live freedom' (Kayhan, P. 1, No. 880, 31 October 2001). Even the pro-Palestine propaganda of the regime was turned against them when crowds accused the mullah-bourgeoisie of 'transforming Iran into Palestine'. The insinuation was that the mullah-bourgeoisie was now indistinguishable from the hated Israeli ruling class.

The carnivalesque mood was captured by the suitably ambiguous slogan levelled at Khamene'i (spiritual leader of the regime) and his disability (his right arm was immobile for many years although it seems to be getting better recently), 'Our leader is an ass, one of his arms is manqué' [my translation]. There were reports from

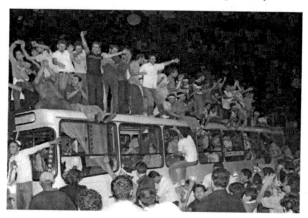

provincial towns regarding clerics caught up in the riots. They were jostled, punched and kicked and in an ultimate act of humiliation had their turbans knocked down (Mojahed, P. 7, No. 563, 30 October 2001). Sarcastic chants of 'Bahrain, Bahrain' added a festive mood to proceedings. Protesters would disrobe and display their 'collective grotesque body' as a direct threat to the Islamic classical body.

A more recent football demo

Music, both western and Iranian pop, blasted from every corner. People generously offering sweets and cakes to passers-by enhanced the carnival mood (Mojahed, P. 6, No. 563, 30 October 2001). The reclaiming of the streets and the demonstrations rapidly spread from the western parts of the capital to include 54 districts.

Government buildings, buses, ticket kiosks, banks (at least 32 in the capital alone), police cars/motor-bikes, traffic lights and public phone boxes were attacked and burnt to cinders. Stone throwing crowds pushed back armed security forces in many places both in Tehran and a number of major and minor urban centres. In some quarters crowds would surround *Basiji* forces (an auxiliary younger militia force, which began as a 'home-defence army' during the Iran-Iraq war, and is mainly responsible for internal security) in a pre-emptive manoeuvre. Eyewitnesses reported some Basiji militia being handcuffed to shop railings in a successful attempt by rioters to immobilise them (Kayhan, P. 1, No. 880, 31 October 2001). The militia was in fact disarmed in places, allowing the crowd to respond to shootings with more than the customary stones and molotov cocktails (Kayhan, P. 9, No. 880, 31 October 2001). The crowds also employed stun grenades, smoke bombs, firecrackers and bricks. In residential areas households practiced an 'open door' policy, taking in rioters to save them from snatch squads. Where rioters were arrested, crowds would surround the security forces' cars and 'de-arrest' their comrades (Kayhan, P. 9, No. 880, 31 October 2001). In more extreme cases, crowds would demand the release of their comrades and smash up police vans to underline their intent (Mojahed, P. 9, No. 564, 6 November 2001).

Barricades went up in Sattar Khan Street (western Tehran). Car tyres were burnt (and more radical) versions of the abovementioned slogans were aired, '[Regardless of] Canons, tanks, rockets, Khamene'i [supreme spiritual leader] must die' (Mojahed, P. 5, No. 563, 30 October 2001). In fact, fire was employed not only to destroy government buildings but also to prevent traffic. Golbarg highway (northern Tehran) was brought to a standstill using such tactics. On the Ba'sat highway in Tehran, a huge refrigerator was used to block the traffic. Buses would then be requisitioned and burned to ensure a complete standstill

Death to the clergy and pass the milkshake mate!

The McDonaldisation of fandom

(Mojahed, P. 6, No. 563, 30 October 2001). Gangs of young motorcyclists would chant anti-government slogans with lights blazing, whistles and horns adding to the cacophony of noise.

Islamic Coca-Cola is groovy!

Khamene'i was a popular starting point although the president Khatami (belonging to the so-called 'reformist' wing of the mullah-bourgeoisie) was soon subjected to similar derision. Comparisons were made between the mullahs and the previous monarchic regime, 'Shame on you, Khamene'i, time to vacate the royal crown', and the more predictable, 'Death to the Basij [militia]', 'Death to the clergy' and the more ominous, '[Our] condolences to the security forces' (Mojahed, P. 5, No. 563, 30 October 2001). Pictures of Khamene'i were burnt throughout the country. Significantly, women would not only egg on the men to engage in evermore daring adventures but also directly insulted and humiliated the police. Outside the headquarters of the 'moral police' in Tehran security guards were forced to break-dance with young protesters. The siren of mobile police vans was a beacon for the malcontent who would then surround and attack the offending noise (Mojahed, P. 5, No. 563, 30 October 2001). The waves of molotov cocktails targeting the class enemy were only exceeded by the amount of rubbish that was piled on roads and highways. Eyewitnesses compared the streets to an earthquake zone.

To counteract all this, a number of oppressive tactics were employed by the regime. Roads to urban centres were blocked to prevent people getting to riot zones. Activists distributing leaflets and writing graffiti were severely dealt with. Tanks were employed by the regime in strategic spaces to control the crowds (Mojahed, P. 9, No. 563, 30 October 2001). Motorbike gangs belonging to the *Hezbollah* (literally, 'Party of God') roamed the streets attacking pedestrians indiscriminately. Students, young workers, couples and mobile owners were favourite targets. In the central city of Shiraz, those arrested were subjected to both whippings and long jail sentences. *Pasdaran* (meaning, '[revolutionary] guards', another paramilitary force) would visibly take down car numbers and issue threats (Mojahed, P. 5, No. 563, 30 October 2001). The anti-riot squad was equipped with electric batons and chains but the 'cattle' were impervious to pain that day. Police vans were equipped with machine-guns. Tear gas was used widely and indiscriminately to disperse the crowds. In the aptly named Coca-Cola crossroad (Tehran), security forces opened fire on demonstrators chanting 'Death to Khamene'i, death to Khatami'. Plain-clothes officers would mingle with the crowd gathering intelligence. Even teenagers were not allowed to 'buy' their way out of the sentence (a common practice under Islam), as the crimes were deemed too sinful. Physical punishment had to be seen to be administrated (Mojahed, P. 7, No. 563, 30 October 2001).

3 . 2 . 2   I r a n   v s .   U n i t e d   A r a b   E m i r a t e s (2 5   O c t o b e r   2 0 0 1)

By the time the Iran-UAE match came around, there were still many teenagers in custody awaiting court appearance from a previous match between Iran and Iraq played on 12 October 2001 (Mojahed, P. 4, No. 564, 6 November 2001). That match had ended in a 2-1 victory for Iran, demonstrating clearly that result was not a determinant of rioting. Information Minister (a euphemism for the secret services), Younesi, walked through the crowds in plain clothes and declared the riots 'apolitical' (Mojahed, P. 4, No. 564, 6 November 2001). Special units were set up to clean up offending graffiti and remove placards throughout this tense period (Mojahed, P. 5, No. 564, 6 November 2001). These units had to endure the derision and hoots of laughter from proletarians whilst conducting their cosmetic operations. Beside this group, there were at least six other security departments involved. The ordinary police were supplemented by Basiji militia, Pasdaran units (a.k.a., revolutionary guards), the anti-riot squads, Hezbollah 'club-wielders', a parachute regiment and, finally, some units of the regular army.

Given the level of oppression involved, some rioters resorted to cunning stratagems. For instance, one method of 'invisible sloganeering' employed in Ardebil (a north-western city near the Caspian Sea) was to leave a tape recorder in a strategic location, switch it on and watch the reaction. The offending slogans would blurt out. The security forces would then run around like headless chickens in order to locate the tape-recorder. And the crowd would just stand back in amusement and enjoy the entertainment. Thousands were rounded up, most of whom were under 18 and a significant proportion in the 13-14 age category (Kayhan Weekly, P. 3, No. 881, 1-7 November 2001). Many women/girls threw away their veils during the riots. Ironically male teenagers would cover up their faces to avoid being photographed (Mojahed, P. 8, No. 564, 6 November 2001). Hundreds were arrested in Isfahan and Tabriz, two cities with a tradition of resistance. In Isfahan, road signs were vandalised and whoever was arrested was treated as a 'political' prisoner and given a minimum sentence of two months in jail (Mojahed, P. 9, No. 564, 6 November 2001). 'Spiritual leader' Khamene'i cancelled his trip to Isfahan, feigning illness. The news of proletarians smashing up the council's decorations in order to prevent Khamene'i visiting their city was suppressed (Kayhan, P. 15, No. 881, 7 November 2001). Whereas in the previous match, dispersal was the preferred method of policing, this time crowds were cordoned off and viciously set upon. Fascist groups of Ansar-ollah (literally, 'God's assistants') worked in tandem with security forces to put down the riots.

The official media attacked the protesters using terms remarkably similar to their western bourgeois counterparts. Rioters were dismissed as 'hooligans' (O'bāsh), 'seditious' (Sharoor), 'rogues' (Arāzel), 'saboteurs' (Ekhlālgar), 'infiltrators' (Nofouzi) and finally, 'thugs' (Khashen) (Kayhan, P. 3, No. 881, 7 November 2001). Authorities seemed petrified of the 'immoral' aspects of the rioting more than anything else. Taking a leaf out of Joseph Goebbels' book, Information Minister Younesi, emphasised that he was not against people having a good time; in fact, the regime had arranged official celebration ceremonies for the fans including music and fireworks (Kayhan, P. 9, No. 880, 25-31 October 2001).[73] What he objected to was behaviour incongruent

---

73 In recent times, under immense pressure from dissidents, the Islamic Republic has been forced to become more sophisticated in recuperating artistic subversion. Classical music (since it has no lyrics), classical Persian music (since a great deal of it is religious and male dominated) and 'western' films (since a great deal of it is as puritanical as its Islamic counterparts) are not censored as much as before. Certain other art forms such as theatre and female concerts are not so much banned as restricted to a handful of intellectuals or exported abroad in the same way the Nazis broadcasted jazz and swing to Allied forces during the War (Morton, 2003: 2). This is in keeping with the Nazi practice of allowing jazz in a restricted form within occupied territories. According to Mike Zwerin (2000: 155), whilst unofficial jazz magazines and clubs were

with Sharia (sacred law of Islam) and 'public decency' (Effat Omoumi). In disbelief he whispered in an interview that, 'the youth had even raised anti-Islamic slogans' (Kayhan, P. 9, No. 880, 31 November 2001).[74]

During half-time the TV showed propaganda reels related to the previous week's rioting, depicting a smashed car and a woman crying, and pleaded with

viewers to stay home after the match. *Crude* emotional blackmail is a stable diet of the media's propaganda against the proletariat in Iran. Rumour had it that TV chiefs had scheduled a popular movie to be shown immediately after the match in order to prevent people from spilling onto the streets (Mojahed, P. 9, No. 564, 6 November 2001). It is even alleged that in the north-eastern city of Nayshāpour, motorcycle caravans of young proletarians were infiltrated

Arāzel and O'bāsh being humiliated as a salutary lesson to 'citizens'!

by security agents who having put themselves at the head of the march would shepherd the crowds out of city boundaries where they posed no threat (Mojahed, P. 9, No. 564, 6 November 2001).

The riots once again ended in mass partying. The Islamic 'public space' was 'contaminated' by techno music (Mojahed, P. 9, No. 564, 6 November 2001). Police cars would routinely drive by and try to intimidate the revellers but the huge numbers involved made the authorities' task impossible. Youngsters would dance half-naked on top of cars. Both men and (unveiled) women would urge women to throw away their veil. Public parks, highly regulated social spaces under Islamic rule, were turned into raves (Kayhan, P. 3, No. 881, 7 November 2001).

---

being banned in former Czechoslovakia, the Nazi regime was establishing its own brand of official jazz, '... the jazz Section of the Czech Musicians' Union was, however, legal. It had been created in 1971, three years after the *Prague Spring*, and was limited to 3,000 members'. Leninist regimes also could see the benefits of a diluted jazz for the elite. To this end they made a spurious distinction between proletarian jazz as the spontaneous expression of pain and bourgeois jazz as mere affectation (Morton, 2003:4).

74 The summer 2007 campaign by the executive against Arāzel (rogues) and O'bāsh (hooligans) has been accompanied by a judicial onslaught which deprives the arrestees from basic rights (supposedly) enjoyed by all citizens.

3.2.3 Republic of Ireland vs. Iran (10 November 2001)

The two regional matches we have covered in detail above could be briefly contrasted to Iran's last abortive attempt at qualification. Only Iranian exiles in Europe could make the journey to Dublin for the away leg. The majority seem to have been rank-and-file zombies of various (bourgeois) leftist parties pathetically jockeying for position for a post-mullah Iran. These parasites tried to feed off the carnivalesque energy of the football riots of the previous weeks but their clumsy attempts failed to have the desired effect. Such bandwagon jumping antics only served to remind people of the opportunistic nature of the Iranian left. The People's Mojahedin Organization (a bourgeois Muslim party / cult aiming to revive the corpse of Islam through a mixture of theatre and technocracy), for instance, used the occasion to promote themselves and sing the praises of a techno-friendly Allah. A social revolt against the totality of Iranian capitalism (including Islam) in previous weeks was turned into a mere political contest with the aim of reforming capitalism and preserving both Islam and nationalism.

The clumsiness of the political imposition was evident in the choice of slogans aimed at the players by the cadre, 'Lads, we want goals, an Iran without mullahs', or just as artificially, 'Attack lads, and overthrow the clergy' (Mojahed, P. 2, No. 565, 17 November 2001). Opposed to these leftist zombies was a group of Hezbollah thugs,

Policewomen women-handling feminists at a recent Tehran demo

shipped for the occasion under the guise of 'official fans' to coerce the enemies of Islam. Devoid of legal powers, the Hezbollah could only plead with the Irish police to arrest 'troublemakers'. Their pleas, however, went unheeded.

On the return leg, the presence of 20 Irish women accompanied by 250 male fans caused quite a stir, as this was the first time since the 1979 'Islamic revolution' that women were allowed to attend a football match. The clergy justified the decision on the grounds that Irish women's sensibilities would not be tainted by the vulgarity and coarseness of Iranian males since none of them could understand Farsi. Both before and after this match, the authorities took revenge on scores of people for the October riots by confiscating their satellite dishes. The move was also intended to reinforce the official line that the whole shebang was orchestrated from outside the country in order to embarrass the clergy.

3.3 BAKHTINIAN INTERPRETATIONS

Based on the preceding newspaper material and the Bakhtinian concepts introduced in section 3.1, I will now attempt a theoretical analysis of the riots. I have chosen to organise this Bakhtinian discussion into five categories for the sake of clarity. In section 3.3.1 (*Communication and Rioting*), I will demonstrate how carnivalesque rioting enrich proletarian inter-communication. I will then look at moments of cultural transgression in the riots and its implications for future struggles (*3.3.2 Cultural Transgressions and Rioting*). In section 3.3.3, I concentrate on some of the salient forms of psychic and physical violence associated with the case-study. I will try to show how they may catalyse or, under certain circumstances, impede the class struggle (*Psychic and/or Physical Aggression and Rioting*). In section 3.3.4, carnivalesque is posited against the spectacle (*Spectacle and Rioting*). The final part foregrounds some of the ways in which the carnival is resurfacing in contemporary Iran, noting both similarities and differences with the classic Bakhtinian model (*3.3.5 Resurgence of Carnival and Rioting*).

3.3.1 Communication and Rioting

Genuine proletarian carnivalesque turns the capitalist world and its values upside down. It does so by creating a zone where the 'purview' of an individual (i.e., the necessarily limited literal and figurative consciousness of an individual under capitalism) becomes momentarily as expansive as the individual's 'environment' (i.e., the entire situation of a person, including the previously inaccessible elements that are now offered up as gift).

One factor that secures the zone is the commonality of the interlocutors' *apperceptive mass* (quoted in Cheyne and Tarulli, 1999: 6). Rioters have common presuppositions (e.g., the need and availability of a 'better world') and mutual knowledge (e.g., the enemies' vulnerabilities). As Vygotsky very rightly pointed out, 'when the thoughts and consciousness of the interlocutors are one, the role of speech in the achievement of flawless understanding is reduced to a minimum' (quoted in Cheyne and Tarulli, 1999: 7). What Bakhtin corrected in this fetishized vision was the false assumption that shared apperceptive mass must be the be all and end all of communication (Min, 2001: 3). Bakhtin argued instead that it is precisely the 'otherness' of the other, which enables productive dialogue. He emphasised that productivity in dialogue does not necessarily mean consensus. His vision is closer in this regard to a genuine proletarian riot, with all its 'impurity' and complexity than Vygotsky's rather anaemic model.

The Iranian riots involved different factions of the proletariat (including at times petty bourgeois and lumpenproletarian elements) who shared an apperceptive mass but employed diverse tactics. Some began with the regenerative aspects of the carnivalesque (e.g., dancing, music and reclaiming the street)[75], others with its destructive dimension (e.g., burning, looting and trashing). It was the merging of these differing tactics that made communication productive and created the 'oceanic feeling' that is a condition of carnivalesque (Roth, 1997: 4). The 'oceanic feeling' is not, as some have suggested, the negation of individuality but the long-awaited expression of (suppressed) individuality through a collective framework.

What Iranian rioters were communicating to each other and the 'outside' world was a sense of what Bloch calls 'concrete utopia' (quoted in Wall and Thomson, 1993: 54). 'Concrete' precisely because it is an essential moment of a communist social movement which self-reflexively propels it-self towards a class-less community and not the abstract, far-off, 'sci-entific' utopia that idealists and non-re-volutionaries are fond of positing. 'Concrete' also in the sense that it is polyphonic, a profusion of voices, signs and languages (Irving and Moffatt, 2002: 4). The rioters consisted of many 'ethnicities' including Persians, Ar-abs, Turks, Kurds and Afghanis. Urban and country, male and female, hetero-sexual and homosexual, old and young took part and created a multiplicity of de-sires and languages which Foucault calls 'heterotopia' (Foucault quoted in Irving and Moffatt, 2002: 4). *Heterotopia* is a site

In a concrete utopia washing machines actually work!

Tehran student demo drowned in blood

where incongruity becomes productive. *Heterotopia, in conjunction with a shared ap-perceptive mass and oceanic feeling are the preconditions of carnivalesque.*

Genuine proletarian carnivals create their own 'carnivalesque time' in op-position to 'official time'. The former is 'aware of *timelessness* and crisis in the version of history which it represents' (Willis, 1989: 131). The latter presents a linear

---

75 For some collective and visible dancing can induce 'oceanic feeling'. As Leslie Gotfrit (1991: 176, quoted in Brabazon, 2002: 22) observes, 'Dancing precipitates an incredible longing. To recover the pleasure - in the imagining and remembering, the connecting again with my limbs, my breath, my body - is to ignite desire. These are rare moments of realising my body and mind as not distinct, and of feeling the power of creativity when embodied'.

and hierarchical teleology of events, which frowns upon change. Official time releg-ates change and crisis to the past. 'Popular festive forms', on the other hand, 'har-ness the *timelessness* of past events in order to project a utopian time' (Willis, 1989: 133). As Bakhtin makes clear (1973: 238), the festive atmosphere of games and sport-ing events underline chance and randomness. In the Iranian context, this element of chance and randomness undermines the 'gloomy eschatological time' of the mullah-bourgeoisie with its emphasis on the 'Day of Judgment' and the return of the 'Hid-den Imam'. There are numerous politico-social factors that determine whether riots erupt or not. However, once we are in a riot situation there are also what Bakhtin calls a 'veritable downpour of *suddenlys*' and 'at just that moment', which shape the outcome (Bakhtin, 1994: 95). 'Gloomy eschatological time' is understandably suspicious of chance and randomness.

The battle between 'biological time' and 'dead time' is expressed in the dicho-tomy between dialogue and monologue. In fact, Bakhtin 'frequently invokes dia-logue as a synonym for *life* and its repression as an allegory of death' (Sandywell,

... a defeated atheism that has been languishing ...

1998: 197). Iranian riots put under erasure the Koranic command, a command that likes to present itself without a human author, standing above society, un-challenged and unvanquished. As Morson (1986: 127) has explained,

... the language of God is absolute and unconditional in the sense that, unlike any utterance of a man, it is not a function of the circumstances that evoked it, and its meaning is not qualified by an audience whose potential reactions have had to be taken into account. A biblical command can be disobeyed, but it cannot be answered. Divine speech does not defend itself or allow itself to be limited by particular historical circumstances.

In so far as 'fundamentalist' discourse does not retreat under pressure but stands firm and steadfast, it is vulnerable to total proletarian rejection. This is more true of Islam and Judaism which attempt to regulate all facets of everyday proletarian activities through petty rites and restrictions than Christianity or Zoroastrianism. Under oppressive circumstances, rejection of religiosity may be slow in coming, but when it finally arrives, it moves fearlessly and with utter disregard for divine iconography.

In the course of these upheavals, since God in his haughtiness was not prepared to budge an inch, the rioters took a mile. The anti-religious impulse of rioters was a novel phenomenon, which will both enrich the social movement in the Middle East and, given favourable circumstances, may even act as a shot in the arm for 'western atheism' – a defeated atheism that has been languishing in unwarranted complacency for more than a century.

The discourse of the mullah-bourgeoisie, just like wills and suicide notes, are 'usually closed to dialogue' (Morson, 1986: 137). There is no sense in a Salman Rushdie, for example, trying to wiggle his way out of a fatwa, since a fatwa is a closed pronouncement. The inflexibility of the monologic fatwa is further strengthened due to the fact that the one person who may be able to rescind it, that is the author, Ayatollah Khomeini, has been dead for some time. The Iranian proletariat may be on the cusp of a seminal historical achievement. Having rejected God's commands and having seen through the diatribes of the ayatollahs, it is now beginning to understand that 'martyrs and sufferers, with rare exceptions, are despots and tyrants' (Maxim Gorky, quoted in Morson, 1986: 142). The pleas of the regime to respect the memory of martyrs, which in the past had prevented strikes, demonstrations and riots, can no longer hold back proletarian anger.

The riots represent the first 21st century call 'for an end to the judgment of God' (Artaud, 1947). The rioters were echoing and with their bodily movements re-enacting Artaud's jibe,

Is God a being?
If he is one, he is shit.
If he is not one
he does not exist.
But he does not exist,
except as the void that approaches with all its forms
whose most perfect image
is the advance of an incalculable group of crab lice.

Terry Eagleton (1989: 185) explains it succinctly, 'a political order in which everything is oppressively meaningful buckles under its own weight'. Islam by providing the believer with every conceivable interpretation and injunction creates a suffocating and excessive meaningfulness that collapses back onto itself, levelling meaning in the process. Carnival then 'releases us from the terrorism of excessive significance' (Eagleton, 1989: 185). It is hardly surprising that the monotony and greyness of official ceremonies in Iran, find a counterpoint in *Kitsch* architecture and shopping malls. In Eagleton's memorable words, '*Kitsch* is all smiles and cheers, relentlessly beaming and euphoric like an aerobics class, marching merrily onward to the future shouting 'long live life!' (Eagleton, 1989: 186).

The mindless shoppers of the Islamic Republic, every bit as addicted to their daily dose of shopping mall voyeurism as 'westerners', are the perfect bourgeois mirror image of the self-flagellating zealots marching in unison during Ashura. What the carnivalesque does is to throw both these modes of non-communication into crisis. Secular *kitsch* and Islamic *taste* are conquered through Bakhtinian celebration. Taking Bakhtin's formulation perhaps even more literally than he intended, Iranian proletarians insist that 'to be means to communicate' (Bakhtin, 1984b: 287).

3.3.2 Cultural Transgressions and Rioting

Bakhtin writes, '… Seriousness burdens us with hopeless situations, but laughter lifts us above them and delivers us from them. Laughter does not encumber man [sic], it liberates him' (Bakhtin, 1986: 134). During the riots, proletarians had the chance to play with God's terror and laugh at it. In Morris's words (1994: 209) 'the awesome becomes a *comic monster*'. The laughter of the proletariat is what makes 'organic atheism' (i.e., a living, fighting atheism which emerges from everyday life and punctures theocracy) so much more radical than the dry, ideological atheism of reactionaries (i.e., the mechanical atheism of the likes of Lenin and Emma Goldman, which can only serve to modernise religion rather than undermine it). 'Organic atheism' refuses to meet religion on the enemy's terrain. Instead it creates its own battlefield and takes on simultaneously both the public and private spheres of divine demagogy. Organic atheism asks, why perpetuate the illusion of the separation of church from state when one has a chance to do away with both?

In the course of the riots, physical attacks on clerics and mosques were augmented by a philosophical and verbal assault on God. The provocative slogan 'Death to God', far more challenging than the tepid Nietzschean pronouncement, 'God is dead', was raised by Iranians both during the riots and on the streets of London during anti-war demonstrations in 2002. 'Death to God', unlike its Nietzschean precursor, acknowledges that there is still work to be done before God can be pensioned off as a museum piece. Slogans such as 'Death to God', 'Death to Islam' and 'Death to the mullahs' may seem one-dimensional if looked at in isolation, but when contextualised within the general festive and celebratory mood of the 7 days that shook Iran, they represent what Bakhtin calls the 'laughing truth, expressed in curses and abusive words, [that degrade] power' (Bakhtin, 1984a, quoted in Solomon, 1979: 297).

It is quite clear that profanities are being employed by proletarians in a conscious bid to undermine Islamic 'taste' and 'decorum'. In his wonderful article about the reaccentuating of the symbolism of the Tyburn tree in Hyde Park, Roberts (2004: 896) shows how the key utterance for the 'patrician' class gradually became one of 'politeness', which was taken as a sign of virtuosity and freedom. He also demonstrates how proletarians,

> ... gained a populist public voice that was neither 'refined' nor 'polite'. Instead, dialogue was frequently fuelled by anger and resentment at a new form of legal regulation that, in the eyes of the Tyburn crowd, constructed innocent customary practices as being illegal (Roberts, 2004: 897).

If anything, the undermining of 'politeness' and 'decorum' by contemporary Iranians seems to be a more conscious project than the description above. By swearing at the referee, the opposing team and the regime during football matches, an anti-hegemonic autonomous zone is created that occasionally finds a continued expression in post-match riots. Profanities should be viewed as part of the struggle between classes over public space. They undermine taste and in so doing weaken hierarchy. Through curses, chants, slogans and music the proletariat lays claim to areas hitherto beyond its control.

It is hardly surprising, therefore, that authoritarian regimes oppose 'erotic' dancing and joyful music. In Trinidad during enslavement dance bands were used by revellers as a cover for attacking the rulers. Enslaved Africans would hold parodies of the Christmas sacrament. Naturally the authorities did everything in their power to ban and when that failed limit carnivals (Liverpool, 1993: 46). Under Nazi rule, Joseph Goebbels 'banned jazz, along with foxtrots and the tango' (Zwerin, 2000: 6). Fights with the Hitler Youth over the 'right' to play music and dance are being repeated in Iran, with the Basiji Youth playing the role of the villain. Nazis referred to those forms of music they disapproved of as *Entartete Musik* (meaning, 'decadent music'). Iranian Muslim clerics call it *Museeghi-ye Mobtazal* (meaning, 'banal and immoral music').

In an article dealing with the connection between music, rhythm and class struggle, Mahabir observes,

> ... rhythm in black music is ideological ... its very deployment in the public sphere illustrates how seriously its listeners consider its ideological function ... for instance the overamplified sound system that emerged in the slums of West Kingston and spread ... the music trucks seen in every Caribbean parade, the maxitaxis that blast music daily for their passengers ... show that the urban and rural

> working classes use music as part of a soundscape of resistance ... participating in
> ... an 'indirect, ad hoc war of position' ... (Mahabir, 2002: 13).

Significantly, Mahabir goes on to explain, 'the Calypso alerts us that to the fact that while the soca [a popular and inter-racial musical form in the 1970s] helps the people cope with their dismal socio-economic conditions, it quickly becomes the cause of riots as the State tries to stop its expression' (Mahabir, 2002: 23).

Although low-level and individualised musical warfare has always been part of the urban 'soundscape' of Iran under the mullah-bourgeoisie, only recently has it been used consciously to provoke the regime. Learning from the more accessible Kurdish and Turkish cultures of musical resistance, as well as the more distant 'western' genres Iranian proletarians are beginning to show signs of appreciating the subversive potential of music and rhythm. Banned Persian music, western rave music and classical music, which were all considered underground entertainment until recently, have begun to resist Islam's colonising impulse within public space. Riots have become spaces for younger generation of proletarians, especially female proletarians, to express themselves sexually. It has been suggested, in a different context, that the very act of moving between a traditional local identity and a cosmopolitan one enhances a sense of personal autonomy (Hannerz, 1992 quoted in Farrer, 1999: 150). Recent reports as well as anecdotal evidence suggest a similar sense of empowerment in young Iranian proletarians. The riot zone seems to provide participants with 'an enlarged repertoire of sexual strategies and styles' (Farrer, 1999: 157). And, finally, in an unofficial inter-classist alliance between proletarians and the secular-nationalist bourgeoisie, even classical Persian 'verse-capping' (dialogue through poetry) has been recruited to the cause of undermining Islamic monologism.[76]

It is crucial to underline that profanities are part of proletarian culture and in certain contexts, a mode of resistance. This may seem an obvious banality to 'western' readers but one cannot overstate the deleterious effects of suppressing proletarian culture by left wing petty-bourgeois Iranian intellectuals in the past. Having romanticised the proletariat as eternally 'good', 'decent', 'clean', 'muscular' and 'angelic' these intellectuals have a hard time matching their construct to reality. Since reality cannot be suppressed or denied indefinitely, the historical solution has been to blame everything 'impure' on the perennial scapegoat- the 'lumpenproletariat'. Iranian leftist discourse is replete with attacks on 'lumpen' elements who are blamed for contaminating the 'upright' proles. Consequently, there have been few attempts to build an

---

76 Alongside musical transgressions, slogans and chants should in addition be studied as external manifestations of what Vygotsky calls 'private speech'. It is significant how the number of slogans would rise and their political content enriched during situations that became emotionally or intellectually complicated. Proletarians were using slogan at these seminal points to complete thoughts and gauge the mood of their fellow rioters, as well as the more obvious expressions of solidarity.

alliance between proletarian and 'lumpenproletarian' elements of the social movement. This cold-shouldering has resulted in 'lumpen' elements feeling alienated from their 'natural allies' and siding with oppression at crucial moments of historical change.

In a sense a great deal of the fault lies with Marx and Engels, especially the latter. In the preface to the second edition of *The Peasant War in Germany* (1850), Engels describes the lumpenproletariat in these unflattering terms,

> The *lumpenproletariat*, this scum of depraved elements from all classes, with headquarters in the big cities, is the worst of all possible allies. This rabble is absolutely venal and absolutely brazen ... Every leader of the workers who uses these scoundrels as guards or relies on them for support proves himself by this action alone a traitor to the movement (Engels quoted in Stallybrass, 1990: 88-89).

Shi'iting on the proletariat

Even Marx has a tendency to 'abstract the lumpenproletariat from any specifiable historical relation and to treat them (as most bourgeois commentators did) as a distinct race' (Stallybrass, 1990: 84). Most of the fear and loathing previously reserved by bourgeois thinkers for the proletariat was now turned upon the lumpenproletariat. Both Marxist and anarchist thinkers are to blame for the present state of affairs, the former for dismissing the lumpenproletariat and the latter for romanticising it. A reassessment of the relationship between proletarian and 'lumpenproletarian' members of society will entail acknowledging their similar cultural heritage. The intermingling of parody, irony, sarcasm, insults and curses from these two groups during the Iranian riots enriched both traditions and rebuilt bridges long damaged by reactionary intellectuals.

Some of the most rebellious elements in Iranian society express their defiance through sexual recoding. Since most leftists are of bourgeois or petty-bourgeois background and still carry a great deal of religious ethical presumptions, sexuality has been marginalised in political discourse. It took the regimentalisation of every facet of sexuality by puritanical Islamic bigots to force the issue. Now that heterosexual and homosexual boys and girls defiantly and brazenly break sexual taboos during riots through drinking, smoking, dancing, consorting or even voyeuristically desiring each other, both the mullah-bourgeoisie and their so-called opponents are lost for words. The transgressions of boundaries by Iranian proletarians (with some help from lumpen and petty-bourgeois elements), coupled to a successful social movement, may even be able to supersede the gains made by 'western' proletarians in the realm of sexuality and provide both western 'feminism' and the 'gay movement' invaluable support during these counter-revolutionary times.

3.3.3 Psychic and/or Physical Aggression and Rioting

Observers have described how Iranian youngsters block the roads either in cars or on foot and simply scream their disgust at the regime. I have already mentioned how this kind of dissent does not involve demands or negotiation. The scream is unadulterated anger which seeks no mediation and puts forward no demands.[77] Class passivity is often associated with lack or suppression of emotions such as anger. Harrington and Flint (1997: 19) have shown the centrality of anger in the mobilisation of energy to overcome a problem. If a belief in the possibility of change is to be attained, one 'must *know,* one must *feel,* and one must be aware of the relationship between the two' (Harrington and Flint, 1997: 19). Cheryl Hercus (1999: 40) shows how important anger is in mediating collective action. Moreover, 'a sense of lost opportunity, defined in the light of feminist discourse, is also behind the anger expressed by [subjects] concerning childhood experiences'.

---

77 The similarities with the punk movement are obvious. Punk was a subversive working class aesthetics characterised by 'active participation, hedonistic pleasure, and the loss of self in an experience of communion, as opposed to a Kantian-bourgeois aesthetic of individualistic and reasoned pleasure' (Jones, 1998). The Iranian phenomenon, however, is more explicitly political and celebratory and less given to the nihilistic negativity of British punk.

Iranian proletarians, especially the youth, are acutely aware of the lost opportunities that have frustrated their 'progress' for decades. The imposed emotional *self-restraint* people feel in their everyday life (and sometime practice 'voluntarily' to avoid conflict) is burst asunder and replaced by emotional *self-assertion* (Hercus, 1999: 44-46) in the course of riots. Since emotional self-restraint requires a great deal of energy and leads to emotional exhaustion, guilt and self-estrangement (Hercus, 1999: 46), a riotous carnival is experienced as empowering.

Anger taken to extremes may seem 'hysterical'. Here again there is a relationship between emotions and carnival. Carnival, it will be remembered, involves celebrating the grotesque body and 'lower bodily stratum' such as sexual promiscuity, alcohol consumption, fattening food and uncontrollable bodily movements. This type of 'hysterical' dissent allows the raising of 'the threshold of shame and embarrassment' (Norbert Elias, quoted in Stallybrass and White, 1986: 188). Stephen Greenblatt's description of how the gradual expulsion of aspects of bodily function, its secretions and fluids, have managed to create 'disgust' in Europeans is equally relevant to Islam,

When it wants martyrs, atheism has only to ask; my blood is ready to flow.

> In this separation, the 'lower bodily stratum' steadily loses any connection with anything other than the increasingly disreputable dreams of alchemists and cranks. Eventually, all the body's

Reclaiming the streets and the fire

products, except tears, become simply unmentionable in decent society (Greenblatt, quoted in Stallybrass and White, 1986: 188).

Nothing could convey Islam's fear of 'dirt' and 'sexuality', fluids and secretions more accurately than the above quote. Tears (and blood) are the only 'clean' secretion that Islam actively encourages; the rest must be shunned, denied or disciplined. Even tears and blood must be secreted in accordance to Islamic protocols. Islam ensures submission by lowering the 'threshold of shame and embarrassment' and by expanding the realm of 'disgust'. Shame in one's 'grotesque' body. Disgust toward the Jew, the homosexual and the foreigner. However, the Islamic veil, especially the all-embracing black *chador*, far from covering the body, constantly foregrounds its 'blemishes'. By contrast, carnivalesque provides participants with images 'through which [they] may recognise [themselves] without disgust' (Stallybrass and White, 1986: 187). The removal of the veil, semi-naked dancing, kissing, eating fatty food, drinking alcohol and swearing during riots are part of a repertoire of tactics designed to remove shame and disgust. 'The body', as Hitchcock (1998: 85) makes clear, 'constantly contradicts the pretensions and ideologies of perfection in its defecation, sneezing, farting, belching, and bleeding ... it wants nothing of discipline and regularity'. Scandals destroy the epic wholeness of the world and 'free human behaviour from the norms and motivations that predetermine it' (Bakhtin, 1963, quoted in Morris, 1994: 191).

There are parallels here with prisons, especially women prisons. In analysing the disruptive behaviour of convict women in 19th century Hobart (Australia), Joy Damousi (1997: 2) shows how,

> Singing and dancing in the wards at night was an effective means of challenging authority. The women's songs were loud and strong, explicitly violating those measures in place which aimed to restrain their pressures and amusements ... These women were indulging in acts deemed vulgar, as their exuberance was deemed 'unfeminine'. To laugh loudly and vociferously in a prison which aimed to regulate and order the very being of its inmates, was an act of impetuousness.

Following a similar trajectory, Islamic morality that aimed to police the private-public split is failing. Proletarian laughter, which may have begun as a response to Islamic dread, gained confidence during the riots and became exuberant, regenerative. The consensual aspect of hegemony, which based itself on 'moral correctitude' and 'sacrifice', has had its comeuppance. This leaves the mullah-bourgeoisie with only one weapon, that of coercion, hence the

I can't go to prison. I have a hot date with an Irish lad!

The Moral Police are at it again!

increasingly militarisation of society under Ahmadi-Nezhad. But coercive tactics, which may work against traditional weapons such as strikes and rallies, are ineffectual against screams or what Bakhtin calls 'festive madness'. The newspaper articles following the riots were reminiscent of puritanical attacks on English alehouses in the 18th century. One such lackey (Clarke, *A Dissertation upon Drunkenness*, 1727) describes what he considers the disgusting environment of the alehouse in the following terms,

The vile obscene talk, noise, nonsense and ribaldry discourses together with the fumes of tobacco, belchings and other foul breaking winds, that are generally found in an ale-room … are enough to make any rational creature amongst them almost ashamed of his being. But all this the rude rabble esteem the highest degree of happiness and run themselves into the greatest straits imaginable to attain it (Clarke, quoted in Stallybrass and White, 1986: 94).

Having been denied the alehouse, Iranian crowds bring the tavern to the streets and in so doing they also negate the liberal coffee-house. By demanding 'laziness' and 'idleness', the rioters undermine the Islamic-fascist work ethic and the moral discipline of the (liberal) coffee-house. The street-parties facilitate the manifestation of the grotesque body. Precisely because 'eastern' capitalism disowns and conceals grotesquerie, it becomes 'vulnerable to the shock of its continued presence or to its unexpected rediscovery' (cf. Stallybrass and White, 1986: 108). Grotesquerie and excess violently oppose the pathos and patient suffering of official Islamic culture. It is hardly surprising that bourgeois merchants and militia forces mobilise to oppose carnivalesque. Likewise, it is of no surprise that we find history replete with similar examples. In discussing the peasant *dashi* festivals of the Edo period (1600-1868) in Japan, Sean McPherson (1998: 8) explains how the festival's 'enormous expenditure of resources and interruptions of productive work flew in the face of the neo-Confucian tenets of thrift and industry espoused by the authorities'. This led to the forging of an alliance against the festival,

As elite merchant concerns with social unrest began to parallel those of the central government, they joined the *samurai* in looking askance at the status inversion and carnivalesque atmosphere of dashi festivals (McPherson, 1998: 8).

These *dashi* festivals were part of the wider '*ee ja nai ka*' peasant movements (translated roughly as 'what the hell', or 'anything goes') which proclaimed 'the end of existing world and the coming of a new world of free association among social equals' (McPherson, 1998: 9). The carnivalesque riots of 21-27 October 2001 in Iran were also part of a wider social movement towards the negation of private property, the state and religion. Laughter and revelry were therefore the appropriate accompaniment of the stones, bricks, stun grenades, molotov cocktails and bullets that the rioters used against the authorities.

3.3.4 Spectacle and Rioting

Carnivalesque is in constant opposition to the spectacle. One such version of the spectacle manifests itself during the official ritual of *Ashura* (enactment of the death of the Shi'a Imam Hussein at the hands of his Sunni rival). Official rituals do 'not lead people out of the existing world order and [create] no second life ... the official feast [looks] back at the past and [uses] the past to consecrate the present' (Morris, 1994: 199). Moreover, it does so by using the mediation of images that have been doctored to misrepresent the actual state of affair. The spectacle is a hierarchical and capitalist set of social relations mediated by performative images in the sense described by Guy Debord (Debord, 1987). It is also the 'material reconstruction of the religious illusion' (Debord, 1987, Chapter 1: thesis 20). He puts it rather well in the twelfth thesis of the first chapter of his book,

> The spectacle presents itself as something enormously positive, indisputable and inaccessible. It says nothing more than 'that which appears is good, and that which is good appears'. The attitude that it demands in principle is passive accept-ance which in fact it already obtained by its manner of appearing without reply, by its monopoly of appearance (Debord, 1987, Chapter 1: thesis 12).

In a similar vein, Ashura reinforce the unstated fear of spectacularised death. The self-flagellation dimension of Ashura is a case in point. The ritual of Ashura is also a regu-latory mechanism for maintaining what Hochschild (1983) calls 'feeling rules',

Passion play of the death of Hussein- looking back to consecrate the present

which are social norms that dictate how we should feel in a given situation. Hochschild points out that these norms benefit the privileged and reinforce the subordinate positioning of the disadvantaged (Hochschild in Summers-Effler, 2002, 46).

Feeling rules were systematically broken during these riots. Group dan-cing and singing, the consumption of al-cohol and sexual liaisons were the most explicit examples of resistance. The riots expose the bankruptcy of Islamic theo-cracy and its cult of death and sacrifice. They do so by taking what is best in oth-er non-religious festivities, such as May Day and *Norouz* (the Iranian New Year's Day) celeb-rations and radicalise them further still using the spirit of carnivalesque.

Football 'hooliganism' works best when it is carried through as a *serious joke*. This is creative play free of ritual. The 'actors' and the history conjured up through ri-oting do not disappear after a week of conflict but become embedded in proletarian collective memory. This text is an additional attempt to preserve the lessons of such struggles. Proletarians are aided in this process of remembering thanks to official media's mishandling of the situation. The attacks on 'hooligans' and 'thugs' launched against the rioters after the events failed to make an impact. When Rafsanjani, Khatami and Khamene'i laid into the rioters as 'traitors' and 'fifth columnists' they were following in the footsteps of reactionaries such as Pope, Hogarth and Fielding who invoked the masquerade as negative (Castle, 1983-1984: 157). The Bishop of London denounced masquerading in 1724 as encouraging 'Licentiousness and Effeminacy', which echoes Rafsanjani's jibe about the rioters as 'susul' (literally, 'effeminate' or 'sissy').[78] Spectacularised Islamic rituals routinely make a connection between 'masculinity and rule, femininity and impurity' (Kelly and Kaplan, 1990: 128).

Bakhtin notes we remember through 'reciting by heart' or 'retelling it in [our] own words' (Bakhtin, 1981: 95). 'In reciting', Parrington (1997: 142) contends,

> the language of others is authoritative and there can be no play with the framing context. One cannot even entertain the possibility of doubting it- therefore one cannot enter into a dialogue with it ... In retelling however, one arrives at *internally persuasive* discourse. Voices that are incorporated in this way will be more critically assessed but once accepted, they will retain much more lasting influence in shaping consciousness.

Renate Lachmann believes 'memory is at the centre of carnival because even when carnival is over, we still remember what it was able to do' (Lachmann, 1988-1989 quoted in Wall and Thomson, 1993: 58). Remembering is not passive. It is an act perpetrated against the past. As Wall and Thomson (1993: 62) make clear,

> ... when we combine memory and carnival - that is, when we see memory as a sort of carnivalesque event- we learn to stress the importance of an indelible social space inscribed in the very process. Memory becomes a complex space where new communities and relationships can be forged through such inscription. It seems entirely appropriate to recall Walter Benjamin's *Theses on the Philosophy of History*, as summarized by Jürgen Habermas: 'there exists a solidarity of those born later with those who preceded them, with all those whose bodily or personal integrity has been violated at the hands of other human beings; and that this solidarity can only be engendered and made effective by remembering' ... Even the most private of memories have a communal power, again because of the carnivalesque aspect. This aspect consists foremost in the erasure of boundaries.

---

78 Rafsanjani (an ex-President of the Islamic Republic of Iran who continues to wield considerable power) needs to prove his masculine credentials more than most. In a patriarchal culture where a masculine identity is deemed a prerequisite for success, Rafsanjani has always been a butt of jokes for not being able to grow a beard. The unintentional irony of him accusing the rioters of being 'sissy' and 'effeminate' is lost on no one other than Rafsanjani himself. The Ahmadi-Nezhad campaign took full advantage of Rafsanjani's lack of masculine credentials with the masses in the 2005 presidential elections.

Remembering is one of the most powerful forms of fighting the separation that the spectacle engenders. By abolishing the separation between inside and outside or between performer and spectator carnivalesque remembering constantly reshapes consciousness in preparation for the next bout of struggle.

3.3.5 Resurgence of Carnival and Rioting

Bakhtin has been immeasurably useful for the evolution of this investigation. However, it is patently obvious that we need to go beyond him on a number of fronts if the radicalism inherent in proletarian rioting is to be fully comprehended. Bernstein (1986: 113) has argued,

> Bakhtin's typology of laughter, for all its richly textured local insights, is haunted, from its inception, by a wistfully nostalgic longing for a realm of pure and ahistorical spontaneity, a rite of universal participation whose essentially affirmative character is guaranteed by its very universality.

In so far as this has been a Bakhtinian reading of rioting, I must accept its limitations in relation to the historic and socio-economic context of the riots. Not only do I find Bakhtin's analysis of carnivalesque ahistorical in places, I also detect certain attempts at sanitisation, which tends to conceal the violence perpetrated during carnivals. Bernstein (1986: 117) again,

> Bakhtin's love for Rabelais and for what he sees as the redemptive energy of the Saturnalia, at times blinds him to the fact that it is only because Rabelais' novels are manifestly nonmimetic that he is able to assimilate them to anthropological and folkloristic records of actual carnivals, many of which, as recent studies have shown, ended in violence that proved devastating both to the innocent victims and to the community as a whole.

The present study should be viewed as part of this project of historical recovery. The violent features of carnival have been thoroughly investigated with the proviso that in our study proletarian violence has proved devastating mostly to capital, religion and the state. But again I concede that traditionally many instances of carnivals have proved reactionary in nature.[79] Violence is not the only entity missing from Bakhtin's account of the carnivalesque. Mary Roth (1997: 6) explains,

---

79 It may be the case that the trend in the 'west' is towards the ever-increasing commodification and spectacularisation of carnivals. A telling example would be the San Fermin fiesta in Pamplona, Spain. Ravenscroft and Matteucci (2003: 3) have shown that the week-long celebrations of this famous carnival have become an occasion for people to 'let off steam'. They also show how the preparation for the carnival reflects routine work-production. They even argue the carnival may disempower the local people by turning them into 'service providers' (Ravenscroft and Matteucci, 2003: 4). All this may very well be true, although I feel the authors overstate their case somewhat. However, I have been at pains to show the 'western' domestication of the carnival does not apply to my case study.

For Bakhtin and other 20th century commentators on carnival and the carnivalesque, drinking and intoxication have passed from the scene. Only Katerina Clarke and Michael Holquist casually mention that the drunken aspect was in fact suppressed by Bakhtin, who desired to 'concentrate primarily on the eating and elide the drinking because of his originary thesis that carnival is a descendant of the aftermath of the hunt'.

Bakhtin has also been charged with robbing carnival of its dark potency. Emerson and Morson, for instance, conclude 'in Carnival he sees only the joy of parody, not the danger of irresponsibility and violence' (quoted in Roth, 1997: 8). It has also been argued that the consumptive and scatological logic of carnival, promoted as transgressive by such theorists as Foucault, Bataille and Bakhtin must be approached with caution in an epoch when rampant consumption is actively encouraged by certain sections of capital (Larsen, 2001: 80).

Muslim 'elite' feeling sorry for themselves!

They've discovered carnivalesque. We're doomed, doomed, I tell you!

Bakhtin has recently been challenged from a feminist perspective. One charge has accused Bakhtin of not paying nearly enough attention to women's dialects and how it differs from men's discourse (Booth, 1986: 154). Bakhtin excuses Rabelais' sexism too glibly,

> The truth is nowhere in Rabelais does one find any hint of an effort to imagine any woman's point of view or to incorporate women into a dialogue. And nowhere in Bakhtin does one discover any suggestion that he sees the importance of this kind of monologue, not even when he discusses Rabelais' attitude towards women (Booth, 1986: 165-166).

Equally absent from Rabelais is a class oriented analysis. Similarly, Bakhtin's liberal and social democratic political ideology in his early years and mystical leanings in later years were oblivious to the importance of a rigorous class analysis. All these shortcomings, I have attempted to overcome by foregrounding the struggles of proletarians on and off the pitch.

Despite these reservations, I feel justified in my choice of a Bakhtinian perspective to demonstrate the significance of seven days of football rioting that shook Iran during October 2001. By opposing the spectacularised aspects of religious performances such as Ashura to carnivalesque riot time, I have shown their inherent antagon ism. Although it is true that every social struggle is pregnant with a mixture of spectacle and carnivalesque, there are genuine moments of liberation when social relationships based on the spectacle are overwhelmed by subversive carnivalesque.

In summary: whilst analysing the response of Scottish proletarians to state sponsored urban 'regeneration' projects at Ferguslie Park in Paisley, Chik Collins (1999: 14) refers to activists who 'seemed not so much to speak as to *spit*' the words at their class enemies, 'almost as if all of the evaluative connotations which expressed their grievance were distilled and conveyed in the intonation' of their curses.

The 7 days that shook Iran between 21 and 27 October 2001 was a proletarian gob spat at the mullah-bourgeoisie. It was a historical turning point, noticed by many, understood in its entirety, by few. It raged and fumed, clarified and concretised, parodied and humbled, brought joy and laughter, and finally, made the tyrants shake in their sandals. With the demise of Iranian theocracy, Islam, and hopefully religion in general, will take a battering throughout the world. The class struggle, long derailed and suppressed, will re-emerge like the 'Many-Headed Hydra', thirsting for revenge as well as regeneration.

Chapter four:

Activity Theory and Social Movements: Two case studies

'If, as a theoretician, one's ears are attuned to the new impulses from the workers, new 'categories' will be created, a new way of thinking, a step forward in philosophical cognition'.

Chapter four:

Activity Theory and Social Movements: Two case studies

All of history is the history of the struggle for freedom.
If, as a theoretician, one's ears are attuned to the new impulses from the workers, new 'categories' will be created, a new way of thinking, a step forward in philo-sophical cognition.

– Raya Dunayevskaya, 1958/2000: 89

I n this section my aim is to compare and contrast two case studies from the perspect-ive of Activity Theory (AT). I have chosen this perspective because 'activity theory offers a theoretical framework to the study of relations between actions, individuals, artifacts, and communities as a whole' (Lindblom and Ziemke, 2003: 85). The two case studies are the 1990 anti-poll tax Trafalgar Square demonstration and the February 2003 one million (plus) anti-war demonstration. Both occurred in London and were covered extensively by the media although in contrasting terms. Both were organised by Leftists (i.e., the left wing of capital), although liberals also played a role in organising the anti-war demo. Both were considered seminal historical watersheds in retrospect.

However, they had very different trajectories. The anti-poll tax demonstration turned into a riot where neither the police nor the stewards (or 'soft-cops' as they are affectionately known amongst radicals) could reign in proletarian rage. Soon after-wards it was granted the privileged historical epithet of The Battle of Trafalgar Square. In contrast, the one million anti-war march passed off peacefully. As ex-plained below, things are not quite as black and white as the preceding sentence sug-gests. It could be argued, after all, that the violence associated with the anti-poll tax riot also acted to camouflage conservatism amongst many of the rioters whilst the 'quiet dignity' of the anti-war demo was not necessarily the 'dignity' of a bourgeois-fied crowd.

I begin by introducing a number of conceptual and theoretical ideas from Activ-ity Theory pertinent to our investigation (section 4.1). The remaining concepts will be introduced throughout the chapter as the necessity arises. I then provide a thumbnail historical sketch of the anti-poll tax rebellion and present the events in terms of Activity Theory (section 4.2). I repeat the process with the anti-war demonstration (section 4.3). In the final section, I discuss the utility and limitations of Activity Theory for the study of our two case studies (section 4.4).

4.1 ACTIVITY THEORY: BASIC CONCEPTS AND IDEAS

Leontiev's *Activity, Consciousness, and Personality* (1978), a key text for Activity Theorists, is a poorly written book. Deliberately ambiguous, it hides its blemishes under a shroud of abstraction. Furthermore, it suffers from reactionary notions such as 'structuralism', 'naturalism' and 'functionalism' (Morss, 1996: 20). The origins of these shortcomings lie in Leontiev's genuine affinity for the bourgeois ideology of Bolshevism and Engels's atavistic take on the dialectics. Activity Theory (AT) emerged in a regimented Leninist-Stalinist society 'against a background of the enslavement of peasants and the organisation of slave-based production (not only in the gulag, but in the country as a whole) that was unprecedented in history' (Zinchenko, 1995: 52). Hardly surprising, therefore, that AT did not adequately discuss contradictions, freedom and emancipation. Moreover, as Stetsenko (1999: 246) has correctly observed, 'the main emphasis in activity theory was placed on exploring the *connection* between consciousness (mind) and activity as if these were two different realities'.

But if these problems, which have most of their roots in Engels-Leninism, are so glaring then how can we explain the wealth of intelligent works inspired by Leontiev in recent years, especially in the West (Engeström, 1987; Rogoff *et al.*, 1995; Aboulafia *et al.*, 1995; Branco, 2001)? We must assume that, despite its inherent flaws, Leontiev's discoveries have filled a void within a critical psychology hitherto lacking an activity-based approach. It is also the case that the ideas of AT have been somewhat refined in recent years. Furthermore, the use of AT in business management and occupational psychology has created a certain demand for its practitioners.

My take on AT will be different from the above applications. I intend to use AT in order to provide a framework for the genesis of proletarian activity but at the same time I emphasise that AT on its own is incapable of providing an adequate solution to the perennial problem of method[80] and interpretation. We still need to integrate its insights into Vygotsky's zoped and Bakhtin's polyphonic carnivalesque if we are to gain from its undoubted insights. AT has its own vocabulary, which needs to be adapted

---

80 *Radical* method is different from *scientific* method, amongst other things, by virtue of the fact that the former does not claim complete control over both the external factors influencing the experiment nor over the experimenters' own operations. In bourgeois science by contrast, 'The idea of gaining full control of the operations of thinking leads to the idea of *method* as a general and universal procedure, by means of which one can produce knowledge' (Lektorsky, 1999: 104).

for the purpose of our discussion. As I explained in the preceding chapters, a useful methodological starting point must always begin by acknowledging and integrating the intra-, inter-, and extra-psychological dimensions of an event. Some Activity Theorists also emphasise this approach. Angela Uchoa Branco (2001: 107), for instance, using different terminologies comes to the same conclusion, 'a necessary starting point, from my perspective, is to integrate contextual, relational and subjective dimensions (or levels of analysis) of the phenomena...'. This is in line with Vygotsky's intended methodological stance even if he failed to provide us with a fully worked out model,

> So the outline of the formation of individual consciousness that Vygotsky created could be represented in the following way: first, collective activity, then culture,[81] then ideal, sign or symbol, and finally individual consciousness (Davydov, 1995: 16).

Once this multi-level approach (i.e., intra-, inter- and extra-psychological planes of analysis) is viewed against the continuum of time (i.e., when the synchronic and diachronic dimensions of time are integrated)[82], we have a useful model for analysing social movements.

In AT, *tools* usually refer to 'all the means, which the different actors have at their disposal for influencing the object to satisfy user's needs' (Hyppönen, 1998: 6). They mediate different forms of activity and are used in gaining self-control of activity (Seeger, 2001: 40). Tools contain the 'intelligence' of past generations (e.g., the sedimented dead labour of past proletarians), although this is not always easy to see since dead labour becomes reified. Tools become 'invisible', their 'intelligence' unacknowledged, 'instead we see intelligence residing in the individual mind using the tool' (Pea, 1993: 53). Different tools result in different ways of thinking (Vygotsky, 1934/1986). Tools are further sub-divided into *concrete* tools (so called what–tools) and *abstract* tools (how- and why-tools).

Concrete tools are different items and resources of the environment, which may help actors in achieving set goals. During a demonstration these could include placards, platforms, leaflets, chains, barricades, flags, molotov-cocktails and communication devices. Writing one's thoughts on such concrete tools turns speech and language into objects of reflection and analysis.[83]

---

81 Activity theorists generally work with a wider definition of culture as a total system of ideas, symbols and meanings that has become fashionable during the reign of identity politics. Unfortunately, identity politics encourages the restriction of culture to 'an unordered aggregate of traits, styles or values that mark off subgroups, social movements, identities or categories of persons from one another' (Turner, 1999: 122). For a useful dialectical take on the notion of 'identity' see McLaughlin, 2003.

82 Some activity theorists (Scribner, 1985) prefer to combine the abovementioned intra-, inter- and extra-psychological planes with successively broader time frames (microgenetic, ontogenetic, sociocultural, and phylogenetic). This approach too has a lot going for it. However, I consider the dialectics of synchronic and diachronic dimensions to be a more manageable temporal framework.

83 It has been suggested by Olson (1995: 98-100) that 'we come to think about our speech, indeed to hear

Abstract tools are 'ways in which the concrete tools are used, reasons for selecting them and using them in particular ways' (Pea, 1993: 53), such as theories, signs, and arguments proletarians employ to convince other members of their class. Some of these abstract tools are used 'to *cause* another subject to perform an action, as in the case of verbal commands and traffic signals. It is in these cases that the sign most closely approximates a material tool in mediating action' (Wells, 2002: 49). Questions that need to be addressed regarding tools may range from old ways vs. new ways of doing things, old division of work vs. new division, etc. Wertsch *et al.* (1995: 25) remind us that abstract tools sometimes 'emerge for reasons other than to facilitate many of the kinds of action they in fact end up shaping'. These accidental and unexpected effects of tools are, to employ contemporary jargon, 'spin-offs' (Wertsch *et al.*, 1995: 26).

Tools have to act on *objects* in order to influence or alter them. An object of activity could be expressed as a state of need, an intention, a feeling, 'which motivates actors to look for different means to satisfy the need' (Hyppönen, 1998: 7). Alternatively, the object can be defined as the 'raw material' or 'problem space' at which the activity is directed and 'which is moulded and transformed into *outcomes* with the help of physical and symbolic, external and internal mediating tools' (CHAT, 1998; Hasan, 1998). Cole (1996) points out that this division between symbolic and material

Even nationalists have to sport a radical pose sometime!

is merely for the purpose of analysis and in reality objects are both symbolic and material at the same time. In the case of a demonstration, the object of activity could be something *specific* (e.g., demand for higher wages, the banning of fast food stores, an end to war, abolition of a tax etc.) or *general* (e.g., demand for the abolition of capitalism and the alienation associated with it). I think it is essential to emphasise this distinction as different demonstrators may have different views about the object of activity and the final object of activity may emerge gradually and in the course of the struggle. It is the *critical* transformation of the

---

our speech, in terms of the categories laid down by our scripts'. In other words, writing systems may initially be developed for mnemonic and communicative purposes, 'but because they are *read* they provide a model for language and thought'.

object into an outcome through mediational tools that 'motivates the existence of an activity' (Kuutti, 1996: 26).

Activities are exercised not in a vacuum but within a framework of *rules*. These refer to societal or local laws, customs, norms, policies, beliefs and strategies, which relate to the issue being foregrounded by the demonstration. *Rules* can change dramatically and in a relatively short span of time. For example, following the overthrow of autocracy in Russia in 1917, 'strikes and other previously illegal forms of work protest were suddenly legal' (Rosenberg and Koenker, 1987: 298). They were soon made illegal again by the Bolsheviks. The changing rules during these three periods (illegality under the autocracy, brief legality during the confusions immediately after the fall of autocracy and renewed illegality under the Bolsheviks) would lead to changing activity systems of proletarian protest.

I feel we should augment Activity Theory's category of 'rules' by using Bakhtin's (1994) distinction between 'official' and 'unofficial' ideology, and Raymond Williams's (1973; 1978) differentiation between 'residual', 'dominant' and 'emergent' forms of rules. Unoffical ideology is the general way in which members of the proletariat view the world and their problems. Official ideologies are,

> the systems of sign organisation where meaning tends to be at its most crystallized or inflexible. They are the accretion of periods of struggle over meaning between the competing social groups within a society (Greenslade, 1996: 123).

However, it is essential to remember that even official ideology could undergo dramatic change. What was considered acceptable behaviour, even customary, could suddenly become illegal. According to E. P. Thompson (1975) the passing of the 1723 Black Acts by Walpole and the Hanoverian Whigs 'created, at a stroke, some 50 new capital offences for crimes against property- particularly in forests' (Collins, 1999: 20). This then limits the activities of peasants and leads to resistance, which in turn transforms consciousness. The introduction of the poll tax and the initiation of pre-emptive hostilities against Iraq are two further examples of a rapid shift in the official ideology of the ruling class. Significantly, neither of these two examples were the culmination of a successful ideological assault on the proletariat. They were 'ready-mades' imposed suddenly and without much preparation. This fact partially explains the bosses' failure to cement their ideological encroachments.

In order to underscore the changing dimension of both 'official' and 'unofficial' cultures it is useful to introduce Williams's distinction between 'dominant', 'residual' and 'emergent' cultural processes. When a cultural process comes to overwhelm its epoch and impose itself on its institutions and modes of behaviour, it becomes in Williams's words 'dominant' (Williams, 1978: 121). Feudal and bourgeois cultures in the zenith of their power could be said to have been dominant. 'Residual' elements belong to a past era but significantly they are still active in the present. Both feudal and Christian ideas are examples of the residual still actively influencing the dominant bourgeois culture. The 'movement' around the issue of fox-hunting in Britain or 'honour' killings in Kurdistan are also *by and large* examples of residual cultural processes. Finally, there are cultural processes Williams calls 'emergent', which refer to 'new meanings and values, new practices, new significances' (Williams, 1973: 41). The various proletarian practices I have described throughout this thesis are examples of emergent cultural processes.

So the addition of these terms form Bakhtin and Williams help to differentiate various forms of activity rules. However and here is where things become slightly complicated, the residual and emergent elements within dominant culture are not always 'alternative' or truly 'oppositional'. Sometimes they may seem that way but in reality they have already been 'incorporated' within dominant culture. Their defiance is in other words a false one which ends up modernising official culture instead of undermine it. Emergent 'youth pop culture' would be an example of 'incorporated' processes.

By 'alternative' Williams means an anti-conformist individual or phenomenon. For instance, the painter Paul Gauguin championed an 'alternative' perspective to bourgeois culture by trying to find a different way to live. He migrated away from centres of capitalist development but ultimately discovered that capital was everywhere. *The only cultural process worth intensifying therefore are those emergent unofficial processes that Williams calls 'oppositional' or those with the potential to become so.* These 'oppositional' individuals/groups refer

Battle of Trafalgar Square

to those who choose a different way of living *and* want to change society in the process. Non-conformists such as Dada, Surrealism, Situationists and many anti-war and anti-poll tax rebels fall into this category.

Activity Theorists use the term *community*[84] as part of their conceptual analysis.

---

84 I assume, following Marx, that 'primitive community' was destroyed with the advent of classes and states, and that the true supercession of capital can only come about if a re-emergent community (*Gemeinwesen*) succeeds in abolishing capitalist society. In the *Economic* and *Philosophical Manuscripts* (1844/1984) Marx explained that community cannot be opposed to the individual and in excerpts from *James Mill's Elements*

As I believe this choice of terminology unfortunate, I have chosen to replace community with *milieu*, which refers to the immediate environment where the activity takes place and the individuals and sub-groups who share the same general object.

Various people involved in a demonstration divide responsibilities related to the achievement of the object of activity. These networks of relationships, views and responsibilities are mapped out using the concept of *division of work*. This refers to both the *technical* division of tasks between activists and the *social* division of power and privilege that may exist (Marx, 1867/1979; Rubin, 1982). It is patently obvious that different members may have conflicting conceptions about means and ends, tactics and strategies. Amongst other things, what differentiates a genuine activity from a pseudo-protest is that, a) proletarians are fully aware of the social and technical division of labour within their ranks, and b) they studiously strive to minimise these divisions in order to diminish the potential for the emergence of specialists (e.g., militant activists who may then set about to 'lead' the 'passive' masses).

As Leontiev (1977: 181) makes clear, one of the methodological advantages of AT concerns its claim to transcend the object-subject dichotomy which characterises idealistic research. It does so by proceeding from a pattern which includes activity as a mediator between subject and object. By activity Leontiev is referring primarily to *practical* social activity,

> The genetically initial and *fundamental* form of human activity is external activity, practical activity. This proposition has important implications, particularly as psychology, traditionally, has always studied the activity of thought and the imagination, acts of memory, and so on, since only such internal activity was considered psychological … In other words, it is *external activity* that *unlocks the circle of internal mental processes*, that opens it up to the objective world (Leontiev, 1977: 183).

This sounds somewhat tautological. As if to pre-empt such criticism, Leontiev elaborates his model,

> The subject-activity-object transitions form a kind of circular movement, so it may seem unimportant which of its elements or moments is taken as the initial one. But this is by no means movement in a closed circle. The circle opens, and opens specifically in sensuous practical activity itself. Entering into direct contact with objective reality and submitting to it, activity is modified and enriched; and it is in

---

of *Political Economy* (1844/1984) he goes further by suggesting that 'individuals are social men and their human beings is their *Gemeinwesen*' (Marx quoted in Camatte, 1978: 18). According to this definition there is no such thing as a community under capitalism, be it a 'European community', a 'mining community', a 'Turkish community' or a 'gay community'. These are examples of *false* communities even if one finds more solidarity amongst its members than the rest of 'civil society'. However, the zone of proletarian development (ZPD) is capable of creating pockets of autonomy where the bourgeois rules of society are temporarily suspended in favour of a 'proto-community'. Genuine strikes, demonstrations, carnivals and riots would be examples of this tendency.

this enriched form that it is crystallized in the product. Materialised activity is richer, truer than the consciousness that anticipates it (Leontiev, 1977: 188).

Now that we have briefly outlined the framework and terminology employed by AT, it may be useful to elaborate on the meaning of activity itself. Tolman (2001: 85), for instance, has traced the origins of the term 'activity' and come to the conclusion that Immanuel Kant represents a seminal figure in this regard. Tolman's position is that philosophical activity prior to Kant was mostly *theoretical* activity. With Kant there is the beginning of a shift away from theoretical towards practical activity. Both Fichte and Hegel began to take practical activity even more seriously than Kant (Tolman, 2001: 86). According to Fichte,

What makes the theoretical appear to come first is that practical principles are first encountered by reflection in their thinkability. But objects that can be thought represent an achievement that results from practical *striving* by the self to make things conform to itself (Tolman, 2001: 86).

Since Fichte's notion of practice was mainly mental, Tolman criticises him for remaining within a subjective idealistic framework. Both Kant and Fichte can also be criticised for basing their concept of activity not on real subjects but on what was termed Transcendental Subject- a certain 'inner essence' of the subject (Lektorsky, 1999: 106). Hegel merely changed the Transcendental Subject into Absolute Spirit. However, he did overcome some of Fichte's problems. For instance, using a master-bondsman allegory, Hegel explains how 'by having to provide for all the masters' needs, the bondsmen must come to master the physical world through labour' (Tolman, 2001: 88). Gradually we are arriving at a definition of 'self' as constituted in the activity- the social practice of labour. However, Tolman goes on to criticise Hegel for an account that remains 'fictional' (i.e., not based on concrete historical circumstances) and one that presumes 'the social relations of the constituting practice are naturally or even normatively oppressive' (Tolman, 2001: 89).

Marx (1844/1964: 110) corrects these deficiencies by basing his analysis on real human practical activity and by extending the investigation into the realm of social relations (instead of limiting himself to the needs of the self alone). So, Marx completed the shift 'initiated by Kant, from the primacy of theoretical activity to the primacy of practical activity by giving a fully concrete account of the latter' (Tolman, 2001: 91). Now 'activity as an object of study and activity as an explanatory principle' become complementary (Fichtner, 1999: 54). In other words, activity is not simply something that individuals do. Rather it could also be a mode of being 'by which organisms establish themselves as subjects of their life processes' (Fichtner, 1999: 55; Graeber, 2005:28). As human beings create a world of artifacts, they double themselves and in so doing 'create the possibility for looking at [themselves] from the outside' (Lektorsky, 1999: 108). Leontiev and others developed the strictly psychological aspects of activity and concluded that,

> ... man's [sic] consciousness, like his activity, is not additive. It is not a flat surface, nor even a capacity that can be filled with images and processes. Nor is it the connection of its separate elements. It is the internal movement of its 'formative elements' geared to the general movement of the activity which effects the real life of the individual in society. Man's activity is the substance of his consciousness (Leontiev, 1977: 202).

Consciousness is thus an indivisible whole, a 'higher integrative system' (Bozhovich, 1979: 7) including the rational, voluntary and emotional aspects of the individual.[85] Its development is both evolutionary and revolutionary. As Frolov (1984: 81-82) has observed 'consciousness must not be identified solely with knowledge and thinking in terms of language'. It develops through a person's activities in a system of social relationships and according to Leontiev these activities are hierarchically organised,

> Life or activity ... is not built up mechanically ... some types of activity are the leading ones at a given stage and are of greatest significance for the individual's subsequent development and others a subsidiary one (Leontiev, 1981: 395).

In fact they constitute a hierarchy of motives and the way individuals handle the conflict existing between these motives shapes consciousness. Activities may become juxtaposed or prioritised. The dialectical relationship between an individual and social activities may very well be asymmetrical but that does not mean the former is incapable of altering the latter, especially if individuals group themselves into a collectivity. In fact, in a recent text Stetsenko and Arievitch

---

85 There is a distinction between the dialectical analysis of consciousness and doctrines such as existentialism and phenomenology. In Ratner's words, '... existentialism and phenomenology study how consciousness is organised but never *what* it is dealing with or *why*. The form of consciousness is described but not its content' (Ratner, 1971: 97).

(2004: 493) have extended Leontiev's theory by looking *at the self as a leading activity*. 'The self is taken to be a process rather than an attribute', state Stetsenko and Arievitch, '[which] is constantly re-enacted and constructed by individuals anew in the ever-shifting balances of life' (Stetsenko and Arievitch, 2004: 493). Finally, an emphasis on activities is not to be misunderstood as devaluing agency and mediating semiotics. There is no direct or mechanistic relationship between consciousness and activity. However, consciousness is directed by activity and is also itself an active agent. As Ratner (1997: 3) has explained,

> … the term activity denotes social relations, systems, structures, and conditions which are actively created and re-created by humans. By definition, activity includes perceiving, analysing, evaluating, planning, imagining, reconceptualising, feeling, and other psychological processes.

In summary: we could link the above reflections on AT back to Vygotsky. His zone of proximal development is now redefined as the distance between the present line of activity (which is experienced as inadequate, reformist or dissatisfying) and a historically possible line of activity (which may resolve the contradiction). An activity system is in other words a 'virtual disturbance and innovation–producing machine' (Engeström, 1999). With this in mind, we can turn to our first case study- the anti-poll tax riot of 1999.

4.2 FIRST CASE STUDY: BATTLE OF TRAFALGAR SQUARE

4.2.1 Outline of The 1990 anti-poll tax riot

Take from the altars of the past the fire, not the ashes.

- French political philosopher, Jean Jaurès (1859-1914)

Around a quarter of a million people took to the streets of London on 31st March 1990 in order to protest against the poll tax. One acute observer commented,

> It was a beautiful day- the bourgeoisie must really learn the need to sabotage the weather! … the atmosphere was wonderful: like a carnival. People were happy, but this wasn't an empty, superficial happiness. This was happiness based on strength and power (Poll tax riot, 1990: 33).

According to Stott and Drury (2000: 253) 'at around 12:30 p.m. a vote was taken in the park, via a public address system and a show of hands, through which the crowd overwhelmingly supported a motion calling for a non-violent demonstration'. As the demonstration passed Downing Street, 'an increasing number began to stop and congregate … verbal abuse and missiles, including two smoke bombs, were thrown at [the police] from the crowed', but the majority were still peaceful at this stage (Stott and Drury, 2000: 255). The day, of course, is remembered for the massive riot that eventually ensued, with hundreds of injuries to the police and widespread looting. More than 400 people were arrested immediately and many more in the coming days. According to the BBC,

> The violence erupted just after 1600 BST following a peaceful march against the poll tax ...
> A group of protesters involved in a sit-in at Whitehall, close to the Downing Street entrance, refused to move after requests from police and stewards. As police arrested offenders, placards and cans were thrown from the crowd and the trouble spread to Charing Cross Road, Pall Mall, Regent Street and Covent Garden (BBC News, 31/3/1990).

The police temporarily withdrew from Trafalgar Square. In truth the state lost control for less than a day. It is worth remembering that during the last poll tax rebellion, Tyler's army had the run of the city for almost a week before he was lured to his death by envoys of King Richard II. It is also not clear exactly who started the riot. The leftists (i.e., left wing of capital) routinely asserted that 'police brutality' triggered the 'troubles'. 'The march came under sustained attack from heavily armed riot police', claimed the Trotskyist organisation *Workers' Power* (Workers' Power Global [a], No. 242, April 2000). The post-hoc analysis of revolutionaries was, as usual, far more honest,

> I don't believe that people need to justify ever attacking coppers and I want to avoid saying that the events were purely self-defence, a lot of it was, but we don't need any more excuses for fighting back ... The political rackets on the left have desperately tried to contain, control and divert this enormous movement. But the limits on their pathetic plans were shown up by the vast array of banners and placards: 'Bollocks to the Poll Tax', 'Bikers Against the Poll Tax' ... 'Yorkshire Miners against the Poll Tax', 'Communities ... charge!' ... From the beginning it was obvious that many people were unwilling to accept the boundaries that normally constrict and control us. The bollards and white tape erected by the police to hem in the masses were soon knocked over and cut to shreds. The march joyously spilled out across the road, leaving the few police to stare in bewilderment and fear. Suddenly, the aura of their uniforms was melting in front of our eyes (Poll tax riot, 1990: 22 and 33).

There was a sense, and not just amongst radicals, that the state had gone 'too far' by imposing a poll tax. There was an unstated feeling that the 'social contract' had been unilaterally renegotiated and now all bets were off. The slightest provocation caused fierce collective response. And there were moments when the police assaulted protesters without provocation. They always seem extremely over the top in the Strand. Four riot vans drove into the crowd for no apparent reason. When just past Lambeth Railway Bridge the cops tried to confiscate an anarchist flag, scuffles broke out (Poll tax riot, 1990: 9). The Parliament was a predictable target of anger,

We walked past the House of Parliament and Downing St, someone started the shout 'burn it down, burn it down, burn it down' just for a laugh, but thousands joined in. And a few hours later we almost did! (Workers' Power Global [b], 21 April 2000).

Anger was punctuated by moments of carnivalesque. Rioters taking time out to explain the intricate politics of the anti-poll tax campaign to baffled (but curious) tourists in the West End. People exchanging passionate kisses amidst a burning Trafalgar Square and protesters hassling not only the police by also the media,

A friend and I piss off a Sky TV crew who are trying to film the trouble by shouting rude things about Rupert Murdoch over each attempt they make to film their reporter. They fuck off to Trafalgar Square (Poll Tax Riot, 1990: 9).

There were moments of tension amongst the rioters as well as between them and the police. The throwing of wayward missiles by inexperienced rioters irked the more experienced protesters. As one protester stated, 'If missiles are thrown, then they must hit their intended target' (Poll tax riot, 1990: 34). Another example occurred outside the South African Embassy when radicals were thwarted in their attempt to generalise the riot to other embassies by 'single issue rioters',

At the South African Embassy some people pick up a crash barrier. I take hold of one end and we push it through an Embassy window. I shout at them to do the next one but they walk away. A punk guy tells me to 'just attack the cop, not property'. I ask him why. 'Because I said so!' he tells me (Poll tax riot, 1990: 10).

It appears that, for at least some of the protesters, attacking 'abnormal' and 'deviant' forms of nationalism was considered legitimate but not an all out assault on nationalism *per se*.

It has been pointed out that one contributing factor to the spread of the rioting was tactical mistakes made by the police on the day. Nowadays, the police make fewer mistakes and possess greater flexibility in dealing with disorder. In the 1990s, however, mistakes were commonplace. One mistake occurred outside the South African Embassy,

The police repeatedly tried to smash us up with cavalry charges up and down the road by the South African Embassy. The cavalry would charge and the crowd would part, let them through and hit the cavalry with every conceivable missile (Workers' Power Global [b], 21 April 2000).

Alternatively, police vans were slowed down by pushing crash barriers underneath them, followed by a volley of bricks and planks thrown at them. But perhaps the crucial blunder comes later in the day, when the police inadvertently spread the rioting to the West End,

... Eventually I rest up on the grass opposite Canada House. Watching the policing whilst eating my grub reveals that the police are like headless chickens. They are attempting to clear the area but instead of pushing us south to the Thames, they are pushing people into the West End (Poll tax riot, 1990: 11).

The law of value is temporarily suspended in favour of commodity liberation. As with visiting destruction on property, the looting is also very selective. The police are attacked but firefighters and ambulance crews are (mostly) left alone. Rioters patiently going through record shops to find that hard to come by Billie Holliday album, then stepping into restaurants for a free lunch. Ratners (a jewellers' shop) was looted but Collets, a trendy leftist (Stalinist to be more precise) bookshop in Charing Cross Road, was left unharmed. It may have had something to do with the huge poster of Marx displayed on the wall. Or perhaps, rioters were too busy looting other shops to burden themselves with heavy tombs of radical wisdom. In St Martin's Lane a Porsche was burnt to cinders. The destruction was again very discriminate. It is important to note that this was not an example of what some sociologists derogatorily refer to as 'flash looting'.[86] Most shops in the Covent Garden area were looted, however,

> ... a kiosk was still open, selling food to the rioters while two door down Barclays Bank had been trashed. Sport cars were forming a burning barricade across the road but 50 yards away motorists were being waved through the crowd. It was wealth that was the target (Poll tax riot, 1990: 52).

Ultimately even the left wing of capital had to concede that the event witnessed a remarkable display of proletarian autonomy,

> The stewards had disappeared but the improvisation of ordinary [sic] people was remarkable. They started organising friends, getting kids and families out of the way and then organising themselves against the police to defend the march (Workers' Power Global [b], 21 April 2000).

---

86 According to Roger Mac Ginty (2004: 859) 'flash looting, rather like flash flooding, is difficult to predict, is often the result of a number of extraordinary factors ...'. This is a dubious metaphor borrowed from meteorology which needs to be queried. First, why should anyone want to 'predict' looting? The dispossessed do not ordinarily worry themselves with such predictions. Vested interests (governments, insurance companies, businesses, armies and Non-Governmental Organisations), on the other hand, seem to spend considerable energy 'predicting' the next eruption in order to install preventive measures. Second, it is the lack of looting in a world characterised by massive poverty, desperation and need that is 'extraordinary' and not its occasional manifestation. Third, unless investigated from a very narrow empiricist, rationalist or positivist perspective, 'flash' lootings usually prove themselves to have a longer historical context. The looting that took place during the anti-poll tax riot in and around the West-End of London is best described as 'planned spontaneity' (i.e., people with grievances and little stake in society *planning* to protest against something they did not like and then *spontaneously* transforming into active looters).

185

There is a danger in trying to classify rioting, since classification could easily turn into a form of control (Foucault, 1994), which in the hands of sociology it invariably does (Korsch, 1971). However, in order to bring out the many-sidedness of the anti-poll tax riot/looting that occurred on the 31st March 1990, it may be helpful to employ a looting typology proposed by Roger Mac Ginty (2004: 866-868). Below I reproduce a table from Mac Ginty (2004: 866).

Table 4.1 – Typologies of looting (Mac Ginty, 2004)

Economic	Symbolic	Strategic	Selective
Absolute need	Trophy	Destructive	Ethnic
Contingency	Celebratory	Occupation	Commodity
Wage augmentation	Recreational		Area
Specialised market			

According to this typology the anti-poll tax rioting/looting contained elements from all four categories mentioned above. In the *economic* category, the anti-poll tax riot/looting was a form of 'wage augmentation'. The social wage of proletarians was under attack and this was combated by an acquisition spree. Under the *symbolic* category of looting, we witness two out of the three elements mentioned by Mac Ginty. There was 'trophy' looting. Rioters took pleasure in looting and later displaying objects without intrinsic value (e.g., one tone-deaf comrade liberated a clarinet from a music store). There was also 'celebratory' looting expressing the sense of power over the ruling class. The third major category of looting, *strategic* looting, refers to looting that is part of a wider politico-social project. Many of the looters, especially disaffected younger ones, saw this as an occasion to resume hostilities against authorities. The destruction associated with strategic looting is usually aimed at inflicting maximum damage on property (e.g., the burning of buildings). There was little occupational looting since the crowds were always on the move. Finally under the *selective* looting category, the anti-poll tax riot witnessed discriminatory attacks on government buildings and West-End businesses.

4 . 2 . 2 A n t i - P o l l T a x R i o t a s A c t i v i t y

The 31st March 1990 anti-poll tax riot in London clearly identified itself with the proletarian uprising against the same method of taxation some 600 years ago, when the Lord Chancellor's head was cut off and placed upon a pole at Tower Hill (Poll Tax Riot, 1990). Many perceived the 'social contract' to have been seriously violated by the introduction of the poll tax. Although the crowd may initially have been made up of a number of sub-groups with different agendas, methods of protest and motivation, the introduction of the poll tax and the fact that 'the police treated the crowd as single unit' created the conditions where 'violence' came to be perceived as a legitimate form of action (Stott and Drury, 2000: 261 and 263).

The rebellion was clearly directed against both political society and civil society, the latter defined as 'the social, economic and judicial relations in which we take part

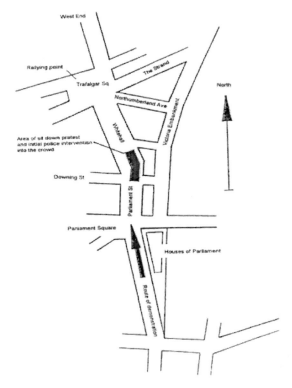

The route showing the latter stages of the demonstration including the area of sit down protest and initial police intervention (Stott and Drury, 2000: 254).

to satisfy' our *individual* needs (Jensen, 1999: 88). For Marx, civil society referred to 'private citizens, families and firms each ensuring their own interests and who all depend upon being able to exchange commodities and services with each other' (Jensen, 1999: 88). Whilst a series of articles and meetings reminded anti-poll tax activists of the significance of 'past glories', most were aware of the need to improve on history. After all,

> To transcend the civil society philosophically, one cannot simply recall forms of community beyond the grasp of civil [and political] society, or recall and reflect upon a harmonious past age, or give utopian visions of possible future forms of

communal life. Philosophical activity was, for Marx, to reflect critically upon the concepts and theories being used in practice and at the same time to take part in practices in order to attempt to overcome limitations and contradictions in practice. Transcending civil society is not partly a conceptual or theoretical matter and partly a practical matter; rather it is theoretical and practical at the same time (Jensen, 1999: 97).

The notion of activity is always best viewed from the perspective of the subject; in this case a typical 'mindless thug', a term employed by politicians and the media to describe demonstrators (Figure 4.1). Sociologists such as Charles Tilly (2003: 132) may more diplomatically refer to them as 'violent specialists' who are responsible for 'signalling spirals' where the feasibility of hitherto risky practices are conveyed to the rest of the crowd.[87] There were two main reasons behind the usage of derogatory terminology by the ruling class:

1)The use of such language was intended to exclude and stigmatise a subset of the proletariat considered problematic by the state. Collins provides an interesting example of the residents of Ferguslie Park (Paisley, Scotland) being treated in a similar fashion. Ferguslie became known in the 1970s as the longest *cul de sac* in Scotland and the derogatory term 'feegy parker' was introduced to describe someone 'living beyond the bounds of respectable and responsible society' (Collins, 1999: 186).

2) The advent of the 'sound-bites' makes gesture politics of this kind almost inevitable. In an empirical study Hallin (1992) has shown 'a steady and striking decrease in the average length of a sound bite from 60 seconds in [the 1968 US presidential election] to less than 9 seconds in 1988' (Hallin, 1992 quoted in Wertsch, 1995: 68). Technological determinism obviously has a role in this phenomenon but Hallin also points out that contemporary journalism has become more active in making the news. This means going beyond merely reproducing the words of politicians and employing sound bites in order to win viewers and beat off stiff competition from rival broadcasters.

---

87 There is a parallel here with the treatment of pupils whose behaviour is regarded as problematic or difficult to categorise. As Daniels and Cole (2002: 312) have pointed out, 'The nomenclature for these pupils has evolved and altered over the years from *the children of the dangerous and perishing class* ... or *Street Arabs* (the later Victorian era) ... to *moral imbeciles* in the early 1900s, to *maladjusted children* from c. 1930 to the 1980s'.

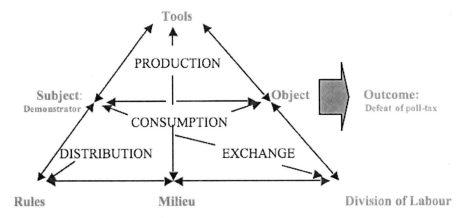

Figure 4.1 - Poll tax riot as Activity System

Figure 4.1 represents Engeström's expanded version of Vygotsky's original ideas. The expanded version enables 'an examination of system activity at the macro level of the collective' (Daniels and Cole, 2002: 314). The *object* of the demonstrator's activities is participation in a demo against the poll tax. The *outcomes* include intended defeat of the tax or failure to defeat the tax, as well as unintended outcomes such as possible extension of the riot to other sectors of the economy, ousting of Thatcher and the overthrow of the government. The *tools* include abstract ones such as theoretical and historical concepts (in the form of political leaflets) that determine the demonstrator's expectations and reactions towards various occurrences, as well as concrete tools such as, megaphones, flags and later in the day, when the demonstration has turned riotous, stones, molotov-cocktails, shields, and anything at hand. These tools as Vygotsky (1934/1986) pointed out serve a dual purpose; they both *mediate* and *transform* psychological processes. Different ways of thinking emerge as a result of the use of tools and the context within which activities are carried out (Cubero and Mata, 2001: 219). Specifically what undergoes qualitative change in thinking is 'the pattern of privileging, ways of speaking [genres] and discourse modes [types of argumentation] that mediate psychological activity through reference to various semiotic [and non-semiotic] tools' (Cubero and Manuel, 2001: 221).

Dialectical learning takes place when the *object* of activity (in this case abolishing the poll-tax) and the *motivation* of the activity (abolition of capitalism or even a vague, wishy-washy desire for a 'better world') coincide.[88] This coincid-

---

88 The analysis of a person's motivation for uttering a word *completes* our understanding of his/her words. Vygotsky emphasised this point. Understanding the speaker's motivation is a criterion by which radical dialogic interaction is distinguished from bourgeois 'dialogue' (an example where the speaker's motivation is deliberately foregrounded can be found in the questionnaires appearing throughout issue number 3 of *The Annual Review of Critical Psychology*, cf. Melancholic Troglodytes, 2003).

ence is the hallmark of an activity. By contrast an action is 'a situation in which the objective and motivation do not coincide' (Dunne, 1995; Leontiev, 1981: 209-210). The problem in most demonstrations (especially 'single issue campaigns') is that the objective and motivation remain separate. Going on a CND demonstration with the objective of achieving nuclear disarmament will not attain the motivation of the participants to live in a safe world because biological, chemical, conventional weapons as well as the everyday routine of capitalist life can kill people with the same venom and because the abolition of nuclear weapons is intertwined with the abolition of states and nationalism.

The *milieu* consists of fellow-minded 'thugs', in this case groups of 'communists', 'anarchists', 'situationists', 'autonomists', and the usual leftist opportunists in the shape of Leninist hangers-on trying in vain to control the 'mob'. The milieu expands during the day as more and more 'ordinary' workers join the demonstrators and are quickly radicalised as a result of their experiences. The *social* division of labour is non-existent as everyone has an equal right to express their views and participate in decision making but there is a *technical* division of labour as different sections of the proletariat bring different competencies to the occasion. Some are better at throwing molotov-cocktails; some engage in hand-to-hand fighting with riot cops; some try to convince fence-sitters to join in through debate whilst others bandage the injured and relay information. At the extreme margin there are those who spend the whole day running from trouble and yet others who suffering from a 'Spartacus Syndrome', fancying themselves as generals, organise their battalions from a safe distance. Finally, the *rules* regulate the use

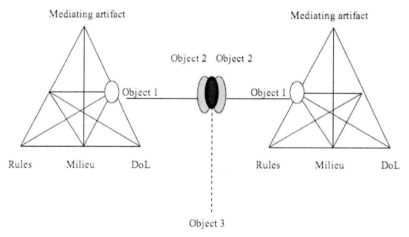

Figure 4.2 – Two interacting activity systems as minimal model (Engeström, 1987) [DoL stands for Division of Labour]

of time and space, with the rebels imposing their own definition of carnivalesque time and space on the proceedings and querying the organisation of society based on the law of value and private property. The poll-tax demonstration was one of the clearest examples of 'prolepsis' seen in recent years- the ability or power of subjects to imagine the future in the light of the past. In a dialectical activity system,

> time is an inherent aspect of events and is not divided into separate units of past, present, and future. Any event in the present is an extension of previous events, and is directed toward goals that have yet been accomplished. As such the present extends through the past and future and cannot be separated from them (Rogoff, 1995: 155).

Figure 4.2 shows two interacting activity systems as a minimal model for understanding dialogues, multiple perspectives and the dynamic flow of time. These are networks of activities within which 'contradictions and struggles take place in the definition of the motives and object of the activity' (Daniels, 2004: 124). Different subjects, depending on their personal histories and position in the division of labour, will construct the object and the other components of the activity in different, partially overlapping and partially conflicting ways (CHAT, 1998). In Ratner's (1997) words, 'individuals occupy different combinations of [activity] fields'. Depending on which combination of activity field the individual occupies and also based on how he/she has socialised the rules of activity and whether contradictions are resolved or not, they may or may not engage in *creative* imaginal thinking. Ratner (2000: 19) states the potential of creative thinking,

> Certainly, not all imagination profoundly understands and advances emotional phenomena or society as a whole. Most imagination works within the system – e.g., to devise a strategy for finding a job or a spouse – without comprehending or changing it significantly [this is what Luria called 'mechanical imagination']. Thus, imagination and creativity are not necessarily emancipating. They only become so if they are cultivated and utilised to critically examine cultural phenomenon. [My addition]

So, in the same way that violence amongst rioters can be a camouflage for a basically conservative political agenda, *mechanical* forms of imagination could also be no more than reinforces of the status quo. *Creative* imagination, on the other hand, allows individuals to go beyond egocentricity and conceive of others around them as real desiring machines,

> Ilyenkov[89] in his writings stated directly that imagination is the only thing that enables a person to conceive others' positions and potentialities. It is imagination

---

89 I quote Ilyenkov advisedly since I find many problems with his formulations, for example, his conception of art. David Bakhurst (2001: 190) in a critical assessment of Ilyenkov's aesthetics (which for me is not critical enough) points out, 'Ilyenkov's dismissal of pop art is undeniably rather crude ... one wonders whether he simply lacked the cultural resources to form a nuanced understanding of the art he derides'. In this regard at least, Ilyenkov strikes me as a 'social realist' with odious moralising tendencies.

that enables a person to look at himself [sic] through other people's eyes (cited in Davydov, 1999: 48).

Ilyenkov's concept of imagination is interesting. Imagination is partly the ability to envisage the potential of things, of what can be. It is partly the ability to 'see particular facts in a way that simultaneously captures their uniqueness and reveals how certain general schema are applicable to them' (Bakhurst, 2001: 193). Finally, it is also the capacity to grasp connections and wholes that were perceived in isolation before. Bakhurst even suggests that for Ilyenkov 'free creativity is a kind of life principle' (Bakhurst, 2001: 196).

To tease out creative imagination from mechanical imagination is useful because it is the former that signifies a genuine zone of proletarian development. The connections made between neighbourhood assemblies and workplace assemblies, the tactics employed by protesters to disrupt the courts and the executive arm of the state, the connections made between an unpopular tax and a full assault on capitalist relationships suggest the anti-poll tax campaign encouraged the development of creative rather than mechanical imagination.

What is essential is that in this multi-voiced activity system there should be constant renegotiation of rules, with reactionary rules altered, abolished and reinterpreted as required. Nodes of activity should constantly move around, otherwise multi-voicedness could become merely a source of conflict instead of achievement.[90] 'What initially appears as object may soon be transformed into an outcome, then turned into an instrument, and perhaps later into a rule', writes Engeström (Engeström, 1996).

Level		Oriented towards		Carried out by	
ACTIVITY	--	OBJECT/MOTIVE	--	MILIEU	ORGANISATION
ACTION	--	GOAL	--	INDIVIDUAL/ GROUP	
OPERATIONS	--	CONDITIONS	--	ROUTINIZED HUMAN OR MACHINE	SPONTANIETY

Table 4.2 – Three level structure of activity proposed by Leontiev

Before going further we need to add two more layers of complexity to our model. Firstly, there is Leontiev's useful distinction between 'activity', 'action', and 'operations' and,

---

90 It would be a mistake to fetishize fluidity, since fluidity within and between activity systems is not an automatic measure of achievement. Racist pogroms, after all, can be described as fluid activity systems. One has to bear in mind all other aspects of the activity (such as rules, the subject-tool-object triangle and the milieu engaged in the activity).

secondly, the introduction of the concept of 'primary', 'secondary', 'tertiary, and 'quaternary' contradiction. Without contradiction then familiar problems would be dealt with in a familiar way 'as long as the requirements of the activity setting continue to be the same as before. In such a setting the need for change does not arise' (Cubero and Mata, 2001: 233). Development could then be redefined as the 'setting up and solving [of] contradictions; it is the form of mobility, the realisation of the contradiction' (Fichtner, 1999: 59).

Leontiev's three-level model of activity assumes that collective activity (the uppermost level) is driven by an object-related motive. In fact, the object of activity is, for Leontiev, its *motive*. This motive, 'may be both material and ideal; it may be given in perception or it may exist only in imagination, in the mind' (Leontiev, 1977: 184). The object of abolishing the poll tax, for instance, drives the activity of demonstrating. The middle level, which can be either individual or group dominated, consists of actions driven by a conscious goal; and the bottom level consists of automatic operations driven by the conditions and tools of the action at hand. A mixture of *spontaneity* and *organisation* determines each level, although the balance alters as we move up and down the model, with the highest level displaying the greatest amount of organisation (and least amount of spontaneity) and the lowest level depending mostly on spontaneous reaction against external conditions. Another way of putting it would be that 'activity systems evolve over lengthy periods of socio-historical times, [whereas] actions are relatively short-lived, with a temporally clear-cut beginning and end ... [and] operations are dependent on the conditions in which the action is performed' (CHAT, 1998: 8). So in our example, abolishing the poll tax would be an activity system consisting of many meetings, debates, and demos over a number of months, the 31st March demonstration would then be an action, which was intended with a clear beginning and a routine endpoint. However, things did not go according to plan because the operations engaged in by both sides (demonstrators and the state) had unforeseen consequences.

Spontaneous operations during a demonstration are not the only source of contradiction. An activity system interacts with a whole array of other activity systems, each of them capable of introducing major contradictions into the system. Both external and internal factors are capable of creating imbalance. This disequilibrium is not necessarily problematic - far from it. 'The activity system is constantly working through contradictions within and between its elements. In this sense, an activity system is a virtual disturbance-and-innovation-producing machine' (CHAT, 1998: 9).

In fact, contradictions help us overcome what Vygotsky called 'fossilised behaviour', that is, behaviour that no longer changes (van der Veer, 2001: 97). Certain behaviours have been repeated so many times, that they have become automatic (e.g., typing or a formulaic march through a well-known route). We need to 'liquefy' the fixed behaviour by working through the contradiction and this involves going back to earlier stages of development. For instance, attending leftists planning sessions prior to the anti-war demonstration of February 2003 was an instructive lesson in 'crowd management'. The organisers spent most of their time discussing stewarding tactics and crowd discipline, since they were anxious to be 'responsible'. Gradually a secular leftist sense of crowd control (associated with counter-revolutionaries like the Socialist Workers' Party) became linked to a religious interpretation of discipline (associated with counter-revolutionaries like CND and the Muslim Association of Britain). The fossilised behaviour of most of the crowd on the march had its origins in the *contradiction-busting* ideology of the organisers.

Il'enkov's (1977) original work on inner contradiction has more recently been categorised into four levels of contradictions that every activity system displays, imaginatively designated as 'primary', 'secondary', 'tertiary' and 'quaternary' contradictions (Engeström, 1999).

The *primary* contradiction permeates all activities in capitalist socio-economic formation because it is the contradiction between exchange and use value. It occurs *within* each constituent of the central activity. The demonstrator who organises against the poll tax, for instance, is bringing to the fore the conflict between a mode of *living* based on human needs and genuine desires as opposed to a mode of *existence* founded on the profit motive. Engeström (1999), for example, has looked at this primary contradiction between the excitement of competitive Finnish baseball (use value) and potential monetary profit (exchange value). He shows how once the activity system of official betting enters the equation, the potential for corruption (in the form of unauthorised changes to the rules of the game of baseball) are immense.

The introduction of new external elements into the central activity creates *secondary* contradictions *between* the constituent elements. For instance, the introduction of a set of 'anti-terrorist' legislatives to oppress anti-poll tax demonstrators may create conflict between the new *object* and traditional *instruments* of protest or the *rules* by which rebels have conducted themselves hitherto.

A *tertiary* contradiction appears when 'a culturally more advanced object and motive is introduced into the activity ... The new ideas may be formally implemented but internally resisted by the vestiges of the old activity' (CHAT, 1998: 10). In our example, the emergence of a new consciousness amongst demonstrators that single-issue campaigns cannot dent the totality of capitalist relationships may be resisted by practitioners of 'single issue campaigns'. Alternatively, law-abiding demonstrators will resist the tactical changes that 'anti-terrorist laws' may force on demonstrators, as they are unable to accept that the rules of the 'game' have been fundamentally altered. Likewise, rebels with a nationalistic or parochial consciousness have historically resisted the introduction of new tactics/strategies from 'abroad'.

Finally, there are *quaternary* contradictions, which appear between the changing central activity and its neighbouring activities when they interact. For instance, during the anti-poll tax campaign, whenever leftist militants came into contact with genuine revolutionaries, there was conflict and tension. Accustomed as they were to hierarchies, 'democratic centralism', vanguardist politics, secrecy and elitism, the leftist militants (e.g. Militant Tendency, Socialist Workers' Party, Green Anarchists, etc) were unable to adjust to new ways of *doing* revolution.

It is important to view these contradictions not negatively but as fruitful sources of learning. Lave and Wenger (1991, cited in Engeström, 1996: 162) propose an approach to the notion of learning based on gradually increasing participation in a 'community of practice' (again I would prefer the term 'milieu' instead of 'community' for reasons explained earlier). Their investigation into different forms of apprenticeship, ranging from Mexican Yucatec midwives to American meatcutters and anonymous alcoholics, shows that although 'there is very little observable teaching [there is] a lot of well-motivated and effective learning. Learning commonly proceeds from less important, simple tasks toward crucial and complete *core* tasks' (Lave and Wenger cited in Engeström, 1996: 162). This is also true of proletarian demonstrations, although here spontaneous innovations play a greater role. Learning is most easily passed on when there is:

Accessibility- when demonstrators have active access to different parts of the activity,

Interaction- when there is abundant horizontal communication between demonstrators, and

Transparency- when the technologies and inner mechanisms of the demonstration are transparent to all and easily inspected (Lave and Wenger cited in Engeström, 1992: 162).

'*... time is an inherent aspect of events and is not divided into separate units of past, present, and future' (Rogoff, 1995: 155).*

If the three criteria outlined above are met then contradictions can be resolved in favour of the proletariat and learning can become 'expansive' (Engeström, 1996: 168). 'The expansive learning approach', writes Engeström, 'exploits the actually existing conflicts and dissatisfactions' among the milieu involved in the activity system, 'inviting them to join in a concrete transformation of the current practice'. This form of learning is a 'process of learning through self-organisation from below'. You go beyond the available information to construct a broader object for your activities. You learn by constructing a new activity. He goes on to explain that as prevalent practices show signs of crisis, collectivities of people must become good expansive learners, so that they can design and implement their own futures.

The radical student movement of the 1960s would be a clear example of expansive learning where the students tried to transcend the limitations of bourgeois education.

This cycle of development goes through various phases. During the first phase a vague sense of discontentment emerges against a limited number of individuals perceived as oppressors/exploiters. In the second phase this discontentment becomes better focused and there is a sharpening of contradiction. Finally, in the third phase, a new object and motive for the activity system are outlined in order to overcome the contradiction. Essentially, 'expansive learning is energised by historically accumulated developmental contradictions within and between activity systems, and it is triggered by disturbances and innovative actions' (Engeström, 2000: 309). It is precisely these 'accumulated developmental contradictions' that are giving way to the emergence of historically specific form of zoped which Newman and Holzman (1993a) call the Zone of Proletarian Development (ZPD).

This type of joint activity not only enhances learning but as Drury and Reicher (1999) have observed from a different perspective, it also empowers participations. This enhanced sense of power during an anti-poll tax demonstration outside a town hall, 'increased the range of collective protest actions which seemed possible' (Drury and Reicher, 1999: 392). This empowered self-perception endured 'and formed a new starting point for subsequent forms of collective actions'. They conclude their study by suggesting, 'empowerment is a product *as well as a precondition* of collective action' (Drury and Reicher, 1999: 392). [Emphasis added]

4.3 SECOND CASE STUDY: THE ANTI-WAR DEMOSTARTION OF FEBRUARY 2003

4.3.1 Outline of the million (plus) anti-war London demonstration (15 February 2003)

> There is nothing more terrible than a class of barbaric slaves who have learned to regard their existence as an injustice, and now prepare to avenge, not only themselves, but all generations.
>
> - Friedrich Nietzsche, *The Birth of Tragedy*, 1872/1994: 8

Britain had never seen anything like it! The numbers took everyone, the police, the media, the politicians, the organisers and the radicals by surprise. The one million plus attendees seem even more remarkable when compared to the

50,000 (plus) who took part in the famous 1968 Grosvenor Square demonstration against the Vietnam War (Dorota Nosowicz, The Observer, Sunday 16 February 2003). Here is how Euan Ferguson of the Observer (16 February 2003) described it,

> It was the biggest public demonstration ever held in Britain, surpassing every one of the organisers' wildest expectations and Tony Blair's worst fears, and it will be remembered for the bleak bitterness of the day and the colourful warmth of feeling in the extraordinary crowds. Organisers claimed that more than 1.5 million had turned out; even the police agreed to 750,000 and rising ... There were, of course, the usual suspects - CND, Socialist Workers' Party, the anarchists. But even they looked shocked at the number of their fellow marchers: it is safe to say they had never experienced such a mass of humanity.

Ferguson even tells us that, 'One group of SWP stalwarts were joined, for the first march in any of their histories, by their mothers', failing to mention that the mothers displayed more radicalism than their children. Incidentally, many people became so disenchanted with the SWP using the Stop The War Coalition as a recruiting ground that they left the Coalition, *without leaving the anti-war movement*. This shows a commendable level-headedness.

In Rome around two million people demonstrated (apparently led by leftists like Italian cinema heroes, Roberto Benigni and Nanni Moretti) and in Glasgow 50,000. All in all Millions marched through more than 300 cities in over 60 countries (Paul Harris *et al.*, The Observer, 16 February 2003). The only anomaly was the muted nature of protests in Middle East countries. Apart from small peaceful marches in Iran, Syria, Bahrain and Yemen, the region's streets were eerily silent. In Britain, the naïve optimism of the majority of protesters was captured in these terms,

> Cheshire fireman nearby said: 'they will take notice of a protest like this. Our MPs, and Blair himself, were voted in by ordinary people like those here today. Blair is clever enough not to ignore this' (Euan Ferguson, The Observer, 16 February 2003).

Ferguson also captures some of the empowerment experienced by inexperienced demonstrators,

> I've never felt strongly enough about anything before. But this is so different; I would have let myself down by not coming and I think this will be something to remember (Euan Ferguson, The Observer, 16 February 2003).

The 'usual suspects' (teachers, firefighters, health and council workers) were joined on the march by first time demonstrators. Marchers included a group of Bedford taxi drivers called Britons Versus Bush and a collection of DJs dubbed Ravers Against the War (Simon Jeffrey and agencies, The Guardian, 15 February 2003). The mix created novel elements,

Swirling kilts, tartan and Saltires mingled with Palestinian, Chilean, Basque flags and even a stars and stripes (albeit with the words 'stop the war' plastered across the stripes). Muslim Alliance placards were carried aloft by groups of middle-aged, middle-class women who admitted they 'hadn't a clue' what the groups' initials stood for (Euan Ferguson, The Observer, 16 February).

The depth of feeling in Scotland was such that two ordinarily reactionary institutions, the Church and the Conservative Party, were forced to side with the crowds. The Church even played an organisational role in the march and rebel Tories went against leadership advice by participating in anti-war protests,

> Iain Duncan Smith may have given his backing for an attack on Iraq, but a solitary banner indicated that the Greenock and Inverclyde Conservatives do not stand shoulder to shoulder with him (Euan Ferguson, The Observer, 16 February).

Yet another bourgeois organisation, the Campaign for Nuclear Disarmament (CND), also felt the impact of people's radicalism when a breakaway group formed the alternative Trade Union CND. The original group lost members and funds to the new TUCND, forcing it to open negotiations for a merger (Jim Barnes, The Guardian, 3 December, 2003). This group in turn became a target for leftist infiltrators. There were allegations of officer positions within CND and TUCND being monopolised by Stalinist and Trotskyist organisations (Patrick Wintour and Rebecca Allison, The Guardian, 1 December 2003). These groups were probably trying to infiltrate CND/TUCND in order to use their position to put pressure on the Stop the War Coalition which, as it is well known, is a front for yet another tawdry opportunistic leftist organisation, the Socialist Workers' Party,

> Mr Barnes [a TUCND bureaucrat] claims the Communist Party and Socialist Action sought control of CND in order to use the campaign as a base from which to exert influence over the Stop the War coalition, the loose body which organised the massive protests against the war in Iraq. Mr Barnes asserts the coalition is increasingly dominated by another Trotskyist group, the Socialist Workers' Party (Patrick Wintour and Rebecca Allison, The Guardian, 1 December 2003).

Thankfully all these middle class bolshevik, social democratic and liberal machinations did not put off the overwhelming bulk of protesters. Mary Riddell (The Observer, 16 February 2003) captured some of the subtle implications of the march succinctly,

> Political leaders hate crowds. Mass meetings have been supplanted by leaks and soundbites. In the fractious build-up to war, lonely societies are encouraged to become more solipsistic. A fearful population, hiding behind its anthrax-proofed windows, is also tractable. There is nothing threatening to government about citizens bickering

over the last roll of duct tape in Wal-Mart ... British marchers have spurned isolation for solidarity, and fear for fury. Their momentum came almost from nowhere. Unlike the Jubilee-trippers, the Soham mobsters and even the Countryside Alliance, they bore no social or political barcode ... Theirs was, and is, a movement without a leader. Its members belong to no obvious political caste. Labour voters who march are deracinated from their leaders, and the Tories have none worth worrying about.

4.3.2 Anti-war demonstration as activity

In this section I would like to briefly analyse the political significance of the million (plus) London anti-war demonstration of February 2003. I will start by drawing upon a useful text, which appeared as a post-hoc study of the demo in the journal *Aufheben* (2004: 28-35). However, the main analysis will be based on the tenets of Activity Theory.

The *Aufheben* text begins by describing the majority of protesters as 'humanist' rather than class conscious (Aufheben, 2004: 28). The prime movers of the march, whether religious (CND, TUCND and Muslim Association of Britain) or secular (Stop the War Coalition of middle class leftists ably supported by sections of the media and the ruling class), were hoisting the banner of pacifism, social democracy or liberalism, bourgeois rights of nations to self-determination, and the international rule of law.

It is, of course, difficult to know what proportion of the protesters were proletarians as opposed to petty bourgeois. It is impossible to deny, however, that revolutionary discourse basing itself on a negation of nationalism and capitalism was marginalised. In Bakhtinian terminology two 'speech genres' addressed the same situation using different mediational means. First-time proletarian protesters came to 'ventriloquate' (Bakhtin, 1986) their opposition through the pacifist genre. Since the overwhelming majority of protesters meekly succumbed to their leaders' agenda and rejected the more radical narratives of the war, it is difficult to disagree with Aufheben's assessment of protestors as 'humanist'. However, it is worth pointing out that this is a shallow and declining 'bourgeois humanism' which having had its heyday during the Enlightenment is today a former shadow of itself (Mattick, 1978: 158).

I also agree with Aufheben's assessment regarding the desire on the part of protesters to go beyond bourgeois media coverage of the events and comprehend the full complexity of the factors involved,

This desire to grasp what was happening would appear to be one of a number of differences between reactions to this Gulf War and that in 1991 ... The lack of a decisive conclusion to the war, with no arsenal of 'weapons of mass destruction' (WMD) being found, and the quick victory turning into a bloody messy occupation, has led to a questioning of motives behind and reasoning for the war (Aufheben, 2004: 29).

199

It is noteworthy how ideologies that have hitherto served the ruling classes well are beginning to act counter-productively. If anti-Arab racism, as manifested in countless Hollywood movies, has clouded the judgment of key policy makers in Washington D.C. (and led to a systematic underestimation of the *enemy's* capabilities), then the obsession with empirical 'facts' has led many 'citizens' to withdraw their support from the state in the absence of evidence for WMD. This blatant racism was also perceived by many 'western' citizens as a direct attack on their 'rights', further eroding support for war. The observation that even racism and empiricism may be transformed from boons to hindrance for the bosses is indicative of a gradual undermining of bourgeois hegemony. I will return to this point presently.

The cold February 2003 anti-war march in USA

Another feature which differentiated the march from previous anti-war demonstrations during the First Gulf War and Kosovo was the presence of many first-time protesters including a vocal and radical contingent of school-students. According to Aufheben (2004: 32-33),

> ... While there were some schoolkid [sic] elements on the 1991 Gulf war demos, and while children have always been involved in protests – both with adults and

on their own – we have to go back as far as the 60s or 70s to find anything on re-motely the same scale ... The kids' demos had their own feel and flavour ... They also showed little respect for adults at times ... This lack of respect applied to the adult protesters as well as to the cops. For example, on the first day of the war, when the Brighton kids' protest march arrived at the location they were due to meet up with other protesters, some of the adults wanted the kids to stay and wait until more numbers turned up. But the kids simply ignored this and carried on sweeping through town. They didn't seem to have time for the experience of adults because they were confident in the effectiveness of their own actions.[91]

The children had created their own zoped without recourse to more experienced adults. The advantages of this sensibility were obvious. The children were not socialised into a

tradition of conformism and defeat as so many of their elders have been. They neither knew their own limitations nor were they aware of the brutality of the state when cornered. Aufheben (2004: 33) continues,

> [The children] brought some cheek and unpredictability to what they did. They also brought some radicality, as demonstrated by their willingness to get stuck in on occasions: kids hurled pen-cils, etc. at the cops for example at Trafalgar Square protests, and stoned an army recruitment of-fice in Oxford.

Perhaps more significant than discov-ering new use values for haberdashery items, is the fact that their protest had an organic element to it and was not purely moralistic[92] in nature. By or-

---

91 Engeström gives an example of 'kid-power' where children consciously entreated (limited and conditional) adult support. A spokesperson for the Children's Campaign for Nuclear Disarmament initiated in the United States in June 1981 stresses, 'We do need adults' support in some way. We need adults to give us money ... to drive us around and feed us when we have meetings ... but it's very important that kids have their own groups, that kids [sic] are speaking directly to kids' (Engeström, 1987: 123).

92 As Aufheben (2004: 34) has correctly noted, 'The dominant slogan on the protests before the war was *Not in my name*, summing up perfectly the individualised, democratic and essentially moral argument against the war ... after Christmas, the dominant slogan became *Stop the War*'.

ganic I mean their anti-war protests were linked to their demands for improved conditions as school children. The graffiti sprayed during their protests is a good example, 'Stop the war! PS We want to wear trainers to school'! School discipline became a target for school children and the dictatorship of time and space they are subjected to in preparation for a life as wage-slaves was exposed in a series of mini-disputes with school authorities. Another example, is how school children 'who massed around Parliament Square on March 12th, ten days before war broke out, not only resisted the police but also underground train fares' (Aufheben, 2004: 33).

We can see how as with the anti-poll tax campaign, the social contract was being questioned and in places abandoned by protesters. However, in the case of the anti-war movement bourgeois hegemony was also put under erasure in a way not realised during the anti-poll tax campaign. Earlier I mentioned how, in places, even empiricism and racism were becoming counter-productive for the bosses. This led them to experiment with alternative methods of deception. Since the initiation of hostilities in a 'preemptive strike' situation required a more comprehensive PR blitz than usual, the official ideology of the ruling class employed its full repertoire to downbeat opposition. Mey (1985) has looked at the manipulative use of language in securing capitalist relationships,

> For Mey the process operates at two levels - the *oppressive* and the *repressive*. Oppressive uses of language seek to exclude or constrain alternative use of language by subordinate groups … Repressive uses of language … function to inhibit the crystallization of alternative uses of language and modes of consciousness in the first place (Collins, 1999a: 105) [emphasis added].

There is yet a more sophisticated method of manipulation, which Mey does not mention. The Situationists called it *recuperation*. What they meant by recuperation was more than mere co-option of subversive ideas. It involved turning them on their head and misusing them in order to strengthen bourgeois hegemony (Debord, 1987).

Repressive uses of language would include religious discourse, especially of the *fundamentalist* variety. When Mussolini, Khomeini and Bush claim that only God can judge them, they are trying to close the door to alternative modes of discourse. When Stalin sanctifies Diamat as the only legitimate form of discourse, he is employing a secular form of repression.

However, once subversive ideas are out in the public domain, repression is no longer an option. Now the bourgeoisie may attempt *oppression*. Radical ideas are constrained, contained, marginalised and excluded from nodes of power. Social democratic leaders who are supposed to be on the side of protesters aid this process by not contesting the dominant meanings of seminal terms. Collins (1999a: 173) provides us with examples of social democratic trade union leaders during the Upper Clyde Shipbuilders Work-In (1971) failing to contest the meanings of 'co-operation' and 'negotiation' as they appeared in the dominant discourse. Similarly, leading social democrats such as Tony Benn and other Labour Party stalwarts refused to contest the meanings of terms like 'peace', 'war' and 'disobedience' during the anti-war campaign. By contrast, the firefighters' dispute (2002-2003) and the post-workers' conflict (2007) in Britain saw the active contestation of terms such as 'modernisation' as related to their industry, forcing union leaders to strike a more radical pose just to keep up. Oppressive use of language has its limits, however, and once the bourgeoisie has regained its confidence it could embark on a more sophisticated project of recuperation. When Situationist inspired detourned cartoons are used by the advertising industry to sell more commodities we witness a classic example of recuperation.

Activity Theory insists that language itself does not have emancipatory potential. 'Rather it is primarily the actual contexts in which speakers are concretely located which either have, or do not have, this potential' (Collins, 1999a: 171). Moreover, in AT context is defined in terms of joint activity unlike cognitive psychology which focuses on the study of individual as a separate entity,

> Context is not an outer container or shell inside of which people behave in certain ways. People consciously and deliberately generate context (activities) in part through their own objectives; hence context is not just 'out there'. Context is both internal to people -involving specific objects and goals- and, at the same time, external to people, involving artifacts, other people, specific settings. The crucial point is that in activity theory, external and internal are fused, unified (Nardi, 1996: 78).

Apart from the participation of school children, the greater number of protesters involved and a more sophisticated bourgeois media campaign, there was also one further feature that differentiated the anti-war campaign from the anti-poll tax struggle, namely, the variety of organisations on offer. The period preceding the war and its immediate aftermath witnessed the generalisation and consolidation of a number of anti-war 'organisations' which practiced different methods of mobilisation. As with Foley (1998) I believe most forms of self-mobilisation are inherently 'educational'. However, we must not homogenise mobilisation and give all its various forms equal weight. Subsequently, following Engeström *et al.* (1999: 346) I would like to classify these mobilisations into three categories: *teams, networks* and *knotworks.*

By *teams* Engeström *et al.* (1999: 346) mean 'relatively stable configurations' with more or less clear division of labour, rules, and lines of demarcation. Teams have a history and a number of formalised rituals and being initiated into a team usually involves mastering these aspects of teamwork. Examples of groups that fetishized teamworking in our context would include leftist organisations such as Stop the War Coalition, CND, the Anarchist Federation and the Muslim Association of Britain.[93]

---

93 Since in general the response of the Muslim 'community' to systematic demonisation by the British press in

However, it is noteworthy that even genuine radical organisations could have a team-working dimension.

Another form of organisation/mobilisation is referred to by Engeström *et al.* (1999: 346) as *networks*. These too are stable structures, although they do not have a centralised leadership and the rules governing its workings are loose, non-hierarchical and informal. The plethora of anti-war groups established by school children, pensioners and non-affiliated citizens, social centres, prisoner support groups, as well as virtual networks on the Internet (e.g., IndyMedia) fall into this category. These networks are faced with the challenge of coordinating complex arrangements of different services which do not rely on each other's advice on a daily basis. Stable teams do not seem to be sufficient for such challenges, particularly as networks demand more time to get acquainted with political issues and reach conclusions.

There is a third form of organisation/mobilisation when participants 'literally [construct] the collaborative relations on the spot as the task [demands]' (Engeström *et al.*, 1999: 346). This is called *knotworking*:

> Hey dude, we're knotworking here. Do you mind?

The notion of knot refers to a rapidly pulsating, distributed and partially improvised orchestration of collaborative performance between otherwise loosely connected actors and activity systems ... we [would] argue that knotworking is a historically significant new form of organising ... connected to the emergence of new co-configuration models of production ... knotworking is characterised by a pulsating movement of tying, untying and retying together other-wise separate threads of activity ... the locus of initiative changes from moment to moment within a knotworking sequence (Engeström *et al.*, 1999: 346).

Emergency knotworking

---

recent years has been the development of an insular culture, some may argue that the genuine interest of a minority of Muslims in teamworking (whether of the Leninist or Anarchist variety) during the anti-war campaign was a positive change. I prefer to reserve my judgment. My position is that this change can only be perceived as 'positive' on condition that once the limitations of Leninist and Anarchist teamworking become obvious, the participants move onto more interesting political terrain.

204

It would be suspiciously convenient if we were to suggest that *teamworking*,[94] with its unresolved divisions of labour and formalised rule structure, was a typical structuralist Leninist organisational form whilst *networking*, characterised by non-hierarchal relations, stood for post-structuralist forms of organisation. Presumably we would then have to round off this cosy narrative by suggesting *knotworking* is harbinger of a new, more radical form of organising that overcomes the limits of both team and networking.

The class struggle, however, is never quite this simple. In reality, most political groupings display the three forms of organising discussed above. We could speculate that what varies is the objective, frequency and sequence in which they are deployed. For example, a Leninist outfit such as Socialist Workers' Party (SWP) specialises in teamworking. Its members are divided neatly into groups with well-defined tasks. Occasionally when it is in its interest the SWP forges various fronts with other organisations. A team from the SWP is allocated the responsibility of networking with outsiders in this front. As part of this front the SWP team may find itself on a demonstration that turns ugly. The team then has to engage in on the spot collaborative knotworking with 'strangers'. The success or failure of this knotworking activity will have reverberations for the rest of the organisation.

A concrete illustration: when during the anti-poll tax riot outside Parliament, protesters began shouting 'Burn it down', Militant stewards were heard shouting back, 'animals go forward, human beings back here' (Poll Tax Riot, 1990: 58). Militant Tendency sealed their anti-working class credentials when following the riot, leading members such as Tommy Sheridan and Steve Nally threatened to 'name names' and 'hold a public inquiry' in order to identify the rioters and bring them to *justice*.[95] It was obvious that they were engaging in some very foolish knotworking. The outcry caused by this act of 'betrayal' dealt a heavy blow to the Militant Tendency's power base within the anti-poll tax federation. It could be argued that the organisation never fully recovered from this knotworking hiccup. Once the command lines were suspended in the mayhem following the riot, the Militant Tendency's over reliance on teamworking and lack of transparency during networking made them vulnerable to a knotworking meltdown.[96]

To conclude this section, let us return to the Aufheben article cited above. They end their analysis by suggesting that,

---

94 This variety of 'teamworking' should not be confused with a relatively recent work regime where management is allowed to increase the rate of exploitation through giving workers the illusion of participation in decision-making.

95 For a brief and useful critique of the concept of *justice* see Melancholic Troglodytes (2001b).

96 Here is a counter example to the above. 'No War But The Class War' (NWBTCW) was the catchy name of a grouping of Anarchists, Left-Communists, Communists, Autonomists, Situationists and Trotskyites who formed an anti-war 'organisation' in Britain before the First Gulf War. This group (now defunct) which also re-emerged in the run up to the Second Gulf War displayed teamworking, networking and knotworking at various stages of its evolution and managed to overcome, albeit temporarily, some of the problems associated with (Leninist) teamworking and (Anarchist) networking. The success was fleeting.

The movement against the war in Iraq in this country [Britain] was essentially focused on extra-workplace activity – the best connections between workplace and anti-war movement organisations being the universities and town halls ... Most proposed strikes and walkouts failed ... the best opportunity of a link between the war and the workplace was the firefighters' strike. In the strike before the war began, the government admitted that, with so many troops busy covering for the firefighters, it would be impossible for them to go to war ... Our experience of the strike was that it was union and union activist led, and when the government showed itself determined to defeat it, no autonomous initiative met the inevitable 'sell out'. [However, despite this setback and] for all the liberal emotional outpouring, bourgeois support and elements of apparent spectacle [manifested during the anti-war movement], there were feelings of genuine power [and] hints of the susceptibility of the state to collective action ... (Aufheben, 2004: 35).

4.4 UTILITY AND LIMITATIONS OF ACTIVITY THEORY

Elhammoumi (2001: 204-205) criticises Activity Theorists and socio-historical psychology, in general, for ignoring the class struggle,

In their analyses of human cognition, socio-historicocultural psychologists (Bruner, Cole,[97] Engeström, Rogoff, Valsiner,[98] van der Veer, Wertsch among others) kept out of theoretical picture any reference to larger forms of human activity and larger processes in social life, such as the realities of economic structure, class struggle, realities of labour activities, and the realities of social interaction.

This is a valid criticism, especially since AT claims to be a form of 'formative experiment' which combines active participation with monitoring developmental change in the object of study (Bannon, 1997: 3). Sawchuk *et al.* (2002) follow up on a similar trajectory by criticising AT for neglecting relations of power. Furthermore, the original

97 Cole's work suffers from further problems. Ratner (1999: 11) is very lucid on this, '[Cole's] abstract approach to activity overlooks important origins and characteristics of psychological phenomena. [His program for enhancing students' reading comprehension disregards] the content and availability of educational materials; the structure and condition of the school buildings and equipment; the educational budget, teaching training, teacher salaries; the students' family lives; the students' family lives; ... the content of media which the children watch ...'.

98 Valsiner's work is the one that perhaps shows the greatest deterioration. Beginning from a Vygotskian stance, he has gradually veered toward an individualistic approach to cultural psychology. This may be a reaction against Activity Theory's propensity to minimise individual agency. In any case, as Ratner (1999: 14) has observed, 'Valsiner's co-construction of culture combines two entirely distinct and separate processes: an impersonal, social component plus a non-social, personal component. The collective part is *alien* while the personal part is *one's own*'. This is the language of liberalism and personal *choice*. For instance, we are perfectly free to either buy advertised products or refuse the charms of an advertising campaign. We, as individuals, have the choice. In Lightfoot and Valsiner (1992: 396) social influences are regarded as 'collective cultural viruses' that 'penetrate personal belief systems'. The individual can fight back if he/she is equipped with 'antibodies' which can 'block or neutralise the attack'!

conception of AT as put forward by Leontiev (1977) also marginalised Vygotsky's notions of the *social situation of development* and *zone of proximal development* (Rey, 1999: 255). Admittedly this shortcoming was later partially rectified by 'third generation'[99] Activity Theorists (Engeström, 1999: 1).

By choosing to concentrate my analysis on the anti-poll tax rebellion and the million strong anti-war February 2003 demonstration, I have attempted to reanimate AT around an explicitly political agenda. In this section, I will evaluate the usefulness and limitations of AT for investigating such instances of social struggle. I have chosen to concentrate on the relationship between activity and collective emotion, discourse, mediational tools and religious influences within social movements. These themes will demonstrate a number of differences between the two case studies and move our investigation into fresh areas. I will also briefly allude to both the gains and failures of our two case studies. After all,

> Revolutionary activity is not a miraculous jump into a practice beyond the complex social practice in which we live; rather it is an ongoing struggle for changing circumstances that undermine our possibilities for developing or sustaining communal practice (or what Marx called 'human society') (Jensen, 1999: 94).

4.4.1 Emotions

At the beginning of this chapter I mentioned how violence at a demonstration could sometimes act as a camouflage for basically conservative motives by rioters. We can now add another rejoinder to this statement. Uninterrupted violence can also hinder reflection,

> As is known from Köhler's works, insight does not occur during violent, strained action. It happens instead during some pauses, intervals, or breaks in activity and actions, which have received various names. Bakhtin ... referred to them as 'the out-of time gappings that are formed between two moments of real time'. These breaks sometimes are also named with terms like 'suspension' ... 'reflection space' ... or 'resting place' (Zinchenko, 2001: 143).

The anti-war march was so huge that there was little room for 'reflection space'. The organisers colonised almost every autonomous temporal and spatial dimension. The few 'reflection spaces' especially constructed on the grass in Hyde Park failed to function as intended due to the volume of marchers. The anti-poll tax demonstration, by

---

99 Engeström (1999: 1) has distinguished between three theoretical generations in CHAT (Cultural Historical Activity Theory). 'The first generation', he writes, 'centred around Vygotsky, created the idea of mediation ... the limitation of the first generation was that the unit of analysis remained individually focused. This was overcome by the second generation, largely inspired by Leontiev's work ... The third generation [which Engeström himself belongs to] ... needs to develop conceptual tools to understand dialogue, multiple perspective and voices, and networks of interacting activity system'.

contrast, was peppered with moments of peace and tranquillity when people gathered in a 'resting place' and discussed the events, drew conclusions and planned further actions. The violence that was manifest did not detract from reflection since it was experienced as an emancipatory extension of reflection. It was as if during,

> a faltering of dominant power subordinate groups seize their moment. Infrapolitical resistance gives way to a public defiance as, often in highly charged emotional states, subordinate actors reveal their hitherto hidden truths (Collins, 1999: 15).

This partially explains why the anti-poll tax ended in a significant portion of the crowds turning riotous whilst the anti-war march (in many ways just as emotional as the fight against the poll-tax) passed off peacefully.

Another factor, which may be relevant here, is the type of discourses available to the protesters. Aristotle divided discourse into *judicial, deliberative* (e.g., political or trade union debate), and *epidictic* speech in praise or blame of someone. When capital feels under serious threat, deliberative discourse is suspended for fear of it opening up a space for something more challenging. Mey (1985) called this method of language manipulation *repressive* where subversive talk is denied expression. Extensive labour laws and institutional mediators are bypassed. Newspapers could be shutdown, television programmes and plays banned. In societies where the proletariat feels powerless, the *unavailability of judicial and deliberative discourse leaves epidictic discourse as the only alternative*. This mode of discourse may begin with a eulogy to soften up the bosses followed by a bargaining session steeped in the rituals of ostentatious reverence. Sometimes if the bourgeoisie proves unresponsive to the proletarian charm offensive, things can turn ugly very rapidly with sabotage and riots piercing the pretence of mutual respectability.

In the case of the poll-tax, we witnessed a joint attack on the proletariat by all branches of the state, be it the executive who initiated the assault or the judiciary and legislative who were only too eager to please their more powerful executive partners. There was no room for judicial or parliamentary manoeuvrings as far as the anti-poll tax rebels were concerned. Furthermore, the stubbornness of the Thatcher government meant that there would be no deliberative discourse either. Since this was such an absolutist policy, there was no point negotiating. By default we were left with an epidictic form of discourse, which as explained above is speech in praise or blame of someone. Whilst in those parts of the world where subordinate groups feel powerless this may involve praise, eulogy and reverential sophistry as an indirect method of negotiation, in Britain it meant blaming the Tories openly. This discourse of blame was the 'soil' (Luria, 1987)[100] of the anti-poll tax demonstration. It created a 'predisposi-

---

100 The 'soil' metaphor refers to 'practical life experience onto which ideas and conceptions *fall* (Collins, 1999: 89). This 'soil' shapes the dialectics of meaning and sense, which in turn affects speech and action.

tion' for violent defiance and once the police started their heavy-handed crowd control tactics (i.e., once the perceived social contract was broken), the riot was inevitable. By contrast, the anti-war march occurred in a 'soil' where judicial and deliberative forms of discourse were not exhausted. Although most of the protesters blamed Bush and Blair for the war using epidictic discourse, they were not unsympathetic to the employment of more 'peaceful' judicial and deliberative discourse. This analysis goes some way in explaining how emotions were contained during the anti-war campaign.

Nonetheless, the behaviour and spoken contradictions of the marchers exposed the extreme division of emotional labour experienced by most western people regarding the impending war. Many experienced difficulty comprehending their own feelings because faced with a complex political situation, they felt an unusual combination of emotions. Perhaps they would have found it easier had they been Ugandans, Aborigines or Samoans. Ratner (2000: 14) explains,

> ... people in Uganda have an emotional concept that combines elements of Western anger and sadness. Australian aborigines have one concept that combines elements of western fear and shame. Samoans have one concept that spans Western hate and disgust and does not distinguish them.

Moments of social rupture have the ability to temporarily suspend social and technical divisions of (mental and physical) labour. The myriad of emotions experienced by people during the run up to the War was testimony to the break up of neat distinctions between emotional states like fear, sadness and shame that are usually compartmentalised. The integration of contradictory affective states influences personality development. This process contains both a conscious and an 'unconscious'[101] element. As Rey (1999: 271) explains,

> In those cases in which contradictions are structured in terms of personality organisation, without the conscious involvement of the subject, contradictions can become a source of anxiety and distress. However, when the subject is aware of the situation, and actively takes part in constructing different alternatives to face the problem, the conflict may turn into an important force for personality development.

---

101 Ratner (1994: 327) has suggested we should abandon the Freudian term 'the unconscious' because 'it connotes a physical thing or a place outside consciousness' and replace it with 'unawareness'. He goes on to explain that there is not a strict separation, as postulated by Freudians, between consciousness and 'unconsciousness', since 'unconscious cognitive processes are functions of consciousness in the sense that they have the same origins, utilise the same symbols and knowledge, and engage in meaning-giving interpretations' (Ratner, 1994: 330). Significantly, explicating and repudiating social concepts such as commodity fetishism that generate unawareness may be very useful but insufficient on its own. Awareness will not automatically follow once old social concepts have been dismantled, as Freud believed. Rather 'such a negative act of deconstruction must be complemented by a positive act which constructs a new sensitising conceptual system' (Ratner, 1994: 338).

Since school children during the anti-war demo and anti-poll tax rebels were actively involved 'in constructing different alternatives to face the problem', they managed to turn the conflict 'into an important force of personality development'. A number of debates between children and politicians on TV as well as confident public speeches organised and carried out by pupils themselves is testimony to 'personality development'.

The nature of demonstrations against the war, especially their ability to supersede divisions of emotional labour as well as the private-public divide, were instrumental in accepting emotions as part of political decision making. Emotions usually marginalised as 'irrational, impulsive, personal, and primitive' and therefore either regulated or 'suppressed in most cultural activities' (Ratner, 2000) were allowed expression.[102] Since there is still a gender[103] differential regarding emotions, with male political activists discouraged from introducing emotions into the process of decision making (perhaps with the exception of displaying anger), there was an opportunity for two groups historically associated with 'emotional outbursts' to be foregrounded.[104] This partially explains the leading role of women and children in many of the anti-war groups set up throughout the country. According to Davydov (1999: 46) the significance of emotions goes further,

> The general function emotions perform is that they enable a person to set a vital task; but this is half the work. The most important thing is that emotions enable a person to decide from the very beginning whether the physical, spiritual and moral means he [sic] needs to fulfil the task are available. If they are – the person starts his analytic apparatus to consider the conditions of achieving the goal. If his emotions say, 'No, the means are not available', the person refuse to take up the task.

Both the anti-poll tax rebellion and the anti-war campaign superseded the given emotional division of labour, although with varying degrees of success. But there was in

---

102 Anger is usually dismissed as irrational. Yet recently investigators have shown the centrality of anger to collective action. 'In an analysis of class passivity, Lee Harrington and William Flint concur, suggesting that anger, as the most agentic emotion, is an essential component of efficacy. They argue that for efficacy -a belief in the possibility of change- to be achieved, *one must know, one must feel, and one must be aware of the relationship between the two*' (Harrington and Flint, 1997 quoted in Hercus, 1999: 36).

103 By *gender* I do not mean a set of traits or attributes. Following Harding (1991) I would argue gender is a *relationship* between men and women and not a distinct property that women and men have apart from the other gender.

104 Social activities reflect the range and expression of emotional expression. For instance, 'controlling emotional expression was important for 18th century middle class [US American] men because it was part of the self-discipline they had to develop in order to compete in the market economy ... An emotional demeanour was also an important way of hiding information from competitors' (Ratner, 2000: 18). In a real sense bourgeois politics is also conducted within a market place. There is a need for its practitioners, therefore, to control emotional expression and avoid the display of 'anxiety, trepidation and even intense desire' (Ratner, 2000: 18), which might be exploited by competitors. Anti-war demonstrations and meetings in the run up to the Iraq War were different because the kind of politics practiced contained an emotional proletarian element lacking in bourgeois politics.

both cases a tension from the outset between the organisers (plus the media) who preferred to see what German critical psychologists call a 'restrictive action potence' and many of the protesters who preferred to go beyond that toward a 'generalised action potence'. The restrictive mode tries to make action effective (potent) within 'the framework of available or conceded conditions' (Maiers and Tolman, 1996: 111). The generalised mode, by contrast, risks 'failure and negative sanctions' in an attempt directed toward extending and developing the framework of action (Maiers and Tolman, 1996: 111). In terms of emotions,

> the restrictive mode is linked to 'emotional inwardness' in which emotions tend to be taken as personal problems [hence the 'Not in My Name' slogan launched by the reactionary wing of the 'anti-war movement']; in the generalised mode, 'generalised emotional engagement' takes emotion as a response to the world requiring corrective action [hence the slogan, 'Bin Bush! Bin Blair! Bin Bin Laden!', launched by Anarchists and left-communists] (Maiers and Tolman, 1996: 112). [My additions]

The restrictive action potence remains within the bounds of 'feeling rules', which are a set of regulations governing people's feelings in bourgeois society (Hercus, 1999: 36). The rioters during the anti-poll tax rebellion and the school children during the anti-war demonstration managed to supersede bourgeois 'feeling rules' but it is true that the organisers of the anti-war demonstration were better equipped in handling people's emotions and managed to suppress anger being directed at the state. Note that the former went beyond bourgeois 'feeling rules' through an angry confrontation with the state, whilst the latter group of school children chose a humorous cat-and-mouse game with the police to achieve the same end. The role of the speakers at Hyde Park (where the rally was held at the end of the anti-war march) was particularly significant in this strategy of containment. Many radicals on the anti-war march engaged in a great deal of 'emotional work'[105] in order to suppress their anger and avoid conflict with other protesters who were resolute in their desire for a 'peaceful' demonstration. In the context of feminists having to suppress their anger, Hercus (1999: 46) has written,

> The costs associated with the emotion work required for the negotiations of feminist identity include emotional exhaustion, guilt, and self-estrangement. Interviewees talked about the energy required to control their anger or restrain themselves from expressing feminist views.

The emotional exhaustion, guilt and self-estrangement one feels as a result of both self-imposed and obligatory emotional work are not merely psychological states. They are

---

105 Hochschild (1979: 561-562) has defined emotional work as 'the act of evoking or shaping, as well as suppressing feeling' which 'can be done by the self upon the self, by the self upon others, and by others upon oneself'.

also determinates of power relations.[106] When an event retains its carnivalesque character, emotional work is reduced to a bare minimum whilst during spectacular state rituals order-givers gain emotional energy at the expense of the rest of us.

4.4.2 Subject, mediational tool, object

Martin Ryder (1999: 3) suggests three possible paradigms for defining the relationship between the subject, mediational means and object. These are:

1. **The Ideal paradigm**- this paradigm is inspired by Marshall McLuhan (1964) and views mediated knowledge in the ideal sense as an instrument of agency. The subject too is ideally portrayed and considered conscious regarding goals. The tool here is considered as a neutral extension of the individual.

2. **The Cynical paradigm**- this paradigm is the polar opposite of the ideal paradigm and is borrowed from Marcuse (1964). Here technology and tools come to dominate passive one-dimensional consumers.

3. **The Dialectical paradigm**- this paradigm finds the abovementioned approaches naïve and basing itself on Marx (1844/1984) sees the individual as enmeshed within

---

106 Laura L. Sullivan (2005: 358) discusses feelings of being 'overwhelmed' and 'burnt out' as a result of activism and how mindless activism is often accompanied by feelings of guilt and urgency. I want to say more about this article because I think it is worthy of serious attention. First, the problems with Sullivan's approach:

1) Political naivety, to which Sullivan openly admits to. For instance, she creates a false division between 'verticals' and 'horizontals' in European Social Forum UK (2004). Obviously there was a real polarity at ESF UK 2004 but to resort to categories borrowed from cartography to explain it, depoliticises the whole debate. The real division at ESF UK 2004 was between two petty-bourgeois tendencies, one represented by Leninists and social democrats (so called verticals aided by Mayor Livingston's office) and the other by anarchists, liberals, libertarians and right-wing hangers-on (so called horizontals). She classifies herself as a 'horizontal' and in so doing fails to see the problems with her own side. The group Wombles are, for example, referred to as 'anti-authoritarian'! (Sullivan, 2005: 346).

2) Epistemological naivety, as expressed in her admiration for Gayatri Spivak's notion of 'strategic essentialism' (Sullivan, 2005: 347). Spivak's attempted synthesis of Feminism and Autonomism through strategic essentialism is wholly inadequate (cf. Melancholic Troglodytes, 2001d: 20-25).

3) Psychological naivety, as expressed in her promotion of the concept of 'emotional intelligence'. It is almost as if various devastating critiques of 'intelligence' never happened (cf. Vygotsky, 1978; Rose, Kamin and Lewontin, 1984; Rose, 1985).

Set against these shortcomings, however, are excellent moments of insight and honesty that recommend the text:

1) Sullivan may start off on alien political terrain at the ESF UK 2004 but she soon navigates her way admirably around problem groups. The process of political development she describes is highly instructive.

2) Sullivan (2005: 365) underscores how emotional distress born out of bureaucratic frustration makes us forget. This has tremendous implications for the kind of organising we should be aiming for.

3) Sullivan mentions how her entire experience at ESF UK (2004) reminded her of past and recent experiences of personal *abuse* (defined broadly as betrayal by a person or people in power).

4) She suggests 'bitching sessions' down the pub after heated meetings is a 'typical way ... for feeling some kind of power in a situation in which you have little' (Sullivan, 2005: 358).

the 'subject-tool-object' nexus. As proletarians we usually engage in activities not of our choosing and beyond our control, hence our alienation. In this paradigm tools are both instrument of agency and the result of activity.

According to this classification the anti-poll tax campaign which displayed a number of dialectical relations had a number of advantages over the anti-war march: First, the tools (both concrete and abstract) available to participants in the anti-poll tax demonstration were both more *varied* (allowing for scaffolding[107] by anonymous others) and more *organic* (in the sense that they were built by protesters from everyday experience over months of campaigning).[108] In contrast, leftist organisations managed to control and limit the tools used for mediation during the anti-war demonstration. Ready-made tools were handed down and came to dominate passive consumers of discourse. Related to the diversity of tools is the diversity of objects or goals, which enables the development of individuals in a number of ways,

> First, goals must be personally meaningful … diversity of goals provide opportunities for boundary crossings and explorations. Second, diversity in objects available to transform into outcomes broaden horizons for development … Last, activities … must have diverse entry paths (Blanton, n.d.).

Second, bearing in mind that the most fundamental developmental medium is another human or another activity system, I would argue that the anti-poll tax rebellion offered greater opportunity for fluid dialectical learning. In this context, humans offered 'themselves as a mirror for the other: affirming the other's values and reflecting differences' (Ryder, 1993: 4).

During the anti-war demonstration, activity systems did not *bleed* into one another and individuals remained opaque, refusing or unable to act as a mirror to fellow protesters. The intersubjectivity achieved during the anti-poll tax campaign foregrounded both the similarities and differences of the protesters. Similarities created a shared sense of oppression and the differences became productive, allowing boundary crossing and exploration of alternative activity systems. For instance, neighbours who had ignored each other for years were invited around to discuss the tax. The movement developed into a unity of opposites. By contrast, the intersubjectivity

---

107 The term scaffolding, which was used frequently in the Vygotsky section, has been all but absent from this part of the analysis, since activity theorists have little use for it. According to activity theorists, the scaffolding metaphor of learning 'implies too strongly that the quantity rather than quality (i.e., content) of the adult's help is the decisive influence on a child's development' (Stetsenko, 1999: 243). Whilst this is a legitimate criticism I still contend scaffolding has some utility in describing the relationship between the more and less experienced members of a collective.

108 As Ratner (1999: 20-21) has explained some activity theorists tend to use tools as if they are devoid of social content. By choosing to talk of *organic* tools I have attempted to underline the origins and history of tools. I am suggesting that *organic* tools (those constructed by past and present generations of protesters) are more useful than *ready-made* tools.

achieved during the anti-war campaign was partial and one-sided. Certain groups such as 'Muslim youths' refused to acknowledge any commonalties with the rest of protesters. In some cases, they even disrespectfully pushed other demonstrators out of the way and marched through them. Likewise, Christian protesters would reject any call for 'direct action'. The cultural differences rapidly cemented into identity-formations and helped maintain alienation.

It could be argued that for intersubjectivity to occur participants need to engage in a combination of speech, gesture or demonstrative action (Wells, 2002: 60). In the anti-poll tax campaign most protesters engaged in all three aspects of intersubjectivity. In the anti-war campaign, however, different aspects of intersubjectivity were practiced by different groups and at different times. Most of the *speech* making was done by Leftist politicians and a minority of Muslim speakers. *Gestures* were the domain of the youth who took advantage of the rare opportunity the campaign offered them to display themselves in a society which has historically ignored them. *Demonstrative actions* (e.g., roadblocks, invading military bases, scaffolding of symbolic buildings and pickets) were carried out by activists. This demarcation explains why despite more than a million participants in the February march, intersubjectivity and solidarity were low.

Dialectical paradigm and systematic thinking were more in evident during the anti-poll tax rebellion.

Wow trippy intersubjectivity!

Are you sure you are reading this right?

"... for intersubjectivity to occur participants need to engage in a combination of speech, gesture or demonstrative action ..."

Third, there was a more prolonged period of 'knotworking' (Engeström *et al*, 1999: 345) prior to the Trafalgar Square anti-poll tax demonstration compared to the anti-war march. This led to more 'tying, untying and retying' (Engeström *et al.,* 1999: 346) of collaborative activity amongst poll tax rebels than the anti-war protesters. It meant the former retained the initiative from Leftist organisers whereas the latter became to some extent hostage to the agenda of political opportunists. So certain aspects of the anti-poll tax rebellion were superior to the anti-war demonstration, however, these three advantages of the anti-poll tax riot (more varied and organic tools, greater speech, gestural and demonstrative intersubjectivity and more prolonged knotworking) are not the whole story. To grasp the dynamics of the situation more fully a linkage with the work of Shawn W. Rosenberg is necessary, as I make clear below.

The three paradigms alluded to by Ryder (the Ideal, Cynical and the Dialectical) find an echo in Rosenberg's (1988: 544-548) distinction between three types of political thinking. The mapping of Ryder's categories onto Rosenberg's may not be exact but it is nonetheless thought-provoking. Rosenberg refers to three types of political thinking as *sequential, linear* and *systematic.* Accordingly,

> Sequential thinkers track the world which appears before them. They reason in terms of both the sequence in which events unfold and the match between current observations and representations of earlier observations ... the sequential thinker is only able to observe a particular political actor performing a particular activity ... objects of thought are understood in light of the role they play in a given sequence of events ... [and] are not thought of as wholes ... (Rosenberg, 1988: 544).

Sequence thinkers therefore fetishize the individual performer as do the advocates of the Ideal paradigm mentioned above. The agency of individuals is assumed unproblematically. This type of political thinking imbues empirical observations with magical qualities and tries to come up with a sequence of events (not a fully fledged narrative) accordingly. In this perspective hidden factors remain hidden and observable factors from a different timescale remain unconnected. The bourgeois commentators of the anti-poll tax rebellion and the anti-war demonstration may suffer from this type of sequential thinking but the vast majority of protesters in both cases had moved beyond this perspective.

The second type of thinking Rosenberg calls *linear* thinking where thinkers move slightly beyond the narrow confines of observable facts and engage with 'temporally and spatially remote considerations' (Rosenberg, 1988: 545). However, there are limitations to linear thinking,

> While [in linear thinking] political action is understood to occur in an organised context, this context is a fragmented one. Some of the parts are pieced together, but an integrated conception of the whole is not forged ... each individual is understood to be the role he or she plays, or the aggregate of the actions he or she performs ... the linear thinker [is also capable of thinking] in terms of groups. These consist of those individuals who perform the same activity or share observable common characteristics.

So clearly, linear thinking is a superior bourgeois type of political thinking compared to sequential thinking. Furthermore, linear political thinking captures the cynicism engendered by war-mongers of both hue and is closely associated with Ryder's Cynical paradigm. It was evident at the aftermath of the anti-war demonstration that most bourgeois commentators and many of the protesters employed this type of linear thinking to make sense of the events. Thus comparisons were made in the media and the 'alternative' press regarding previous incursions into Iraq by the British ruling class. The fact that even bourgeois commentators had to rise above sequential thinking and employ a linear perspective suggests the general level of political *knowledge* (as distinct from consciousness) was higher during the cycle of anti-war demonstrations. Cynicism had become trendy.

Finally, there is a third type of political thinking which Rosenberg calls *systematic* thought. This is the one most closely related to Ryder's Dialectical paradigm. Accordingly,

> Systematic thinkers juxtapose the relationships that exist between actions. They analyse these relationships by examining them relative to one another, by considering each in its context … [observable relations are conceived of as] embedded in a system of relationships that is the product of either objective conditions or subjective associations (Rosenberg, 1988: 546).

Of course, in reality there is usually a blending of sequential, linear and systematic thinking during social movements. Even revolutionaries do not always think through dialectical categories.[109] Sometimes the linear and even the sequential types of thinking get the better of revolutionaries. But what I find significant is that whilst it is true that the anti-poll tax rebellion itself displayed more dialectical analysis (or in Rosenberg's words, systematic thinking) than the one-million anti-war march, the subsequent events have introduced interesting complexities. The anti-poll tax event was, after all, a national campaign with limited generalisability across the borders. Even nationally, many failed to make the necessary dialectical links between the anti-poll tax campaign and other proletarian struggles. Once the poll tax was abolished, the struggle ended. However, the anti-war campaign has not disappeared. Many people have become radicalised as a result of early participation in protests and the dialectical linkages being made between war, oil, suppression of labour power, water shortages, prisoner abuse, and media deceit have led to 'expansive learning'. In this sense, the legacy of the anti-war demonstration may prove more significant than the dramatic riot at Trafalgar Square.

4.4.3 Discourse and activity theory

Neither the anti-poll tax rebellion nor the anti-war march ended in the overthrow of capitalism. Had they done so, this investigation would have been superfluous. What we can say with certainty is that they temporarily disrupted the stable bourgeois equi-

---

109 Engeström (1987: 131) has distinguished between three types of human *development* (i.e., three types of real production of new societal activity systems). The *individual-explosive*, the *invisible-gradual* and the *collective-expansive*, He goes on to claim, 'it is the third type which is the one which requires intuitive or conscious mastery …'.

librium that had hitherto existed between *meaning* and *sense*. As Collins (1999: 64) has put it,

> Today consciousness may have a certain sensible structure – a particular merging of senses and given meanings which have acquired a level of stability. Tomorrow some personal experience or some newly emerging development in the system of social relations might disrupt this structure, setting the meanings in consciousness in motion afresh.

The anti-poll tax rebellion radically shifted the meaning of a limited number of terms such as 'fair taxation' and 'justice', whilst the anti-war march succeeded in permeating a wider constellation of seminal words with fresh sense- words such as 'terrorism', 'dissent', 'disobedience' and 'freedom'. In the case of the anti-poll tax rebellion the disenchantment remained, by and large, focused on an unpopular tax and an aggressive Tory party, whereas the anti-war 'movement' polarised society to a greater extent and on a larger number of issues.

    The discourse shaping the anti-poll tax campaign remained mostly 'defensive' whereas the anti-war campaign using less fiery terminologies attacked more than a policy. It put under temporary erasure an entire system. The anti-war protesters 'rearmed' (Luria, 1987) themselves with more powerful mediational means. These mediational means helped them develop a more complex political discourse compared to their supposed leaders. It seems as if both questions and answers were arrived at collectively to a greater extent in both these two cases than, say, the miners' strike of 1984-85 when the framework of discourse was tightly policed by both media and trade unions.

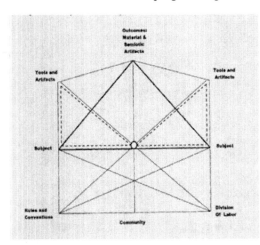

Discourse as tool in joint activity (Reproduced from Wells, 2002: 59)

    Despite the above analysis, I think it would be fair to say that AT has said little about dialogue and discourse (see Collins, 1999; Daniels, 2004 and Jones, 2002 as counter-examples to this general neglect). According to Wells (2002: 43),

> Activity Theory as formulated by Leont'ev and expanded by Engeström has tended to emphasise activity systems in which the objects to which subjects' actions are directed are material in form. In such accounts, discourse -if considered at all- is treated as just one of the artifacts or practices that mediate the subject's object-directed actions.

This brand of AT has difficulty dealing with the process of dialogic meaning making, where narratives and explanations in speech and writing are used to work through problems. In Wells's words, even Engeström's sound improvements to Leontiev's original model 'still appears to prioritise a unidirectional form of artifact-mediated, object-oriented action' (Wells, 2002: 47). For example, a recent study of changing communication principles between Chinese managers and workers provides very little opportunity for the workers to explain themselves in their own words (Hong and Engeström, 2004). The study claims that during 'joint' meetings between bosses and workers, '[the latter] had little to say about work but talked mainly about other issues such as complaints and suggestions concerning food, accommodations, and entertainment' (Hong and Engeström, 2004).

The political naivety of the investigators is such that they do not see this indirect approach as a strategy by workers to talk about work without being flagged as troublemakers by managers. The fact that the only 'problem' worth investigating is the problem of workplace modernisation and productivity which is ultimately traced to lack of vertical and horizontal communication, speaks volumes for the priorities of contemporary Activity Theorists. Even when language is discussed by Activity Theorists, most tend to direct their attention towards 'contradictions with specific emphasis on the object of the activity and the outcomes. The production, distribution and selection of [dialogue] tend not to be highlighted in the analysis' (Daniels, 2004: 124).

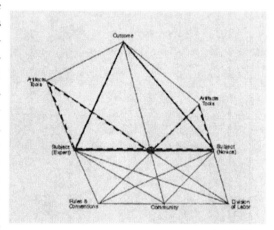

Discourse in the zone of proximal development (Reproduced from Wells, 2002: 61)

Perhaps there are understandable reasons for this neglect. Wells (2002: 58) concedes that representing the multi-dimensional complexity of dialogic interaction diagrammatically is no easy matter. For Wells,

> One thing seems to be clear, however, and that is that to represent each phase of action as either object-oriented, mediated by tools, or subject-oriented, mediated by signs, does not do justice to the nature of collaborative joint activity (Wells, 2002: 59).

Wells's attempt to represent this complex dialogic interaction within an activity system is reproduced here. This is a major elaboration of Engeström's model. First, note that the diagram shows a dyad engaged in a joint activity such as preparing a picket of an oil company. The two subjects have their own activity system (shown as dotted lines), which is subsumed under a larger triangle (thick line), representing the joint action. Second, both subjects share the same base (i.e., they have the same rules of convention, milieu, and are subjected to the same division of labour). Third, they act on the same object (i.e., the picket outside an oil company). This object is shown as a circle in the middle of the diagram. Four, each subject brings his/her own personal tools and artifacts (resources) to the interaction. Fifth, the diagram is shown symmetrically because it is assumed both subjects possess the same amount of resources and experiences.

However, as we have already seen a zone of proximal development contains subjects with varying expertise. In order to show this asymmetry, the diagram could be tilted towards the more experienced subject initially. As expertise is shared the eschewed diagram becomes more symmetrical.

4.4.4 Religion and social movements

> Nothing is easier than to give Christian asceticism a Socialist tinge. Has not Christianity declaimed against private property, against marriage, against the State? Has it not preached in the place of these, charity and poverty, celibacy and mortification of the flesh, monastic life and Mother Church? Christian Socialism is but the holy water with which the priest consecrates the heartburnings of the aristocrat.
>
> - K. Marx, *The Communist Manifesto*, 1847-48 / 1986: 108.

We must discard the habit of using 'violence' and 'peace' as abstractions. Both 'violence' and 'peace' could, of course, act as a mystifying force concealing social relations. Ironically the priest's call for *reflection* can be an excuse to deflect anger from the ruling class. The passive religious call for 'peace' during the anti-war demonstration tended to negate a politico-historical critique of the causes of war. The obligatory 'one minute silences' for reflection and prayer was, in fact, a mechanism for anger-management.[110] This basically moralistic stance is an expression of the unstated feelings of guilt that have been systematically imposed on people by religion, and it partially explains the lack of political discussion during candle burning processions organised by

---

110 During the First Gulf War, one-minute silences called for by the CND and other religious groupings were not always adhered to. One such call outside Parliament Square on the first night of bombings was punctuated by radicals with the slogan, 'No war but the class war'. In a sense these radicals were opposing the false dichotomy between bourgeois 'war' and bourgeois 'peace'. The impact of this intervention was quite dramatic!

the church or CND. In those parts of the world where monotheism's victory over polytheism has been belated and incomplete- places such as Africa -missionaries have had a difficult task convincing people of feeling guilty. As Ratner observes,

> ...until recently [sub-Saharan Africans] attributed their misfortune to witchcraft by hostile others; they did not blame themselves and did not feel guilt. The adoption (imposition) of Protestant religious beliefs was one factor that has spurred the development of guilt in younger Africans (Ratner, 2000: 11).

What was interesting about the anti-war demonstration was the inability of religious forces to create guilt amongst the vast majority of participants. Most saw the war as an external imposition garnished by lies in pursuit of power and profit. The Church's failure to create guilt through civil society paralleled the British state's inability to renew a sense of patriotism through institutions of political society.[111]

Another point worth dwelling upon is the competition between the two major religions in the anti-war campaign, namely, Christianity and Islam with the secular Left. Pablo del Rio and Amelia Alvarez (1995: 236-237) have discussed the thin line that divides animism, religion and rationalism from the perspective of Activity Theory. Animism is concerned with *natural* situations (the relationship of nature and humans) and *instrumentalist* actions with objects (e.g., magic and relics). Religion is concerned with *social* situations (but mystified through powerful narratives) and *cultural* action (e.g., prayer, liturgy and rituals). Finally, Left Rationalism attempts to provide an explanation of both natural and social situations (e.g., evolutionary theory and sociology) through *scientific/rational* action (e.g., empirical investigation).

In Britain, the same thin line discussed by del Rio and Alvarez was criss-crossed many times throughout the campaign by Christianity, Islam and the Rational Left. Christianity in its organised form (Church of England and CND) seemed the closest fit to animism. The reasons for this 'regression' are not clear to me.[112] Christian relics

---

111 This failure is indicative of the waning powers of 'Puritanism' in Britain. Puritanism was a solution 'adopted by dominant groups [in the late 18th and early 19th centuries] to deal with the problems created by the nature of early capitalist production, and in particular the proximity which it engendered between employer and employed at a time when the latter had only recently lost immediate control over their labour' (Collins, 1999: 22). The passage from formal to real phase of capitalist domination, the rise of polyphonic subjectivities, the prevalence of 'consumerism' and the need to engage in Keynesian policies from time to time have all conspired to make Puritanism redundant in Britain (except for some marginal ethnicities such as 'Asian' and 'Muslim' sweat-shop workers). It is vital to emphasise that the waning influence of Puritanism does not mean religion in general has been weakened in Britain. The demise of residual forms of religiosity such as Puritanism and dwindling church attendance are not a true indication of religious beliefs.

112 The only time Christianity moved beyond animistic behaviour and discourse and reverted to its more familiar monotheistic status was when it was trying to impose collective guilt on 'westerners' in relation to the war. Since many protesters did not view themselves as 'westerners' and in any case were too proactive in their denunciations of the ruling class to feel guilty, Christianity failed to influence events throughout the campaign. Their failure was further marked a year after the campaign when a CND demonstration drew a paltry number of protesters.

such as crosses and candles were in evidence throughout the demonstration. Shrines imbued with magical qualities were the sites of congregation by the devout. All this, of course, could be put down to the fact that most Christian demonstrators followed a bourgeois mode of protestation which privileges symbolic resistance over literal resistance. The 'one minute silences' and 'candle burning processions' then come to symbolically represent a very bourgeois form of Christian 'defiance'. Ironically, Christianity did not posit a powerful narrative to explain the causes of the war nor did it try to engage non-believers in dialogue. These tasks were left to Islam and Leftist Rationalism.

These two latter ideologies engaged strangers (and each other) in proselytising narratives and performed liturgical and ritualistic actions. But narratives are not merely tools for proselytising. They are also in Hung's words, 'effective instructional tools for the appropriation of cultural knowledge' (Hung, 2002: 125). In other words, by failing to posit a comprehensive narrative of the war, 'western' Christianity lost the opportunity to come to grips with and understand it. The same is true of the 'fundamentalists' occupying the White House. Their simplistic narrative of 'good' versus 'evil' is proving counterproductive for the US ruling class's ability to control events after the demise of Saddam Hussein. The anti-working class and racist tendencies within 'western' Christianity and 'western' politicians which served them well for centuries are becoming blinkers. Ironically, the very same mechanisms of prejudice and simplicity embedded in the narratives of 'eastern' Islamicists remain productive in terms of mobilisation and political impact.[113]

Ultimately the anti-capitalist movement needs to be very wary of ideas emanating from religious circles even when they present themselves as 'liberation theology'. For example, Parker (2005: 99) has shown how many researchers in Latin America have drawn on 'liberation theology' to turn psychology into 'liberation psychology' (e.g., Martin-Baró, 1994). Parker goes on to advise caution regarding hasty alliances. For instance he wonders if,

> Is this just another opportunity for those with a religious agenda to get a foothold in scientific psychology and turn it into something worse … Is there a danger that the power of the priests, shamans and spiritual leaders of different kinds would be reinforced … Is there a danger that drawing on theology will also draw in the host of other reactionary ideas that mainstream religions tend to propagate about the role of women and the supposed pathology of certain sexual practices? (Parker, 2005: 99).

Obviously these are meant to be 'rhetorical' questions and, therefore, it stands to reason that the author would answer his own questions in the positive. If so I would con-

---

113 There are exceptions to this rule. The recent execution of working class hostages in Iraq by Islamic groups as well as discriminate bombings of civilians has clearly dented their support amongst the region's proletariat.

cur. I would go further and suggest one of the reasons radicals and revolutionaries displayed so much confusion in their relationship with religious elements within the anti-war movement was due to their reliance on a mechanical and atavistic notion of atheism. As indicated above, the propagation of *organic atheism* (one basing itself on the everyday activities of proletarians and not on any ideological presumptions) would be a significant step toward undermining institutionalised religiosity without alienating 'religiously inclined' individuals.

In summary: this chapter has attempted to conceptualise proletarian development in terms of expansive learning which may take place if certain contradictions between and within activity systems are resolved. Not all proletarian instances of joint-activity become expansive learning but strikes, demonstrations and riots are miniature cycles of innovative learning which have the *potential* to do so. Study-extension identifies these contradictions and pushes them forward, challenging participants to use new tools for achieving goals which themselves may be transformed in the process. Following Engeström (1999: 3), I have tried to show that development is not always linear, vertical or irreversible. It is not always benign and may very well 'be viewed as a partial destruction of the old' (Engeström, 1999: 3). AT allows us to reconceptualise the development of individuals within collectivities.

The study of the anti-poll tax rebellion and the anti-war February 2003 protests confirms Engeström's claim that,

> [Proletarian] *activities are becoming increasingly societal* … To become increasingly societal means, first of all, that activity systems become gradually larger, more voluminous, and denser in their internal communication. Consequently, activity systems have impact on growing numbers of people. Secondly, it means that different activity systems, and the people within them, become increasingly interdependent, forming ever more complex networks and hierarchies of interaction. Thirdly, this interdependency is not just a formal affiliation. Activity systems are increasingly penetrated and saturated by the basic socio-economic laws and by the corresponding contradictions of the given society (Engeström, 1987: 120). [My addition]

It is the proletarian ability to resolve contradictions innovatively that propels the social movement to supersede the 'basic socio-economic laws' of capitalist society. In the process, the subject-object of activity undergoes expansive learning and reconstructs itself. Increasingly the proletariat is becoming able to influence every aspect of the expansive learning cycle, from pre-production (i.e., planning of protests) to production (i.e., the actual protest), to distribution (i.e., interaction of various protests and communication within and between them) and finally consumption (i.e., how protest are received and represented by the media).

Chapter five:

Towards a new kind of revolutionary organising

Together we can!
Working together as a team
means winning together as a team.

'The formal organisation ... is not the heart of the question of the organisation of the working class.'

Chapter   five :

Towards a new kind of revolutionary organising

*The formal organisation- how many work-
ers organised into unions and parties, how
many subscriptions to the newspapers,
how many political candidates nominated
and elected, how much money collected
for dues and so forth- is not the heart of
the question of the organisation of the
working class.*

- George Rawick, 1969: 4

In this final chapter I wish to demonstrate how the three strands of sociocultural psychology discussed thus far (Vygotsky, Bakhtin and Activity Theory), could be combined effectively as a method for the study-extension of the class struggle. The
model will be applied to the problem of revolutionary proletarian organisations.
This task will be carried out in two distinct sections (sections 5.1 and 5.2).

In section 5.1, I intend to look at both historical and contemporary radical organisations and evaluate their strengths as well as weaknesses. The examples, which may
be textual works of individuals dealing with organisational matters or actually existing organisations, have been chosen for their originality and/or seminal impact on
proletarian movements.

The *methodology* employed is a Marxian one which brings out the contradictions of organising within capitalism and foregrounds the alienation, dualism, fetishism and divisions of labour that have historically acted to undermine proletarian joint
activity. The *methods* of study will include literature review and to a lesser extent
participation action research in the cases where I have had direct experience of the
problems involved over the course of the organisation's evolution. These cases will be
grouped under two broad subsections representing those writers and ideas that prefigure (or forewarn us regarding the dangers of) the Zone of Bourgeois Development
(5.1.1.) and those prefiguring the Proletarian Zone of Development (5.1.2).

The Zone of Bourgeois Development (ZBD) was a convergence space for modern science, technology and academia (Newman and Holzman, 1993a: 91). Its end-

227

point was the creation of instrumentalist knowledge and bourgeois individualism. Its midwives were rationalism, positivism and empiricism. To quote Newman and Holzman (1993a: 91),

> That 'universal zone' served a particular class at a particular historical moment. The 'ZBD' (Zone of Bourgeois Development) required an urban-based research-educational community directly connected to the most progressive forces in the social environment (the bourgeoisie) while simultaneously being protected from the most regressive (the church and the nobility). The European-style university ('ZBD') played such a bourgeois revolutionary role. But the 'ZPD' (Zone of Proletarian Development) could not, ultimately, be the 'ZBD'.

The authors go on to claim that nowadays universities are less a place of development and 'more a zone of bourgeois stagnation' (Newman and Holzman, 1993a: 92). The Melancholic Troglodytes judge the state of affair similarly,

> With the exception of a few 'pure science' subjects, such as computing, nano-technology and genetic engineering, academia has entered a process of irreversible decomposition (Melancholic Troglodytes, 2003: 3).

Some of this stagnation is surely due to resistance conducted in the ZBD by proletarian elements. The rest is perhaps more to do with the inherent shortcomings of the ZBD itself. Since the ZBD is in crisis, it is hardly surprising that those pseudo-radical tendencies (Anarchist as well as Leninist) which imitate its mode of organising are also experiencing stagnation. The ZBD, which was characterised by specialism at its birth and more recently has attempted to partially lower some of the barriers separating disciplines in order to encourage 'cross-fertilisation' (the way Leninists and Anarchists partially lower nationalist cordons in order to conjure up a lame *inter*nationalism), can never be a useful model for proletarian revolution. This is largely because the aim of our revolution is not the conquest of political power but its abolition.

Furthermore, the ZBD is a tool for the maximisation of profit and the creation of increasing layers of control and surveillance. The Zone of Proletarian Development (ZPD), by contrast, is a tool-and-result. The ZPD may not be a blueprint of the future the way utopian socialists falsely envisaged it to be, but Mattick and Hakim Bey are basically correct in assuming that it is about the here-and-now (Bey, 1985: 19) and may in fact be a manifestation of 'embryonic communism' (Mattick, 1938:4). Given this postulate we could assume that the ZPD is qualitatively different from the ZBD and that the latter can never be restructured to aid the formation of the former.[114]

---

114 This is not to say phenomenon such as the 19th century working class Sunday school movement were wholly counter-productive but it does suggest proletarian 'meaning-making' is inherently different in terms of its aims, procedures, protocols and organisation.

I begin section 5.2 by distilling what is living and what is dead in these organisational prescriptions. The distinction will be categorised in terms of the differences between the Zone of Bourgeois Development (5.2.1.) and the Zone of Proletarian Development (5.2.2.). I will employ Vygotsky, Bakhtin and Activity Theory to suggest a radically alternative method of proletarian organising. This may not be a universal cure-all for the impasse proletarians find themselves in and it certainly will not be applicable to every terrain but in demarcating both the actual and potential levels of development, it will, at the very least, highlight the 'zone of proximal development' (zoped) encompassing today's struggles.

In writing on revolutionary organisations I am very much mindful of the mistakes of past thinkers who fetishized the organisational form as a solution to the lack of class struggle.[115] The correct organisation would, it was believed, develop consciousness which would then subvert capitalism. Lukács (1971) is a typical example of this naïve tendency. As Barrot (1987: 30) has correctly noted,

> Lukács knew (with the help of Hegel and Marx) that capitalism is the loss of unity, the dispersion of consciousness. But, instead of concluding from this that the proletarians will recompose a unitary world view by means of their subversive practice (concluding in the revolution), he thought that consciousness must be reunited and rediscovered first in order for this subversion to happen. As this is impossible, he too fled back into magic and theorised the need for a concretisation of consciousness which must be incarnated in an organisation before the revolution is possible. This organised consciousness is the 'party'.

Furthermore, the party is a form 'of disciplining class struggle, of subordinating the myriad forms of class struggle to the overriding aim of gaining control of the state' (Holloway, 2002: 17).

Since the aim of revolution is not the conquest and wielding of state power on behalf of the proletariat but the abolition of the state and the very concept of 'power', our approach to the problem of organisation is fundamentally at variance with recipes emanating from the left wing of capital. In section 5.2.2, I intend to demarcate the boundaries of the ZPD through a close reading of revolutionary literature on organisation and a reworking of the critical psychology of Vygotsky, Bakhtin and Activity Theory. The goal is neither to come up with a perfect blueprint for an organisation nor to engage in a 'consciousness-raising' exercise but to take the concrete realities of anti-capitalist practice all around us and facilitate its extension. In the olden days this exercise might have been called the charting of the dialectics of social being and consciousness.

---

115 Try as I may, I cannot refrain from having a dig at the reactionary ideology of Engels-Leninism here. A fundamental problem with mechanical materialism of the Engels-Leninist variety resides in its attempt to treat consciousness as a mere reflection of social reality- a separation with far reaching consequences. As Bickley (1977: 201) has correctly pointed out: 'The intellectual and philosophical roots of the ossification of Marxism can be traced back to Engels' *Dialectics of Nature* and Lenin's *Materialism and Empirio-Criticism*'.

5.1 HISTORICAL AND CONTEMPORARY MODES OF PROLETARIAN ORGANISING

5.1.1 Prefiguring the Zone of Bourgeois Development (ZBD)

Two groups of writers are discussed in this section, those who promote the Zone of Bourgeois Development (such as Kautsky and Lenin) and those who are forewarning us about the dangers of bourgeois principles creeping into the social movement (such as Joe Freeman and Jacque Camatte). Together, their writings constitute a prefiguring of the Zone of Bourgeois Development.

> *Sounds complicated! On the question of organisation, can't we just tail-end the European bourgeoisie whilst feeling inspired by the genius of St Francis of Assisi? Wouldn't that be easier?*

Kautsky (1854-1934) on organisation

As the leading theoretician of the Second International, Karl Kautsky is an easy target for revolutionaries. His brand of materialism, inspired by Engels' *Anti-Dühring* (1876-1878), was shaped by his orientation towards the natural sciences and a determinist out-

Fools, beware the ZBD!

look which reduced Marxism to a method of analysis and not a praxis (Goode, 1988: 249). He wrote the theoretical section of the infamous reformist dirge known as the Erfurt programme in 1891. He was also responsible (alongside Engels, Plekhanov, Lenin and to a lesser extent Marx himself) for various reactionary alliances the 'metropolitan' working classes were cajoled into throughout the twentieth century (e.g., alliances with national liberation movements in 'peripheral' societies). Finally, his equivocal stance towards the First World War and support for parliamentarianism earned him a ticking off from his one time disciple, Lenin, who branded him a 'renegade'. Since Kautsky was at no time a revolutionary it is hard to know exactly what he was reneging from and bearing in mind that Lenin also advocated strategic parliamentary action, his criticisms of Kautsky seem rather expedient[116].

---

116 Kautsky kept spilling the beans and embarrassing fellow ex-travellers to the bitter end. This may explain the venom with which he was attacked by Lenin. In his analysis of *Hitlerism*, Kautsky writes, 'A revolution is greatly strengthened when it combines revolutionary with national enthusiasm. This was a factor that

Kautsky's disdain for the 'politically illiterate masses' (Kautsky, 1934: 34) reflected in his elitist conception of organisation. His collaborationist policies with the 'lesser of two evils' also shaped the need to engage organisationally with various factions of the bourgeoisie.[117] Kautsky was contemptuous of 'low rabble proletarians' (Kautsky, 1934: 29), those who were not educated or organised within Social Democratic Parties. It may even be possible that he was influenced by Le Bon's reactionary crowd psychology. He also displayed a touch of moral self-righteousness that set him apart from many rank-and-file members of his party. According to Kautsky, the 'intellectually developed proletariat' abhor 'violence' because they are 'morally uplifted by their Socialist convictions' (Kautsky, 1934: 24). He made a distinction between those who were willing to engage in a long fight for their freedom and those (infantilised) workers who were seeking immediate gratification of their desires,

> ... [the First World War] reduced, at least relatively and often also absolutely, the number of educated and organised workers and increased the number of uneducated and unorganised proletarians. It diminished the number of those who were sufficiently developed to set themselves a new goal for which they were ready to put up a long and stubborn fight. It enlarged the number of those who could not wait and were often looking for immediate spoils (Kautsky, 1934: 33).

Wars and crisis 'impeded the proper political training of new generation of workers' and 'furthered their brutalisation' (Kautsky, 1934: 33). Kautsky was at heart a missionary who wished to impart knowledge and *consciousness* onto the proletariat,[118] preferably those organised like sheep around his organisation, after all 'as an isolated individual, the proletarian is a nonentity' (Kautsky, 1903: 1). His conception of education was a narrow one based on formal monologic schooling. His comments on intellectuals and those skilled sections of the proletariat he referred to as the 'aristocracy of labor' remained unresolved. He naively believed '[the intellectual] fights not by means of power, but by arguments'[119] (Kautsky, 1903: 2). The 'aristocracy of labor' must

---

proved of great help to the Bolsheviks in 1920, who drew new power from the war with Poland ... Of course, in the end democracy is the loser under such an awakening of the warlike spirit, even when the revolutionists emerge as the victors' (Kautsky, 1934: 4).

117 To his credit he was prepared to admit after the victory of fascism that his policies were misplaced, 'It is quite true that the *policy of the lesser of two evils* of supporting Hindenburg for the presidency against Hitler and tolerating the quasi-dictatorial government of Bruening as the last available bulwark against Nazism, did not avert the ultimate greater evil and that it proved a failure' (Kautsky, 1934: 6). This was only a partial apology since he considered the Communists' approach to have been even worse. At the very least, believed Kautsky, his social democratic tactics bought the German proletariat some time!

118 Kautsky himself would disagree with this analysis, I am sure. He is on record as claiming, '... it is impossible to conceive of science being handed down to the proletariat or of an alliance between them as two independent powers. That science, which can contribute to the emancipation of the proletariat, can be developed only by the proletariat and through it' (Kautsky, 1903: 3).

119 Paul Mattick writes, 'Instead of demanding the end of capitalistic science, [German Social Democracy]

not leave the unskilled workers because they can then easily succumb to becoming 'scabs' (Kautsky, 1903: 4). Hence, there must be the closest dual relationship between the economic trade union and the political party. Kautsky (and this is also true of Lenin) postulated that the proletariat had to go through the detour of scientific consciousness in order to become revolutionary. Subsequently he 'authorised the existence of organisations to enclose, direct and control the proletariat' (Barrot, 1985: 9).

His conception of organisation became clearer during his heated debates within the Second International regarding parliamentarianism and the 'dictatorship of the proletariat'.

In a letter to Franz Mehring he goes as far as saying that for him the English parliamentary system with a social democratic majority (perhaps even one which retained the monarchy) would be the best form of the 'dictatorship of the proletariat' (cf. Draper, 1987: 54). As Debord correctly concludes,

> The ideology of the social-democratic organisation gave power to *professors* who educated the working class, and the form of organisation which was adopted was the form most suitable for this passive apprenticeship (Debord, 1987: thesis 96).

Lenin (1870-1924) on organisation

Lenin was a fortunate man. Not every *petty* bourgeois is rewarded with the opportunity to become a *grand* bourgeois presiding over as huge a capitalist Leviathan as was the USSR. His ideas on organisation have influenced generation after generation of power-seeking petty bourgeois activists and sometimes even permeated the proletariat. Lenin learned a great deal from his mentor, Kautsky. In fact, the personal and ideological ties of continuity between them are such that, Barrot (1985: 9) has coined the pejorative term 'Kautskyism-Leninism' to describe the social democratic phenomenon spanning Germany and Russia. The other major intellectual influence was Plekhanov who moved away from Narodism (Russian populism) toward an emasculated version of Marxism in the early 1880s (Zarembka, 2003: 277).

Lenin was also a technician in the sense of being a constructionist of the 'revolution'. Since the Party was for him almost synonymous with the social movement, he used every available tool instrumentally to build the Party. For instance, the newspaper *Iskra* was not just a means of disseminating propaganda for Lenin but 'the best practical method of uniting the scattered centres' of the Party (Hill, 1985: 52). In opposition to German revisionists such as Bernstein and what was later called the Menshevik (minority) faction of Russian so-

---

asked for labour scientists; instead of abolishing capitalistic law, it trained labour lawyers; in the increasing number of labour historians, poets, economists, journalists, doctors and dentists, as well as parliamentarians and trade-union bureaucrats, it saw the socialisation of society...' (Mattick, 1978: 4).

cial democracy, Lenin attempted to reduce the number of rank-and-file members[120] since he believed that,

> the rapid numerical expansion of the German and other parties had been accompanied by a progressive debasement of Marxist theory rather than by an education of the membership up to the theory (Hill, 1985: 53).

Lenin's thoughts regarding these issues were encapsulated in slogans such as, 'little and good' or 'make smaller to make greater' (Hill, 1985: 57). Various obstacles were put in the way of potential recruits to ensure only the pure of heart would get through. As Hill (1985: 63) makes clear, 'Lenin insisted on a long period of probation and frequent purges' of unsuitable elements including careerists. Like all technicians Lenin needed to be in charge, controlling the ascent of the 'malleable' spontaneous masses 'up to the theory'. This approach demanded a tightly organised, disciplined, hierarchical cadre of activists ably supported by 'sympathisers', who had not yet passed the rigours of recruitment.

I'll be back!

This explains why although Russian social democracy discarded terrorism as a method of struggle, the Bolshevik faction, under Lenin's direct influence, absorbed much of the specifically Russian tradition of strict secrecy and centralised activities of 'professional revolutionaries' practiced by *Narod-*

The dustbin of history

naya Volya (the Party of People's Will). Lenin's critique of capitalism was so superficial that he, in fact, recommended the factory with discipline and organisation based on collective work as the basis of the Party. There is little in Lenin to suggest he understood the need to expose and struggle against various social and technical divisions of labour within proletarian organisations. As Trotsky (1947: 61) observed many years later, these practices led to the emergence of perennial problems within the Party,

> The habits peculiar … to a political machine were already forming in the underground. The young revolutionary bureaucrat was already emerging as a type. The conditions of conspiracy, true enough, offered rather meagre scope for such formalities of democracy as elections, accountability and control … [The Committee men] were far more intransigent and severe with revolutionary working men than with themselves, preferring to domineer …

---

120 On at least two occasions the doors of the Party were flung open and recruits encouraged to join. According to Hill, 'the first was in August 1919, the blackest moment of the war of intervention … [and] after Lenin's death in 1924 there was an even larger mass enrolment' (Hill, 1985: 64).

Trotsky is even honest enough to admit that the autonomy of proletarian organisations was a source of concern for the Bolsheviks,

> The Petersburgh Committee of the Bolsheviks was frightened at first by such an innovation as a non-partisan representation of the embattled masses. It could do nothing better than to present the Soviet with an ultimatum: immediately adopt a Social-democratic programme or disband. The Petersburgh Soviet as a whole, including the contingent of Bolsheviks working men as well, ignored the ultimatum without batting an eyelid (Trotsky, 1947: 64-65).

Any worker who showed competence and organisational ability was a target for poaching. In an early example of 'corporate head-hunting', Lenin instructed that,

> A worker-agitator who shows any talent and is at all promising *should not work in the factory*. We must see to it that he lives on Party support ... and goes over to an underground status (Lenin quoted in Brinton, 1975: xii).

The severance of the organic link between the proletariat and Bolshevik 'professional revolutionaries' was a long and non-linear process, which had its roots in Lenin's dualistic approach to organisation and his struggle toward a Russian road to capitalism. His concept of *democratic centralism* was ultimately a bourgeois mode of controlling the rank-and-file in order to use them in the conquest of power. As Dauvé and Martin (1997: 64) have concluded, 'For Lenin, the main problem was to forge a *leadership* capable of leading the workers to victory'. Victory as endpoint (and a very bourgeois conception of *victory* at that) was already mapped out by the leaders. Creativity, if indeed it exists, is reduced to means not ends. Politics becomes a matter of administration. This kind of politics as Tormey (2005: 399) states,

> ... conforms to the logic of a military operation: we are to be coordinated, organised, galvanised. It is not a practice with room for doubt or ambivalence, of uncertainty or unknowability. These are signs of 'weakness' and 'vacillation'... Politics in this sense is paradoxically the end of the political, or the end of the political as a creative act.

Hakim Bey on organisation

Hakim Bey (a.k.a. Peter Lamborn Wilson) is one of the few individuals who have attempted to take Situationist ideas on organisation further. The fact that he is also influenced by (individualist) Anarchism, (bourgeois and petty bourgeois) Sufism, (postmodern) libertarianism and (romantic) Shamanism has meant that Situationist notions have undergone strange transformations under his influence. Hakim Bey is not a revolutionary. He is handicapped by a lack of class analysis. His vision of the 'orient' veers unashamedly into 'orientalism'. Some of his writings seem tailor made for the student-bohemian[121] crowd in search of Nirvana (or at least the self-delusion that their 'gap-year' could be imbued with a sense of dangerous radicalism). And yet I have decided to include him in my study since he touches on a number of key issues that have a direct bearing on revolutionary organisations.

Bey's central idea regarding organisation is the notion of the *Temporary Autonomous Zone* (TAZ). More recently, he has tried to supplement TAZ by positing

a more durable concept which he calls a *Permanent Autonomous Zone* (PAZ). Bey believes Temporary Autonomous Zones (TAZs) already exist. He gives examples of this type of phenomenon but also augments actually existing TAZ by extrapolating from historical and sci-fi narratives. The TAZ is a kind of 'free enclave', or 'islands on the net'. It is an actual space which may have a certain dimension of it represented in cyber virtuality. In Bey's own words,

> The TAZ is like an uprising which does not engage directly with the State, a guerilla operation which liberates an area (of land, of time, of imagination) and then dissolves itself to re-form elsewhere/elsewhen, before the State crushes it ... Getting the TAZ started may involve tactics of violence and defence, but its greatest strength lies in its invisibility - the state cannot recognise it because History has no definition of it ... The TAZ is therefore a perfect tactic for an era in which the State is omnipresent and all-powerful and yet simultaneously riddled with cracks and vacancies ... in most cases the best and most radical tactic will be to refuse to engage in spectacular violence, to withdraw from the area of simulation, to disappear (Bey, 1985: 3).

For the Bey of the 1980s we were living in the *Jahaliah* (the age of ignorance or the medieval Dark Ages according to Islamic thinking) and the proper response to such overwhelming ignorance was to drop out and disappear, as a hermit would. Bey's TAZ, it turns out, could be a geographic, social or imaginal space. Examples of such partial 'liberated zones' are,

---

121 In a study of *bohemia*, Enzo Traverso (2002: 123-153) claims the term has always contained a tension between revolutionary and counter-revolutionary tendencies. He writes, '... the rebellious spirit of bohemia can find an outlet in an active participation in the 1848 revolution, as well as feeding reactionary subversion, leading to Bonapartism and fascism in the twentieth century'. I would argue that there is also the third tendency within bohemia – the non-revolutionary. The student-bohemian followers of Bey are mostly non-revolutionaries with a pernicious minority of counter-revolutionaries at the margin of his 'Temporary Autonomous Zones'.

> The sixties-style 'tribal gatherings', the forest conclave eco-saboteurs … Harlem
> rent parties of the twenties, nightclubs, banquets, old-time libertarian picnics …
> (Bey, 1985: 5).

By invoking a number of proto-TAZ enclaves such as the above as well as more romantic historical events such as the mediaeval Assassins of the Middle East and the
sea-rovers and Corsairs of the 18th century, Bey is trying to glimpse the outline of an
'archetype'. These 'drop-outs' would find themselves an isolated space where they
would gradually dispose of accumulated layers of civilisation and turn 'wild'. The
'psychic nomads' would employ the policy of 'race mixing' as a founding principle
and create 'a pirate economy' ('living high off the surplus of social overproduction',
Bey, 1985: 16). Following Foucault, Bey suggests that 'the TAZ is in some sense a *tactic of disappearance*' (Bey, 1985: 17). The TAZ has both a negative aspect ('an element
of refusal' to use Zerzan's phrase- cf. Zerzan, 1988) that is directed against the status
quo and a positive aspect, which suggests an alternative to current institutions,

> For example, the negative gesture against *schooling* is 'voluntary illiteracy'…
> There are however positive alternatives which make use of the same energy of dis-
> appearance. Home-schooling and craft-apprenticeship, like truancy, result in an
> absence from the prison of school. Hacking is another form of 'education' with cer-
> tain features of 'invisibility' (Bey, 1985: 17).

It is noteworthy that most of the examples provided by Bey to illustrate negative and
positive aspects of resistance emphasise 'individualism' and shun collective struggle.
Bey is 'suspicious' of collective resistance and 'Revolution', as are most of his petty-
bourgeois readership. However, there are certain attributes of his TAZ that continue
to intrigue. For example, Bey emphasises that TAZ as a conscious radical tactic will
appear when there is genuine attempt at 'psychological liberation'. That is,

> We must realise (make real) the moments and spaces in which freedom is not only
> possible but actual. We must know in what ways we are genuinely oppressed, and
> also in what ways we are self-repressed or ensnared in which ideas oppress us
> (Bey, 1985: 19).

Significantly, TAZ is about the here-and-now and not some pie-in-the-sky Social
Utopia. So in line with the Situationists, Bey is against the notion of 'sacrifice' for
a vague far-off dream. Instead of sacrifice, the TAZ promotes conviviality and
face-to-face meetings (or 'immediatism'). Without mentioning Bakhtin, Bey talks
about the 'healing laughter' which he opposes to the 'poisonous and corrosive
laughter' of 'cynical nihilists' (Moorish Orthodox Radio Crusade Collective, 1992:
30). Only a serious (but not sober) TAZ can produce the healing laughter.

However, like any door-to-door salesman Bey has a tendency to make exaggerated claims for his face-to-face meetings,

> We're not kidding or indulging in hyperbole when we insist that meeting face-to-face is already the 'revolution' ... Immediatism is a picnic- but it's not *easy*. Immediatism is the most natural path for free humans imaginable- & *therefore* the most unnatural abomination in the eyes of Capital. Immediatism will triumph, but only at the cost of *self-organisation of power*, of *clandestinity*, & of *insurrection*. Immediatism is our delight. Immediatism is *dangerous* (Moorish Orthodox Radio Crusade Collective, 1992: 13).

No doubt the knowledge that they are being 'dangerous' and 'revolutionary' is a great solace to hordes of bohemian Hakim Bey fans who armed with a basketful of hummus sandwiches and vegetarian samosas plant their flag of autonomy on the shores of the Central Parks of the world!

As the chorus of criticisms of his TAZ scheme became louder, Bey was forced to acknowledge that the Temporary Autonomous Zone may need to be supplemented

by the Permanent Autonomous Zone (PAZ). Certain cracks in capitalism, it was now conceded, were so 'vacant that whole groups can move into them and settle down', more-or-less permanently (Bey, 1993: 1). The *Jahaliah* (Age of Darkness and Ignorance according to elitist Islamic revisionism) may very well be coming to a close and a more proactive strategy was called for- the *Jihad*. According to some of his critics for the later Hakim Bey, 'capitalism and the state are no longer the central enemies ... instead colonialism in the form of globalisation that produces sameness (homogenisation) is what we must confront ...' (Killing King Abacus, 2000: 1).

The 'festival' aspect of TAZ might even be able to refresh and renew the PAZ. Bey gives examples of the PAZ: MOVE in Philadelphia, the Koreshites of Waco, computer hackers, the Chinese Tong Secret Society and squatters. The PAZ should aim at creating a 'truly alternative economy' whilst avoiding confrontational attitude,

> People probably ought to choose the people they live with. 'Open-membership' communes invariably end up swamped with freeloaders and sex-starved pathetic creeps [a slightly moralistic attitude given Bey's own sexual preferences]. PAZs must choose their own membership mutually- this has nothing to do with

'elitism'. The PAZ may exercise a temporarily open function- such as hosting festivals or giving away free food, etc.- but it need not be permanently open to any self-proclaimed sympathizer who wanders by (Bey, 1993: 2). [My additions]

The above passage could be read as an updating of the 1970s hippy communes Bey is so fond of. The updating involves a measure of control over the evolution of the commune with presumably Hakim Bey himself acting as the 'invisible Sufi', pulling all the strings from behind the curtain. He will need all the control mechanisms he can lay his hands on if he is to suppress the clamour of dissent that has greeted his latest views in certain quarters.

For instance, Bey's views on nationalism are proof yet again that Anarchism and Leninism are mirror-images of each other. In *Millennium* (1996) Bey resurrects the Leninist distinction between 'oppressed' and 'oppressor' forms of nationalism. He calls 'oppressed' countries examples of 'true' nationalism and gives the Zapatistas, Bosnia, Slovenia, Macedonia, the Ukraine and the Kurds as examples. By contrast 'oppressor' countries are referred to as 'negative' or 'hegemonic' nationalities and he cites the Serbs and Russians in this category. Regardless of the exact terminology employed and the examples posited, Bey's analysis 'tends to naturalise nationalities and thus nationalism' (Killing King Abacus, 2000: 2). Bizarrely Bey seems to be supporting the state against capitalism in some of his latest works. As the Killing King Abacus (2000: 3) magazine has sarcastically observed,

> While in TAZ Bey, unlike many other anarchists, was simply waiting for the state to 'go away' on its own, in *Millennium* he has decided that, since it didn't disappear, we could use it to fight Capitalism.

The same article pours further scorn on some of Bey's romantic misappropriations of history. For example, the pirates of North Africa that Bey is so keen on and in fact credits with creating 'pirate utopias' had their ships powered by slaves. A minor historical point Hakim Bey just forgets to mention! Likewise, he champions the Chinese Tong as revolutionaries when they were nothing of the sorts. His opportunistic use of religion reaches nauseating extremes when he proclaims, '... it seems clear that without religion there will be no radical revolution' (Bey, 1996: 84). This sad quote is reflective of Bey's recent degeneration, a degeneration that has seen him cuddle up to Libya's Colonel Qadafi as a neo-Sufi. Let me end this section on Hakim Bey's contribution to organisational question with the scathing attack levelled at him by Killing King Abacus (2000: 4),

> Unfortunately, just as TAZ, with its implicit suggestion that anarchists wait in the cracks for the state to crumble, was an expression of the weakness of the anarchist movement of the late [1980s], Millennium, with its more explicit demands that anarchists align themselves with nationalism, religion, and the state, is a measure of its weakness in the early [1990s].

Autonomists on organisation

The shear breadth of autonomist writing on political matters is so great as to make any attempt at generalisation futile. The best I can do in this section is to provide a thumbnail account of a sample of autonomist works on organisation. I will begin with traditional literature on organisation and move onto cyber-autonomist discussions related to more recent struggles.

First permit me to make it clear that I do not accept Autonomist Marxism as a genuinely revolutionary tendency. Yet I have undeniably learnt greatly from its teachings and will continue to do so irrespective of its Leninist origins and its current languishing within the mire of Leftism. As a reaction against the almost theological method of citations and the negation of subjectivity favoured by Stalinists, the generation of 1950s and 1960s Autonomist dissenters began by launching a series of investigations into the objective *and* subjective conditions of working class life. Interviews, questionnaires and oral history became widely used tools of analysis (Wright, 2002: 24).

Justice for Janitors demo (USA)

Based on these 'worker enquiries' one leading advocate, Mario Tronti, came up with the concept of the *social factory* in order to conceptualise recent capitalist developments. According to Tronti, 'When all of society is reduced to a factory, the factory – as such – seems to disappear …' (Tronti quoted in Wright, 2002: 38). A methodological tension soon developed with some Autonomists such as Panzieri, using such insights to broaden the definition of *productive labour* whilst others, Tronti himself included, continued to emphasise manual labourers.

Autonomism's problems with the concept of organisation began because of its inherent Kantian dualism. Organisation for some like Alquati was all about 'the transformation of objective forces into subjective forces' (Alquati quoted in Wright, 2002: 51). Organisation was, therefore, a function of 'class composition' and for Autonomists class composition was defined as 'the various forms of behaviour which arise when particular forms of labour-power are inserted in specific processes of production' (Wright, 2002: 49). In other words, first determine what type of worker the production process has thrown up, whether they are 'professional workers' (the highly skilled factory workers at the beginning of the 20th century) or 'mass workers' (semi-skilled assembly workers produced by Taylorism and Fordism), or the 'socialised worker' (a new political subject bound up with the proletarianistaion of intellectual labour). Then you will know how to harness their subjective and behavioural energies (i.e., their class composition) within the right kind of organisational framework.

As if this reductionism was not bad enough there was also a tendency within Autonomism from the outset to find the elusive 'vanguard of the proletariat' and build around them. For Alquati this was the technician within factories, since their greater mobility within the firm 'granted them a global vision of sorts' (Wright, 2002: 57). However, a number of tensions with the official labour movement forced Autonomism to 'break' with its past. Whilst some (e.g., Panzieri) experienced this as traumatic and looked for every opportunity to return to the fold of official labourism, others (e.g., Alquati) experienced it as a release (Wright, 2002: 59-60). But the 'break' was in many ways illusionary. For instance, Autonomism arguably remained within a Leninist ideological framework even though it was now putting greater emphasis on working class struggle. The poles had been reversed but the maintenance of a 'scientific' outlook, with ready-made independent and dependent variables, detracted from the conclusions. Tronti could not have realised how much he was exposing about Autonomism when he confessed,

> We too have worked with a concept that puts capitalist development first, and workers second. This is a mistake. And now we have to turn the problem on its head ... and start again from the beginning: and the beginning is the class struggle of the working class (Tronti, 1964, quoted in Wright, 2002: 64).

The obvious conclusion for Tronti was that the classical Leninist distinction between political and economic struggles was no longer applicable [was it ever?] and since according to him we must always begin with working class struggle then, '... the chain will break not where capital is weakest, but where the working class is strongest' (Tronti quoted in Wright, 2002: 66). One can see in these comments the same theoretical arrogance, the same haughty generalisations that simple-minded Leninists are so fond of. To illustrate once more that their 'break' with Leninism was as superficial as it was temporary we could remind ourselves how Tronti still persisted with Lenin's views on trade unions,

In certain instances, some of which are very much present, tying the union to the party via a transmission belt seems the most practicable path for the class struggle (Tronti quoted in Wright, 2002: 69).

Tronti still believed in the 'vanguard party' and the 'intervention of revolutionary will' and the intellectuals' duty to 'measure, control, manage and therefore to organise the political growth of the working class'. As Wright (2002: 71) makes clear this is the same arrogance displayed by the likes of Trotsky 'with his analogy of the party as piston and the class as steam'.[122] Tronti made a valid distinction between strategy and tactics but then suggested a fatuous division of labour with strategy already embryonic within the working class and tactics the preserve of the party. Since Tronti fetishized working class 'activity' even their 'passivity' was now seen as a threat to the ruling class, a form of 'organisation without organisation' (Tronti quoted in Wright, 2002: 77). Of course, resistance through 'passivity' was not the preferred option. Many trends within Autonomia 'formulated a brand of Leninism' which sanctified armed struggle 'as the pinnacle of the class struggle' (Wright, 2002: 161). Other Autonomists became enamoured of instances of self-organisation among young workers in the small shops of Milan and Turin. As Wright (2002: 165) explains,

> Known as 'proletarian youth circles', these precursors of today's social centres attempted to co-ordinate disputes in different firms, whilst also engaging in new forms of self-reduction such as the mass gatecrashing of cinemas, concerts and other cultural activities.

During the 1970s these 'proletarian youth circles' managed to provide linkage between different sections of the Italian proletariat and Autonomists were rightly impressed by their ability to organise themselves without outside assistance. Autonomists like Negri were also calling for 'the reconstruction of a participatory civil society outside the state, the building of networks of localised, user run social services, radical innovation and rearrangement of the working day, and the passage of production into communal, cooperative forms ...' (Witheford, 1994: 108). This is a co-operative form of organisation 'dictated by the immaterial paradigm of production' (Hardt and Negri, 2004: 142).

Most Autonomists believe computerisation marks 'a watershed in the relation between worker and machine- a quantum leap in the predominance of fixed over variable

---

122 A similar (but more sophisticated) metaphor is employed by Bronfenbrenner (1983: 175). As Engeström (1987: 108) has explained for Bronfenbrenner, '... development takes place like in a moving train. One can walk forward and backward through the cars, but what really matters is where the train is going ... The train metaphor exemplifies the central problem embedded in most of the available societally and ecologically oriented analysis of development, including that of [Bronfenbrenner himself]. The environments or societal contexts are seen as historically changing, but not as being constructed and reconstructed by the people living in these contexts'.

capital, dead labor over living labor' (Dyer-Witheford, 1999: 94). Autonomists are also mindful of the reactionary origins of electronic networking. As Nick Dyer-Witheford (1999: 78) notes,

> Electronic networking, originally developed as part of preparations to fight a nuclear war, receives its first large-scale civilian application in the emergency management systems used by the Nixon administration to monitor its wage-price freeze and picket line violence in a truckers strike.

However, despite these murky origins Autonomists like Negri believe as computers and machines become more pervasive the new 'socialised worker' will enjoy 'an increasingly *organic* relation to technoscience' (Dyer-Witheford, 1999: 84). That is why, according to Negri, tactics such as sabotage and neo-Luddism which might have made sense during the era of the 'mass worker' are increasingly superfluous.[123] I disagree with this analysis but Negri is correct when in a vein similar to Bakhtin he alludes to the conflict between *communication* and *information*. This has direct relevance to the problem of organisation. Again Dyer-Witheford[124] makes this point clear,

> Information [read: monologic discourse] is centralised, vertical, hierarchic, communication [read: dialogic interaction] is distributed, transverse, dialogic. Capital tries to capture the communicative capacity of the labor force in its technological and organisational form ... (Dyer-Witheford, 1999: 86). [My additions]

In many ways the dispersed nature of computer work and the service industry founded on its success made organising resistance problematic. In the USA the divided ethnic composition and high turn over pose additional problems. However,

> In the early 1990s ... following a wave of worker complaints, Justice for Janitors, an organisation of the Services employees International Union, began a series of campaigns fighting for union recognition, pay raises, and settlement of sexual harassment grievances ... Moreover, in some respects the Justice for Janitors campaign went beyond familiar models of shop-floor activism. They made

---

123 Here once more Negri's overemphasis on what he considers to be the privileged (or leading edge) section of the proletariat leads to neglecting that capital employs a variety of methods of surplus value extraction, production processes and therefore methods of surveillance and repression. To suggest that sabotage of the work process is now passé represents yet another dogmatic and arrogant Negri final judgment.

124 Nick Dyer-Witheford (1999: 174) traces Negri's distinction between 'dominative information and insurgent communication' to Habermas's theory of communicative action 'which upholds an *ideal speech situation* of democracy, symmetrical dialogue unobstructed by inequities of power and skill as a yard-stick against which to measure emancipatory social change'. The parallels between Negri and Habermas are real and disconcerting but I have chosen to foreground Bakhtin since I believe his work to be more productive. Bakhtin's nuanced interpretations of dialogic interaction displays a more realistic account of human communication than Habermas's rather anaemic liberal model.

connections between workplace conditions and issues of race and gender discrimination, and forged alliances with feminist and ethnic community organisations (Dyer-Witheford, 1999: 97).

During the mobilising effort at Apple they even threatened to take their struggle into schools and universities (a major market for Macintosh computers). Nick Dyer-Witheford (1999: 125) also mentions the importance of network activism, 'mailing lists such as ACT-IV-L, LEFT-L ...' for a variety of social movements. During strikes the Web can become a means of communication as well as a mode of organising. For instance,

> In 1994, some twenty-six hundred workers from eight unions struck San Francisco's two daily papers. During the strike they produced their own paper- the *San Francisco Free Press*. This was not only distributed within the city but was also made electronically accessible via the World Wide Web, thus making it probably the most widely circulated strike bulletin in the history of civilisation (Dyer-Witheford, 1999: 127).

The centre of 'information activism' has shifted in recent years toward a proliferation of grassroot initiatives which try to engage with both local and global rulers. More examples are provided by Dyer-Witheford (1999: 148),

> Brazilian street television, video training for Korean trade unionists, township-based South African community radio stations ... the radio activism of Solidarno-sc, underground music and media permeating Eastern Europe, the role of computer networks ...

In fact so successful has computer networking been in publicising some key struggles such as the Zapatista movement that Peter Waterman (1990) suggested they could become the bedrock of a 'fifth international' described as,

> A transitional connection of oppositional groupings that does not, like the four previous socialist Internationals, rest on the hierarchical directives of a centralised vanguard party, but rather arise from the transverse communications of multiplicitous movements (Dyer-Witheford, 1999: 153).

The suggestions conveniently ignores that in most countries computer access is still restricted to bourgeois and petty-bourgeois members of society.[125] Lately, some Auto-

---

125 There is another issue that promoters of the 'networking' metaphor usually avoid and that is the mathematical origins of the term. Some of the most important theorists of networking are bourgeois ideologues at the RAND Corporation such as David Ronfeldt. 'Cognitive psychology' is yet another metaphor 'anti-globalisers' employ uncritically. Cognitive psychology is a positivist doctrine which deskills people. As Parker says, 'If your ideal world is a giant office with arrows leading you from one cubicle to the

nomists have become concerned about the dangers of cyber-activism. The European Counter Network, for instance, has noted the pitfalls of computer activism,

> Technical fetishism, new hierarchies of expertise, health risks, and the ultimate night-mare, a simulated international radical network in which all communication is medi-ated by modems and in which information circulates endlessly between computers without being put back into a human context (Dyer-Witheford, 1999: 128).

In summary, the groups that claim the heritage of the Movement of '77 (a cycle of fierce struggle in Italy which peaked in 1977) have proposed a number of organisa-tional models (see Wright, 2005). In my view none go beyond orthodox modernist Leninism or (at best) unorthodox postmodernist Leninism and whilst some are more thought-provoking than others, none offers a genuine alternative to past failures.

Camatte on organisation

Jacques Camatte furnishes us with a flawed but interesting cri-tique of the formal political party as rackets. Ultimately, his solution is disappointing because it amounts to a rather lame call for purity (albeit a call wrapped in fluffy humanism) and a rejection of the proletariat (which shares disturbing commonalities with Negri's recent foregrounding of the notion of *multitudes*). However, the road to Camatte's hell is paved with both good inten-tions and pertinent criticisms of all hitherto Leninist and An-archist organisations. It is, there-fore, a hell well worth visiting.

Camatte edited the journal *In-variance*. He collaborated with Amadeo Bordiga but broke with him over a number of major dis-agreements including the party form. His criticisms were not con-fined to Leninism, Anarchism and Italian Left Communism (Bordi-

'The gang seduces its recruits, then vampirizes their creative abilities ...'

next, then cognitive psychology is for you' (Parker, 2007: 44). A bit more care in our choice of metaphors is essential if clarity is not sacrificed in favour of trendiness.

gism) but were also directed against smaller groups such as the Situationists, Social-isme ou Barbarie and Council Communists. One writer has explained how Camatte compared political parties to gangs:

> The gang seduces its recruits, then vampirizes their creative abilities and sup-presses their desires and their individuality in the name of an illusory community (Trotter, 1995: 9).

Where Bordiga confidently declares communism an objective possibility at least since 1848, 'Camatte's modification holds that communism has always been possible throughout history' (Trotter, 1995: 8). Since communism is an objective possibility it is all the more necessary to supersede the party form and the notion of *representation* which Camatte denounced as the essence of politics. In fact, he follows Marx in mak-ing a distinction between the *formal* party and the *historic* party. Having made the distinction he then modifies Marx too. According to Trotter (1995: 10),

> For Marx, the formal party is an actual, but ephemeral and contingent organisation that exists during a time of heightened revolutionary activity. In times of counter-revolution, when there is little activity, revolutionaries should maintain loose net-works of personal contacts to maintain the continuity of critical theory. These networks he called the historic party. For Camatte, the formal party is now a use-less concept, having degenerated into numerous sectarian rackets.

Camatte is arguing that during counterrevolutionary times the split between theory and practice becomes accentuated. His solution is to turn 'revolutionaries' into guardians of critical theory and keep the fires of the temple burning like some Zoroastrian magi charged with lighting the path for the eventual return of Ahura-Mazda. For Camatte, theoretical clarity is not at all the same as proposing a polit-ical programme (Bordiga) or bringing consciousness to the proletariat from the outside (Kautsky and Lenin) or proletarian pedagogic self-education (council communism). It will, however, magically resurrect the equation between prolet-arian movement = theory = communism. The party can 'only be the party-Ge-meinwesen and it will not be able to function when it appears by appealing to the principle of centralisation, or the opposite, federalism' (Camatte, 1972: 5). One can only marvel at Camatte's ability to wish problems away and dispense with the need to struggle using a deft linguistic turn of phrase.

His negativist attitude toward any kind of political activity could be traced back to his belief that since social democracy has repressed consciousness of the historic goal of the proletariat in favour of immediate goals and since the further 'racketization of con-sciousness' through specialisation has all but disintegrated consciousness, the historic party becomes the only method of preserving a total critique. In other words,

The revolutionary must not identify himself [sic] with a group but recognise himself in a theory which does not depend on a group or on a review, because it is the expression of an existing class struggle. This is actually the correct sense in which anonymity is posed as the negation of the individual ... Moreover, the desire for theoretical development must realise itself in an autonomous and personal fashion and not by way of a group which sets itself up as a kind of diaphragm between the individual and the theory (Camatte and Collu, 1969: 23-24).

So individuals must retain their 'autonomy' whilst maintaining a network of personal contacts (i.e., the historic party) with people who have reached the same level of theoretical clarity. He also links this historic party to the *real* phase of capital's domination when capital has become representation (cf. Debord, 1987) and 'escaped from human control, including that of the dominant classes' (Trotter, 1995: 13). In the real phase of domination 'politics as an instrument mediating the despotism of capital' simply disappears (Collu and Camatte, 1969: 32).

This is an explicit call for 'anti-activism'. Camatte is arguably distorting Marx's notion of the historic party here, since the latter never tired of arguing for the proletariat constituting itself as a class and at the same time inevitably getting dirty in the mire of 'politics'.[126] However, to his credit, Camatte does reject the bane of some left communist groupings, namely the theory of 'decadence'. Influenced by Rosa Luxemburg, these groups suggest capitalism has been in decline since the beginning of the twentieth century (1914 is a popular break-off point) and therefore no longer 'progressive'. Camatte rejects the 'progressive-decadent' dichotomy and suggests the 'wandering of humanity', which began at least as early as the 6th century B.C. with the advent of the Greek *polis*, will end by 'abandoning' the capitalist mode of production and not necessarily because capitalism has become 'decadent'.

Finally, what is significant in Camatte (and also Bordiga) is their critique of democracy. This sets them apart from left-communism, the S.I. and a whole host of radicals who employ the concept uncritically. For Camatte (1969: 1),

... one can define democracy as the behaviour of humans, the organisation of those who have lost their original organic unity with the community. Thus it exists during the whole period which separates primitive communism from scientific communism ... Democracy was born from the moment that there was a division between men [sic] and the allocation of possessions. That is to say, it arose with private property, individuals and the class division of society, with the formation of the state.

Apart from its quasi-mystical overtones, the above definition also has the side-effect of making the struggle for organised activity redundant. Conveniently for Camatte,

---

126 Camatte does refer to this dimension of the historic party (Collu and Camatte, 1969: 39) but only tangentially.

... the revolution is not a problem of forms of organisation. For capitalist society, everything is an organisational question. At the beginning of its development, this appears as the search for good institutions; at the end as the search for the best structures to enclose men [sic] in prisons of capital (Camatte, 1969: 3).

However, Camatte is careful not to reject democracy and parliamentarianism entirely. He believes during the *formal* phase of domination,

[democracy] is a mechanism used by the capitalist class to attain domination over society ... That is why the proletariat can also for a certain time intervene on this terrain ... The proletariat can use parliament as a platform to denounce the demo-cratic mystification and can use universal suffrage as a means to organise the class ... when capital arrived at its real domination, and constituted itself as a material community, the question was resolved: it seized the State. The conquest of the state from the inside no longer poses itself ... (Camatte, 1969: 6).

In summary, whilst Camatte foregrounds a useful series of flaws in the party and the clique, his smug rejection of proletarian self-organising activity smacks of the kind of elitism one has come to expect from grumpy, old left-communists. No, it is more than that, isn't it? It is cowardly! Yes ... cowardly.

Jo Freeman on organisation

Joe Freeman's text, *The Tyranny of Structurelessness*, was originally published in 1970 to address organisational issues related to the US women's movement. However, in puncturing certain cosy myths it found itself addressing a wider readership than its intended target audience and since many of the problems it discussed are still with us today, it has retained most of its relevance. Freeman (1970: 1) began her critique by pointing out that,

Contrary to what we would like to believe, there is no such thing as a 'structure-less' group ... The structure may be flexible, it may vary over time, it may evenly or unevenly distribute tasks, power and resources over the members of the group. But it will be formed regardless of the abilities, personalities and intentions of the people involved.

To pretend otherwise, as many informal groups still do, is to be indulging in wishful thinking at best and shear duplicity at worst. Freeman insists (1970: 1),

The [myth] of 'structurelessness' becomes a way of masking power, and within the women's movement it is usually most strongly advocated by those who are the most powerful ... Those who do not know the rules and are not chosen for initi-ation must remain in confusion, or suffer from paranoid delusion that something is happening of which they are not quite aware ... [Therefore] the rules of de-cision-making must be open and available to everyone, and this can only happen if they are formalised.

In other words a Leninist organisation based on the precepts of democratic centralism is a *formal* structure whereas a whole host of anarchist and autonomist organisa-tions that are not explicitly and openly structured still have an *informal* or covert structure. Both the formal and informal structures create elites. Freeman is in-sistent, however, that elites are not always con-spiratorial students of Machiavelli. Most of the time, she believes, elites emerge organically as a by-product of friends who engage in joint political activity. She also believes this is inevitable and since it is unavoidable the 'healthiest situation' would be to aim for a formal struc-ture with two or more of such friendship networks com-peting with each other for power (Freeman, 1970: 2). Presumably this way everything would be in the open and the power games may even cancel each other out creating a space for useful joint activity. What is dan-gerous is to have an informal elite which actively promotes the myth of 'structurelessness'. In these cir-cumstances power becomes capricious.

... then the anarchists tried to hijack the meeting and copulate with the situationists but the autonomists had come prepared ... honestly reverend, they are more dysfunctional than my family!

There are further problems with self-acclaimed 'structureless' groups. For example, Freeman (1970: 3) believes that 'the idea of structurelessness' is respons-ible for creating the 'star' system. Since movements such as the feminist movement do not put forward any

Gossiping as a form of structurelessness tyranny

official spokespersons and since 'the public is conditioned to look for spokespeople', certain women of public note are propelled into stardom. The 'sisterhood' usually purges these stars 'who then become free to commit all of the individualistic sins of which [they] have been accused' (Freeman, 1970: 3).

Another problem occurs when a group cannot find a local project to devote themselves to. Freeman believes the group members 'turn their energies to controlling others in the group ... and spend their time criticising the personalities of the other members...' (Freeman, 1970: 3). Subsequently, alienation may set in and the group begins to haemorrhage membership. It is noteworthy that both of these problems surface within proletarian groups as well and both difficulties become more acute at times of low class struggle.

In the final part of the essay, Freeman attempts to describe the organisational traits necessary for the 'healthy functioning' of any political group. She counsels rejecting the ideology of 'structurelessness' without going to the other extreme of blindly imitating traditional political organisations. Experimenting with different kinds of structuring for different situations seems the most sensible way of proceeding. Whilst advocating experimentation, Freeman believes certain principles are essential: *delegation* of specific authority to individuals; *rotation* of tasks in order to avoid specialism; *diffusion* of information to everyone on a frequent basis; and *equal access* to resources.

... and since 'the public is conditioned to look for spokespeople', certain women of public note are propelled into stardom....

One of the problems with Freeman's formulation is her artificial stages theory, separating 'consciousness-raising' from 'movement building'. The zone of proximal development not only does away with this false dichotomy but also questions the very notion of 'consciousness-raising'. Consciousness is not mere awareness. Rather consciousness, in Vygotskian terminology, is the organising matrix of higher mental functions such as emotions, thinking and language. It can, therefore, no sooner be raised than lowered. It can, however, be re-arranged, developed, made self-revelatory. It can also pass from a form where most of its dialectical links are severed, concealed or marginalised to one where these linkages are foregrounded. In the process of collective struggle (and not in 'consciousness-raising' groups that mimic the ZBD), polarities such as public-private, concrete-abstract, immediate-long term and emotion-intellect are superseded and dialectical consciousness becomes generalised.

Another problem with Freeman is her emphasis on form at the expense of content and motivation. For Freeman once you have stopped denying the structured nature of your group and initiated certain sound principles of management (such as delegation, diffusion and equal access) the group begins to function healthily. The neglect of both the political and psychological dimensions of collective action is the Achilles' heel of this formalist approach.

Finally, Freeman has a tendency towards reductionism. Her simplistic analysis of the causes of 'elitism' and the 'star system' ignore the contribution of Marxists in relation to the social and technical division of labour and the Situationist critique of the emergence of stars as part of the spectacularisation of society. All these points will be further elaborated in the second section of this text.

5.1.2 Prefiguring the Zone of Proletarian Development (ZPD)

Having looked at some of the writers promoting the Zone of Bourgeois Development (Kautsky and Lenin for instance) and some of the obstacles that could potentially prevent revolutionary praxis (as brilliantly outlined by Joe Freeman and Jacques Camatte), we can now turn our attention to a more positive area. Below I discuss writers and ideas that are conducive to revolutionary organising.

Karl Marx (1818-1883) on organisation

Thankfully Marx has left us no blueprint for the perfect revolutionary organisation- only a smattering of vague concepts and his political practice during his phase of activism. I say thankfully since, given the conformity of most of his followers, one can only imagine how a carefully constructed blueprint would have ossified the notion of change and innovation in relation to this most thorny of problems.

So let us begin our brief consideration of his thoughts on the subject with *The Poverty of Philosophy* (Marx, 1846-47/1978), a devastating attack on Proudhon's anarchism and the utopian socialism of the likes of Fourier[127]. Marx sees proletarian organisation as tied up with the general development of history. In order to underscore his point he occasionally goes overboard and displays a certain determinism,

> [In spite of bourgeois economists and utopian socialists], in spite of manuals and utopias, combination has not ceased for an instant to go forward and grow with development and growth of modern industry (Marx, 1846-47/1978: 167).

At this stage Marx's views are still tinged with a teleological fervour which associates economic *progress* with evermore radical forms of proletarian combination,

> England, whose industry has attained the highest degree of development, has the

---

127 Marx was at times extremely dismissive of utopias and yet as Tormey (2005: 396) argues close inspection shows 'the other suppressed dimension of Marx's own work, which is its deep, thrilling utopianism'. As Bloch (2000) observes Marx's utopia was rooted in the flow of historical process, it was a 'concrete utopia' and not an 'abstract utopia'. The point is joint-activity should not be about the deferral of people's needs and desires to a distant, vague future. It is mostly about the here and now with an eye on both the past and the future. Nor should it emasculate the social movement within 'sacred' programmes but encourage a continuous inspection and reaccentuation of the aims and methods of the movement.

biggest and best organised combinations ... In England they have not stopped at partial combinations which have no other objective than a passing strike ... Permanent combinations have been formed, trade unions, which serve as bulwarks for the workers in their struggle with the employers (Marx, 1846-47/1978: 167).

Even here Marx is fully aware of the reactionary role trade unionists can play as, for example, when employers sabotage the struggle with the aid of foremen. At the time of agitation against the Corn Law in England, employers openly recruited foremen in Bolton (the most radical town in England according to Marx),

Alright so I screwed up once or twice...

> What did the manufacturers do? To save appearance they organised meetings composed, to a large extent, of foremen, of the small number of workers who were devoted to them, and of the real *friends of trade* (Marx, 1846-47/1978: 164).

So foremen as well as 'small number of workers' could be deployed to strengthen capitalism and oppose combinations. Moreover, bourgeois reformers (e.g., Eduard Bernstein) can invade proletarian organisations, bringing with them remnants of bourgeois and petty-bourgeois thought. There was a need to contest this 'invasion' continuously. Marx also understood that organising into collectivities reduces the bosses' ability to divide and rule the proletariat. In fact,

> ... combination always has a double aim, that of stopping competition among the workers, so that they can carry on general competition with the capitalist (Marx, 1846-47/1978: 168).

This in itself is uncontroversial until a few lines further down Marx states the division between economic and political demands as an inevitable given. Borrowing from Hegel, he talks about this in terms of 'a class in itself' and 'a class for itself'. The economic struggle increases until it has reached a certain point. Only then does it take on a political character, only then the mass that is already a class against capital becomes a class for itself.

However, this class for itself cannot be a permanent state of affairs since unlike previous revolutions 'the condition for the emancipation of the working class is the abolition of all classes' (Marx, 1846-47/1978: 169). The 'communist party' distinguishes itself from other working-class parties by virtue of its ability to 'bring to the fore the common interests of the entire proletariat, independent of all nationality' and sectional interests (Marx, 1847-48/1986: 95). In a famous sentence prefiguring Vygotsky's zoped Marx writes, 'we shall have an association, in which the free development of each is the condition for the free development of all' (Marx, 1847-48/1986: 105). In later writings Marx was adamant that in the militant state of the working class, its economical movement and its political action are indissolubly united.

Although Marx had a predilection for hierarchical organisations, this involved a tolerance for different types of groupings. For instance, The Communist League (established 2 June 1847) consisted of concentric formations 'of communities, circles, leading circles, a central committee and a congress' (Engels, 1847: 1). These formations may have been placed in a hierarchy but they were different types of groupings playing a variety of functions. Marx did, however, manage to transform the League from a conspiratorial secret society into a semi-open revolutionary organisation. The change in slogan from the almost Masonic 'All Men are Brothers' to the imperfect 'Working Men of All Countries, Unite!' signified this change. Marx enjoyed complete power over the League but the First International (established 28 September 1864),

> was a union of independent (and jealously independent) organisations of working men in various different countries. Marx had no dictatorial powers; he was only one among a number of members of the general council (Werner Blumenburg quoted in Callinicos, 1987: 33).

It is interesting to note that unlike many of his disciples, Marx was flexible enough in his outlook not to get obsessed with organisational purity. His attitude towards the Paris Commune is a case in point. Although Marx detected many shortcomings in the Commune and despite the fact that the Commune did not represent Marx's idea of communism, he supported it to the hilt,

> It was not the particular programme adopted by the Commune that mattered -whether it was of a centralist or a federalist nature, whether it actually or not potentially implied the expropriation of the bourgeoisie- but the fact alone that segments of the working class had momentarily freed themselves from bourgeois rule, had arms at their disposal, and occupied the institutions of government (Mattick, 1983: 227).

What mattered was not merely the actual level of development but the potential of the Commune, the fact that it was a 'thoroughly expansive political form, while all previous forms of government had been emphatically repressive' (Marx, 1871/1974: 212). To use Vygotskian language what mattered was that the Paris Commune represented a zone of proletarian development (ZPD). Ten years later Marx's passions regarding the Commune had cooled somewhat. Now he described it as an 'uprising of a single city under very special conditions, with a population which neither was nor could be socialistic' (Marx in a letter to Domela Nienwenhuis, quoted in Mattick, 1983: 230).

Pannekoek (1873-1960) on organisation

Pannekoek's writings on organisation have enjoyed a resurgence lately. He was derogatorily referred to by Lenin as an 'ultra-left' communist suffering from an 'infantile disorder', as were a number of his close associates (Lenin, 1975). Anyone who has been sensitised to the use of pathologising arguments in the field of therapy and diagnosis should be equally appalled by Lenin's underhanded way of dismissing political opponents.

Organisational form, according to Pannekoek, depends on 'the conditions of society and the aims of the fight. They cannot be the invention of theory, but have to be built up spontaneously by the working class itself ...' (Pannekoek quoted in Bricianer, 1978: 269). Pannekoek gradually came to oppose formal political parties in favour of autonomous proletarian organisations. This brought him into conflict with both the Second International and the Third International:

> The old labour movement is organised in parties. The belief in parties is the main reason for the impotence of the working class; therefore we avoid forming a new party- not because we are too few, but because a party is an organisation that aims to lead and control the working class. In opposition to this, we maintain that the working class can rise to victory only when it independently attacks its problems and decides its own fate (Pannekoek quoted in Antagonism Press, 2001: 31).

He was a pragmatic who believed if old methods are not working, they should be unceremoniously ditched in favour of new ones. He was not too hung up on terms and designations so long as the joint activity under considerations involved self-reflective practice,

> If ... persons with the same fundamental conceptions unite for the discussion of practical steps and seek clarifications through discussions and propandise their considerations, such groups might be called parties, but they would be parties in an entirely different sense from those of today (Pannekoek quoted in Antagonism Press, 2001: 32).

Old formal parties are primarily concerned with the seizure of political power whereas the groupings Pannekoek describes, in a manner reminiscent of Vygotsky's zone of proximal development, have the task of 'developing the initiative of the workers' and aim to 'be an aid to the working class in its struggle for emancipation' (Antagonism Press, 2001: 33).

Victory demands 'unlimited intellectual freedom' whereas the formal parties rule by suppressing dissent (Pannekoek quoted in Antagonism Press, 2001: 33).

He was just as scathing regarding trade unions. Union bureaucrats who began by haggling with the bosses, 'became the specialists acquainted with methods of organisation, masters of money as well as the press, while the members themselves lost much of their power (Pannekoek quoted in Bricianer, 1978: 271). The problem of trade

> The main weakness of the American working class is its bourgeois mentality, its total submission to bourgeois ideas, to the black art of democracy.

> Lovely pancakes!

Toni Pancake and chum!

unions was partly the problem of any organisation that grows too large- the masses lose control of them. Pannekoek is not always clear whether formal political parties and trade unions have been reactionary from the outset or whether they gradually degenerated and became an obstacle to the development of class struggle. Perhaps this is the reason he was wary of employing a loaded term such as 'decadence'. But in general his position suggests a historical break between the ascendant phase of capitalism (when parties and unions still had a positive function) and the phase of decline (when they became reactionary and replaced by workers' councils)[128],

> The old forms of organisation, the trade union and political party and the new form of councils (soviets), belong to different phases of the development of society and have different functions. The first has to secure the position of the working class among the other classes within capitalism and

---

[128] He further confuses the issue by using the distinction between private and state capitalism synonymously with the ascendant-decadent phases of capitalist development, 'The trade unions were and are indispensable as organs of struggle for the working class under private capitalism. Under monopoly or state capitalism, towards which capitalism increasingly develops, they turn into a part of the ruling bureaucratic apparatus, which has to integrate the working class into the whole' (Pannekoek, 1952: 1).

belongs to the period of expanding capitalism. The latter has to secure complete dominance for the workers, to destroy capitalism and its class divisions, and belongs to the period of declining capitalism (Pannekoek quoted in Bricianer, 1978: 275).

Workers' councils were the organs that did away with the artificial separation between the judiciary, legislative and executive. They were a higher form of 'democracy',

For the working class, parliamentary democracy is a sham democracy, whereas council representation is real democracy: the direct rule of the workers over their own affairs (Pannekoek quoted in Bricianer, 1978: 276).

Parliamentarianism inhibits 'the autonomous activity by the masses that is necessary for revolution' (Pannekoek quoted in Shipway, 1987a: 110). In fact his critique of 'democracy' goes further when he denounces the fetishisation of majority decision-making,

We are by no means fanatics of democracy, we have no superstitious respect for majority decision nor do we render homage to the belief that everything the majority does is for the best and must succeed. Action is crucial, activity overpowers mass inertia. Where power enters as a factor, we want to use and apply it. If, nonetheless, we firmly reject the doctrine of the revolutionary minority, this is just for the reason that it must lead to a mere semblance of power, to merely apparent victories, and thus to serious defeats (Pannekoek, 1920).

Pannekoek, therefore, emphasised three forms of organisation: the wildcat strike (where workers decide and choose revocable and temporary delegates who carry out their wishes, disbanding the strike committee as soon as the strike is over), the informal political discussion and propaganda grouping (which aids the development of consciousness without imposing itself on the rest of the proletariat) and, finally, workers' councils (that become the productive organs of this and the future classless society). Historically, he based his thoughts on two seminal case studies: the Russian revolutions of 1905 and 1917 and to a lesser degree the Spanish revolt of 1935-36.

On the question of 'violence' and destruction as part of the struggle, Pannekoek was not squeamish. Rather he gauged its effect on the overall level of class struggle. It was, in short, a tactical issue. On the burning of the Reichstag he wrote,

First of all, it must be said that no one will cry over the disappearance of the Reichstag. It was one of the ugliest buildings in modern Germany, a pompous image of the Empire of 1871 (Pannekoek, 1933: 1).

Pannekoek knows full well 'all revolutionary class struggle, when it takes the form of civil war, will always provoke destruction' (Pannekoek, 1933: 1). However, 'from a revolutionary point of view, [Van Der Lubb's] gesture appears valueless and from different points of view one could speak of a negative gesture' (Pannekoek, 1933: 1). If an act of destruction strengthens the bourgeoisie in the long term by for example legitimising counter-measures, then it has been worse than pointless- it has been counter-revolutionary. Moreover, if at all possible, we should 'try to pass on a world as rich and intact as possible to [our] descend-ents, to future humanity' (Pannekoek, 1933: 1). Pannekoek discusses the failed tactics of the Russian nihilists,

> At certain moments, it even appeared that by a series of well organised attendats, the ni-hilists would overthrow Tsarism. But a French detective, engaged to take over the anti-terrorist struggle in place of the incompetent Russian police, succeeded by his personal energy and his entirely western organisation in destroying nihilism in only a few years. It was only afterwards that a mass movement developed and finally overthrew Tsarism (Pannekoek, 1933: 1).

Pannekoek has been accused of fetishising the council form of organisation but he is on re-cord as saying,

> 'Workers' councils' do not designate a form of organisation whose lines are fixed once and for all, and which only requires a subsequent elaboration of the details. It means a principle – the principle of the workers' self management of enterprises and of produc-tion (Pannekoek, 1952: 2).

For Pannekoek revolution was 'not a single event of limited duration' but rather 'a process of organisation, of self-education' (Pannekoek quoted in Shipway, 1987a: 111). However, it is true that in places Pannekoek's insistence on maintaining rational book-keeping and labour time accounting is indicative of outdated thinking. His rejection of all forms of 'permanent' organisation was perhaps also a phase revolutionaries had to go through in their battle against Leninism. And although his definition of consciousness as the *collective will of the proletariat* was superior to Kautsky and Lenin's conceptions since it was not tainted by re-flection theory, it was nonetheless rather atavistic compared to contemporary notions. It is also true that Pannekoek's definition of consciousness contained contradictions. At times he reduced the concept to individualised 'self-education', going against his earlier formulations. At his best, however, Pannekoek always attempted to demonstrate the dialectical relation-ship between consciousness and organising (Shipway, 1987a: 4).

Mattick (1904-1981) on organisation

Paul Mattick employed a periodisation of capitalism which distinguished an ascendant and a decadent phase of capitalist development. His views of old labour movements in the dec-adent phase of development were as harsh as those of Pannekoek. However, if anything, he was even more critical than his Dutch fellow-traveller regarding labour organisations in the ascendant phase of capital expansion. Their limited objectives (better wages and conditions) could only be realised whilst capitalism was 'expanding'. According to Mattick (1938: 2) 'the parties of the workers like those of the capitalists became limited corporations …'. He went as far as making comparisons between old labour and fascism that seem slightly glib and superficial with the benefit of hindsight (Mattick, 1978: 74). More pertinently on the eve of the Second World War he wrote,

> Not only capital, as Marx said, is its own grave digger, but also the labour organisations, where they are not destroyed from without, destroy themselves. They destroy themselves in the very attempt to become powerful forces within the capitalist system (Mattick, 1978: 77).

A revolution was, therefore, only possible outside and against the old labour organisations. The autonomous organisations Mattick envisaged should 'combine … legislative and executive powers whilst developing the self-action of the workers' (Mattick, 1938: 4). As he pointed out,

> A rebirth of the labour movement is conceivable only as a rebellion of the masses against 'their' organisations. Just as the relations of production … prevent the further unfolding of the productive forces of society, and are responsible for the present capitalistic decline, so the labour organisations of today prevent the full unfolding of the new proletarian class forces … (Mattick, 1978: 76).

First clarity, then unity … then chocolate!!

The only old labour organisation Mattick seemed to have had any affection for was the Industrial Workers of the World (IWW), perhaps because he had a hand in drafting its constitution. He also lauds the example of anti-parliamentarian council communist organisations associated with 'left-communism' for whom slogans such the abolition of wage slavery and classes ceased to be mere slogans and became immediate ends in themselves (Mattick, 1978: 83). However, if the conditions are not suitable for such organisations then,

> Critique and propaganda [become] the only practical activities possible … and their apparent fruitlessness only reflects an apparent non-revolutionary situation (Mattick, 1978: 84).

So social change is impossible unless anti-capitalist forces grow stronger than pro-capitalist forces. Until then it would be impossible to organise any genuinely anti-capitalist force against the status quo. When the balance finally shifts against capital, a new organisational framework based on councils will be adopted. His injunction became, 'First clarity, then unity' (Mattick, 1938: 3). This convenient fatalism is only slightly alleviated through Mattick's humility and pragmatism. He was humble enough not to substitute his struggle for that of the workers and pragmatic enough to know revolutionaries have to be present whenever the workers are struggling in order to push things forward (Mattick, 1978: 85).

Mattick identified the organisation vs. spontaneity debate as one superseded by history. This is in keeping with Leontiev's charting of activity, action and operation along the spontaneity-organisational axis, discussed in chapter four. Wildcat strikes, for instance, are not disorganised since they 'form picket lines, provide for the repulsion of strike-breakers, organise strike relief, create relations with other factories ...' (Mattick, 1938: 5). In fact, Mattick went as far as stating that wildcat strikes are 'embryonic communism' (Mattick, 1938: 5). Writing in 1949 Mattick asserts,

> The whole discussion around the question of organisation and spontaneity which agitated the old labour movement has now lost its meaning. Both types of organisations, those depending on spontaneity and those trying to master it, are disappearing ... [However] for some time to come the results of all types of resistance and struggle will be described as spontaneous occurrences, though they are nothing but the planned actions or accepted inactivities of men (Mattick, 1978: 123 and 136).

The desire for control over spontaneity originates from fear of the uncontrollable, a fear shared by most structuralist and bizarrely also post-structuralist ideologies. Mattick was concretely familiar with structuralist organisations. With the benefit of hindsight we could detect similar impositions created by post-structuralist organisations. In fact both ideologies attempt, albeit with different mechanisms, to bring bourgeois order to proletarian chaos. 'The socialists and bolsheviks considered capitalist society inefficiently organised with regard to production and exchange', says Mattick which is why once every social layer submitted to their authority, 'they became society's most thorough organisers. And it was precisely this organising activity that they designated with the term *socialism*' (Mattick, 1978: 135). This may be banal but it is vital. Mattick is saying the form of the organisation is dialectically related to the contents of one's ideology. The Bolsheviks' atavistic definition of *socialism* and *communism* was perfectly in tune with their structuralist *democratic centralism*.

Ironically, the same argument regarding the dialectics of form and content can be turned against Mattick. After all, although certain vital tasks such as the abolition of wage slavery and money remain as relevant now as before, our definition of communism is constantly evolving since proletarian desires and needs do not remain static. Since the content of communism as the existing social movement against this state of affairs is developing, it follows that the form and function of organisations are also in a state of permanent flux. Here Mattick's fetishization of the council form becomes anachronistic.

On a more positive note, Mattick was aware of the limitations of the term *inter-nationalism* and how such shortcomings adversely impact organisations. This is relevant in an age of 'anti-globalisation' or 'de-globalisation' politics,

> Nationalism is merely the instrument for large-scale competition; it is the 'internationalism' of capitalist society. [Old] proletarian internationalism was based on an acceptance of the fictitious 'free-trade' principle of the bourgeoisie. It conceived of international development as a mere quantitative extension of the familiar national development. Just as capitalist enterprise broke through national boundaries, so the labour movement gained an international base without changing its form or activities … Large-scale business, cartelisation, trustification, financial control, state-interferences, nationalism, and even imperialism were held to be signposts of the 'ripening' of capitalist society toward social revolution (Mattick, 1978: 126).

I hope I am not inadvertently distorting Mattick when I suggest that in this paragraph he is claiming three crucial points: First, for Mattick *inter*-nationalism (i.e., the maintenance of nationalisms within an interactive framework) is a non-starter since it only apes bourgeois organisational tendencies; second, there is a qualitative distinction to be made between genuine proletarian *internationalism* and all hitherto organisations falsely claiming this designation; and third, Mattick gets involved in a posthumous debate with the currently fashionable notion of *empire* proposed by Hardt and Negri (2000), siding against those who see in the supposed transformation from 'imperialism' to 'empire' a positive harbinger of things to come. Even if what is nowadays referred to as 'globalisation' tends towards centralised totalitarian control,

> It would [only] correspond to the socialist and bolshevik goal of world-government, planning the whole of social life. It would correspond also to the limited 'internationalism' of capitalists, fascists, socialists and bolsheviks who envision such partial organisations as Pan-Europe, Pan-Slavism, Latin-Bloc, numbered internationals, Commonwealth, Monroe-Doctrine, Atlantic Charter, United Nations and so forth, as necessary steps towards world government (Mattick, 1978: 128).

Although the over-generalisation of the preceding paragraph detracts somewhat from its impact and renders nuanced differences between various forms of reactionary *internationalism* invisible to our gaze, it is nonetheless a prescient critique of contemporary journals such as both Green Pepper and Red Pepper (who promote *Euro*-May Days), groups like Chain-Workers (who desire to reanimate a collective European identity on top of the dung heap of

Green-Anarchism),[129] organisations such as the People's Global Action (which consciously mimic bourgeois continentalism), IndyMedia (which organises itself around linguistically disputed national entities), the European Social Forum (whose organisers seem to treat non-European locations as potential tourist destinations), and Non-Governmental Organisations (NGOs) that have all but become a repressive arm of the military establishment.[130]

Earlier worker organisations were either inherently reactionary because they materialised in the ascendant phase of capitalism or simply did not know 'how to go about organising a socialist society', as was the case with Russian soviets and socialist parties (Mattick, 1983: 225). What is paramount for Mattick is workers' self-activity. The Spanish CNT (National Confederation of Labor, the Anarcho-Syndicalist trade union federation) is castigated, for example, for stifling this self-activity,

> The CNT never approached the question of revolution from the viewpoint of the working class, but has always been concerned first of all with the organisation. It was acting for the workers and with the aid of the workers, but was not interested in the self-initiative and action of the workers independent of organisational interests (Mattick, 1937: 3).

Despite Mattick's emphasis on autonomy in organisational matters he has been criticised for treating the proletariat as a passive object in his economic treaties. Although it is possible to ignore the shortcomings of Mattick's economics without ditching his writings on organisation, there is undeniably a certain amount of negative spillage from the former into the latter. Ron Rothbart (1980: 1) explains,

> From Mattick's point of view, the dynamics of capitalism can be comprehended by an understanding of the laws of capital accumulation. These laws ultimately lead the process of accumulation to an impasse ... In this sort of analysis, the working class is only 'tacitly present'.

The human factor, the proletariat as subject is therefore left out of Mattick's equations. In other words he 'deals with the economy in abstraction from the class struggle' (Rothbart, 1980: 8). Mattick's politics and organisational recipes remained for the most part on the terrain of negation. Having correctly identified Leninism as counter-revolutionary, he and his followers were incapable of proposing anything other than a knee-jerk reaction against its tenets. This explains the confusion which abounds

---

129 See interview with Alex Foti (Mute, 2005: 47).

130 In a brilliant analysis of the changing nature of war Silvia Federici (2004: 47) writes, 'In many cases, what arms could not accomplish was achieved through *food aid* provided by the USA, the UN and various NGOs to the [Angolan] refugees and the victims of the famines which the wars had produced ... food aid has become a major component of the contemporary neo-colonial war-machine, and the war economy generated by it ... in 1988 the UN passed a resolution asserting the right of donors to deliver aid ... It is on this basis that the US/UN military intervention in Somalia in 1992-93 (operation Restore Hope) was justified'.

whenever its current adherents gather to engage in 'joint-activity'. Sometimes they work as a 'discussion group' seeking the holy grail of 'clarity'. At other times, the discussion group feels the urge to 'do things' and having half-heartedly intervened in a demonstration or strike, it may transmute into a 'book club'. Finally, (and this is a criticism that could be levelled at most council communists and 'left' communists, past and present), there is a systematic tendency in their writings to emphasise politics and economics at the expense of culture, psychology and sexuality. No major theoretician of these two traditions endeavoured to comprehend capitalism in its *social* totality[131] and in so doing they neglected vital dimensions of proletarian existence.

Paul Cardan (1922-1997) on organisation

Paul Cardan (a.k.a. Cornelius Castoriadis) began his youthful politics as a Greek Stalinist but became disillusioned with the Greek Communist Party when they joined bourgeois Greeks during W/W II. He became a Trotskyite and having survived both the Nazis and the Stalinist purges following the end of the Second World War, he moved to Paris. There he gradually became critical of Trotsky's critical support of the USSR and eventually broke with Trotskyism. According to Marcel van der Linden (1997: 5),

> Castoriadis and Lefort [Castoriadis' co-thinker] proposed that a new elite, a 'social layer' of bureaucrats, had achieved power in the USSR and that this elite exclusively defended its own interests rather than those of the Soviet workers. For this reason the Soviet Union was a new kind of society, which strove for expansion just as much as Western capitalism ... In a later stage Castoriadis and Lefort abandoned the characterisation of the Soviet Union as a new type of society and described it as 'bureaucratic capitalism'. According to them this was a society based on exploitation, without the classic laws of competitive capitalism but with the surplus value formation typical of capitalism. [My addition]

Having reached this point Cardan then concentrated on the problem of organisation and prefigured a number of future trends. He denounced trade unions and political parties as 'cogs in the system of exploitation' (Cardan, 1959: 1), without giving up on the need to organise (as some radicals had). He emphasised that future organisations have to be *autonomous*, in other words 'self directing' and 'responsible only to itself' (Cardan, 1959: 3). He condemned vanguardism and substitutionism as the return of 'all the old rubbish'. He pointed out that it is a Leninist fallacy to argue the working classes have only created economic organisations thus far. For instance, in Germany 'the workers began by building a political movement, and the trade unions emanated from this' (Cardan, 1959: 5). The pro-

---

131 I guess Maurice Brinton (usually referred to as a libertarian socialist) would be an exception to this rule.

letariat did not remain unscathed from his criticisms since capitalism's spirit was forever reborn in its activities. He was also aware that,

> The workers may score the enormous victory of building a revolutionary organisa-
> tion that expresses their aspirations and immediately turn victory into defeat if
> they think that once the organisation is built it remains only for them to have con-
> fidence in it for it to solve their problems … The proletariat's struggle against cap-
> italism is, therefore, in its most important aspect, a struggle of the working class
> against itself, a struggle to free itself from what persists in it of the society it is
> combating (Cardan, 1959: 6).

Cardan insisted that the problem with trade unions and political parties was not one of 'betrayal' or 'corrupt' leaders or 'mistakes' but a historical process of *bureaucratisation*. By bureaucratisation he meant the gradual formation of 'stratum of irremovable and uncon-trollable leaders' within labour organisations (Cardan, 1959: 7). Bureaucratisation does not consist merely of a set of bureaucrats but a set of social relationships and the reality and ideology corresponding to this set of social relationships. When bureaucratic leaders talk of 'revolutionary politics' it becomes clear their vision has been transformed into a *tech-nique*. Engineers become the privileged caste within this stratum. Cardan believes,

> It would be false to present the bureaucratisation of workers' organisations simply as a
> result of the evolution of capitalism toward concentration and statification … [or] to
> present [bureaucratisation] as an inevitable result of their numerical expansion …
> (Cardan, 1959: 11).

Regrettably, the proletariat has a role in the degeneration of its own organisations. Capital-ism survives within the proletariat by re-enacting the director/executant distinction. 'Be-trayal' cannot be entirely the work of Machiavellian outsiders. There must be an element of self-delusion, an element of complicity. In a manner reminiscent of Marx, Lukács and more recently the Melancholic Troglodytes, Cardan foregrounds the proletariat as the simultaneous *subject-object* of history. As he states, 'the working class is neither a totally irresponsible entity nor the absolute subject of history' (Cardan, 1959: 12).

This subject-object of history must, therefore, carry out a struggle on two fronts sim-ultaneously. It must undermine and expose bureaucratised labour rackets whilst building its own autonomous organisations. Prefiguring Activity Theory, Cardan writes:

> … [Consciousness] is not recording and playing back, learning ideas brought
> in from the outside, or contemplating ready-made truths. It is activity, creation
> and capacity to produce. It is therefore not a matter of 'raising consciousness'
> through lessons, no matter how high the quality of the content or of the teach-
> er … (Cardan, 1959: 15).

If learning and development is to take place within autonomous organisations 'the questions asked, and the methods for discussing and working out these problems, must be changed' (Cardan, 1959: 17). In other words, if a subject cannot be linked 'organically with the workers own experience', then the chances are it is not a fundamental concern of revolutionary theory (Cardan, 1959: 18). According to Cardan, new proletarian organisations have three main tasks:

1. To bring to expression the experience of workers and 'to help them become aware of the awareness they already possess' (Cardan, 1959: 18). Vygotsky (1978) would concur with the need 'to bring to expression', in other words, complete a thought process by verbalising it;
2. To place before the rest of proletariat a critique of contemporary capitalism and a positive communist alternative;
3. To aid other workers in their struggle to defend their immediate interests and positions.

In order to achieve these tasks, Cardan recommends 'grassroot organs [should] enjoy as much autonomy as is compatible with the general unity-of-action of the organisation' (Cardan, 1959: 19). Thus a productive equilibrium between centralisation and decentralisation needs to be established through 'direct democracy', which he defines as 'collective decision making by all those involved wherever it is materially possible'. When collective decision making is not materially possible, responsibility should be delegated to instantly recallable 'representatives' (Cardan, 1959: 19). For Cardan the contradiction between living within capitalism and the wish to supersede it is partly resolved when,

> an organisation proposes a form of struggle and this form is taken up, enriched, and broadened by the workers. It is resolved when genuine collective works become inaugurated within the organisation; when each person's ideas and experiences are discussed by the others, and then surpassed, to be merged in a common aim and action; and when militants develop themselves through their participation in every aspect of the life and activity of the organisation (Cardan, 1959: 21).

This is a vision remarkably close to Vygotsky's 'zoped', Bakhtin's 'dialogic politics' and Engeström's 'expansive learning'. In fact, there is a great deal in Cardan that prefigures my approach in this chapter. His notion of the 'radical imaginary', the sense of what it takes to confront the bourgeois world order and his promotion of 'auto-poeisis' (usually interpreted as self-imagining or self-invention) are interesting precursors. His critique of post-structuralism (i.e., the death of the subject, the death of history and the unsurpassability of power), pointed out how by offering a seductive aura of subversiveness, post-structuralism legitimised depoliticisation (Whitebook, 1998: 6).

However, one needs to be very careful with Cardan. His 'auto-poeisis' was not a collective but an individualised act of transformation. Despite his later criticisms of Lacan, his notion of autonomy is still enmeshed in psychoanalytic terminology and described as a struggle against the 'unconscious'. Many of his ideas are presented ahistorically. His predilection for the Greek classical tradition led him toward a nauseating Eurocentrism and an uncritical celebration of the Greek notion of democracy. This, it is claimed, even led him to support US 'democratic' imperialism against 'Russian totalitarianism'. And finally, the Situationists were correct in asserting that despite his great learning, there was a tendency with Cardan toward specialisation.

The Situationist Internationalists (S.I.) on organisation

For a group renowned for their flowery language and Sufi-like machinations, the Situationist Internationalists could be remarkably lucid at times,

> When bureaucratic leaders talk of 'revolutionary politics' it becomes clear their vision has been transformed into a technique.

> Bureaucratisation does not consist merely of a set of bureaucrats but a set of social relationships ...

Our central idea is that of the construction of situations, that is to say, the concrete construction of momentary ambiances of life and their transformation into a superior passional quality (Debord, 1957 in Knabb, 1981: 22).

Arafat ♥ Albright

Situations are products of imaginal creativity. New situations are created to encourage new forms of interrelationship. Old (bourgeois) situations are analysed in order to foreground hidden contours of power and the adverse influence of the environment on individuals. The technique is called *psychogeography* and was defined as,

The study of the exact laws and specific effects of the action of the geographical environment, consciously organised or not, on the emotions and behaviours of individuals (Debord, 1957, in Knabb, 1981: 23).

Note that psychogeography is not very concerned about the 'specific effects of the actions' of individuals on the environment. The conceiving of the relationship between the individual and the 'environment' as a one-way process has led to a degree of positivism creeping into psychogeographic research. The technique also suffers from insensitivity toward the inter-psychological and intra-psychological aspects of interaction since it concentrates almost exclusively on extra-psychological influences.[132] However, the fact that the Situationists were consciously analysing the relationship between organisation and individuals sets them apart from most other radicals who have given the problem scant attention. In a statement reminiscent of both Vygotsky's concept of collaborative work and Luria's privileging of *creative* imagination over mere *mechanical* imagination, Debord underscores the relationship between organisation and creativity,

> It must be understood once and for all that something that is only a personal expression within a framework created by others cannot be termed a creation. Creation is not the arrangement of objects and forms, it is the invention of new laws on that arrangement (Debord 1957, in Knabb, 1981: 22).

Again in parallel with Vygotsky's work on the interconnection of play and imagination, the Situationists emphasised the role of play in organisational matters.[133] However,

> the Situationist game is distinguished from the classic conception of the game by its radical negation of the element of competition and of separation from everyday life. The Situationist game is not distinct from a moral choice, the taking of one's stand in favour of what will ensure the future reign of freedom and play (Debord 1957, in Knabb, 1981: 24).

The ideal revolutionary organisation as far as the Situationists were concerned was a workers' council. They distinguished this from previous rank-and-file organisations where the local general assembly consisted of mere electors. This was to be overcome by 'making the local general assemblies of all the proletarians in revolution *the council itself*, from which any delegation must derive its power at every moment' (Riesel, 1969 in Knabb, 1981: 271). As Shipway (1987b: 164) explains,

> By workers' councils the SI meant 'sovereign rank-and-file assemblies, in the enterprises and the neighbourhood', federated locally, nationally and internationally through recallable, mandated delegates controlled by the base assemblies. These

---

132 In an attempt to overcome such shortcomings Melancholic Troglodytes (2003: 66) have recently proposed a synthesis between *psychogeography* (which is good at investigating extra-psychological factors), Bakhtin's concept of the *polyphonic traveller* (which successfully puts under erasure the inter-psychological dimension) and Walter Benjamin's notion of the *flâneur* (which can be adapted for the study of the intra-psychological plane).

133 The Situationists emphasised the festive character of the struggle as, of course, did Bakhtin. This festivity they contrasted with the seriousness of counter-revolutionary leftist organisations. Following the occupation of the Sorbonne a Situationist influenced committee wrote, '[The leftist bureaucrats] counterpose their lying seriousness to *the festival* in the Sorbonne, but it was precisely this festiveness that bore within itself the only thing that is serious: the radical critique of prevailing conditions' (Council for Maintaining the Occupation 1968a, in Knabb, 1981: 348).

would be 'unitary' organisations, concentrating and unifying all functions … there would be no representation, no specialists, no separation or externalisation of powers, and no hierarchy.

The councils are offensive instruments which fight for conquest of power as opposed to unions that were 'organisms of resistance … crystallized in a bureaucratic form'[134] (Riesel, 1969 in Knabb, 1981: 273). Although the S.I. were not after *pure* councilism (since that would be tantamount to a reified ideology), they were seeking organisations radically different from those proposed by Lenin,

> For Lenin, then, the councils, like charitable institutions, should become pressure groups correcting the inevitable bureaucratisation of the state's political and economic functions, respectively handled by the Party and the unions … Gramsci himself merely cleanses Lenin in a bath of democratic niceties (Riesel, 1969 in Knabb, 1981: 275).

The S.I. thought very highly of the German Communist Workers Party (the Kommunistische Arbeiter Partei Deutschlands, KAPD) since the latter adopted the councils as its programme as early as the 1920s. They did criticise the KAPD, however, for remaining tied to the hierarchical model of the vanguard party and for limiting itself to propaganda and theoretical tasks whilst leaving the role of federating the factory organisations to another organisation (the AAUD, General Workers Union of Germany). This dualism in a Marxist organisation was akin to the organisational arrangements of the Anarchist CNT-FAI in Spain. In short, the federated factory committees should become the sole deliberative and executive power over the course of the struggle. Riesel also mentions that all should be welcomed to participate in council decisions and not just local wage-earners although 'the dubious importance [intellectuals] may assume should be severely restricted' (Riesel, 1969 in Knabb, 1981: 282).

The Situationists went to great lengths to try to avoid organisational problems. Despite the arrogant posturing of some of its leading members, they were basically genuine when they claimed not to be interested in becoming leaders. They even stated categorically that a genuine revolutionary organisation must dissolve itself at the moment of victory to avoid bureaucratisation and degeneration. They certainly did not view the S.I. as a vanguardist party[135],

---

134 Elsewhere the S.I. is more critical of unions and leftist parties, 'The fundamental struggle today is between … the mass of workers … and the leftist political and union bureaucracies …These bureaucracies are not workers' organisations that have degenerated and betrayed the workers, they are a mechanism for integrating the workers into capitalist society. In the present crisis they are the main protection of this shaken capitalism' (Council for Maintaining the Occupation, 1968b in Knabb, 1981: 349).

135 Again there seems to have been a real gap between words and deeds for as Stewart Home (1988: 30) makes clear many Situationists, including Debord himself, suffered from elitist tendencies which also explains their need to 'eliminate sectarianism'.

We have never considered the SI as a goal, but as a moment of a historical activity ... The SI's 'coherence' is the relationship ... between all our formulated theses and between these theses and our actions; as well as our solidarity in those cases where the group is responsible for the action of one of its members (this collective responsibility holds regarding many issues, but not all) ... Coherence is acquired and verified by egalitarian participation in the entirety of a common practice ... This practice requires formal meetings to arrive at decisions, transmission of all information and examination of all observed lapses (Debord, 1969 in Knabb, 1981: 199).

The real test of programmes is of course the cauldron of the class struggle and when May 1968 erupted, it provided the Situationists the opportunity to put their ideas into practice. Now the very principles of the *spectacle*, non-intervention and separation, were being challenged by huge sections of society. Their analysis of organisational problems was usually far more advanced than leftist parties which spent most of May 1968 trying to catch up with the 'masses'. For instance, regarding the occupation of Sorbonne which began on 13th May 1968 they had this to say,

The Sorbonne was given over to the students in the hope that they would peacefully discuss their university problems. But the occupiers immediately decided to open it to the public to freely discuss the general problems of the society. This was thus a prefiguration of a *council*, a council in which even the students broke out of their miserable studenthood and ceased to be students (Council for Maintaining the Occupation, 1968a in Knabb, 1981: 346).

The Occupation Council had to deal with mundane organisational matters that armchair strategists usually tend to ignore or delegate to junior members of the group,

It had to take over or recreate from scratch all the services that were *supposed* to be under its authority: the loudspeaker system, printing facilities, interfaculty liaison, security (Council for Maintaining the Occupation, 1968a in Knabb, 1981: 347).

The Situationists preferred policy decision to be ratified by all. However, if there is disagreement then,

Majority decision is executed by everyone; the minority has the *duty* to break if the issue in dispute seems to it to concern a fundamental matter among the previously recognised bases of agreement (Situationist International, 1969 in Knabb, 1981: 355).

The S.I. had national sections which at least in theory were meant to make decisions autonomously, including financial autonomy, publication of texts and the right to expel individuals. They would come together in international gatherings as often as possible to hammer out issues. However, it is worth putting all these grandiose schemes and protocols into perspective. The S.I. had an inflated idea of itself. As Mark Shipway (1987b: 152) observes,

> At no time was the SI ever a large organisation, at least in terms of numbers. Only 70 individuals ever became members during the fifteen years of its existence, and never more than ten or twenty belonged to the group at any one time. Frequent 'exclusions' were used as a means of preserving the group's theoretical coherence, while aspiring members were just as regularly turned away ...

Amadeo Bordiga

Why are old revoltuionaries so aesthetically challenged?

Cornelius
Castoriadis

Paul Mattick

Guy Debord

Deleuze and Guattari on organisation

Following Foucault, a genealogical outline of ruling class organisation is presented by Deleuze and Guattari. *Societies of sovereignty* whose goal and function was 'to tax rather than to organise production, to rule on death rather than to administer life' (Deleuze, 2002: 1), gradually gave way to *disciplinary societies* in the 18th and 19th centuries. The latter 'initiated the organisation of vast spaces of enclosure' (Deleuze, 2002: 1). Particularly in the factory, these disciplinary societies comprised of productive forces 'within the dimension of space-time whose effect [was] greater than the sum of its component forces' (Deleuze, 2002: 1). These environments of enclosure (e.g., factory, prison, hospital, school, family, etc.) are in crisis and will soon be replaced by the *societies of control*. In a society of control, the corporation has replaced the factory, and 'the corporation is a spirit, a gas' (Deleuze, 2002: 2). The old enclosures of disciplinary societies were moulds or distinct castings whereas the new controls are 'modulations, like a self-deforming cast that will continuously change from one moment to the other' (Deleuze, 2002: 2). Structures become rhizome-like- an underground network of horizontal roots and above ground stems. The rhizome, they argue, is conducive to human connectivity and multiplicity.

One significant question raised by this transformation from *discipline* to *control* relates to the role of unions. Since their history is tied to the whole struggle against disciplines within the spaces of enclosure, 'will they be able to adapt themselves or will they give way to new forms of resistance against the societies of control?' (Deleuze, 2002: 4). Deleuze and Guattari's ambivalence towards trade unions stands in sharp contrast to the more sophisticated critique of unionism presented earlier by left-communist currents. This confusion may have its roots in their Freudian perspective on the relation between instinct and institution,

That which one calls an instinct, and that which one calls an institution, essentially designate processes of satisfaction ... That [instinct] may satisfy itself in the institution is not to be doubted: sexuality in marriage, avidity in property ... [However] there is a difference between institution and law: the latter is a limitation of actions, the former, a positive model of action ... tyranny is a regime where there are many laws and few institutions; democracy, a regime where there are many institutions and very few laws (Deleuze, 2003: 1).

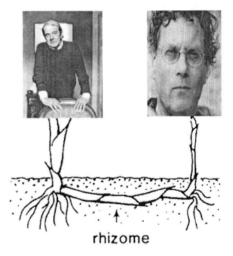

rhizome

'The rhizome, Deleuze and Guattari argue, is conducive to human connectivity and multiplicity'.

Despite their Freudian reductionism the mere inclusion of emotions, imagination and desires as factors involved in the shaping of organisations takes us a step forward from the pedantic insistence in denying such influences. They insist those with authority desire repression for others whilst the people possess libidinal desires for freedom. In recent years, the collaboration of Deleuze and Guattari with Antonio Negri has also yielded some (but only some) interesting ideas related to the emergence of new forms of revolutionary organisation. I agree wholeheartedly[136] with Guattari and Negri (1990: 103-104) when they write,

---

136 It is essential to point out that although Guattari and Negri's conclusions in rejecting Leninist and anarchist methods of organisation are sound, the same cannot be said of their rationale. They seem to believe centralist Leninist organisations have to be rejected since the law of value no longer functions (Guattari and

The transformations which trouble a society require a new type of organisation. Leninism or anarchism are no longer anything today but fantasms of defeat, voluntarism, and disenchantment, a forced faith or solitary rebellion, an antithetical form of repression or a simple abstract assertion of singularity ... Obviously, we have no model of organisational replacement, but at least we know what we no longer want. We refuse everything which repeats the constitutive models of representative alienation and the rupture between the levels where political will is formed and the levels of its execution and administration.

Deleuze and Guattari insist so long as we alternate between the impotent spontaneity of anarchy and the bureaucratic and hierarchic coding of a party organisation, our desires will not be liberated. We need 'machines of desire' to win the 'war' against capitalism. These 'machines of struggle', the term Guattari and Negri use to designate new forms of organisation, are re-emerging alongside a new form of revolutionary subjectivity. Machines of struggle must be able to both neutralise the destructive powers of capital (their negative aspect) and articulate the multidimensional needs and desires of subjectivities (their positive aspect),

This is the first positive characteristic of the new revolutionary subjectivity. Its co-operative, plural, anti-centralist, anti-corporatist, anti-racist, anti-sexist dimensions further the productive capacities of the singularities ... the positive starting-point of a revolutionary method of organisation [becomes] a scientific method in its mode of analysis, yet open to historical processes and capable of imagination (Guattari and Negri, 1990: 108-109).

Machines of struggle are charged with the daunting historical task of uniting what Guattari and Negri (1990: 18) call 'molar' and 'molecular' struggles. 'Molar antagonisms' refer to workplace struggles over exploitation, safety and health issues. Occasionally these 'molar antagonisms' expand into the outside world- what they call 'molecular proliferation'. It is at this seminal junction that a revolutionary transformation occurs during which a new subjective consciousness is born of the collective experience.

It is noteworthy that 'machines of struggle' can be radical without being radicalising, unless they engage in demasking identity and promoting the desire for a non-utilitarian existence (Slater, 2004: 89).

Libertarian Organisation and Structure (LOS) on organisation
The overwhelming majority of Anarchists are as intellectually vacuous, disgusting, dishonest and anti-working class as their Leninist counter-parts. Occasion-

---

Negri, 1990: 106). In other words, Leninist organisations were fine once but since postmodernism they have become anachronistic! This is vacuous.

ally, however, a group or an individual from these tendencies breaks the mould. When that happens, they become worthy of the attention of revolutionaries.

In 1987 the group Libertarian Organisation & Structures brought out a pamphlet entitled, *The Future in the Present*, that tried to grapple with 'some of the things which prevent groups with basically anarchist intentions from achieving them' (LOS, 1987: 2).[137] The pamphlet questions some of the most cherished holy writs of Anarchism such as its naïve rejection of 'authority' and its even more simple-minded glorification of the 'autonomous individual'. As the pamphlet states in the preface,

> ... we feel that the classical anarchist concept of authority as something a minority inflicts on an unwilling majority is only relevant in a limited number of situations. Our experience is that there are many more subtle ways in which authority can develop, such as people getting bored, personal links inhibiting challenge or criticism, etc ... Also it reflects an over-simplified nineteenth century concept that a group is a collection of autonomous individuals who decide everything through rational processes that they completely understand (LOS, 1987: 2).

Before presenting the psychological aspects of organisation, LOS discusses a number of historical examples (not dissimilar to the approach I have chosen in this section of my research). For example, they point out how during the 1917 Russian turmoil 'the regional organisations were not strictly non-hierarchical but the peasants side-stepped this by ignoring ... decisions they disagreed with' (LOS, 1987: 7). On the other hand, both peasants and urban proletarians failed to deal with the vexed problem of 'internal' leadership.

LOS is arguing it is relatively easy to see 'external' leaders (the state, mediators of all sorts) for what they are. It is much more difficult to expose and control 'internal' leaders (those who have risen from our own ranks such as leading militants). It is even more difficult to acknowledge that in times of crisis a certain amount of leadership from competent 'leaders' may be necessary for the success of the enterprise. They also believe that,

> During revolutionary periods the organisation should be, and should be seen to be, nothing more than the expression of class co-ordination, mutual aid and solidarity. It should not be seen as some additional layer ... (LOS, 1987: 17).

The pamphlet then goes on to discuss the ways the capitalist market and its values affect the radical 'scene' by introducing the element of competition into activities. So much so that 'even anarchist groups, despite their avowed dislike of recruit-

---

137 My thanks to Dermot (a Spurs supporter) for bringing this pamphlet to my attention.

ment, have to engage in this competition' (LOS, 1987: 24). Groups end up 'acting' certain about their politics in order to impress potential recruits. In short,

> competition acts to drive groups and their members into the corner of certainty- a certainty which might at first be only superficial, for the purposes of the sell, but which in time comes to resound in the make-up of both groups (their internal structure) and members (some form of authoritarian psychology). As regards structure, certainty assures that the prevailing organisational form becomes unquestioned: the vanguard party, the [consciousness raising]-type group, the bottom-up assembly, are the -only- means to assert the politics. They become absolute structures whose usefulness does not alter with changing conditions (LOS, 1987: 25).

Since even being aware of these problems is not sufficient protection against their malign influence, one has to accept that a certain amount of 'authority', 'individualism' and 'competition' will creep into the most radical of organisations. Consequently 'all we can do is work for a constantly shifting *dynamic balance* which minimises the amount of' these negative factors' (LOS, 1987: 30). Therefore, there is a need to question the absolute faith radicals have traditionally invested in classical 'egalitarian' methods of organising- tactics such as 'rotating the delegates' for instance. LOS believes that,

> No mandate can ever be complete, so there will always be a need for interpretation even before you allow for the fact that the unexpected, urgent issues are always going to crop up (LOS, 1987: 33).

Having questioned various anarchist dogmas regarding organisation, the pamphlet then moves onto the psychological terrain. Basing itself on group-oriented psychoanalysis (especially the work of Bion) and work with small therapeutic groups, the LOS pamphlet talks about the problems of the *Social Identity Group*. This is a group with similar world views (e.g., a group of anti-capitalist radicals). Accordingly, the Social Identity Group has two dimensions, a conscious, rational dimension and an unconscious, irrational one. The former is referred to as *Work Group* and engages with the primary task according to a 'scientific spirit'. The latter, called the *Basic Assumption Group*, refers to the latent aspect of the group and consists of wishes, desires, anxieties, impulses and projections. Bion (1961) suggests this Basic Assumption Group believes in 'magic'. For Bion the Work Group was positive and the Basic Assumption Group was to be contained.

Each of these two types of organising (Basic Assumption Group and Work Group) consist of a number of subgroups.[138] Let us take the Basic Assumption

---

138 Later in this chapter we will see that there is an uncanny similarity between Bion's Basic Assumption Group and Work Group with my distinction between the Zone of Bourgeois Development and the Zone of

Group, with its unconscious- irrational-magical qualities, first. According to Bion (1961: 91) the Basic Assumption Group has three subgroups:

1. *Basic assumption fight-flight* which according to Stokes (1994) and Thompson and Hoggett (2001: 355) 'corresponds to a culture of paranoia and aggressive solidarity', in which the group unites to smash real and imaginary threats to its survival. Under 'basic assumption fight-flight' feelings such as fear, suspicion and hatred abound and anyone who questions the level or existence of the threat is marginalised.

2. *Basic assumption dependency* which 'corresponds to a culture of willed and willing subordination, a resourceless dependency on an accepted wisdom (a bible … a party leader…)' (Thompson and Hoggett, 2001: 355). Under 'basic assumption dependency' obedience and gratitude flourish and dissent is suppressed.

'… it is relatively easy to see 'external' leaders (the state, mediators of all sorts) for what they are. It is much more difficult to expose and control 'internal' leaders …'

I love you Dr Evil!

3. *Basic assumption pairing* corresponding 'to a salvationist culture in which a promised future is preferred to an unbearable present …' (Thompson and Hoggett, 2001: 355). Naïve optimism is the order of the day in such groups and voices questioning the coming of paradise are hushed up.

All three basic assumption subgroups mentioned above represent a certain type of 'emotional tyranny' (Thompson and Hoggett 2001: 355). These negative aspects of the Basic Assumption Group are opposed by the positive attributes of the Work Group. These are categorised by Bion under four headings:

1. A clear goal or sense of common purpose;
2. The absence of rigidly defined internal subgroups;
3. The contribution of every member valued;
4. Members with clearly defined and fully accepted roles.

The last part of the LOS pamphlet is also productive since it discusses praxis, rituals and self-objectification. Basing itself on Anthony Giddens, *praxis* is defined

---

Proletarian Development. Even the number of subgroupings mentioned by Bion find an almost exact match with my subgroupings. However, the substance and dynamics of my categories (based as they are on Vygotsky, Bakhtin and Activity Theory) are very different from Bion's, as are my motives for the categorisation.

as regular patterns of enacted conduct by active actors who interact with each other in situations in habitual, reflexive, reflective, and more conscious ways. Praxis has various components. It could be *discursive* (when actors are engaged actively in reflecting on the meaning of their conduct), *practical* (a set of routine and habitual behaviour that the actor may not be fully conscious of) and finally *unconscious* praxis (which refers to a primordial need to gain practical control of the stable features of the social world) (LOS, 1987: 59). The pamphlet tries to map the discursive and practical forms of praxis onto the categories subject and object. Although the mapping procedure is rather forced, it does have the advantage of underlining the simultaneous subject-object existence of the proletariat. Those ideologies that glorify the subject, such as Anarchism, 'serve to obscure a profound objectification of both the self and others' (LOS, 1987: 60).

Finally, the pamphlet discusses rituals. Ritual 'pervade political groups and it is part of the individual members' practical consciousness' (LOS, 1987: 61). Ritual, therefore, renders individuals passive and produces self-objectification. However, this self-objectification may have certain pay-offs for the individual. Firstly,

> In allowing the individual to be passive, ritual provides an opportunity for them to be lazy. They don't have to think very strenuously, to exert themselves ... [secondly] ritual can generate a sense of certainty ... (LOS, 1987: 61).

Furthermore, rituals may also be responsible for lack of creativity within political groups as well as a contributing factor to sectarianism, 'whereby subgroups ritualistically oppose one another' (LOS, 1987: 62).

Kamunist Kranti on organisation

Kamunist Kranti is an interesting Indian 'left-communist' grouping with a presence amongst the factory workers of Faridabad (a town of 1 million inhabitants 300,000 of whom are factory wage workers). As Goldner (1998: 1) has amusingly observed,

> The world has its share of revolutionary P.O. boxes but Kamunist Kranti stands out as one of the few, if not the only ultra-left current with a genuine, year-long working-class presence ...

Faridabad, we are informed by Goldner (1998: 2), may appear like a 19th century Dickensian industrial town but certain sections of it are extremely opulent in contrast to the slums and shanties surrounding it. The origins of Kamunist Kranti are to be found in 'the fallout and regroupment of the Indian Maoist milieu' following Indira Gandhi's declaration of the state of emergency in 1975. Gradually it moved away from Maoism and took on an anti-vanguardist 'affinity group' outlook. Its negative experiences with management-provoked-strikes convinced the group that strikes have become in the 20th century a weapon of the ruling class (Goldner, 1998: 4). They, therefore, 'refuse to be provoked into confrontations that are rigged in advance' (Goldner, 1998: 9). It is undeniable that management at times initiate hostilities in order to defeat a section of the proletariat and prepare the ground for massive restructuring of the labour process. Accordingly,

> [Kamunist Kranti] tells stories of management calling in groups of perceived 'troublemakers' and insulting them in the most personal way, calling them wimps and cowards who stand there and take such insults, while the workers refuse to be provoked; in the middle of the management's tirade the police van, which had been called in advance, pulls up at the factory gate.

Numerous similar encounters convinced Kamunist Kranti that the era of vanguardist, spectacularised, 'unifocal' showdowns with the bosses is over. In 'unifocal' confrontations the state can utilise its entire executive and judiciary might against ring-leaders in order to smash strikes. Instead they propose a strategy of 'small steps' like 'termites' taken by 'affinity groups'. Goldner (1998: 10) provides us with examples of such 'small steps',

> Workers assigned to work dangerous machinery for which they are not trained, instead of openly refusing and making themselves vulnerable to discipline and dismissal, work the machinery, let it break down, paralyze the factory, and force management to establish guidelines for training. Workers denied bathroom breaks from the assembly line start pissing on the shop floor and win bathroom breaks. They confront management over in-plant complaints in groups and refuse to delegate leaders who could be singled out or co-opted.

These small acts of sabotage are augmented by non-compliance with management overtures. For instance, Kamunist Kranti suggests a refusal to talk or even greet managers and supervisors (Kamunist Kranti, 1997: 53). Kamunist Kranti rejects out of hand secret meetings between workers' delegates and management,

> The process of closed door talks between bureaucrats and representatives begins wrapped in theatrical performances (hunger strikes, token strikes and threatening thundering speeches). Behind closed doors representatives and bureaucrats cut and edit workers demands and sign agreements. Parts of these agreements are hidden and parts are presented to the wage-workers (Kamunist Kranti, 1997: 57).

The 'affinity groups' or 'collectivities' Kamunist Kranti propose take decisions willingly and not as a result of instructions from the top. Collectivities have no heroes or martyrs. They have neither centre nor periphery. Collectivities are,

> embedded in the daily activity of wage-workers. Collectivity recognises differences, it does not suppress them. Its strength lies in recognising multiplicity, diversity, dissidence, doubt and criticism. Collectivity accepts varying levels of helplessness, weakness, fear, hesitation, ignorance, lack of articulation and insignificance within wage-workers ... There is no attempt at face-saving and steps back and forth are taken for granted. There is no desperation as it is an everyday affair. Sentiments and rhetoric of 'now or never', 'do or die' find no echo here. Openness and continuous discussions are its lifeblood (Kamunist Kranti, 1997: 57).

The importance of these guiding organisational principles for all societies but especially for societies such as India, the Middle East and most of Africa cannot be overstated. Political organisations in these parts of the world have historically suffered from a preponderance of hierarchical tendencies (exacerbated by fierce state repression which tends to create an underground existence inevitable), an extreme separation of the political and the social spheres (which leaves large swathes of people's 'private' lives inaccessible to analysis and change), accommodation to performative and gestural politics (with all the negative issues associated with the cult of personality, sacrifice in the name of a 'higher' cause, and machismo), and a disregard of the 'subjective' dimension of organising (such as people's feelings, fears, dreams and desires). The fact that Kamunist Kranti addresses these issues is indicative of a genuine desire on their part to learn from history.

However, as Goldner has observed there are a number of problems with the organisational blueprint Kamunist Kranti has proposed which cause concern,

> Kamunist Kranti, as a current, is overly focused on worker struggles at the point of production. The lessons of their Faridabad experience, however rich, are not as generalizable as KK thinks. They offer only so much ... to revolutionaries in countries where a large part of the proletariat has never made it to the shop floor, or has more recently been downsized out of it. In breaking totally (and mainly rightly) with 'unifocal struggles' in the context of a city, Kamunist Kranti has also broken with the CLASS-FOR-ITSELF ... (Goldner, 1998: 11) [emphasis in original].

The problem is not 'unifocal struggles' *per se* but losing them, since the adverse effects of defeat in a unifocal struggle (e.g., the 'Great' Miners' Strike of 1984-85 in Britain) is rapidly generalised to other sectors of society and this process tends to inaugurate a massive shift in the balance of class forces. As others (e.g., Guattari and Negri, 1990) have noted it is the osmosis of 'molar' and 'molecular' struggles which create the dialectics of resistance capable of defeating the ruling class. By concentrating solely on 'small step' struggles on the shop floor, Kamunist Kranti fails to achieve this osmosis.

Open-source on organisation

In modern times, the idea of *openness* as a guiding principle for organisations has been traced back to 'the founding of the Free Software Foundations in 1985 ... and the Open Source Initiative in 1998' (King, 2004: 80). Stalder (2003) had identified the key elements of 'openness' as,

> ... communal management and open access to the informational resources for production, openness to contributions from a diverse range of users/producers, flat hierarchies, and a fluid organisational structure.

The idea of openness travelled rapidly from software programming to political organisations so much so that in certain circles, 'openness is now seen as paradigmatic' (King, 2004: 80). The idea of openness seems to have 'appeal across rather different constituencies', including 'both the reformist-liberal and the radical activists' (King, 2004: 81). According to King (2004: 83) there are five key areas of correspondence between groupings that deploy openness. These five key areas are:

Meetings and Discussions- the meetings are publicised both online and offline and are open to all comers. Summaries of meetings are posted on the World Wide Web.

Decision-making- Most decisions are arrived at by those who turn up to the physical meetings through 'consensus' with dissenters having the right to veto or block decisions, although in practice the block is rarely used due to peer pressure.

Documentation- Documents related to organisational matters are usually published online using a content management system such as wiki.

Demonstrations- These are 'open' to all comers with self-discipline and 'soft' policing the preferred option.

Actions- Even some actions (which may involve disobedience or damage to property) are openly advertised in advance.

King (2004: 84) mentions the People's Global Action (PGA) as a primary example of an 'organisation' based on 'openness'. Another example would be ATTAC mentioned above. The PGA 'owes its genesis to an international encounter between activists and intellectuals that was organised by the Zapatistas in Chiapas in 1996', writes Paul Routledge (2004: 5). The PGA, it is claimed, has intentionally rejected 'organisational models based on representation, verticality and hierarchy' (King, 2004: 84), although it still sees fit to base its network on various dubious continental boundaries and to avoid calling itself an 'organisation' (the preferred designation is 'a tool of coordination').

Nonetheless, the emphasis on organisational matters has resulted in marginalising political debate and a disregard for content of activities. In fact, the PGA quite blatantly suppresses certain political issues and considers anything beyond its 5-point programme to be an 'over-complication'. There is a tendency to claim the future in the present network of open relations. It is unproblematically assumed that the networks being set up today are prefigurative of future modes of organisation. As King (2004: 84) notes,

> [The claim is that] it is the open, networked, horizontal form of the movement that produces its radical potential for social change: the message, yet again, is the medium. In the case of self-described 'open-publishing' project Indymedia, for example, the open submission structure is said to collapse the distinction between media producers and consumers, allowing us to 'become the media'.

Indeed Indymedia is at this stage of its development no more than a liberal/libertarian project aimed at mostly middle class operators with pretensions of being radical (the less kind analyst may go as far as saying it is no more than job-placement, a training environment for future journalists, lawyers and artists). The fact that one has to plough through inane weblog comment after comment before finally coming across something approaching revolutionary clarity is testimony to these shortcomings.

It is also the case that having created a network that is, at least in theory[139], horizontal (in other words having decided on a format that is different from mainstream bourgeois news coverage), little attention is given to either the style or content of news making. Subsequently, the style and content of the Indymedia websites tend to replicate leftist bourgeois models almost to a tee. The fact that there are no officials in charge may make the security services' task of keeping tabs on activists *slightly* more difficult, but ironically it also causes problems for the social movement. This is what the group Sans Titre had to say after one PGA meeting,

> Whenever we have been involved in PGA-inspired action, we have been unable to identify decision-making bodies. Moreover, there has been no collective assessment of the effectiveness of PGA-inspired actions ... We wanted to start a process of strategic thinking about the validity of counter-summits. The issues we raised never appeared on the agenda. No debate ever took place. And to this day we do not know who took the decision not to make time for it ... If the PGA-process includes decision-making and assessment bodies, where are they to be found? How can we take part? (Sans Titre, 2002: 1).

It is no surprise to the present author that certain sections of PGA show such a marked reluctance in discussing strategy and anything that undermines their summit hopping tourism. After all, a serious debate could expose their cosy power base. In fact the horizontal

---

139 King (2004: 85) concludes that, '... Indymedia channels are often politically censored by a small group of more-or-less anonymous individuals to quite a high degree'.

phraseology is tailor-made for concealing power asymmetry. The power exercised by the mailing-list moderators and domain-name owners has been described by some as 'feudal or propriety' (Neilson and Rossiter, 2006: 407). For PGA everything is a matter of logistics. By ignoring substantial political issues, logistical problems when they occur (and they invariably do), become insurmountable. Technology is treated as a neutral tool, a perspective which tends to maintain power in the hands of the powerful individuals within the organisation.[140] Power tends to gravitate and become enmeshed in what King (2004: 86) calls 'supernodes'- small groups of individuals who do most of the work and consequently end up making most of the vital decisions about how, where and when actions occur. Within the PGA supernodes consist of mostly bourgeois, white, neo-libertarians with little or no grasp of the class struggle.

There are two imperatives propelling these supernodes: one is the deliberate pursuit of power which is today seen amongst both Leninist and (most) anti-Leninist (i.e., Anarchist, Autonomist, Situationist, Left-communist, Libertarian Socialist) circles, and the other happens almost by default without a malicious *will-to-power*, usually due to personal qualities such as *charisma* and *commitment*. It is ironic that the latter imperative (i.e., the crypto-hierarchical 'open' structure of groups like PGA and Indymedia) is proving more of a hindrance to the establishment of zones of proletarian development than the naked pursuit of power which can be easily identified and resisted by most political activists. The Sans Titre group come up with further searching queries that, as far as I know, have never been adequately addressed by PGA. For example they ask,

'Within the PGA supernodes consist of mostly bourgeois, white, neo-libertarians with little or no grasp of the class struggle.'

How can mutual trust be proposed as an organising principle … when clearly

---

140 This is eerily similar to the way in which the development of a website for the European Social Forum 2004 was subcontracted to a profit driven company (GreenNet) by the Greater London Authority (GLA) elite (cf. Dowling, 2005: 208). The fact that there should be a tender process was also decided by the GLA. In the same year (2004) the WSF at Mumbai faced tremendous computer problems. One of the main reasons for this, according to Caruso (2005: 173) was the separation of technical from political decisions. As he explains the choice of design, operating system and software are all inherently political issues which need to be decided by all rather than the technical staff. To ignore these issues would be tantamount to accepting the Aristotelian misinterpretation of *technics*.

people do not know each other, nor much about each other's practices? ... [How can PGA claim to be against lobbying] when PGA members have been involved in lobbying public institutions ... [We need to look into the real effects of counter-summits as they] make us dependent on the calendar of capitalist institutions ... the surprise is no longer there, counter summits have become a predictable performance ... counter-summits privilege certain classes of activists: those able to travel freely throughout Europe, in a kind of anti-capitalist tourism[141] (Sans Titre, 2002: 3). [Comments in original]

Borrowing from critiques of feminist and libertarian organisations put forward by Freeman and Camatte, King writes (2004: 87),

Freeman's insight is fundamental: the idea of openness does not in itself prevent the formation of the informal structures that I have described here as crypto-hierarchies; on the contrary, it is possible that it fosters them to a greater degree than structured organisations. Underneath its rhetoric of openness, the non-hierarchical organisation can thus take on the qualities of a 'gang'. As Jacque Camatte and Gianni Collu realised in 1969, such organisations tend to hide the existence of their informal ruling cliques to appear more attractive to outsiders, feeding on the creative abilities of individual members, whilst suppressing their individual contributions, and producing layers of authority contingent on individuals' intellectual or social dominance.

The creation of a 'gang' mentality occurs both consciously and inadvertently. The latter process is catalysed by the technological determinism of the Net. Paul Routledge (2004: 8) is quite succinct on this point,

The reliance on the Internet to organise grassroots globalisation networks raise other problems. First, is that of the circulation of excessive amounts of information, or 'information blizzard'... Second, the abstract, disembodied character of Internet discussions (and protest post-mortems) can accentuate what become quite vitriolic debates ... that might otherwise reach compromise if conducted in a face-to-face manner, with the attendant visual and verbal clues and nuances.

This reliance on Internet communication accentuates yet another problematic tendency- that of 'Eurocentrism'. On a related topic, Latin American delegates complain that the European perspective is 'obsessed with particular forms of *process* and *consensus*' (Routledge, 2004: 13). These tendencies are not as universal as European delegates think. For example,

---

141 One must not be too cynical about this 'tourist' predilection amongst (mostly) European activists. It may be as Routledge (2004: 8) has argued, 'Rather than being forms of political tourism, the PGA caravans are organised in order for activists from different struggles and countries to communicate with one another, exchange information, share experiences and tactics, participate in various solidarity demonstrations, rallies, and direct actions, and attempt to draw new movements into the convergence'. Of course, all of the above may occur not because but despite of PGA's leadership!

Quechua delegates commented that in indigenous meetings participants would often repeat issues constantly, while in international meetings, where there was much participation by 'Northern' activists, repetitions by speakers were frequently silenced (Routledge, 2004: 13).

Finally, Paul Routledge conceives of networks such as PGA as 'convergence spaces'. This is a useful term which has also been deployed by Newman and Holzman (1993a: 91). These convergence spaces comprise a heterogeneous affinity between various social formations that have a collective vision. The collective visions are representative of a prefigurative politics- a better way of engaging with others in a post-capitalist world. However, given the reactionary nature of PGA (its anti-working class and Eurocentric tendencies), the term convergence space cannot serve as an accurate description of this particular network. If PGA has a collective vision, it is no more than capitalism with a human face.[142] And its dictatorial behaviour (e.g., its initiation of show-trials against revolutionary who dare challenge its mindset), turns the potential of heterogeneous affinity into a nightmare of innuendos and whispers directed at critics. In fact, a recent critic (with whom I find myself in agreement) observes,

> Despite claiming to be a Network, PGA turns out to be a federation of these regions [North American, Latin American, Asia and Europe] with power centralised in the regional bodies ... The fetishisation of regional autonomy as opposed to the autonomy of all constituent elements is undermining the claim of the PGA to be a network (Blissett, 2004: 114).

5.2 WHAT IS LIVING AND WHAT IS DEAD IN ORGANISATIONAL ISSUES?

Hopefully my survey of writings on radical organisations has been thorough without becoming encyclopaedic. It is time to take stock. What I propose to do in this section is to outline what is dead (or if not quite dead then at least reactionary and counter-productive) and what is still living (or if not quite living then at least on the verge of being born) in relation to proletarian organisations. The dead elements represent the Zone of Bourgeois Development (ZBD) and the living will be grouped under the rubric of the Zone of Proletarian Development (ZPD). These two zones will be expounded below. Once again I underline that the intention is not to come up with an ideal organisational blueprint but to suggest characteristics and practices conducive to

---

142 This is a criticism not exclusive to the PGA. Most of the main players in the 'anti-globalisation' movement aim for nothing more radical than capitalism with a human face which is why they are supported by a section of the world bourgeoisie. For instance, ATTAC (Association for the Taxation of Financial Transactions in the Aid of Citizens), originally set up in 1998 by the editors of Le Monde Diplomatique, relies on the political naivety of those who do not know any better and the financial desperation of those who do, in order to promote the ZBD.

revolutionary activity. It would be an error to universalise these characteristics since different terrain may require different organisational strategies.

5.2.1- Zone of Bourgeois Development (ZBD) or what is dead (or at least bloody well ought to be) in organisational matters?

Since we are forever condemned to know the past and the present with more clarity than the future, it stands to reason that the contours of our proto-model revolutionary organisation will manifest itself both through default and conjecture. In other words, our approach has a negative element of refusal of all past and present organisational failures and a positive element in the shape of what we hope to achieve in the future. Based on the preceding literature review, some of the main problems which have traditionally beset proletarian organisations are presented below. These problems will be discussed under the heading of the Zone of Bourgeois Development (ZBD). The ZBD has three main characteristics, namely, *organisational dualism, organisational fetishism* and *organisational religiosity.*

1. Organisational Dualism: Dualism ranks high on the ZBD's list of sins. Organisationally it manifests itself in a number of dichotomies as for instance the one between intellect and emotion which Leninist and Social Democratic parties have historically resolved through the mind-body metaphor. The mind or brain (the party's central committee) takes care of decision making whilst the rank-and-file provide the emotional demiurge for enacting the committee's decisions.

As already mentioned, Trotsky's analogy portrayed the party as the piston and the class as the steam. Kautsky was more upfront about his contempt for proletarian self-organisation. His description of the working class as 'politically illiterate masses' (Kautsky, 1934: 34) or 'low rabble proletarians' (Kautsky, 1934: 29) is testimony to an elitism which has, either by hook or

Hopefully my survey of writings on radical organisations has been thorough without becoming encyclopaedic.

Oh God.... Can't this idiot just shut up!

by crook, kept proletarians away from mechanism of decision making. Regardless of the simile employed, the point is to create a false duality and then control the (by and large one-way) interface between the brain and the body.

Once dualism is accepted as part of the movement's epistemology and methodology, it may occur in a variety of shapes. For instance, most hitherto movements have enacted a split between the 'political' and 'economic' spheres of resistance. This is not only true of Leninism and Social Democracy but also has disturbing parallels amongst some 'Left-Communist' and Anarchist movements. The Situationists' astute criticisms of German 'Left Communists' and Spanish Anarchists are pertinent here. As explained above, the German KAPD limited itself to theory and propaganda whilst leaving the role of federating the factory organisation to the AAUD (General Workers Union of Germany) - a split similar to the organisational arrangement of the Spanish Anarchist CNT-FAI. Autonomist Marxism display the same basic Kantian dualism when it attempts the 'transformation of objective forces into subjective forces' (Alquati quoted in Wright, 2002: 51). Jo Freeman was guilty of something similar when she postulated a stages theory separating so-called 'consciousness raising' groups from the process of movement building. Camatte's distinction between the *formal* party

and the *historic* party[143] is a response (an incorrect one in my opinion) to the accentuated split between theory and practice in 'non-revolutionary' times. Tronti assigned tactical decisions to the party and suggested strategic decisions are to be found in embryonic form within working class activities.

A further feature of the Zone of Bourgeois Development is to be found in the way the concrete and abstract aspects of discourse are kept apart. The dialectical flow between the concrete and abstract aspects of discourse is interrupted. Bernstein (1971, 1972), for instance, believes working class people use a *restricted* form of discourse characterised by an emphasis on concrete

The ZBD fosters dualism

aspects of the situation whereas bourgeois subjects use an *elaborated* form of discourse focusing on abstract aspects of the situation.[144] However, during our ana-

---

143 As mentioned in the section on Camatte this is, in fact, a distorted version of Marx's distinction between the formal and historic party. To use Vygotskian terminology Camatte may be employing the same 'meaning' but is imbuing the formal and historic party with his own personal 'sense'. Following Leontiev, one could also add that Camatte has a different motivation to Marx. Marx wanted to underline the changes that occur in the functioning and essence of a revolutionary organisation diachronically, whereas Camatte is looking for an excuse to push his 'anti-activist' agenda during 'non-revolutionary' times.

144 Elaborated discourse (containing a high element of abstraction) is assumed to possess positive qualities and conversely restricted discourse (contained a high element of concreteness) is perceived negatively. This is indicative of Bernstein's bourgeois fetishisation of the 'word'.

lysis of the rich and dialogic proletarian discourse related to the 'desecration' of Winston Churchill's statue on May Day 2000 we saw a counter-example to this. Our conclusions suggest discourse operates dialectically within a Zone of Proletarian Development allowing for fresh reflection on complex problems.

In other words, unlike the Zone of Bourgeois Development, the ZPD attempts to overcome artificial separations regardless of where it starts from. A discourse characterised by a high degree of concrete codes may quickly become a platform for the dialectical interplay of the concrete and abstract. A wildcat strike may nominally begin life on the 'economic front' but if it is to succeed it must soon acknowledge its own political imperatives whilst a grouping of artists may begin as a response to 'political' and 'cultural' censorship but rapidly gain 'economic' significance when they withdraw their labour-power (e.g., a BBC staff strike or a film crew's go-slow tactics). In brief, the ZPD emphasises social convergence (of the political, economic, cultural and sexual) whilst the ZBD obfuscates the social nature of the movement by creating and retaining artificial demarcations.

Besides dualistic tendencies, the ZBD also suffers from deterministic predispositions. There is at times a rigid tendency to link an organisation's features to arbitrary historical periods. For example, in some of his less nuanced writings Marx displayed a certain determinism when he confidently claimed that there is a linear correlation between the notion of industrial *progress* and ever bigger and stronger combinations (Marx, 1846-47/1978: 167). This blinded Marx to the historically contingent nature of trade unions. Pannekoek's suggestion that trade unions were indispensable under 'private capitalism' but become part of the problem under 'state capitalism' (Pannekoek, 1952: 1) is a more sophisticated response but ultimately fails because of the problems with the very notion of 'historical periodisation'. Mattick distinguished between 'ascendant' and 'decadent' phases of capitalism but failed his own logic by denouncing trade unions and political parties even during the ascendant phase of development. All these periodisations become deterministic because they register their analytical concepts as mere tools and not as *tool-and-result*. In section 5.2.2, I will explain how Marx's distinction between formal and real phases of capital domination can first be extended and then used as tool-and-result in order to grasp the heterogeneous organisational forms currently operational.

The learning that takes place within the ZBD is, needless to say, subject to capitalist rules of acquisition.[145] The social nature of knowledge-making is unacknow-

---

145 The American Leninist, James P. Cannon, provides us with a nauseating example of aping the ZBD. In a short essay on 'How to Organise and Conduct a Study Class', Cannon (1924) instructs, '... Enthusiasm for [educational work] among party members must be aroused and maintained ... the next move must be to appoint a leader for the class ... [the teacher must] establish his authority at the very beginning ... Nothing is more fatal to the success of such a class than for the opinion to grow up amongst some of the students that the teacher knows less than they do about the subject ... the [study class] must be conducted in a businesslike fashion from start to finish ...'! Many political conferences and public talks still employ this basic template to this day.

ledged and the end product is usurped in favour of exchange value. The LOS group is correct in suggesting that even 'revolutionary' groups are affected by capitalist competition and simply being aware of these problems is not sufficient to neutralise their adverse influence. As Kamunist Kranti have observed delegating responsibility or rotating spokespersons do not necessarily overcome tendencies toward power-formation and may very well create new problems such as providing easy targets for bosses to attack. The problem with the ZBD is that it is structured in such a way as to conceal most of these issues (I will discuss commodity fetishism and alienation under the next heading), or alternatively, to promote tendencies such as hierarchy and division of labour as unproblematic and inevitable.

This can be illustrated by reference to the work of Peter Good (2001). Equipped with a Bakhtinian perspective, Peter Good has surveyed the landscape of psychiatry. In fact, he did more than survey from afar. He actually masqueraded as a patient in order to experience the 'gaze' of psychiatry firsthand. He has attempted to make sense of his subsequent experiences as an object of psychiatry through distinguishing between what he calls the *Care Chronotope* as opposed to the *Patient Chronotope*. For Bakhtin (1981: 84),

> *Chronotope* (literally, 'time-space') [is] the intrinsic connectedness of temporal and spatial relationships that are artistically expressed in literature. This term (space-time) is employed in mathematics, and was introduced as part of Einstein's Theory of Relativity ... In the literary artistic Chronotope, spatial and temporal indicators are fused into one carefully thought-out, concrete whole. Time, as it were, thickens, takes on flesh, becomes artistically visible; likewise, space becomes charged and responsive to the movements of time, plot and history.

Good takes this definition and extends it to the bodily experiences of a 'polyphonic traveller' such as himself going through the time-space of psychiatry. As a pseudo-patient, Good had to negotiate the boundaries of the Care Chronotope and the Patient Chronotope using techniques such as 'cunning' and 'deception' (Good, 2001: 48). The Care Chronotope

> refers to a 'variety' of practitioners and official spaces' and its distinguishing feature is the 'sheer speed of its time flow'. It projects a faith onto a future time as a way of dealing with the 'disappointments of the present and the shame of the past'. The practitioners travel confidently around this time-space nexus armed with the unitary lexicon of psychiatry ... The Care Chronotope is committed to resolving the problem within the boundaries of the individual. What goes on between bodies is generally obfuscated (Melancholic Troglodytes, 2003: 159).

Within the ZBD the practitioners of the Care Chronotope are the (official or unofficial) party leaders and union bureaucrats. If they do not have the solutions to problems then 'every past hero or heroine can be called upon to rescue a current uncertainty' (Good, 2001: 24). Even when past gurus are invoked, 'each generation of practitioners is anxious to claim their own timespace as the one that will herald the onset of the awaited vision' (Good, 2001: 24). These official voices are 'determined to arrive at a planned and systematic

'A prerequisite for the polyphonic traveller is to fraternize with a wide range of voices and this requires the realisation that some aspects of the Patient Chronotope have a subversive aspect to them.'

resolution' (Good, 2001: 26). In the same way that the Care Chronotope creates and maintains a dependent Patient Chronotope, the dictatorship of timespace within the ZBD subjects the proletariat to a regime calculated to perpetuating the status quo. As Good explains (2001: 27),

> Time, in the Patient Chronotope, has a much more unstable quality than that found in the Care Chronotope. It is given to sudden accelerations or alarming tangents and its direction can go backwards or downwards or simply resolve into endless repetitions. But the form of time that most characterises this chronotope is the kind of time that has a slowed-down almost viscous quality to it ... The divisions that mark public and private timespaces are more pronounced in this chronotope. In any patient voice there is a weakened addressivity towards a public relationship but a much stronger addressivity directed to the private voices of inner dialogue.

So power is intrinsically linked to the chronotope and any new power that wishes to be taken seriously has to build its own chronotope including a myth about how Time began with it and not its rivals. The Great French Revolution's creation of a new calendar is a primary example of this but the same project can be carried out with more subtlety as when Johnny come-lately 'radicals' like Tony Cliff, Alex Callinicos and

Chris Harman attempt to become the story-tellers of the anti-poll tax campaign or the anti-capitalist movement.

The 'polyphonic traveller' (whether a pseudo-patient on a psychiatric ward or a radical at a Leftist meeting) has the daunting task of exposing all of this palaver. A prerequisite for the 'polyphonic traveller' is to fraternize with a wide range of voices and this requires the realisation that some aspects of the Patient Chronotope have a subversive aspect to them. For instance, time experienced within a Zone of Proletarian Development too may seem 'unstable', at times accelerated alarmingly (e.g., during a riot) or deliberately slowed-down (e.g., during a go-slow by factory workers or May Day celebrations).

One final problem with the ZBD that needs to be mentioned is its instrumental-ist usage of technology and the concomitant ideology which views technology as a neutral ahistorical tool. This is hardly surprising given the tool-orientedness of the ZBD itself and the way it turns everything in its path into exchangeable objects. The 'dominative information' (Negri, 1989) is centralised and hierarchic. In shunning face-to-face encounters it creates mediators that require specialists to maintain them (cf. Bey, 1985). This damning judgment, however, cannot be the whole story and in sec-tion 5.2.2, I will discuss technological environments that are conducive to revolution-ary activity.

2. Organisational Fetishism: John Holloway (2002: 43) criticises radicals for ignoring the seminal importance of fetishism. As for those Engels-Leninists who do engage with Marx's concept of fetishism, he charges them with viewing fetishism as a static, stable given rather than a site of contestation. In other words there exist,

> two different ways of understanding fetishism, which we can refer to as 'hard fet-ishism' on the one hand, and 'fetishisation-as-process', on the other. The former understands fetishism as an established fact, a stable or intensifying feature of cap-italist society. The latter understands fetishisation as a continuous struggle, always at issue (Holloway, 2002: 78).

It is the latter understanding of the concept, 'fetishisation-as-process', that interests us here.[146] In his outstanding contribution, *The Devil and Commodity Fetishism in South America*, Michael T. Taussig writes:

> The concept of commodity fetishism is meant to point out for us that capitalist so-ciety presents itself to consciousness as something other than what it basically is,

---

[146] Holloway (2002: 88) makes another salient point with regard to fetishisation as an established fact. He believes this all-pervasive take on fetishism 'leads to the conclusion that the only possible source of anti-fetishism lies outside the ordinary- whether it be the Party (Lukács), the privileged intellectuals (Horkheimer and Adorno), or the *substratum of the outcasts and the outsiders* (Marcuse)' [emphasis in original].

even though that consciousness does reflect the superficial and hypostatized con-
figuration of society. Fetishism denotes the attribution of life, autonomy, power,
and even dominance to otherwise inanimate objects and presupposes the draining
of these qualities from the human actors who bestow the attributions. Thus, in the
case of commodity fetishism, social relationships are dismembered and appear to
dissolve into relationships between mere things ... (Taussig, 1980: 31).

As mentioned in the introduction there has been a tendency amongst leftists (and
even revolutionaries) to make up for a perceived lack of class struggle by proposing a
new form of organisation as a vessel for the development of consciousness which will
then magically lead to a higher level of struggle. Lukács (1971) was a perfect example
of this fallacy. Even revolutionaries were not immune to such temptations. Paul Mattick (1978), and to a lesser extent Pannekoek (1944-47), were guilty of fetishising the
workers' council as the only revolutionary form. However, since communism is an
evolving social movement, no form can capture its dynamics forever. To insist otherwise, would be to rigidify temporality and imbue organisational form with magical
qualities capable of superseding historical contingencies. Perhaps this is the reason
Marx was careful not to repeat the mistakes of utopian socialists in proposing an ideal
way of organising society.

The proposal for a new form of organisation also bespeaks of a puritanical urge
to break with not just past failures but also with everything that is not black and
white. The slogan proposed by Mattick and taken up by some contemporary British
Left Communists with regard to making a revolution 'outside and against the old labour organisations' is a convenient radical pose which does away with all shades of
grey, ambiguity and complication.[147] But is it realistic? Even diehard revolutionaries
may find themselves embroiled in trade union issues from time to time. To suggest
one must do nothing (or confine one's activities to 'critique and propaganda' work
during 'non-revolutionary' periods, as Mattick did) is tantamount to cowardice.

We are, therefore, constantly struggling against fetishism- one form of which
manifests itself in *bureaucratisation*. This process of bureaucratisation could either be
imported from the 'outside' or initiated by workers themselves under mediated (indirect) bourgeois influences. In either case, as Cardan (1959) observed, it leads to the
formation of a separate and uncontrollable layer of specialists whose interests gradually diverge from the proletariat.

The LOS group furnished us with an account of how much more difficult it has
been historically for proletarians to see through 'internal' leaders (those who have
arisen from our own ranks, e.g., Lech Walesa in Poland, Arthur Scargill in Britain, Ah-

---

147 An example of a British Left Communist group that elevates the slogan 'outside and against unions' to a
religious mantra is Wildcat (Wildcat, 1992). Having degenerated into a Left Communist Fundamentalist
outfit (i.e., a Left Communist grouping that combines a panache for conservatism and word-reverence with
moralism), Wildcat dissolved itself in the late 1990s.

madi-Nezhad in Iran, Lula in Brazil or Louis Farrakhan in the USA) as opposed to 'outside' leaders.[148] As the S.I. noted, one crucial factor in avoiding such degeneration is to ensure the new organisation dialectically links 'defensive' (or possibilist) demands with 'offensive' (or impossibilist) demands. The 'stars' or 'celebrities' of the 'anti-globalisation movement', individuals such as Naomi Klein and George Monbiot, systematically sabotage this dialectical linkage. Self-righteous musicians, such as Sir Bob Geldof, manage the same feat whilst toiling outside the 'anti-globalisation movement'. Hence Debord's reflections on the rise of the celebrity in an age when 'dissatisfaction itself has become a commodity' are more pertinent than ever,

> The celebrity, the spectacular representation of a living human being, embodies this [modern day] banality by embodying the image of a possible role. Being a star means specialising in the *seemingly* lived ... Celebrities exist to act out various styles of living and viewing society- unfettered, free to express themselves globally ... In one case state power personalises itself as a pseudo-star [think of the jet-setting Tony Blair or the Pope here]; in another a star of pseudo-consumption gets elected as pseudo-power over the lived [think of Arnold Schwarzenegger]. But just as the activities of the stars are not really global, they are not really varied (Debord, 1987: thesis 60). [Comments added]

Every fetishized organisation needs a living fetish totem as its centre point. Related to the issue of bureaucratisation and stardom within proletarian collectivities is the vexed problem of *subtle vanguardism*. By subtle vanguardism I am not referring to the crude Bolshevik tactic of gaining control over the class which usually involves the imposition of a layer of 'politically correct' petty bourgeois commissars over the proletariat.

Subtle vanguardism does not demand explicit power for itself at the expense of the proletariat but rather stands back from the fray and simply nominates a section of the proletariat as privileged over others. The privileged section is then glorified and put on a pedestal in the hope it acts as a role model for the rest of the class. The leadership uses this romanticised privileged section as ventriloquists use their dummy. Words are put into the dummy's mouth which gain magical currency precisely because they emerges from a fetish object. This top-down enforced 'ventriloquation' is

---

148 A particularly offensive and nauseating defence of such 'internal' leaders comes from a vacuous activist by the name of Gianpaolo Baiocchi (2004). He defends the sponsorship of the Third World Social Forum (WSF) in Porto Alegre by Brazil's Workers' Party on the grounds that it supports 'participatory solutions' and 'non-instrumentalist relationships to the social movement'. He then describes approvingly the jubilant reception of President Lula by the reactionary crowd assembled at Porto Alegre: '[Lula] closed by promising he would not deviate *one comma* from his socialist ideas. The crowd went wild and started to chant, holding up two hands to signify the number eight, a call for Lula's re-election barely three weeks into his first term' (Baiocchi, 2004: 200). The tolerance of such outlandish counter-revolutionary theatrical performances by wankers like Lula is testimony to the bourgeois character of the WSF. During the fifth WSF the star system was retained but the target of the delegates' affections became the valiant Hugo Chavez. Apparently the bourgeois prick was cheered by a twenty-thousand strong crowd of boot-lickers (cf. Glasius, 2005: 247).

then used to ensure subtle vanguardism. The criteria employed for measuring the privileged status may include tradition, heroic deeds or influence over the production process. For instance, in Romania and Russia miners are usually treated as the vanguard of the movement because of their tradition of struggle. In the USA firefighters and steel workers are viewed through rose-tinted spectacles since their heroic struggles have gained legendary status. Finally, Middle Eastern oil workers are believed to constitute a vanguard since their position in the production process offers them a unique vantage point for sabotaging the economy.

There are a number of problems with the notion of subtle vanguardism. Firstly, since this myth is founded on a partial truth its demystification proves difficult. It just so happens that Romanian and Russian miners, US firefighters and steelworkers and Middle Eastern oil workers have at times been at the forefront of the struggle against exploitation. At other times, when these groups have fallen short of revolutionary standards or sided with reaction (as in the case of Romanian miners) their transgressions tend to be ignored or rationalised away. Secondly, the fact that at any given time a section of the proletariat may prove more capable or better organised should not confer on them the status of permanent leadership. Thirdly, the concept of subtle vanguardism forgets that no section of the proletariat has sufficient experience and power to overcome capitalism and only interaction between different strata within the ZPD can ensure success. Autonomist Marxists in particular have a tendency to forget this lesson. Alquati and Negri, for instance, designate a section of the proletariat as the 'most advanced', then attempt to impose that group's organisational criteria on the rest of the class. Fourthly, by setting the scene for what the group Kamunist Kranti calls 'a spectacular unifocal struggle', subtle vanguardism hands over the initiative to the state.

'Words are put into the dummy's mouth which gain magical currency...'

This top-down enforced 'ventriloquation' is then used to ensure subtle vanguardism.

Organisational fetishism as the general ideology responsible for imbuing certain forms with magical eternal properties is also guilty of reifying certain organisational principles into mere techniques. For instance, King (2004) and Freeman (1970) have noted how organisational principles such as 'openness', 'horizontal relations' and 'structurelessness' can reify dynamic processes and prevent individual and collective development. 'Supernodes' and 'crypto-hierarchies' in the case of 'open' structures and 'elites' in the case of 'structureless' groups emerge and go unnoticed precisely because process has been reified. Even when such problems are avoided, organisational fetishism tends toward the fetishization of *democracy*. Democracy whether defined as 'majority rule' (Cardan, 1959) or separation between decision making and action (Kautsky, 1903) is often used to prevent a 'minority' of proletarians taking the initiative against capitalism. Democracy creates mediations which intensify organisational fetishism and reduce the efficacy of transparent direct action (Camatte, 1969).

3. Organisational Religiosity: Once organisation has been fetishized (i.e., once alienation has taken hold of the organisation, its processes reified, its objectives infused with magical qualities and the notion of fetishisation-as-process suppressed), it is but a short step to complete degeneration and organisational religiosity. In many cases, it would be inaccurate to classify such groupings as representatives of zones of bourgeois development since *development* (even in its narrow bourgeois sense) has ceased to exist.

In this phase, the organisation displays increasing signs of decomposition. It comes to be viewed as a safe haven from the ravages of the 'outside' world, a *community* whose falsehood and imaginary status is denied by adherents. Camatte and Collu (1969) referred to such organisations as 'gangs' which having seduced their members, vampirize their creativity. Fundamentalist outlooks become prevalent. This 'fundamentalism' manifests itself in terms of *conservatism* in thought and action, theological/legalistic notions such as *precedence* (the dictatorship of dead words) and *moralism*

Personal and ideological ties of continuity!

(which is employed to control the rank-and-file and distinguish the in-group from rival out-groups).

The group is encouraged to lay low and wait out the storm in the 'safety' of this imagined community. Hakim Bey's reintroduction of the Shi'a concept of *Taqiya* (concealment of one's faith in oppressive times) into radical circles is a particularly obnoxious example of this trend.[149] There is a gulf separating revolutionaries who refuse to

---

149 Hakim Bey chooses his reactionary interventions with care. It so happens that there is superficial commonalities between the way revolutionaries have to conceal their identities and ideas from the state

be provoked by bosses into a fixed fight or do not advertise their ideas for fear of persecution (e.g., Kamunist Kranti) and reactionaries (be they Muslims, Christians, Anarchists or Leninists) who lie in order to gain access to positions of power or use underground activity as an excuse for maintaining cults.

The degeneration of the ZBD into a cult goes hand in hand with the adoption of missionary doctrines that see the group as saviours of the corrupt world. Since waiting for the future paradise is increasingly seen as the solution to contemporary ills, revolutionary praxis becomes redundant. Most activities are now directed towards maintaining the organisation. A number of Leninist, Anarchist, Left-Bolshevik and 'Left-Communist' groupings in Britain fall under this category. A hallmark of such groups is the use of rituals to create passive members who trade off the possibility of development and creativity for the illusionary 'safe-haven' promised.

Organisational religiosity has its own discourse and modes of regulating in-group and inter-group communication. In chapter 4, I looked at what Mey (1985) called the 'repressive' uses of language which attempt to inhibit alternative/oppositional modes of discourse from emerging. I provided the examples of Mussolini,

Khomeini and George W. Bush who by claiming that only God can judge their actions close the door to many forms of dissent from being voiced. The simple trick is to make sure 'official' consciousness prevents utterances by unofficial consciousness. By preventing 'motives of inner speech to turn into outward speech' (Vološinov, 1987: 89) clarity and rigour are denied to unofficial consciousness. Stalin acted in this man-

Jonestown (Guyana) in 1978

ner by murdering or imprisoning his rivals and ensuring the existence of only one form of discourse- his precious Diamat. Lenin, perhaps due to his relatively weaker position, only attempted 'oppressive' usage of language intermittently (e.g., the cam-

---

apparatus and the Shi'a concept of *Taqiya*. This is even true for 'western' revolutionaries. Since Shi'ites have been weaker than Sunnis for long stretches, Taqiya has become a useful method of self-preservation. However, although renouncing one's 'faith' under torture may be a sensible precaution against execution for atheists who do not believe in an after-life, it seems a strange tactic for believers who glorify martyrdom. What Bey ignores is that Taqiya is permissible under Shi'a jurisprudence only if a believer's life is threatened. Bey, on the other hand, seems to prescribe the tactic of concealment and denial as a matter of course for 'non-revolutionary' times. Bey also conveniently ignores the dialectics of means and ends, how inappropriate means distort a movement's ends in the long term. By making a virtue out of necessity, Bey forgets that revolutionary activity is at its most subversive when it is out in the open, transparent to everyone's gaze and constructive criticisms. Political conditions may exclude openness as a strategy in certain periods and certain parts of the world but Bey's predilection for secrecy and underground activity smack of the romantic adventurism of an old man with too much imagination and too little sense.

paign against the Kronstadt rebellion and its sympathisers in 1921). During his reign, oppositional ideas were already in the public domain and therefore the only viable method of censorship was the 'oppressive use of language', which seeks to marginalise and constrain alternative uses of language by recalcitrant elements (Mey, 1985).

The significant point about organisations that have degenerated towards religiosity is that the leadership can employ 'repressive' techniques *within* the group by denying the possibility of alternative modes of discourse from emerging, whilst at the same time it uses 'oppressive' techniques to constrain and regulate *inter*-group communication. In this way its own rank-and-file will remain safely within the organisational fold whilst new members can be recruited from the outside.

The classical example of a rapidly decomposing ZBD which employed both 're-pressive' and 'oppressive' techniques is the Jonestown 'commune'. Jonestown was a prison-town built by James Jones who ruled over his disciples with an iron-fist. In the name of socialism 'people were drugged and beaten, brainwashed and forced to indulge in slave labour, sexually manipulated and annihilated as individuals...' (Brinton, 1978: 1). James Jones began as a preacher and became 'radicalised'. His followers believed him to be 'the reincarnation of Lenin and Jesus Christ' (Brinton, 1978: 8).

What concerns us here is how easily a 'religio-political' organisation degenerated into a suicide-cult. How easily, critical judgment was abdicated, rhetoric replaced arguments and slogans took the place of debate (Brinton, 1978: 2). Just like today's 'Jihadists', James Jones (b. 1931) used to play 'religious games' as a child. He learned techniques of manipulation from Father Divine, the legendary pastor from Philadelphia, e.g., interrogation committees and how to make himself the object of sexual desire of the whole congregation. He claimed to be able to cure cancer, raise the dead, etc. In 1963 he organised an exodus of his people to the Promised Land to build 'socialism', first to San Francisco and eventually to Guyana (1973).

In order for the commune to be economically viable, 'people worked from 12 hours or more a day- after which they had a right to *self-criticism* sessions. Whoever expressed doubts ... was punished. He (or she) either had the head shaved, or had to wear a yellow hat or a special badge to signal *dishonour'* (Brinton, 1978: 7). Children who wet their pants were administered electric shocks. One survivor explained the reason why so many meekly went to their death: 'Only months after we defected from the Temple did we realize the full extent of the cocoon in which we'd lived. And only then did we understand the fraud, sadism, and emotional blackmail of the master manipulator' (quoted in Osherow, 1981: 84). The physically and emotionally draining cycle of work-self-criticism-sexual-manipulation, left little room for reflection and resistance.

Brinton (1978: 10) reminds us that 'historically, cults and sects have usually flourished at times of social crisis, when old values were collapsing and new ones had not yet asserted themselves'. Today we live in similar crisis-ridden times. In addition, 'cults offer three benefits: ultimate meaning, a strong sense of community and rewards either in this world or the next' (Brinton, 1978: 11). The leader and the followers come to forge a symbiotic relationship since they both need each other. This is as true of so-called 'anti-authoritarian' informal anarchist groups as Leninist organisations. Rituals then come to play a vital role in providing the followers with the illusion of movement. James Jones used to run 'white-nights' which were dress rehearsals for the mass suicide which eventually took the lives of 921 members. Anarchist 'horizontals' run preparatory anti-summit meetings, followed by a mass (political) suicide at a pre-designated time and place, after which the survivors organise themselves into defence campaigns. The perpetuation of the cycle maintains the power of the anarchist elite.

The Militant Tendency is another good example of an entryist organisation that employed 'repressive' techniques within its own ranks whilst using 'oppressive' techniques to silence Labour Party members. Lesser examples of this double-censorship approach have been employed with varying degrees of success by the propagandists of the Revolutionary Communist Group (a bizarre British Stalinist grouping of postgraduate students whose anti-working class credentials has endeared some of their ex-members to certain sections of the 'anti-globalisation' movement such as 'anarchists' gathered around the journal *Schnews*), and the even more bizarre 'left-Bolshevik fundamentalist' outfit known as the International Communist Current. The latter gang takes 'repressive' measures to the extreme by banning pictures and graphics (in fact anything with a trace of imagination) from their dire bi-monthly, *World Revolution.*

5.2.2 - Zone of Proletarian Development (ZPD) or what is living (or at least on the verge of being born) in organisational matters?

The preceding section demarcated a bourgeois zone where praxis is denied, dualism and organisational fetishism rule and creativity is defined in very narrow terms. In this section I intend to draw out the contours of an alternative mode of organising based on proletarian interests. The Zone of Proletarian Development (ZPD) is a historically specific variety of Vygotsky's zone of proximal development (zoped) and consists of four main features. These are *joint-dialectical-activity, heterogeneity, carnivalesque* and *empowerment.*

1. Organisational Joint-Dialectical-Activity: In *The Communist Manifesto* (1847-48) Marx wrote,

> In place of the old bourgeois society, with its classes and class antagonisms, we shall have an association, in which the free development of each is the condition for the free development of all (Marx, 1847-48/1986: 105).

As remarked earlier this quote and similar passages suggest a concordance with Vygotsky's seminal notion of the zoped. Marx was interested not only in the actual level of development but in a movement's potential. This potential could only be discerned through collaborative activity. Thus Mattick and the Situationists were correct in emphasising that proletarian organisations should carry within them seeds of the future. However, to designate an actual proletarian organisation as 'embryonic communism' should not be at the expense of limiting its potential. The historically emerging ZPD has three elements that must be kept in mind simultaneously- the dead labour of past generations embedded in tools, the immediate or everyday activities and needs of proletarians and the long-term goals and desires of the social movement. Only organisations that link the three can lay claim to being revolutionary. Engeström's (1991: 168) concept of 'expansive learning' identifies the contradictions that lead to double bind situations and encourages people to design alternative practices in order to resolve these contradictions. A revolutionary organisation that is durable has a greater potential to initiate 'expansive learning' than a short-term riot or demonstration. However, precisely because it is more durable there may be a marked tendency towards *teamworking* and *networking* rather than *knotworking* practices (see chapter 2 and Engeström, 1999: 346). This tendency calls for a great effort to minimise the negative aspects of both teamworking (e.g., the creation of specialists) and networking (e.g., the emergence of powerful supernodes).

In chapter 4, during my discussion of the anti-poll tax and the anti-war demonstration of February 2003, I mentioned that there are three basic paradigms for analysing the relationship between subject, tool and object (Martin Ryder, 1999: 3). The first is the Ideal paradigm that idealises the subject as autonomous, the tool as neutral and the object as unproblematically attainable (cf. McLuhan, 1964). The second is the Cynical paradigm and represents the exact opposite. Here the tool is demonised and comes to dominate the passive and helpless subject, thus making the attainment of the object impossible (cf. Marcuse, 1964). The third paradigm is the dialectical one which supersedes the limitations of the Ideal and Cynical paradigms by positing the individual simultaneously as the 'subject-tool-object' of activity (cf. Marx, 1844). Here tools have a history. Furthermore, they act both as 'instruments' of agency and the result of activity.

It is through dialectics that the ZPD overcomes the dualism that besets the ZBD. The concrete everyday events that embody proletarian struggles are the bedrock of zones of proletarian development. But demands cannot simply be defended. The task of the ZPD is to extend and escalate everyday demands until all capitalist social relations are put under erasure. To use terminology from German Critical Psychology, the *restrictive action potence* which tries to make action potent (effective) within 'the framework of given or conceded conditions' (Maiers and Tolman, 1996: 111) must reach *generalised action potence* if the struggle is to be extended. For instance, restrictive action potence is linked to emotional inwardness whereas a generalised action potence 'takes emotion as a response to the world requiring corrective [collective] action' (Maiers and Tolman, 1996: 112). Similarly, as Guattari and Negri (1990) pointed out, 'molar' antagonisms (workplace fights over exploitation and safety) need to be expanded until they reach 'molecular proliferation' into the outside world. When the Justice for Janitors organisation threatens to take its struggle against Apple into schools and universities they are consciously crossing this threshold. The molecular proliferation changes the nature and tempo of the initial molar antagonism as was the case in 1968 France with students and workers feeding off each others' efforts. The ZPD must become a place where strategies as well as tactics are discussed and decided upon and where emotions and intellect are seen as irreversibly interconnected. In this regard, Kamunist Kranti seem to have attained an impressive level of honest clarity. As quoted earlier,

> Collectivity accepts varying levels of helplessness, weakness, fear, hesitation ... within wage-workers ... There is no attempt at face-saving and steps back and forth are taken for granted (Kamunist Kranti, 1997: 57).

The ZPD brings to attention two interrelated kinds of activity, one concerning the overthrow of capitalism and the other concerning the reconstruction of human beings. After all if we are correct in assuming that the proletariat is the subject-tool-object of history or to put it differently both product and producer of this world, it stands to reason that 'the transformation of this world and the transformation of ourselves as human beings are one and the same task' (Newman and Holzman, 2004: 10). The ZPD in contradistinction to the ZBD is primarily a convergence space tending toward the social. Whilst the ZBD throws up artificial barriers between politics, culture, sexuality, psychology and economics, the ZPD transcends these demarcations by foregrounding the social aspect of praxis. Holloway (2002: 102) echoing Vygotsky puts it like this, 'Thinking on the basis of doing means, then, thinking against-and-beyond our own thought'.

2. Organisational Heterogeneity: Kamunist Kranti reminds us, 'collectivity recognises differences, it does not suppress them. Its strength lies in recognising multiplicity, diversity, dissidence, doubt and criticism' (Kamunist Kranti, 1997: 57). Guattari and Negri (1990: 107 and 120) would concur,

> This is the first positive characteristic of the new revolutionary subjectivity. Its co-operative, plural, anti-centralist, anti-corporatist, anti-racist, anti-sexist dimensions further the productive capacities of the singularities ... From now on organising signifies first: work on oneself, in as much as one is a collective singularity [there is no need to agree with this ontological prioritising of self-development, to agree with the gist of the quote]; construct and in a permanent way re-construct this collectivity in a multivalent liberation project. [My addition]

Whilst avoiding determinism it is essential to understand that different modes of capitalist accumulation tend to throw up differing organisations of resistance. If grasped productively, this heterogeneity could be a source of strength and not division. Marx (1846-47/1978), Pannekoek (1952), Camatte and Collu (1969) and Hardt and Negri (2000) may not have furnished us with a workable model of this relationship but at least they were aware of it. In order to theorise this heterogeneity more effectively we must make a distinction between *visible* and *invisible* heterogeneity.

Visible heterogeneity describes all those differences that are discernible through the 'naked' eye. They are perceived and differentiated largely because capitalist society has conditioned us into observing these categories. For instance, it took the experience of colonialism and slavery to make 'people of colour' see themselves as a 'race' apart. Similarly it took the social and technical division of labour to engineer gendered differences based on empirically verifiable biological variation. The fact that these categories are constructed does not make them any less 'real'. In the past 'visible gender heterogeneity' has found capable theorists in the shape of radicals such as Mariarosa Dalla Costa and Selma James (1975) and Leopoldina Fortunati (1995). If you consider the community as first and foremost the home (as Mariarosa Dalla Costa does) and demand wages for house work, then your organisation will need to adapt accordingly if it is to be viable. Alternatively, if you believe (as Fortunati does) that most houseworkers produce *absolute* surplus value as opposed to factory workers who produce *relative* surplus value, then you must draw out the organisational implications of this distinction. The way houseworkers resist capital differs from factory workers because their labour process is constructed differently,

> If technological innovation can lower the limit of necessary work, and if the working class struggle in industry can use that innovation for gaining free hours, the same cannot be said of housework; to the extent that she must *in isolation* procreate, raise and be responsible for children, a high mechanisation of domestic chores doesn't free any time for women. She is always on duty, for a machine doesn't exist that makes and minds children (Dalla Costa and James, 1975: 29).

It is also noteworthy how it has traditionally been in the interest of trade unions (even those created by workers themselves) not to organise domestic work. Most domestic workers were ignored by the traditional labour movement until recently when a fall in the number of union membership has made new recruitment efforts indispensable. As Dalla Costa and James (1975: 34) observe,

> The organised parties of the working class movement have been careful not to raise the question of domestic work. Aside from the fact that they have al-

ways treated women as a lower form of life, even in factories, to raise this question would be to challenge the whole basis of the trade unions as organisations that deal (a) only with the factory; (b) only with a measured and 'paid' work; (c) only with that side of the wages which is given to us and not with the side of the wages which is taken back, that is, inflation.

Dalla Costa and James (1975: 38) also talk about certain demands that have the potential to unite houseworkers and factory workers since it is in the interest of both groups for these demands to be met. For instance,

> If women demand in workers' assemblies that the night-shift be abolished because at night, besides speaking, one wants to make love - and it's not the same as making love during the day if the women work during the day - that would be advancing their interests as women against the social organisation of work, refusing to be unsatisfied mothers for their husbands and children ... [but crucially] to make love and refuse night work to make love, *is in the interest of the class* (Dalla Costa and James, 1975: 38-39). [Comments in original]

Love making, therefore, can become a bridge between what Guattari and Negri (1990) refer to as the osmosis of 'molar antagonisms' into 'molecular proliferations'. In order to investigate the relationship between gender and class, Dalla Costa and James put forward the following nuanced distinction,

> Sexuality after all is the most social of expressions, the deepest human communication. It is in that sense the dissolution of autonomy. The working class organises itself as a class to transcend itself as a class; within that class [women] organise autonomously to create the basis to transcend autonomy.

Gender, race, colour, culture and at times sexual orientation and physical impairment can be used as *visible* markers to identify groups sharing a set of interests. These groups may decide to come together to discuss their problems and organise autonomously within the class to achieve their aims. However, there is another group of markers that tend to be *invisible* since capitalism conceals their existence. These markers are the ways in which surplus value is extracted and the corresponding labour processes that emerge to regulate the extraction process. Delineating them may help to show how certain organisations emerge under certain conditions. This in turn will help to create a horizontal contact zone across them. In this way heterogeneity becomes productive.

Marx (1867/1979) provided us with the most incisive analysis of the labour process. His distinction between the *formal* and *real* subsumption of labour under capital is the ideal starting point. During the formal phase of subsumption capital gradually takes over a mode of labour developed before the emergence of capitalist relations. This is carried out,

> as a form of *compulsion* by which surplus labour is exacted by extending the duration of labour-time ... [Under formal subsumption] surplus-value can be created only by lengthening the working day, i.e., by increasing absolute surplus-value (Marx, 1867/1979: 1021).

Marx goes on to distinguish the formal phase of domination from preceding pre-capitalist relations. In his view these features are,

> [Firstly] the pure money relationship between the man who appropriates the surplus labour and the man who yields it up ... [secondly, the worker's] *objective conditions of labour* (the means of production) and the *subjective conditions of labour* (the means of subsistence) confront him as *capital*, as the monopoly of the buyer of his labour-power (Marx, 1867/1979: 1026).

These features result in the increase of the continuity and intensity of labour, creating evermore versatile workers and divisions of labour. This new phase is called the *real* subsumption of labour and is characterised by *relative* surplus value extraction. Compulsion does not disappear but is increasingly combined with an element of consent in order to guarantee profits. Science and technology constantly reinvent the labour process and increase the rate of surplus value (sometimes at the same time as wages). As Geoffrey Kay (1979: 50) has noted,

> [The social interdependence of capital] is vastly more important when the production of relative surplus value is the main mode of exploitation, since the success and failure of the individual capitalist enterprise becomes increasingly dependent upon the success or failure of social capital as a whole.

Kay (1979: 52) goes on to explain that in reality the distinction between absolute and relative surplus value extraction is blurred and that even under real domin-

'... *because at night, besides speaking, one wants to make love ...*'

ation capitalism employs both absolute and relative surplus value extraction side by side (see also Tomba, 2007). In fact, as Fortunati (1990) has explained the same family unit can be divided along gender specific lines in this regard with the (female) house-worker producing, by and large, absolute surplus value and the (male) factory work-er, by contrast, relative surplus value. We can roughly claim that in the 'west' prior to 1850 absolute surplus value production was dominant and after 1950 there was a switch to relative surplus production.

As if things were not complicated enough, I earlier postulated the emergence of a new phase of capital domination, named the *surreal* phase. The surreal phase is characterised by four methods of surplus value extraction (pre-formal, formal, real, post-real).

If this is true we could further postulate that various methods of surplus value extraction correspond to specific labour processes such as Taylorism or post-Taylor-ism. Furthermore, Autonomist Marxist literature suggests there is a rough corres-pondence between these labour processes and the emergence of various subjectivities. For instance, the formal phase of domination is characterised by absolute surplus value extraction and the beginnings of a Taylorist labour process. The subjectivity most prevalent in this period is the 'mass worker'. As capitalism becomes more gener-alised and Taylorism gives way to post-Taylorism, the 'socialised worker' comes to represent the more social dimension of production.

It is beyond the scope of this investigation to describe this tendency in any more detail but I am convinced it is essential to understand these underlying mechanisms if we are to create linkage between different organisational methods. *The ZPD must en-deavour to flag both visible and invisible markers of heterogeneity in order to facilit-ate horizontal linkage between subsets of proletarians.*

If we are to achieve horizontal linkage across subsets of proletarian groupings then a degree of 'intersubjectivity' becomes essential. In chapter 2, I described 'inter-subjectivity' in the sense put forward by Maiers and Tolman (1996: 105) 'not as mere contemplation or self-reflection but as effective agency, which is achieved only in co-operation with others, that is, in societal, historical relations'. This effective agency is not due to a complete agreement between participants in a joint activity. In fact, Wertsch (1980) has demonstration that effective communication (in his case between mother and child) comes about through *partial* rather than complete intersubjectivity. So although a shared *presuppositional knowledge between collaborators* (Lock, 2000: 117) is necessary, this does not amount to complete agreement on analysis or choice of activity.

The establishment of intersubjectivity itself depends on a number of factors, chief amongst them *sensitivity* to the verbal and non-verbal cues of fellow group members (Kermani and Brenner, 2000: 19). Sensitivity depends on the *quality* of inter-actions between learner-teachers and not necessarily the content or winning of argu-ments. Again what this suggests is that the maintenance of horizontal linkage depends primarily on solidarity amongst participants, a solidarity born of trust and a *general* shared set of values/interests and encouraged by sensitivity to others' point of view. Once people become sensitive to others' points of view they can freely ponder the complex nuances that exist between *meaning* and *sense* in everyday speech.

Chik Collins (1999: 62) reminds us that *meaning* refers to the abstract, stable, dictionary definition of words whilst *sense* is much more fluid and personal since it derives from actual use in everyday speech. Leontiev (1977: 198) elaborated on this by (a) emphasising the importance of *motivation* to the meaning-sense polarity, and (b) relating the meaning-sense polarity to the rise of commodification and alienation. For the mineral trader, as Marx observed, the commodity he monopolises has an objective meaning realised on the market but not a personal sense. This split promotes alienation in both worker and capitalist. In chapter 2 we observed how the May Day 2000 mohicanisation of Churchill's statue overcame alienation by bringing the meaning and sense of the statue into closer harmony. This was an example of what Bakhtin called 'life-as-authoring'. It is clear, therefore, that life-as-authoring by dialectically linking meaning and sense and encouraging empowerment overcomes alienation and produces the preconditions for intersubjectivity to create horizontal linkage amongst a heterogeneous proletariat.

3. Organisational Carnivalesque: Carnivalesque is an alternative mode of social being and consciousness that aims to subvert all hierarchies. In the words of Robert Stam (1992: 86),

> The carnivalesque principle abolishes all hierarchies, levels social classes and creates another life free from conventional rules and restrictions. In carnival, all that is marginalised and excluded … takes over the centre in a liberating explosion of otherness.

In chapter 3 on Bakhtin and Iranian football riots, I opposed carnivalesque to the Debordian concept of the spectacle. In fact most proletarian collectivities will consist of a mixture of carnivalesque and spectacular relationships (see figure below). The trick is to promote the former and fight the latter. The carnivalesque consists of elements such as laughter, mocking, parody, irony, aggression, sexual overtones, dialogic interactions, grotesquerie and polyglossia that make it, at least potentially, an emancipatory 'ready-made'. It is important not to reify these characteristics as technique. They are process rather than product. In other words, each subversive act will require different types of laughter, parody, irony grotesquerie and sexual overtones. In relation to laughter, for instance, Bakhtin has remarked,

> Laughter has the remarkable power of making an object come up close, of drawing it into a zone of crude contact where one can finger it familiarly on all sides, turn it upside down, inside out, peer at it from above and below, break open its external shell … doubt it, take it apart, dismember it, lay it bare and expose it, examine it freely and experiment with it (Bakhtin, 1981: 23).

Leftism has traditionally been devoid of the healing laughter, the kind of *laughing-with-people* that soothes whilst helping to emancipate.[150] Even mere humour seems to be beyond the reach of most of its protagonists. As for an entire mode of social being and consciousness conducive to subverting hierarchies (i.e., carnivalesque), nothing can be more horrifying to the average Leftist. In a devastating assessment of Leftism, John Holloway (2002: 16) has sarcastically commented,

> At the top of the hierarchy we learn to place that part of our activity that contributes to 'building the revolution', at the bottom come frivolous personal things like affective relations, sensuality, playing, laughing, loving.

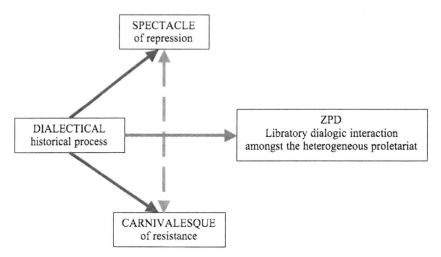

Dialectics of spectacle and carnivalesque with ZPD as a possible synthesis (adapted from Boje, 2001).

Bourgeois ideologies prefer if the controlling of emotions is carried out 'voluntarily' by atomised individuals. Each person can become his/her emotion-controller. This explains why Leftists feel so uncomfortable in the presence of what I would call the 'undomesticated proletariat' (vagabonds, gypsies, ne'er-do-wells and prostitutes) and what is mislabelled and marginalised as 'lumpenproletariat'. Self-control, as Goffman has pointed out, is a 'precondition for successful interaction' in a bourgeois world (quoted in Kuzmics, 1991:1). This self-control is connected to the need to avoid embarrassment. The sombre and serious affectation of Leftist activists is further proof of the emotional self-control they practice and attempt to impose on others. And yet their at-

---

150 Laughter related to a person or event can, of course, be both an example of *laughter-at-people* and laughter-with-people. The desecration of Churchill's statue is a case in point; it was laughter *with* fellow demonstrators directed *at* Churchill and all he represents.

tempts are rarely successful and subsequently Leftist gatherings are infused with embarrassing moments: the speaker who runs out of arguments and refuses to acknowledge the fact; the chairperson who dictatorially silences 'emotional' critics; the 'plants' who forget their prepared speeches half way through delivery; the paper-sellers who self-consciously peddle the party's latest tomes of wisdom, and so on. Even when Leftists decide to discuss affective conditions, the style of presentation betrays their discomfort. Witness the dry, sombre treatise of a Fortunati (1995: 75) or a Negri (2003: 209) on the concept of 'love', the one 'human condition', if there ever was one, that demands a humorous approach.

In contradistinction to the Leftist opposition to carnivalesque, most proletarians realise that it is precisely the excessive attributes of carnivalesque which 'destroys all alienation' (Bakhtin, 1984a: 381). Carnivalesque allows everyone to participate instead of passively consuming. This in turn leads to the creation of a shared social purview and solidarity. Carnivalesque provides participants with images 'through which [they] may recognise [themselves] without disgust' (Stallybrass and White, 1986: 187).

That is why it is crucial to *socialise* political gatherings. For example, the simple act of food sharing at a meeting may allow members of a group to recognise each other and themselves without 'political' masks. Crucially the carnivalesque provides proletarians

Carnivalesque provides participants with images 'through which [they] may recognise [themselves] without disgust.'

Oh, lovely dick!

with a repertoire of alternative techniques of resistance (alongside the more traditional strike and picket) which enables a rapid change of tactics when circumstances demand it. Even when grotesquerie is promoted it is what Bakhtin called 'grotesque realism' which both degrades and regenerates. Grotesque realism lowers all that is pretentious and high, including unnecessarily abstract ideas, thus allowing for concrete ideas to express themselves. The grotesque and laughing qualities of carnivalesque are useful in overcoming the body-mind dualism favoured by Leftist organisations. Peter Hitchcock (1998: 85) neatly sums it up,

The body in revolt is often a revolting body ... The body constantly contradicts the pretensions and ideologies of perfection in its defecation, sneezing, farting, belching, and bleeding ... The body's materiality, especially the materiality of what Bakhtin calls its 'lower stratum', conspires against the codes of order and rationality issued by the 'head'. It wants nothing of 'discipline' and 'regularity'; it prefers, inestimably, the excessive process of waste, procreation, and decay.

For all the abovementioned reasons therefore, it is essential for a proletarian organisation to create a 'convergence space' (Routledge, 2004: 8) which is infused with carnivalesque. The Situationists understood this more profoundly than most. Emotions, creativity, imagination and unconscious desires (defined socially and not individualistically) rely on a carnivalesque space for their very survival. In a rather romanticised manner, Hakim Bey (1993: 2) too talks about the 'festival' aspects of TAZ (Temporary Autonomous Zone). In Caribbean Islands during enslavement the white authorities 'feared that the horns and drums that accompanied the dance were being used [by slaves] for communication purposes' (Liverpool, 1993: 103). Some refer to a meeting's *vibe*, loosely defined as the meeting's atmosphere (as in 'good/bad vibes'). Some collectivities, according to Gordon (2003: 17)

> have experimented with the designation of a *vibe-watcher* who notes how people are feeling during the meetings- (over-emotional, angry, upset, uncomfortable, etc.) and deals with these feelings by suggesting a time-out if things get too emotional or an *energizer* (moving around, playing a game) if people are getting restless.

Although there are major problems with the abovementioned 'experiment' (including the creation of new specialisms in the shape of the 'vibe-watcher', the cognitive bias in judging certain states as 'over-emotional' and the imposition of emotive games on participants, and an unstated anti-intellectualism), there is at least the acknowledgment of the significance of group emotions and the way a meeting's 'vibe' can be as decisive in determining outcome as the political content under discussion. It is no exaggeration to claim that the carnivalesque ZPD works by reaffirming the forces of life and suspending seriousness and death.

4. Organisational empowerment: Empowerment has proved a contentious issue for social scientists. Empowerment theory itself has been justifiably criticised as 'overly individualistic and conflict-oriented resulting in an emphasis on mastery and control rather than cooperation and community' (Speer, 2000: 51).

However, empowerment does not have to be trapped within an individualistic framework or for that matter to treat 'mastery' and 'cooperation' as mutually exclusive. 'Mastery' could be achieved *through* collective cooperation. Rappaport's definition is a case in point, '[Empowerment is] a process: the mechanism by which people, organisations, and communities gain mastery over their lives'

(Rappaport, 1984: 3). Similarly, the Social Identity Model (Reicher, 1996) defines 'empowerment' as a

> subjective sense of ability or confidence; it exists on a continuum (greater or lesser) rather than being dichotomous (either absent or present). *Collective empowerment* is therefore ... the perceived degree of control that members of one group have over their fate and that of other groups (Reicher, 1996 quoted in Drury and Reicher, 1999: 384).

Speer (2000: 59) has shown 'that critical awareness and knowledge of resources required to change community are necessary elements of empowerment' whilst proponents of Social Identity Model suggest that 'empowerment is a product as well as a precondition of collective action' (Drury and Reicher, 1999: 381).

It stands to reason, therefore, that the ZPD should endeavour to enhance individual and collective empowerment and avoid any process or mechanism that may impede it. Various revolutionaries have pointed out how mediatory bodies and institutions are erected to undermine empowerment. Pannekoek (1933) and Mattick's (1978) critique of trade unions is a case in point. Unions by initially positing themselves as a mediating layer between capital and labour and later on elevating themselves to the level of labour-regulating capital, act to *dis*empower proletarians. All initiative and spontaneity is taken out of the struggle to be replaced with negotiating tactics carried out by specialists. Gradually even defending workers' interests takes second place to restructuring labour and maximising profit.[151] The parliament is another mediating institution with similar characteristics. As Pannekoek (in Bricianer, 1978: 26), Mattick (1938: 4) and the Situationists (in Knabb, 1981: 346) have observed it is to the advantage of proletarians to do away with the separation of power between the executive, judicial and legislative branches of the state. Hakim Bey's (1992: 13) rejection of mediations and preference for face-to-face meetings may also be perceived as a mechanism for enhancing empowerment through transcending the dichotomy between decision making and action.

However, not all meetings can be arranged face-to-face and likewise it would be naïve to assume that 'representation' and 'delegation' of responsibility can be dispensed with overnight. In fact the privileging of small, local, face-to-face meetings can be an excuse for nationalistic and parochial tendencies to downgrade the need for transnational cooperation. Such meetings are neither always possible nor always desirable. Making a connection to like-minded activists in dis-

---

151 Dowling (2005: 209) describes how during the preparation for the European Social forum 2004 in the UK, 'participants found themselves being held to ransom by promises of trade union and GLA [Greater London Authority] money'. For instance, proposals drawn up by trade union lawyers had to be accepted by participants, otherwise there would 'be no ESF' (Dowling, 2005: 209). Political empowerment is impossible without economic independence.

tant parts of the world through cyber-space may prove more empowering than meeting the same circle of friends and fellow local activists over and over again. Whilst accepting mechanisms such as 'rotation', 'minute-taking'[152] and 'diffusion of information' (Freeman, 1970) or technologies such as the Internet (Dyer-Witheford, 1999) as empowering under many circumstances, it is essential not to fetishize such protocols. After all, even delegation of responsibility which normally suggests at least a temporary shifting of power from proletarians to their delegates may be preferable to a lack of representation. This is true of any 'nation wide' factory committees' organisation or any 'international' conference of radical groups.

What determines whether an organisational framework is empowering or disempowering is both the process participants engage in and the product of their activities. Empowering proletarian organisations play a dual role in both subverting bourgeois organisations and offering alternatives. This is the reason why organisations such as IndyMedia (http://www.indymedia.org/or/index.shtml) or Media Workers Against the War (http://www.mwaw.org/) cannot be classified as part of the 'zone of proletarian development'. In mimicking a bourgeois style and format of broadcasting and news generating, such organisations have forfeited any claim to radicalism. They neither attack bourgeois media *in its totality* nor provide us with a qualitatively different mode of 'broadcasting'.[153] This goes some way in explaining why so many activists find working with IndyMedia and Media Workers Against the War alienating rather than empowering.

Organisations that seek to conquer power, rather than empower proletarians, understand the class struggle instrumentally. John Holloway (2002: 130) contextualises the problem in the following terms,

> Class struggle is understood instrumentally, not as a process of self-emancipation but as the struggle to create a society in which the proletariat would be emancipated: hence the pivotal role of 'conquering power'.

Ultimately the ZPD and ZBD differ with regard to their attitude toward power. The ZPD seeks *power-to* in order to change the world and do away with Power.

---

152 An example of how something as innocuous as 'minute-taking' can become a tussle about power is provided by Emma Dowling (2005): 'My minutes [of a European Social Forum preparatory meeting] included an account of what people had said at the meeting, as well as points of discussion and disagreement, rather than merely listing abstractly what had been agreed at the meeting, which was how the verticals wanted minutes to be published'.

153 A great deal of IndyMedia broadcasting, for instance, is indistinguishable from mainstream media's vox-popping technique. Mainstream media uses vox-popping to enshrine neo-liberal common sense and Indymedia uses it to reinforce neo-libertarian common sense. This explains why dissent in Indymedia manifests itself in ethnomethodological clownish behaviour by radicals who feel overwhelmed by reactionary chatter.

The ZBD emphasises *power-over* to maintain its hegemony. Holloway (2002: 29) explains the difference,

> Whereas power-to is a uniting, a bringing together of my doing with the doing of others, the exercise of power-over is a separation. The exercise of power-over separates conception from realisation, done from doing, one person's doing from another's, subject from object. Those who exercise power-over are Separators, separating done from doing, doers from the means of doing.

This 'uniting', this 'bringing together of my doing with the doing of others' must involve, amongst other things, the act of collective remembering. Vygotsky believed the relationship between remembering and thinking to be crucial. For the adult at least, 'to remember is to think' (Vygotsky quoted in Luria, 1987: 370). I demonstrated in the case of Churchill's desecrated statue (chapter 2) that what followed the event on May Day 2000 was a gigantic effort to remember collectively the significance of Churchill to the evolution of class struggle.

The organisational attributes necessary for promoting the ZPD (i.e., dialectical joint activity, heterogeneity, carnivalesque and empowerment) are not entities that can be measured, quantified or engineered through tests and protocols. Rather they are social processes that all participants need to be aware of, discuss and collectively promote if we are to escalate and intensify the class struggle. Failure to achieve this can only lead to the reinforcement of its nemesis- the ZBD.

Epilogue: I began this book by mentioning how in the 18th century 'mobs' in the USA initiated an unprecedented imperial crisis and how this crisis was translated into political discourse by Sam Adams (Linebaugh and Rediker, 2001: 137). It is fitting that I conclude the work with another (imperfect) historical analogy.

Marcus Rediker (2004) has penned a marvellous history of the 'Golden Age of Piracy (1716-1726)'. He describes how 'pirates acted the part of a floating mob, a *flying gang*, as they called themselves, with its own distinctive sense of popular justice' (Rediker, 2004: 86). Sailors in general occupied a strategically vital niche within the emergent capitalist economies of the 18th century since, 'whether by moving commodities or waging war by sea, the sailor provided the labor power of transatlantic endeavour' (Rediker, 2004: 22). So when some four thousand of them took to piracy, the disruption to the maritime process of primitive accumulation of capital was immense (Rediker, 2004: 9).

Their ships and the culture they built around them exemplify an 18th century version of the ZPD and one that was consciously anti-ZBD. For instance, just like the 'ideal' revolutionary organisation outlined in the preceding pages, these multiracial marooned pirate communities were proudly anti-dualistic. They had minimised (and in some cases done away with) the distinction between the ship captain and the crew. Decisions were made collectively and the common council's pronouncements were 'sacrosanct' (Rediker, 2004: 69). Skills were transferred as widely as possible and in fact pirates were considered the best sailors in the world. Even the space aboard the ship was reorganised in order to remake bourgeois maritime social relations. Pirates took 'the liberty of ranging all over the ship', a practice known as 'laying rough' (Rediker, 2004: 65). Food and booty was shared far more equally. Egalitarianism had replaced the strict hierarchy of merchant ships. There were even a small number of legendary women pirates such as Anne Bonny and Mary Read who fought alongside their male comrades. They were highly respected and ballads were sung in their honour.

Pirates did away with another attribute of the ZBD, namely, commodity fetishism and as far as they could avoid it with exchange value too. Above all it was the use value of items that interested them. They were also fiercely anti-religious. The death speech of many included sacrilegious tirades. When in 1726 the infamous William Fly was sent to the gallows in Boston he 'cursed the very heavens & in effect the God that judged him' (Rediker, 2004: 4). Pirates opposed God as 'the king of terrors' with their own vengeful form of terror which punished dictatorial captains and profit-mongering merchants (Rediker, 2004: 5).

Cognisant of the fact that survival from enemy ships and hostile governments required joint-activity, the pirates reorganised their ships. A new position- that of the quartermaster- was invented in order to facilitate executive decision-making and regulate onboard behaviour. As mentioned earlier the crew was multiracial and anti-nationalistic. Rediker (2004: 8) observes,

> When hailed by another ship, pirates, who were multinational in origin, usually answered that they came 'from the seas,' not from any particular country. Some pirates explained to captives that they had 'sold their nation' for booty.

Besides joint-activity and a heterogeneous composition, pirate communities (both in convergence spaces such as Madagascar and aboard the ships) also manifested the remaining two attributes of the ZPD. They were carnivalesque and they fostered empowerment. Rediker again,

> … many observers of pirate life noted the carnivalesque quality of pirate occasions- the eating, drinking, fiddling, dancing, and merriment- and some considered such 'infinite Disorders' inimical to good discipline at sea (Rediker, 2004: 71).

Sexual freedom was a hallmark of pirate communities. Both heterosexual and homosexual relations were pursued without most of the taboos and restrictions of bourgeois morality. The carnivalesque nature of their existence led them to 'Curse the King and all the Higher powers' whilst cherishing 'the life of liberty' (Rediker, 2004: 37).

Despite its achievements, this proto-ZPD remained numerically insignificant and was finally crushed by the concerted efforts of key states determined to re-establish their power-over. The historical lesson it bestowed upon us can be encapsulated thus: escalate and intensify the class struggle through the promotion of zones of proletarian development or face ever-increasing subjugation by the forces of capital and its lackeys.

Appendix one:
Mindful Thuggery and the Spectacularisation of Drama

(slightly edited version)
(by Melancholic Troglodytes)

2 May 2000

t *was a good day to be alive!* May Day 2000 was, in Vygotskian terminology, a 'Zone of Proximal Development' (ZPD). The ZPD is the distance between what a person can do or understand independently and what they can potentially do and understand with the guidance of other capable peers. In short, it is a dialectical learning zone. Different sections of the proletariat brought their experience, competence and sense of humour to a glorious festival and learned to share them with other working class people. There art certain truths that are best decoded collectively. In the event, the hardened 'molotov-cocktail brand of revolutionaries' learned the value of psycho- geographic urban landscaping from street reclaimers, the 'veggie brigade' understood that a gulf of blood separates us from the police, media and all sections of the state, the 'theory freaks' came to know the joys of critiquing the law of value through unmediated action and the 'fetishizers of spontaneity' came to recognize the value of mind-*ful* thuggery. Oh, yes, brothers, sisters and fellow hermaphrodites, *May Day 2000 was a good Jay to be alive!*

> *To be imprisoned in the viewless winds,*
> *And blown with restless violence round about*
> *The pendant world!*

It was good that the proletariat ignored the Houses of Parliament, and attacked Ten Downing Street instead. After all, during the *real* phase of capital domination, it is the executive and not the legislative (or the judiciary) that reigns supreme. A Scottish prole began kicking the crowd control barriers outside Leviathan's residence. Soon, he was joined by a middle eastern giant of a man who was carrying his kid on his shoulders. They had an entertaining father and son routine. The son would throw bottles at the cops from above, whilst the father helped his Scottish comrade demolish Leviathan's lines of defence, from below.

It was good that the trafficking of commodities was brought to a temporary halt, by people deciding to picnic on the grassy concrete. The process foregrounded contours of power masquerading as innocent circulation. It was also good that the crowds dispersed in order to let a distressed pregnant woman drive through.

It was good that photographers were dealt with more forthrightly than usual. One cameraman was chased and beaten up by a small group, another thrown off the roof of a bus shelter. The simple precaution of acquainting the evil celluloid inside these infernal damnations with the purifying rays of Sol Invictus should now be added to our defensive repertoire, as a matter of course. It was also good that revolutionaries targeted *professional* image looters who work hand in glove with the state, and not every 'militant-tourist' armed with a cheap *camera obscura*.

It was good that a money exchange was set on fire. What better critique of "yellow, glittering, precious gold", than to torch the den in which all currencies gather to decide our fate? Likewise, it was a joy to see an establishment as anti-working class and unhealthy as McDonald's subjected to a spot of imaginative DIY redecorating. Contrary to media lies, at no time were the employers at risk from the demonstrators, although admittedly, french fries, burgers and apple pies *were* subjected to the ruthless dictatorship of the proletariat!

It was good that graffiti was employed as a form of communication. Since ancient Greece, proletarians have found graffiti a convenient method of bypassing official monologism. The media's spitefulness towards this form of discourse stems from its obsessional need to regulate all information. It was particularly gratifying to find a detourned version of that anti-working class cunt, Winston Churchill, providing the festival with a suitable focus of contempt. Churchill was hated before W/WII, tolerated as 'a necessary evil' during the war, and kicked out of office at the earliest opportunity, after the war, by the British proletariat, May he rest in hell! The defacing of the Cenotaph brought into sharp focus the contested nature of signs. For whereas, the bourgeoisie claims it as a sign of respect for the war dead, the proletariat sees in it a constant reminder of our defeats at the hands of the bosses. It was *our* weakness that allowed capital to initiate two world wars, and countless others, during the last century. Three commonalities have manifested themselves in all modem wars. First, they were fought for profit, resources, and land. Second, they ended up punishing and disciplining *all* proletarians irrespective of which camp they were forced to join. *And,* third, whilst the proletariat always does the fighting and the dying, it is the bourgeoisie that always reaps the benefit. In recent years, the Cenotaph has come to celebrate two mid-twentieth century victories: a) the intra-classist victory of old capitalists (Britain, USA, USSR) over upcoming capitalists (Germany, Italy, Japan); and, b) the inter-classist victory of capital over the *whole* proletariat.

As flies to wanton boys are we to the gods;
They kill us for their sport.

Oh, but the generosity of the bourgeoisie knows no bounds! Having butchered millions of us in battlefields, they graciously provide us with reified monuments as a constant reminder of the *dictatorship of capital.* Adam Smith once advocated the leaching of a personal 'song of death' from childhood, to help acclimatise the proletarian rogue to his/her inevitable fate, as with native American 'savages'. The Cenotaph is the stone of Kaaba which the congregation must circumambulate ritualistically, to renew faith in bourgeois *hegemony,* whilst chanting their 'song of death'. On May Day 2000, we sang a different tune, one that strikes at all nationalists and war-mongers. We despise the scum who start wars for capital accumulation, cajole us into uniforms and force us to open fire on our proletarian brothers and sisters. We recognise no 'imagined communities'. *We recognise no war, but the class war.* The choice between fascism, liberalism, social democracy and Leninism is a false one. As false a choice as that between supporting a liberal prime minister, with social democratic tendencies (Blair), or a social democratic Mayor, with liberal tendencies (Livingstone). Large sections of the proletariat are superseding such deceits, hence, the bosses' fear.

Monster, I do smell all horse-piss, at which my
nose is in great indignation.

The state stratagem for containing the new generation of radicals, seems to be two-fold: 1) to escalate the usual modes of surveillance, classification, and punishment with a view to breaking our will to fight; and, 2) to allow a partially revamped left wing of capital (i.e., labourism in its social democratic manifestation plus a few Leninist organizations), to police and marginalize revolutionaries at future events. British patriots associated with the industrial faction of capital have been emotionally manipulated to perceive May Day 2000 as a personal affront. In this context, the artificial conflation of cenotaph and synagogue, and the broadcasting of May Day nazi demonstrations in Berlin is calculated to confuse and mystify the politically naive. The state's deliberate separation of the 'trade union sponsored' march from the 'anti-capitalist' march, was a strategy of confinement. Likewise, *violence* was posited as a de-contexualised metaphysical entity, so that the media could equate the subversive *violence* directed against private property and the state, with the reactionary attacks of racists on blacks and asylum seekers. The *dictatorship of the proletariat* can be 'violent' or 'peaceful', it can be 'silent' or 'deafening', it can be expressed 'individually' or 'collectively', with a 'frown' or a 'smile'. But it must always be out in the open, for all to see, debate and critique. And it must oppose *thanotocracy* (regime based on death) with *life* and joy.

Whenever the bourgeoisie preaches *morality* from its pulpit so vociferously, two conclusions can be drawn: firstly, that the private-public spheres of behaviour are dangerously out of synch, and must, therefore, be brought into harmony with *common sense*, and secondly, this intensity of moral panic and indignation, is usually a prelude for a new offensive against the working class.

As May Day 2000 came to a close, it became clear that what began as *dramatic theatre* (characterized by genuine antagonism, unpredictability, free-flowing and playful subversion), had metamorphosed into a *spectacle* (characterized by ritualistic confrontation with oh, so, predictable rules and outcomes). We will do well to look at the evolution of the medieval festival, which over centuries was gradually institution-alised in three directions: toward the *fair* (which commercialised the gift-exchange di-mension of the festival); the *circus* (which used clowns and performers to sanitize the festival); and, the *carnival* (which after a period of retaining the spirit of rebellious-ness, has been, more or less, 'cleaned up'). Unless we are careful, this is the fate the bourgeoisie has in store for *our* May Day.

The Glorious Proletarian Siege of Oxford Street

a Revisionist Misinterpretation of the May Day 2001 Debacle!

(slightly edited version)
(by Melancholic Troglodytes)

3 May 2001

"Do not repeat the tactics which have gained you one victory, but let your methods be regulated by the infinite variety of circumstances." *The Art of War,* Sun Tzu

Fellow *mindful* thugs: In London at least, May Day 2001 was NOT a good day to be alive! It is our understanding that elsewhere, proletarians had more success in gorging themselves on the entrails of the Leviathan! This is an attempt to analyse the mistakes committed by a small section of the world proletariat who were involved in various actions throughout London. Although our experience was an overall defeat, May Day 2001 still qualifies as a Vygotskian 'zone of proximal development'- a dialectical learning zone, if you prefer. So, let's take stock and see what we can learn from this debacle.

Proletarian crowds, perched forever on the threshold of mobility (from where the term *mob* originates), have always petrified the bourgeoisie- Earlier in the day, at Elephant & Castle, the police became animated only once the crowd decided to become a *mob* (by spilling from the enclosed square onto the adjacent roads). At Oxford Circus, the policy of *im*mobilization was pursued with even greater urgency. As collectivities, we are at our strongest when we are dynamic, fluid, moving and unpredictable.

The Glorious Proletarian Siege of Oxford Circus shares two commonalities with the Mother of All Battles fought more than a decade ago in the Gulf: (1) In both cases, the victorious side enjoyed a *qualitative* superiority over the vanquished, and, (2) The war was won through a proxy media blitz even before proper hostilities were initiated. Most of you will remember how the victory of the Great anti-poll tax riot was immediately followed by the damp set-back of the Brixton Prison demonstration. Here too, the partial victory of May Day 2000 had to be reversed by the state, otherwise the movement would have gained irreversible momentum.

We are in danger of being ghettoized. Our strategy should have included a concerted effort to make ambulance workers and fire-fighters understand that we perceive them as members of the working class and quite distinct from the police. This must become an integral aspect of our discourse. If it turns out that the state was successful in alienating postal workers (who were told we intend to attack them!) and transport workers (who did not feel sufficient affinity to join us), then we have a great deal of bridge-building to do.

"The rising of birds in their flight is the sign of an ambuscade." - Sun Tzu

We are in danger of losing clarity. The real divisions that exist within our movement are not built around the fluffy-crusty axis (as inane journalists contend) nor about peace vs. violence. No doubt there are imbeciles who fit these categories perfectly. But most of us have seen through identity politics as methods of infantilization and pacification, and likewise, most have no intention of fetishizing either peace or violence, which as metaphysical concepts can only obfuscate our process of decision-making. The real division is between those who are prepared to negotiate with capitalism for limited reform and those of us who refuse to contemplate anything short of the complete abolition of capitalism.

The latter grouping must be clear and open about its aims: revolutionaries have always started from the premise that the main objective is to extend and intensify the class struggle and we achieve this by dialectically linking the specific to the general. To the 'fluffies' and single issue campaigners we must say: "Demonstrate to us how you intend to link your specific objections to a company or brand name to a full assault on the entire capitalist system. Because if you can't, then we reserve the right to denounce you as either non-revolutionaries, or worse, counterrevolutionaries." To the "crusties" and violence worshippers, we must say: "The rule of the working class is the social imposition of a self-conscious class over the bourgeoisie. Yes, at times this might be expressed violently, at other times peacefully; collectively or individually; as part of a riot or a revel. But if you continue to fetishize violence you are, a) re-animating a divisive demon that was slain years ago- the demon of machismo, and, b) you are reducing the scope of the struggle to the military terrain *alone*- a terrain where the class enemy will always enjoy a decisive advantage over us. *We are in danger of being militarised.* If you do not desist from childish tactical and strategic errors, you too will be denounced as counterrevolutionaries and treated with the contempt you deserve."

"If there is an outbreak of fire, but the enemy's soldiers remain quite, bide your time and do not attack." - Sun Tzu

If there are two broad strands within our movement (reformists and revolutionaries), then in relation to the media, the *Melancholic Troglodytes* discern at least three loose groupings: (i) the 'pro-situ-Taleban' tendency- basing themselves more on theology than revolutionary theory, the pro-situ-Talebans believe the media to be the incarnation of the Devil and, therefore, preach complete abstinence. Yet, we know in a world dominated by bourgeois hegemony, escape from the clutches of image-looters is but a fairy-tale. This fundamentalist outlook ignores that we are re-presented to the rest of our class via the distorted prism of bourgeois prejudice whether we like it or not (ii) the 'journo-groupie' tendency- obsessed with getting their ugly mugs on TV, this tendency misses no opportunity to ingratiate itself with the media. In the process, the 'journo-groupies' dilute and recuperate our critique of capitalism. They also *inoculate* (in the Barthesian sense) the proletariat against genuinely subversive ideas. The British media is using this tendency to, amongst other things, modernize itself. This approach may do wonders for the future career prospects of various individuals but it damages the working class, (iii) the 'very-very-clever' tendency- although not thoroughly demarcated yet, this tendency understands that the media, just like everything else under capitalism, is a *site of contestation.* It understands, we must go beyond mere *criticism* to a full *critique* if capital is to be undermined. It understands, we must self-reflexively underscore not only the formation of our ideas but deconstruct the very mechanisms through which Liberalism manipulates political debate. It understands, the morons who have taken it upon themselves to speak on our behalf thus far are doing untold damage to our cause. It also understands that if we are to defeat the class enemy on its own terrain, we must gradually change the 'rules of the game'.

But how do we do that? How can we change the rules of the game? How can we use the media to connect with other proletarians? How can we subvert *common sense* (Giambattisla Vico) with out revolutionary sense? First, we can initiate a real debate amongst ourselves as to the best way of proceeding. Second, we can learn from the mistakes of French, Italians and North American comrades who have more experience of dealing with the media. Third, we can try to impose certain ground-rules on the media. For instance, we need more control over the output and editing. We must prevent them from using us as sound or image-bites. We must insist on the inclusion of more than one revolutionary on each panel (at present we are outnumbered during media 'debates' and the lone revolutionary can be easily depicted as a cuckoo shouting in the wilderness). We must demonstrate linkage between various aspects of the social movement and prevent fragmentation of issues. They will resist this tooth and nail. Those who are chosen to express our views must do so on a rotational basis (so that no individual is tempted to become a celebrity), and on the basis of immediate recall. Their contributions must be constantly scrutinised and openly critiqued. These measures are far from being full-proof but they are an essential starting point.

"The host thus forming a single united body, it is impossible either for the brave to advance atone, or for the cowardly to retreat alone." - Sun Tzu

The three abovementioned strands resurface again in relation to the Law and judiciary: (i) the 'anti-Perry Mason' tendency, believes we must have no truck with the law. Sadly, the moment one of their members is invited to put his/her feet up courtesy of Her Majesty's prison services, they crack and are completely overwhelmed by the judiciary's aura, (ii) the 'Ally McBeal' tendency, who see themselves as courtroom warriors and who may in the short term help a few individuals beat the rap. However, in the process bourgeois law is reinforced, as none of its political underpinnings are questioned, (iii) the 'very-very-clever' tendency, understands that as soon as demonstrators are arrested, the working class has entered the realm of bourgeois law, whether we approve or not. But we also understand that the legal defence of our comrades must never overshadow the struggle but must become an extension of it. Thus far we have only attacked the executive and legislative branches of the state. If the state decides to break us through long and arduous legal battles, then the judiciary too must become a focus of our anger. This must be done through laying bear the mechanisms of liberal 'injustice' without jeopardizing arrested comrades. Our approach must show the anti-working class nature of 'Zero Tolerance Policing', and how what began as an assault on refugees is now being extended to the whole class. In short, our attitude towards the law -must be neither *conformist* nor *anti-conformist* but *nonconformist.* The 'rules of the game' must be altered even in the court-rooms.

"So in war, the way is to avoid what is strong and to strike what is weak." - Sun Tzu

Although we have failed to extend 'molar antagonisms' (workplace struggles at the point of production), to 'molecular proliferations' (the osmosis of isolated instances of struggle into the outside world), we have achieved a great deal during the last two years. We are better organized, informed and equipped than we were. The political agenda has been transformed. A new proletarian vocabulary is slowly being forged.

It is nice to be able to avoid traps. On May Day 2001 we quite consciously walked into one because the only alternative was abject surrender. *And the proletariat does not surrender.* In the future we must be flexible enough to side step show downs that are fixed. But should we find ourselves enclosed, caged and enslaved again, we must turn the situation around by creating zones of autonomy within our prison. Sensory deprivation is not conducive to revolutionary action. On May Day 2001 the whole psychogeography of the event was against us. Alienating surroundings, bad weather, concrete ground, intimidating scum both encircling us and sowing confusion within our ranks. We must choose demonstration sites with more care. And finally, there were those comrades with weak bladders who redecorated central London with their bodily fluids. *What a waste of ammunition, comrades!* In the future, our urine must be collected in plastic bags, made into 'urine-bombs' and thrown at the enemy. Molotov-cocktails are just angry, urine-bombs are both angry and the perfect expression of the contempt we have for the bourgeoisie and their lackeys. *Comrades, your urine is glory to the revolution!*

References

Abbasqoli, M. (1999) 'Iranian Football Players in Europe: A Bridge Over Amateurism (Parts I and II)', Tamashagaran (Fans): Soccer Monthly, No. 44, 5-13, also available at http://www.netiran.com/?fn=artd(959), [accessed on 22nd October 2003].

Aboulafia, A., Gould, E. and **Spyrou, T.** (1995) *Activity Theory vs Cognitive Science in the Study of Human-Computer Interaction.* IRIS Information systems research seminar in Scandinavia, Gjern, Denmark. Available at http://iris.informatik.gu.se/conference, [accessed on 12th June 2003].

Abrahamian, E. (1982) *Iran Between Two Revolutions.* (Princeton, New Jersey: Princeton University Press).

Abrahamian, E. (1993) *Khomeinism: Essays on the Islamic Republic.* (Berkeley, Los Angeles, London: University of California Press).

Afrasiabi, K. L. (1995) 'Islamic Populism', *Telos,* (summer), No. 104, 97-125.

Ahmed, M. K. (1998) *Private speech: A cognitive tool in verbal communication.* English Language Program, International University of Japan. Available at http://www.iuj.ac.jp/faculty/mkahmed/privatespeech.html, [accessed on 19th August 2004].

Akyeampong, E. (1996) 'What's in a drink? Class struggle, popular culture and the politics of akpeteshie (local gin) in Ghana, 1930-67', *The Journal of African History,* (July), Vol. 37, No. 2, 215-236.

Alabarces, P. (1999) 'Post-Modern Times: Identities and Violence in Argentine Football', pp. 77-85, in G. Armstrong and R. Giulianotti (Eds.), *Football Culture and Identities.* (London: Macmillan Press Ltd).

Aljaafreh, A. and **Lantolf, J.** (1994) 'Negative feedback as regulation and second language learning in the zone of proximal development', *Modern Language Journal,* Vol. 78, 465-483.

Altheide, D. and **Johnson, J.** (1994) 'Criteria for assessing interpretive validity in qualitative research', pp. 485-499, in N. Denzin and Y. Lincoln (Eds.), *Handbook of Qualitative Research.* (London: Sage).

Anderson, B. (1990) *Imagined Communities: Reflections on the Origins and Spread of Nationalism.* (London and New York: Verso).

Anonymous (2004) *Mayday cancelled! Comments from some members of the London Mayday Collective.* Also available at www.ourmayday.org.uk, [accessed on 14th December 2004].

Antagonism Press (2001) *Bordiga and Pannekoek.* (London: Antagonism Press).

Argyle, M. (1988) *Bodily Communication.* 2nd edition. (Madison, CT: International Universities Press).

Armstrong, G. and **Giulianotti, R.** (Eds.) (1999) *Football Culture and Identities.* (London: Macmillan Press Ltd).

Aronson, E. and **Gonzalez, M.H.** (1988) 'Desegregation, Jigsaw, and the Mexican-American Experience', pp. 301-314, in P. A. Katz and D. A. Taylor (Eds.), *Eliminating Racism: Profiles in Controversy.* (New York: Plenum).

Arshinov, P. (1987) *History of the Makhnovist Movement: 1918-1921.* (London: Freedom Press).

Artaud, A. (1947) *To Have Done with the Judgment of God (Pour en finir avec le jugement de* *dieu).* A radio play by Antonin Artaud, excerpted from the collection: *Antonin Artaud Selected Writings,* Edited and with an Introduction by Susan Sontag, Translated from the French, *Oeuvres complètes,* by Helen Weaver. (Los Angeles: University of California Press Berkeley).

Artaud, A. (1977) *The Theatre and its Double.* (London: Calder).

Aufheben (2004) *A phenomenal anti-war movement?* No. 12, 28-35.

Baiocchi, G. (2004) 'The Party and the Multitude: Brazil's Workers' Party (PT) and the Challenge of Building a Just Social Order in a Globalizing Context', *Journal of World-Systems Research,* Vol. x, No. 1, (Winter), 199-215.

Bakhurst, D. (2001) 'Ilyenkov on Aesthetics: Realism, Imagination and the End of Art', *Mind, Culture, and Activity,* Vol. 8, No. 2, 187-199.

Bakhtin, M. M. (1973) *Rabelais and His World.* Translated by Hélène Iswolsky. (1st ed., Cambridge: MIT Press).

Bakhtin, M. M. (1981) *The Dialogic Imagination: Four Essays.* Translated by Caryl Emerson and Michael Holquist. (Austin: University of Texas Press).

Bakhtin, M. M. (1984a) *Rabelais and His World.* Translated by Hélène Iswolsky. (Bloomington, IN: Indiana University Press).

Bakhtin, M. M. (1984b) *Problems of Dostoevsky's Poetics* Ed. and trans. Caryl Emerson. (Minneapolis: University of Minnesota Press).

Bakhtin, M. M. (1986) *Speech genres and other late essays.* (Eds.) C. Emerson and M. Holquist. (Trans.) V. W. McGee. (Austin, TX: University of Texas Press).

Bakhtin, M. M. (1993) *Towards a Philosophy of the Act.* With translation and notes by Vadim Lianpov. Edited by M. Holquist. (Austin, TX: University of Texas Press).

Bakhtin, M. M. (1994) 'Forms of Time and of the Chronotope in the Novel', in M. M. Bakhtin, *The Dialogic Imagination: Four Essays.* Translated by Caryl Emerson and Michael Holquist. (Austin: University of Texas Press).

Bambery, C. (1996) 'Marxism and Sport', *International Socialism,* No. 73, (Winter), 35-54. Also available at http://pubs.socialistreviewindex.org.uk/isj73/bambery.htm, [accessed on 27th September 2004].

Bannister, P., Burman, E., Parker, I., Taylor, M., and **Tindall, C.** (1994) *Qualitative Methods in Psychology: A Research Guide.* (Buckingham: Open University Press).

Bannon, L. (1997) *Activity Theory.* Available at http://www-sv.cict.fr/cotcos/pjs/TheoreticalApproaches/Actvity/ActivitypaperBannon.htm, [accessed on 3rd September 2002].

Barbrook, R. (2005) *Imaginary Futures: from thinking machines to the intergalactic network.* Also available at www.imaginaryfutures.net, [accessed on 25th September 2005].

Barfurth, M. A. (1995) 'Understanding the Collaborative Learning Process in a Technology Rich Environment: The Case of Children's Disagreements', pp. 8-13, in J. L. Schnase and E. L. Cunnius (Eds.), Proceedings of the first international conference on Computer Support for Collaborative Learning. (Hillsdale, NJ: Lawrence Erlbaum Associates).

Barker, C. (2002) *A Modern Moral Economy? Edward Thompson and Valentin Volosinov Meet in North Manchester.* Paper presented to the conference on Making Social Movements: The British Marxist Historians and the study of social movements, June 26-28. (Edge Hill College of Higher Education).

Barker, J. (2005) 'Armchair Spartans and The Spectre of Decadence', *MetaMute: culture and*

politics after the net. Also available at
http://www.metamute.com/look/article.tpl?IdLanguage=1&IdPublication=1&NrIssue=24&NrSection=5&NrArticle=1515, [accessed on 20th July 2005].

Barthes, R. (1973) *Mythologies.* (London: Paladin).

Barrot, J. (1985) *Leninism or Communism?* (London: Wildcat).

Barrot, J. (1987) *What is Situationism?* (London: Unpopular Books).

Bataille, G. (1985) *Visions of Excess: Selected Writings, 1927-1939.* In David Larsen (2001) '*South Park's* Solar Anus, or, Rabelais Returns: Cultures of Consumption and the Contemporary Aesthetics of Obesity', *Theory, Culture & Society*, Vol. 18, No. 4, 65-82.

Baudrillard, J. (1983) *Simulations.* (New York: Semiotext(e) Foreign Agent Series).

Baudrillard, J. (1994) *The Illusion of the End.* (Polity Press).

Bedny, G. and **Karwowski, W.** (2004) 'Meaning and sense in activity theory and their role in the study of human performance', *Ergonomia IJE&HF*, Vol. 26, No. 2, 121-140.

Beeman, W. O. (1976) 'Status, Style and Strategy in Iranian Interaction,' *Anthropological Linguistics*, No. 18, (October), 305-322.

Bennett, T. (1979) *Formalism and Marxism.* (London: Methuen).

Berger, P. L., Berger B. and **Kellner, H.** (1974) *The Homeless Mind* (Harmondsworth, Middlesex: Penguin Books).

Berk, L. E. (1986) 'Private speech: learning out loud; talking to themselves helps children integrate language with thought', *Psychology Today,* (May), Vol. 20, 34-39.

Bernard-Donals, M. (1998) 'Knowing the Subaltern: Bakhtin, Carnival, and the Other Voice of the Human Sciences', in Bell and Gardiner (Eds.), *Bakhtin and the Human Sciences: No Last Words.* (London: Sage Publications in association with *Theory, Culture & Society*).

Bernstein, B. (1971) 'Education cannot compensate for society'. In B. Cosin *et al.* (Eds.), *School and Society.* (London: Routledge and Kegan Paul).

Bernstein, B. (1972) 'Social class, language and socialization', in P. P. Giglioli (Ed.), *Language and Social Context.* (Harmondsworth: Penguin).

Bernstein, M. A. (1986) 'When the Carnival Turns Bitter: Preliminary Reflections Upon the Abject Hero', pp. 99-121, in Gary Saul Morson (Ed.), *Bakhtin: Essays and Dialogues on His Work.* (Chicago: The University of Chicago Press).

Bey, H. (1985) *The Temporary Autonomous Zone.* (Autonomedia: Brooklyn). Also available at http://www.hermetic.com/bey/taz3.html, [accessed on 9th June 2004].

Bey, H. (1993) *Permanent TAZs.* Also available at http://www.hermetic.com/bey/paz.html, [accessed on 9th June 2004].

Bey, H. (1996) *Millennium.* (New York and Dublin: Autonomedia and Garden of Delight).

Bickley, R. (1977) 'Vygotsky's contribution to a dialectical materialist psychology', *Science & Society*, Vol. 41, 191-207.

Billig, M. (1978) *Fascists: A Social Psychological View of the National Front.* (London and New York: Harcourt Brace Jovanovich).

Billig, M. (1995) *Banal Nationalism.* (London, Thousand Oaks and New Delhi: Sage Publications).

Billig, M. (1997) 'The Dialogic Unconscious: psycho-analysis, discursive psychology and the nature of repression', *British Journal of Social Psychology*, No. 36, 139-159.

Billig, M. (2001) 'Humour and Embarrassment: Limits of the 'Nice Guy' Theories of Social Life', *Theory, Culture & Society*, Vol. 18, No. 5, 23-44.

Bion, W. R. (1961) *Experiences in groups and other papers.* (London: Tavistock Press).

Black Flag (1999) 'May Day on the Tube: International Workers Day 1999', No. 217, also available at http://www.flag.backened.net/blackflag/, [accessed on 20ᵗʰ April 2003].

Blanton, W. E. (n.d.) 'Theoretical framework'. The Virtual Fifth Dimension Clearing House and Propagation Center. Also available at http://129.171.53.1/blantonw/5dClhse/theoretical.html, [accessed on 24ᵗʰ October 2004].

Blissett, L. (2004) 'Peoples Global Action: Network or Federation', *Mute: Culture and Politics after the Net*, No. 28, 114-115.

Bloch, E. (2000) *The Spirit of Utopia.* (Stanford CA: Stanford University Press).

Bloch, M. (1989) *Ritual, History and Power: Selected Papers in Anthropology.* (London: Athlone).

Blunden, A. (1997) *Vygotsky and the Dialectical Method.* Also available at http://www.marxists.org/archive/vygotsky/works/comment/vygotsk1.htm, [accessed on 18ᵗʰ August 2004].

Blunden, A. (2001) *The Vygotsky School.* Talk at Spirit, Money and Modernity Seminar, 23/24th February 2001, also available at http://home.mira.net/~andy/seminars/chat.htm, [accessed on 19ᵗʰ August 2004].

Boje, D. M. (2001) 'Carnivalesque Resistance to Global Spectacle: A Critical Postmodern Theory of Public Administration', accepted for publication for September issue of *Administrative Theory and Praxis*, special issue on Radical Organization Theory. At http://cbae.nmsu.edu/~dboje/papers/carnivalesque_resistance_to_glob.htm, [accessed on 23ʳᵈ April 2003].

Bonefeld, W. (2002) 'History and Social Constitution: Primitive Accumulation is not Primitive', *The Commoner*, Debate 01, available at http://www.thecommoner.org.uk/debbonefeld.pdf, [accessed on 5ᵗʰ August 2004].

Booth, W. C. (1986) 'Freedom of Interpretation: Bakhtin and the Challenge of Feminist Criticism', pp. 145- 176, in Gary Saul Morson (Ed.), *Bakhtin: Essays and Dialogues on His Work.* (London and Chicago: The University of Chicago Press).

Bottomore, T., Harris, L., Kieran, V. G. and **Miliband, R.** (Eds.) (1988) *A Dictionary of Marxist Thought.* (Oxford: Basil Blackwell Ltd.).

Bourboulis, P. P. (1964) *Ancient Festivals of 'Saturnalia' Type.* (Thassalonike: Hetairea Makedonikon Spoudon).

Bowers, J. (1996) 'Hanging around and making something of it: ethnography', in J. Haworth (Ed.), *Psychological Research: Innovative Methods and Strategies.* (London: Routledge).

Bozhovich, L. I. (1979) 'Stages in the formation of the personality in ontogeny', *Soviet Psychology*, Vol. 17, No. 3, 3-24.

Brabazon, T. (2002) 'Dancing through the revolution', *Youth Studies Australia*, Vol. 21, No.1, 19-24.

Bradshaw, L. and **Slonsky, B.** (2005) '*Get Off the fucking Freeway.* The Sinking State Loots its Own Survivors', *MetaMute*. Also available at http://www.metamute.com/look/article.tpl?IdLanguage=1&IdPublication=1&NrIssue=24&NrSection=5&NrArticle=1523, [accessed on 13ᵗʰ September 2005].

Branco, A. U. (2001) 'Contextual, Interactional and Subjective Dimensions of Cooperation and Competition: A Co-Constructivist Analysis', pp. 107-121, in S. Chaiklin (Ed.), *The Theory and*

Practice of Cultural-Historical Psychology. (Aarhus, Oxford, Oakville: Aarhus University Press).

Bricianer, S. (1978) *Pannekoek and the Workers' Councils.* (Saint Louis: Telos Pres).

Brinton, M. (1975) *The Bolsheviks and Workers' Control: The State and Counter-Revolution, 1917 to 1921.* (London: Solidarity & Detroit: Black and Red).

Brinton, M. (1978) *Suicide for Socialism? Parts one and two.* Available at http://www.uncarved.org/pol/brinton1.html, [accessed on 15th August 2005].

Bristol, M. D. (1983) 'Carnival and the Institutions of Theatre in Elizabethan England', *ELH,* Vol. 50, No. 4, (winter), 637-654.

Brohm, J. M. (1978) *Sport: A Prison of Measured Time.* (London: Ink Links).

Bromberger, C. (1998) 'Sport as a touchstone for social change: A third half for Iranian football', *Le Monde Diplomatique,* (April). Also available at http://mondediplo.com/1998/04/04iran, [accessed on 24th August 2004].

Bronfenbrenner, U. (1983) 'The context of development and the development of context', pp. 147-184, in R. M. Lerner (Ed.), *Developmental Psychology: Historical and philosophical perspectives.* (Hillsdale: Lawrence Erlbaum).

Brown, D. (1974) *An Indian History of the American West: Bury My Heart at Wounded Knee.* (London and Sydney: Pan Books Ltd.).

Bruner, J. S. (1965) 'The growth of the mind', *American Psychologist,* No. 20, 1007-1017.

Burman, C. (2004) 'The Culture of Management or the Management of Culture: technical systems or social processes? The role of culture, capital and creativity in development interventions in Limpopo Province, South Africa'. Unpublished PhD Thesis. (University of the North, Limpopo Province).

Burman, E. (1994) *Deconstructing Developmental Psychology.* (London and New York: Routledge).

Burman, E., Gordo-Lopez, A. J., Macauley, R. and Parker, I. (Eds.) (1995) *Cyberpsychology: Conference, Interventions and Reflections,* (Manchester: Discourse Unit, the Manchester Metropolitan University).

Butterworth, M. L. (2005) 'Ritual in the *Church of Baseball* Suppressing the Discourse of Democracy after 9/11', *Communication and Critical/Cultural Studies,* Vol. 2, No. 2, June, 107-129.

Cabrejas, J. (2003) 'Behind Bush's drive to war', *The Humanist,* Vol. 63, No. 6, (Nov-Dec), 20-24.

Caffentzis, G. and Federici, S. (1982) 'Mormons in Space', *Midnight Notes,* No. 5, also available at http://www.geocities.com/redgiantsite/mormons.html, [accessed on 1st August 2004].

Callinicos, A. (1987) *The Revolutionary Ideas of Karl Marx.* (London, Chicago and Melbourne: Bookmarks).

Callinicos, A. (1990) *Against Post-Modernism: A Marxist Critique.* (New York: St. Martin's Press).

Camatte, J. (1969) 'The Democratic Mystification', originally appeared unsigned in *Invariance,* Serie I, No. 6, (April-June), also available from http://www.geocities.com/~johngray/demyst.htm, [accessed 26th May 2004].

Camatte, J. (1972) 'About the Revolution', first appeared in *Invariance,* Serie II, No. 2, (April), also available from http://www.geocities.com/~johngray/abtrev.htm, [accessed on 26th May 2004].

Camatte, J. (1975) *The Wandering of Humanity.* (Detroit: Black and Red).

Camatte, J. (1978) *Community and Communism in Russia.* (London: Unpopular Books).

Camatte, J. (1995) *This World We Must Leave and Other Essays.* (New York: Autonomedia).

Camatte, J. and Collu, G. (1969) 'Letter On Organization', pp. 5-30, originally appeared in 1972 in the French journal *Invariance*, Annee V, Serie II, No. 2, (reprinted in Chicago and Detroit: Black and Red).

Cannon, J. P. (1924/2003) 'How to Organise and Conduct a Study Class'. First published in the *Daily Worker* magazine supplement, December 13, 1924. Also available at http://www.marxists.org/archive/cannon/works/1924/class.htm, [accessed on 10th May 2006].

Cardan, P. (1959) 'The Proletariat and Organisation'. Excerpts from *Socialisme Ou Barberie*, (27 April 1959). Also available at http://www.geocities.com/cordobakaf/proleorga.html, [accessed on 24th October 2004].

Caruso, G. (2005) 'Open Office and Free Software: The Politics of the WSF 2004 as Workplace', *ephemera: theory & politics in organization*, Vol. 5, No. 2, 173-192. Available at www.ephemeraweb.org, [accessed on 14th August 2005].

Castle, T. (1983-1984) 'Eros and Liberty at the English Masquerade, 1710-90', *Eighteenth-Century Studies*, Vol. 17, No. 2, (winter), 156-176.

Cazden, C. B. (1979) 'Peekaboo as an instructional model: Discourse development at home and at school'. In papers and reports in child language development, No.17. (Palo Alto, CA: Stanford University, Department of Linguistics).

Chak, A. (2001) 'Adult Sensitivity to Children's Learning in the Zone of Proximal Development', *Journal for the Theory of Social behaviour*, Vol. 31, No. 4, 383-395.

Chan, G. and Sharma, N. (2007) 'Eating in Public', pp. 180-188, in S. Shukaitis and D. Graeber (Eds.), (2007) *Constituent Imagination: Militant Investigations, Collective Theorization.* (Oakland, Edinburgh, West Virginia: AK Press).

C.H.A.T (Cultural-Historical Activity Theory) (1998) *The Activity System.* Available at http://www.edu.helsinki.fi/activity/pages/chatanddwr/activitysystem/, [accessed on 22nd September 2004].

Chehabi, H. E. (2001) Yahūdiān-e Irāni dar Arseyeh Varzeshi (Farsi), [Iranian Jews in sporting fields], Irān Nāmeh, (Winter and Spring), Vol. 18, Nos. 1-2, 125-149.

Chehabi, H. E. (2002a) 'The Juggernaut of Globalization: Sport and Modernization in Iran', *The International Journal of the History of Sport*, Vol. 19, Nos. 2 and 3, (June-September), 275-294.

Chehabi, H. E. (2002b) 'A Political History of Football in Iran', *Iranian Studies*, Vol. 35, No. 4, (Fall), 371-402.

Cheyne, J. A. and Tarulli, D. (1999) 'Dialogue, Difference, and the *Third Voice* in the Zone of Proximal Development', *Theory and Psychology*, Vol. 9, 5-28.

Chomsky, N. (1994) *Secrets, Lies and Democracy.* (Tucson: Odonian Press).

Churchill, W. (Ed.) (1992) *Marxism and Native Americans.* (Boston: South End Press).

Clark, K. and Holquist, M. (1984) *Mikhail Bakhtin.* (Cambridge, Mass: Harvard University Press).

Cleaver, H. (2000) *Reading Capital Politically.* (Leeds and Edinburgh: Anti-Theses and AK Press).

Clifford, J. and Marcus, G. (Eds.) (1986) *Writing Culture: The Poetics and Politics of Ethnography.* (Berkeley: University of California Press).

Cole, M. (1985) 'The zone of proximal development: where culture and cognition create each other', pp. 146-161, in J. V. Wertsch (Ed.), *Culture, communication and cognition: Vygotskian perspectives.* (Cambridge: Cambridge University Press).

Cole, M. (1996) *Cultural psychology: A once and future discipline.* (Cambridge, MA: The Belknap Press).

Cole M. and Wertsch, J. V. (1996) *Beyond the Individual-Social Antinomy in Discussions of Piaget and Vygotsky.* Also available at http://www.massey.ac.nz/~alock/virtual/colevyg.htm, [accessed on 19th August 2004].

Collins, C. (1999a) *Language, Ideology and Social Consciousness: Developing a sociocultural approach.* (Aldershot, Brookfield USA, Singapore, Sydney: Ashgate Press).

Collins, C. (1999b) 'Applying Bakhtin in Urban Studies: The Failure of Community Participation in the Ferguslie Park Partnership', *Urban Studies* (January), Vol. 36, No. 1, p. 73.

Collu, G. and Camatte, J. (1969) 'Transition', pp. 31- 39, originally appeared in 1972 in the French journal *Invariance,* Serie I, No. 1. (reprinted in Chicago and Detroit: Black and Red).

Council for Maintaining of the Occupation (1968a) 'Report on the Occupation of the Sorbonne', pp. 346-348, in K. Knabb (Ed.), *Situationist International Anthology.* (Berkeley: Bureau of Public Secrets, 1981).

Council for Maintaining of the Occupation (1968b) 'For the Power of Workers Councils', pp. 349-350, in K. Knabb (Ed.), *Situationist International Anthology.* (Berkeley: Bureau of Public Secrets, 1981).

Coupland, P. (2000) 'H. G. Welss's *Liberal Fascism', Journal of Contemporary History,* Vol. 35, No. 4, 541-558.

Cubero, M. and Mata, M. L. de la (2001) 'Activity Settings, Ways of Thinking and Discourse Modes: An Empirical Investigation of the Heterogeneity of Verbal Thinking', pp. 218-237, in S. Chaiklin (Ed.), *The Theory and Practice of Cultural-Historical Psychology.* (Aarhus: Aarhus University Press).

Dalla Costa, M. (2005) 'Development and Reproduction', *The Commoner,* No. 10, (Spring/Summer), 172-199. Available at www.thecommoner.org, [accessed on 7th July 2005].

Dalla Costa, M. and James, S. (1975) *The Power of Women and the Subversion of the Community.* (Bristol: Falling Wall Press).

Damousi, J. (1997) Disrupting the Boundaries: Resistance and Convict Women, *Australian Humanities Review,* (August), also available at http://www.lib.latrobe.edu.au/AHR/copyright.html, [accessed 21 July 2004].

Daniels, H. (1996) *An Introduction to Vygotsky.* (London and New York: Routledge).

Daniels, H. (2004) 'Activity Theory, Discourse and Bernstein', *Educational Review,* Vol. 56, No. 2, (June), 121-132.

Daniels, H. and Cole, T. (2002) 'The Development of Provision for Young People with Emotional and Behavioural Difficulties: an activity theory analysis', *Oxford Review of Education,* Vol. 28, Nos. 2 and 3, 311-328.

Darnton, R. (1988) *The Great Cat Massacre: and other episodes in French cultural history.* (London: Penguin Books).

Dauvé, G. and Martin, F. (1997) *The Eclipse and Re-Emergence of the Communist Movement.* Revised Edition. (London: Antagonism Press).

Davies, N. Z. (1975) *Society and Culture in Early Modern France: Eight Essays.* (London: Stanford University Press).

Davydov, V. V. (1995) 'The influence of L. S. Vygotsky on education theory, research, and practice', *Educational Researcher,* Vol. 24, No. 3, 12-21.

Davydov, V. V. (1999) 'A New Approach to the Interpretation of Activity Structure and Content', pp. 39- 50, in S. Chaiklin *et al.* (Eds.), *Activity Theory and Social Practice.* (Aarhus, Oxford, Oakville: Aarhus University Press).

Davydov, V. V. and **Zinchenko, V. P.** (1993) 'Vygotsky's contribution to the development of psychology', chapter 5, pp. 93-106, in H. Daniels (Ed.), *Charting the Agenda.* (New York: Routledge).

Day, J. D. and **Cordon, L. A.** (1993) 'Static and dynamic measures of ability: An experimental comparison', *Journal of Educational Psychology,* Vol. 85, 75-82.

de Angelis, M. (1999) 'Marx's Theory of Primitive Accumulation: a suggested reinterpretation', also available at http://libcom.org/library/marx-primitive-accumulation-reinterpretation-massimo-de-angelis, [accessed on 12th August 2005].

de Angelis, M. (2001) 'Marx and primitive accumulation: The continuous character of capital's *enclosures*', *The Commoner,* No. 2, available at http://www.thecommoner.org.uk/02deangelis.pdf, [accessed on 7th August 2004].

de Cillia, R., Reisigl, M. and **Wodak, R.** (1999) 'The discursive construction of national identities', *Discourse & Society,* Vol. 10, No. 2, 149-173.

Del Rio, P. and **Alvarez, A.** (1995) 'Tossing, praying, and thinking: the changing architecture of mind and agency', pp. 215-247, in J. V. Wertsch, P. del Rio and A. Alvarez (Eds.), *Sociocultural studies of mind.* (Cambridge: Cambridge University Press).

de Saussure, F. (1974) *Course in General Linguistics.* (Glasgow: Fontana, Collins).

de Shazer, S. (1991) *Putting difference to work.* (New York: Norton).

Debord, G. (1957) 'Report on the construction of situations and on the International Situationist tendency's conditions of organization and action', pp. 17-25, in K. Knabb (Ed.), *Situationist International Anthology.* (Berkeley: Bureau of Public Secrets, 1981).

Debord, G. (1969) 'The Organization Question for the S.I.', pp. 298-301, in K. Knabb (Ed.), *Situationist International Anthology.* (Berkeley: Bureau of Public Secrets, 1981).

Debord, G. (1987) *Society of the Spectacle.* (Exeter: Rebel Press, AIM Publications).

Deleuze, G. (2002) *Postscript on the Societies of Control.* Available from http://info.interactivist.net/article.pl?sid=02/11/18/1941201, [accessed 15th May 2004].

Deleuze, G. (2003) *Instincts and Institutions.* Available from http://info.interactivist.net/article.pl?sid=03/12/08/1614209, [accessed on 15th May 2004].

Dentith, S. (1995) *Bakhtinian Thought: An Introductory Reader,* chapter 3, pp. 65-87. (London and New York: Routledge).

Donato, R. (1988) *Beyond group: A psycholinguistic rationale for collective activity in second-language learning.* Unpublished doctoral dissertation. (Newark: University of Delaware).

Douglas, M. (1973) 'The Abomination of Leviticus', pp. 54-72, in *Purity and Danger.* (London: Penguin Books).

Dowling, E. (2005) 'The Ethics of Engagement Revisited: Remembering the ESF 2004', *ephemera: theory & politics in organization,* Vol. 5, No. 2, 205-215. Available at www.ephemeraweb.org, [accessed on 14th August 2005].

Draper, H. (1987) *The Dictatorship of the Proletariat: From Marx to Lenin.* (New York: Monthly Review Press).

Drury, J. (2003) 'What critical psychology can('t) do for the *anti-capitalist movement*', *Annual Review of Critical Psychology,* No. 3, 88-113.

Drury, J. and Reicher, S. (1999) 'The Intergroup Dynamics of Collective Empowerment: Substantiating the Social Identity Model of Crowd Behavior', *Group Processes and Intergroup Relations*, Vol. 2, No. 4, 381-402.

Drury, J., Reicher, S. and Stott, C. (2003) 'Transforming the Boundaries of Collective Identity: from the *local* anti-road campaign to *global* resistance?', *Social Movement Studies*, Vol. 2, No. 2, 191-212.

Drury, S. B. (2007) 'Leo Strauss and the American Imperial project', *Political, Theory*, Vol. 35, No. 1, 62-67.

Dunayevskaya, R. (1958/2000) *Marxism and Freedom: From 1776 Until Today*. (Humanity Books).

Dunne, R. (1995) *Activity Theory*. Available at http://www.ex.ac.uk/telematics/T3/maths/actar01.htm, [accessed on 19th August 2004].

Durkheim, E. (1915) *The Elementary Forms of Religious Life*. (New York: Free Press).

Dyer-Witheford, N. (1999) *Cyber-Marx: Cycles and Circuits of Struggle in High-Technology Capitalism*. (Urbana and Chicago: University of Illinois Press).

Eagleton, T. (1989) 'Bakhtin, Schopenhauer, Kundera', pp. 178-188, in Hirschkop and Shepherd (Eds.), *Bakhtin and Cultural Theory*. (Manchester: Manchester University Press).

Elhammoumi, M. (2001) 'Lost-or Merely Domesticated? The Boom in Socio-Historicocultural Theory Emphasises Some Concepts, Overlooks Others', pp. 200-217, in S. Chaiklin (Ed.), *The Theory and Practice of Cultural-Historical Psychology*. (Aarhus: Aarhus University Press).

Elhammoumi, M. (2002) 'To Create Psychology's Own Capital', *Journal for the Theory of Social Behaviour*, Vol. 32, No. 1, 89-104.

Elias, N. (1983) *The Court Society*. (Oxford: Blackwell).

Ellis, B. and Fopp, R. (2001) 'The Origins of Standpoint Epistemologies: Feminism, Marx and Lukács', *TASA 2001 Conference*. (The University of Sydney, 13-15 December 2001).

Ellyatt, W. (2002) *Action Guide: Story Telling and the Power of Narrative*. Available at http://www.pathsoflearning.org/library/storytelling.cfm, [accessed on 3rd August 2004].

Emerson, C. (1996) 'The outer word and inner speech: Bakhtin, Vygotsky, and the internalization of language', pp. 123-142, in H. Daniels (Ed.), *An Introduction to Vygotsky*. (London and New York: Routledge).

Emerson, C. and Morson, G. S. (1987) 'Penultimate words', pp. 43-64, in C. Koelb and V. Lokke (Eds.), *The Current in Criticism*. (West Lafayette: Purdue UP).

Engels, F. (1847) *The Communist League*. Also available at http://www.marxists.org/archive/marx/works/1847/communist-league/index.htm, [accessed on 1st May 2004].

Engels, F. (1876-1878) 'Anti-Dühring'. In *Marx-Engels Collected Works*, Vol. 25.

Engels, F. (1850) *The Peasant War in Germany*. Also available at http://www.marxists.org/archive/marx/works/1850/peasant-war-germany/, [accessed on 28th June 2003].

Engeström, Y. (1987) *Learning by Expanding: An activity-theoretical approach to developmental research*. (Helsinki: Orienta-Konsultit). Also available at http://lchc.ucsd.edu/MCA/Paper/Engestrom/expanding/toc.htm, [accessed 6th March 2004].

Engeström, Y. (1995) 'Innovative organizational learning in medical and legal settings', pp. 326-356, in L. Martin, K. Nelson and E. Tobach (Eds.), *Sociocultural Psychology: Theory and practice of doing and knowing*. (Cambridge: Cambridge University Press).

Engeström, Y. (1996) 'Non scolae sed vitae discimus: Toward overcoming the encapsulation of school learning', pp. 151-170, in H. Daniels (Ed.) *An Introduction to Vygotsky*. (London and New York: Routledge).

Engeström, Y. (1999) 'Learning by Expanding: Ten Years Later'. Introduction to the German edition of Learning by Expanding, published in 1999 under the title Lernen durch Expansion (Marburg: BdWi-Verlag; Translated by Falk Seeger) Available at http://lchc.ucsd.edu/MCA/Paper/Engestrom/expanding/intro.htm, [accessed on 20th April 2003].

Engeström, Y. (2001) 'The horizontal dimension of expansive learning: weaving a texture of cognitive trails in the terrain of health care in Helsinki'. Paper presented at the international symposium *New Challenges to Research on Learning*, (March), 21-23. (Helsinki: University of Helsinki).

Engeström, Y., Engeström, R., and Vähäaho, T., (1999) 'When the Center Does Not Hold: The Importance of Knotworking', pp. 345-374, in S. Chaiklin *et al.* (Eds.), *Activity Theory and Social Practice*. (Aarhus: Aarhus University Press).

Estep, Jr., J. R. (2002) 'Spiritual formation as social: Toward a Vygotskian developmental perspective', *Religious Education*, Vol. 97, No. 1, 141-164.

Farrer, J. (1999) 'Disco *Super-Culture*: Consuming Foreign Sex in the Chinese Disco', *Sexualities*, Vol. 2, No. 2, 147-166.

Federici, S. (2004) 'War, Globalization and Reproduction', pp. 44-53, in *The Neo-Liberal Wars*. Canberra: A Treason Press Pamphlet. Also available from http://www.treason.metadns.cx, [accessed on 28th April 2004].

Federici, S. and **Caffentzis, G.** (2007) 'Notes on the Edu-Factory and Cognitive Capitalism', *The Commoner*, No. 12, (Summer), 63-70. Available at www.thecommoner.org, [accessed on 17th July 2007].

Fernandez, N. C. (1997) *Capitalism and the Class Struggle in the USSR: A Marxist Analysis*. (Aldershot, England: Ashgate Press).

Feuerstein, R. (1991) 'Cultural difference and cultural deprivation', pp. 21-23, in N. Bleichrodt and P. Drenth (Eds.), *Contemporary issues in cross-cultural psychology*. (The Netherlands: Swets and Jetliner).

Fichtner, B. (1999) 'Activity Revisited as an Explanatory Principle and as an Object of Study – Old Limits and New Perspectives', pp. 51-65, in S. Chaiklin *et al.* (Eds.), *Activity Theory and Social Practice*. (Aarhus: Aarhus University Press).

Foley, G. (1998) *Learning in Social Action: A contribution to understanding informal education*. (London: Zed Books).

Forman, E. A. and **Cazden, C. B.** (1985) 'Exploring Vygotskian perspectives in education: The cognitive value of peer interaction', pp. 323-347, in J. V. Wertsch (Ed.), *Culture, Communication, and Cognition: Vygotskian Perspectives* (Cambridge: Cambridge University Press).

Fortunati, L. (1995) *The Arcane of Reproduction: Housework, Prostitution, Labor and Capital*. Translated by Hilary Creek. (New York: Autonomedia).

Fortunati, L. (2007) 'Immaterial Labor and Its Mechanization', *ephemera: theory & politics in organization*, Vol. 7, No. 1, 139-157. Available at www.ephemeraweb.org, [accessed on 15th July 2007].

Foucault, M. (1977) *Discipline and Punishment: The Birth of the Prison*. (London: Penguin Books).

Foucault, M. (1984) *The History of Sexuality: Volume 1, An Introduction*. (Harmondsworth,

Middlesex: Penguin).

Foucault, M. (1994) *The Order of Things: An Archaeology of Human Sciences.* (Vintage).

Fox, D. and Prilleltensky, I. (1997) *Critical Psychology: An Introduction.* (London, Thousand Oaks, New Delhi: Sage Publications).

Freedman, J., and Combs, G. (1996) *Narrative therapy: The social construction of preferred realities.* (New York: Norton).

Freeman, J. (1970) *The Tyranny of Structurelessness.* Also available at http://struggle.ws/pdfs/tyranny.pdf, [accessed on 7th June 2004].

Freud, S. (1929-1930) 'Civilization and Its Discontent', pp. 64-145, in J. Strachey (Ed.), *The Standard Edition of the Complete Psychological Works of Sigmund Freud, Vol. 21.* (London: The Hogarth Press and the Institute of Psycho-Analysis).

Frey, J. H. and Eitzen, D. S. (1991) 'Sport and society', *Annual Review of Sociology,* Vol. 17, 503-522.

Frolov, I. (Ed.) (1984) *Dictionary of Philosophy.* (Moscow: Progress Publishers).

Gardiner, M. (1992) *The Dialogics of Critique: M. M. Bakhtin & The Theory of Ideology.* (London and New York: Routledge).

Gegenstandpunkt (2003) *Warning. Communism is not exactly dead!* Available at www.gegenstandpunkt.com/english/en_index.html, [accessed on 24th December 2004].

Gerami, S. (2003) 'Mullahs, Martyrs and Men: Conceptualizing Masculinity in the Islamic Republic of Iran', *Men and Masculinity,* Vol. 5, No. 3, 257-274.

Gergen, K. J. and Gergen, M. M. (1997) 'Tales that wag the dog: Globalization and the emergence of postmodern psychology', pp. 98-112, in M. H. Bond (Ed.), *Working at the Interface of Cultures: Eighteen Lives in Social Science.* (London: Routledge).

Gillen, J. (2000) 'Versions of Vygotsky', *British Journal of Educational Studies,* Vol. 48, No. 2, (June), 183-198.

Girard, R. (1977) *Violence and the Scared.* Translated by Patrick Gregory. (Baltimore: The John Hopkins University Press).

Glasius, M. (2005) 'Deliberation or Struggle? Civil Society Traditions behind the Social Forums', *ephemera: theory & politics in organization,* Vol. 5, No. 2, 240-252. Available at www.ephemeraweb.org, [accessed on 14th August 2005].

Gleeson-White, S. (2001) 'Revisiting the Southern Grotesque: Mikhail Bakhtin and the Case of Carson McCullers', *The Southern Literary Journal,* Vol. 33, No. 2, 108-123.

Goffman, E. (1972) 'Embarrassment and Social Organisation'. In *Interaction Rituals.* (London: Allen Lane).

Goldner, L. (1998) 'Revolutionary Termites in Faridabad: A Proletarian Current in India Confronts Third Worldist Statism, Kamunist Kranti/Collectivities: Presentation and Critical Dialogue'. Originally appeared in *Collective Action Notes* (Baltimore, USA), Fall 1998. Also available from http://home.earthlink.net/%7Elrgoldner/kk.html, [accessed on 2nd June 2004].

Goldner, L. (2005) 'China in the Contemporary World Dynamic of Accumulation and Class Struggle: A Challenge for the Radical Left', also available at http://home.earthlink.net/~lrgoldner/china.html, [accessed on 2nd August 2007].

Good, P. (2001) *Language for Those Who Have Nothing: Mikhail Bakhtin and the Landscape of Psychiatry.* (New York, Boston, Dordrecht, London, Moscow: Kluwer Academic/Plenum Publisher).

Goode, P. (1988) 'Karl Kautsky', pp. 248-249, in T. Bottomore, L. Harris, V. G. Kiernan and R. Miliband (Eds.), *A Dictionary of Marxist Thought.* (Oxford: Basil Blackwell Ltd).

Gordon, U. (2003) 'Consensus Games: Towards a Democratic Theory of Consensus Decision-making' pp. 11-22, in C. Baker and M. Tyldesley (Eds.), *Ninth International Conference on Alternative Futures and Popular Protest: Vol. II.* A selection of papers from the Conference 22-24 April 2003. (Manchester: Manchester Metropolitan University).

Gorer, G. (1935) *Nobody Talks Politics: A Satire with an Appendix on Our Intelligentsia.* (London).

Gotfrit, L. (1991) 'Women dancing back: Disruption and the politics of pleasure', in H. Giroux (Ed.), *Postmodernism, Feminism and Cultural Politics.* (Albany: State University of New York).

Graeber, D. (2005) 'Preface: Spring 2005 – Value as the Importance of Action', *The Commoner,* No. 10, (Spring/Summer), 4-65. Available at www.thecommoner.org, [accessed on 7th July 2005].

Gramsci, A. (1971) *Selections from the Prison Notebooks,* (London: Lawrence & Wishart).

Greenblatt, S. (1982) 'Filthy rites', *Daedalus,* Vol. 3, No. 3, 1-16.

Greenslade, L. (1996) 'V. N. Voloshinov and Social Psychology', pp. 116-127, in I. Parker and R. Spears (Eds.), *Psychology and Society: Radical Theory and Practice.* (London, Chicago: Pluto Press).

Griffin, P. and **Cole, M.** (1984) 'Current activity for the future: The Zo-ped', *New Directions for Child Development* Vol. 23, 45-63.

Gross, D. (1977-78) 'Irony and the Disorders of the Soul', *Telos,* No. 34, (winter), 167-172.

Gross, D. (1978) 'Culture and negativity: notes towards a theory of the carnival', *Telos,* No. 36, 127-132.

Guattari, F. and **Negri, T.** (1990) *Communists Like Us.* (New York: Semiotext(e) Foreign Agents Series).

Hallin, D. C. (1992) 'Sound bite news: Television coverage of elections, 1968-1988', *Journal of Communication,* Vol. 42, No. 2, 5-24.

Hannerz, U. (1992) *Cultural Complexity: Signs of Identity, Defiance, and Desire.* (New York: Columbia University Press).

Harding, S. (1987) *Feminism and Methodology.* (Milton Keynes: Open University Press and Bloomington, Indianapolis: Indiana University Press).

Harding, S. (1991) *Whose Science? Whose Knowledge? Thinking From Women's Lives.* (Buckingham, England: Open University Press and Ithaca, New York: Cornell University Press).

Harding, S. (1993) 'Feminist Philosophy of Science: The Objectivity Question', in *Out of the Margin Conference Report.* (Amsterdam 2-5 June, 1-28).

Hardt, M. and **Negri, A.** (2000) *Empire.* (Cambridge, Massachusetts: Harvard University Press).

Hardt, M. and **Negri, A.** (2004) *Multitude.* (New York: The Penguin Press).

Harrington, C. L. and **William, C. F.** (1997) 'Anger, resentment and class (in)action: explaining class passivity through micro-emotional processes'. Paper presented at Emotion in Social Life and Social Theory Conference, Humanities Research Centre, Australian National University, Canberra.

Hasan, H. (1998) 'Integrating IS and HCI using Activity Theory as a philosophical and theoretical basis', *Foundations of Information Systems,* November 4. Available at http://www.bauer.uh.edu/parks/fis/hasan.htm, [accessed on 12th January 2005].

Hasse, C. (2001) 'Institutional Creativity: The Relational Zone of Proximal Development', *Culture and Psychology*, Vol. 7, No. 2, 199-221.

Hartsock, N. C. M. (1997) 'Standpoint Theories for Next Century', in S. J. Kenney and H. Kinsella (Eds.), *Politics and Feminist Standpoint Theories* (New York: Haworth Press).

Harvie, D. (2005) 'All Labour Produces Value For Capital And We All Struggle Against Value', *The Commoner*, No. 10, (Spring/Summer), 132-171. Available at www.thecommoner.org, [accessed on 7th July 2005].

Hayes, G. (1996) 'The Psychology of Everyday life', pp. 153-163, in I. Parker and R. Spears (Eds.), *Psychology and Society: Radical Theory and Practice*. (London, Chicago: Pluto Press).

Henwood, K. and Pidgeon, N. (1994) 'Beyond the qualitative paradigm: a framework for introducing diversity within qualitative psychology', *Journal of Community and Applied Social Psychology*, 4, 225-238.

Herbert, F. (1968) *Dune.* (London: New English Library, Hodder and Stoughton).

Hercus, C. (1999) 'Identity, Emotion, and Feminist Collective Action', *Gender & Society*, Vol. 13, No. 1, (February), 34-55.

Hill, C. (1972) *The World Turned Upside Down: Radical Ideas in the English Revolution*. (London: Penguin Books).

Hill, C. (1985) *Lenin and the Russian Revolution.* (Middlesex: Penguin Books).

Hirschkop, K. and Shepherd, D. (1989) *Bakhtin and cultural theory*. (Manchester: Manchester University Press).

Hirst, W. and Manier, D. (1995) 'Opening vistas for cognitive psychology', pp. 89-124, in (Eds.) L. Martin, K. Nelson and E. Tobach, *Sociocultural Psychology: Theory and practice of doing and knowing*. (Cambridge, New York, Melbourne: Cambridge University Press).

Hitchcock, P. (1998) 'The Grotesque of the Body Electric', pp. 78-94, in Bell and Gardiner (Eds.), *Bakhtin and the Human Sciences*. (London: Sage).

Hochschild, A. R. (1979) 'Emotion work, feeling rules, and social structure', *American Journal of Sociology*, No. 85, 551-575.

Hochschild, A. R. (1983) *The Managed Heart: Commercialization of Human Feeling*. (Berkley, CA: University of California Press).

Hollis, H. (2001) 'The Other Side of Carnival: Romola and Bakhtin', *Paper on Language & Literature*, (Summer), Vol. 37, No. 3, 227-246.

Holloway, J. (2002) *Change the World Without Taking Power: The Meaning of Revolution Today.* (London, Sterling-Virginia: Pluto Press).

Holquist, M. (1981) Introduction to *Speech genres and other late essays*, by M. M. Bakhtin. (Austin: University of Texas Press).

Holzman, L. (1996) 'Newman's Practice of Method Completes Vygotsky', pp. 128-140, in I. Parker and R. Spears (Eds.), *Psychology and Society: Radical Theory and Practice*. (London, Chicago, IL: Pluto Press).

Holzman, L. (2001) 'Lev Vygotsky and the New Performative Psychology: Implications for Business and Organizations', to appear in D. M. Hosking, and S. McNamee (Eds.), *Organization Behaviour: Social Constructionist Approaches*. (Amsterdam: John Benjamins), also available at http://www.ex-iwp.org/docs/2001/lh_vygoperf.htm, [accessed on 6th August 2004].

Holzkamp, K. (1992) 'On doing psychology critically', *Theory and Psychology*, Vol. 2 No. 2, 193-204.

Home, S. (1988) *The Assault on Culture: Utopian Currents from Lettrisme to Class War.* (London: Aporia Press and Unpopular Books).

Hong, J. and Engeström, Y. (2004) 'Changing Principles of Communication between Chinese Managers and Workers: Confucian Authority Chains and *Guanxi* as Social Networks', *Management Communication Quarterly,* Vol. 17, No. 4, (May), 552-585.

Hook, D. (2001) 'The *disorders of discourse.* (misuse of discourse analysis as proposed by Michel Foucault)', *Theoria,* (June), 41-69.

Hung, D. W. L. (2002) 'Learning through video-based narratives within the cultural Zone of Proximal Development', *International Journal of Instructional Media,* Vol. 29, No. 1, 125-140.

Hutcheon, L. (1984) 'Authorized transgression: The paradox of parody'. In Groupar (Ed.), *Le singe á la port: Vers une thé oriede la parote.* (New York, Bern, Frankfurt/M.: P. Lang).

Hyppönen, H. (1998) *Activity theory as a basis for design for all.* Presentation for 3rd TIDE Congress 23-25 June1998. Also available at http://www.stakes.fi/tidecong/213hyppo.htm, [accessed on 12th January 2003].

Il'enkov, E.V. (1977) *Dialectical logic: Essays on its history and theory.* (Moscow: Progress).

Inghilleri, M. (2002) 'Britton and Bernstein on Vygotsky: divergent views on mind and language in the pedagogic context', *Pedagogy, Culture & Society,* Vol. 10, No. 3, 467-482.

Irving, A. and Moffatt, K. (2002) 'Intoxicated Midnight and Carnival Classrooms: The Professor as Poet', *Radical Pedagogy,* Vol. 4, No. 1. Also available at http://www.icaap.org/iuicode?, [accessed 2nd April 2003].

Ivanchenko, G. V. (2002) *The concept of zone of proximal development of personality in the context of possible/impossible dichotomy.* Available at http://krantzj.hanover.edu/vygotsky/ivanch.html, [accessed on 18th August 2004].

Jaggar, A. (2004) 'Feminist Politics and Epistemology: The Standpoint of Women', in S. Harding (Ed.), *The Feminist Standpoint Theory Reader: Intellectual and Political Controversies.* (New York and London: Routledge).

Jahn, K. (2000) *Leo Strauss and the Straussians.* Also available at http://home.earthlink.net/~karljahn/Strauss.htm, [accessed on 20th August 2004].

Jakubowski, F. (1976) *Ideology and Superstructure in Historical Materialism.* Translated by Anne Booth. (London: Allison and Busby Limited).

James, C. L. R. (1964) *Beyond a Boundary.* (London: Stanley Port; reprint, Durham, N.C.: Duke University Press).

Jameson, F. (1990) *Postmodernism, or the Cultural Logic of Late Capitalism.* (London: Verso).

Jaramillo, J. A. (1996) 'Vygotsky's sociocultural theory and contributions to the development of constructivist curricula', *Education,* Vol. 117, No. 1, 133-140.

Jensen, U. J. (1999) 'Categories in Activity Theory: Marx's Philosophy', pp. 79-99, in S. Chaiklin *et al.* (Eds.), *Activity Theory and Social Practice.* (Aarhus: Aarhus University Press).

Jiménez-Domínguez, B. (1996) 'Participant action research', pp. 220-229, in I. Parker and R. Spears, (Eds.), *Psychology and Society: Radical Theory and Practice.* (London: Pluto Press).

Jinxia, D. and Mangan, J. A. (2001) 'Football in New China: Political Statement, Entrepreneurial Enticement and Patriotic Passion', *Soccer & Society,* Vol. 2, No. 3, 79-100.

Johnson, Laird, P. N. (1986) 'An artist constructs a science', *The Times Literary Supplement,* 15th

August, 879-880.

John-Steiner, V. (1992) 'Private speech among adults'. In Diaz and Berk (Eds.), *Private Speech: From Social Interaction to Self-Regulation*. (Hillsdale, NJ: Lawrence Erlbaum Associates).

John-Steiner, V. and Tatter, P. (1983). 'An interactionist model of language development', pp. 79-97, in B. Bain (Ed.), *The sociogenesis of language and human conduct* (New York: Plenum Press).

Jones, P. (1998) 'Anarchy in the UK: '70s British Punk as Bakhtinian Carnival'. Available at http://www.pcasacas.org/SPC/spcissues/24.3/Jones.htm, [accessed on 10th May 2006].

Jones, P. (2002) 'Discourse, Social Change, and the Materialist Conception of History'. Paper delivered at the Fifth Conference of the International Society for Cultural Research and Activity Theory. (Amsterdam: Vrije Universiteit).

Juvan, M. (1997) *The Parody and Bakhtin*. Also available at http://www.zrc-sazu.si/mjuvan/bakhpar.htm, [accessed on 11th July 2003].

Kagan, C. and Burton, M. (2000) 'Prefigurative Action Research: an alternative basis for critical psychology?', *Annual Review of Critical Psychology*, Vol. 2, 73-87.

Kamunist Kranti (1997) *A ballad against work*. (Majdoor Library, Autopin Jhuggi, N.I.T., Faridabad 121001, India: A Publication for Collectivities).

Kautsky, K. (1901) 'Trade Unions and Socialism'. Originally appeared in *International Socialist Review*, Vol. 1, No. 10, (April). Also available form http://www.marxists.org/archive/kautsky/1901/04/unions.htm, [accessed 8th May 2004].

Kautsky, K. (1903) 'The Intellectual and the Workers'. Originally appeared in *Die Neue Ziete*, Vol. XXII, No. 4. Also available from http://www.marxists.org/archive/kautsky/1903/xx/int-work.htm, [accessed 8th May 2004].

Kautsky, K. (1934) 'Hitlerism and Social democracy'. Originally appeared in Joseph Shaplen and David Shub (Eds.), *Socialism, Fascism, Communism*. Also available from http://www.marxists.org/archive/kautsky/1934/hitler/, [accessed 7th May 2004].

Kay, G. (1979) *The Economic Theory of the Working Class*. (London and Basingstoke: Macmillan).

Kāzemi, B. (1999) Melli-garāyān Va Afsāneye Democrācy (Farsi), [Nationalists and the Myth of Democracy], (London: Nazm-e Kārgar Publishing).

Kelly, J. D. and Kaplan, M. (1990) 'History, Structure and Ritual', *Annual Review of Anthropology*, Vol. 19, 119-150.

Kendon, A. (1990) *Conducting interaction*. (Cambridge: Cambridge University Press).

Kenrick, D. (2004) *Gypsies: from the Ganges to the Thames*. (Hatfield: University of Hertfordshire Press).

Kermani, H. and Brenner, M. E. (2000) 'Maternal scaffolding in the child's zone of proximal development across tasks: Cross-Cultural perspective', *Journal of Research in Childhood Education*, (Fall-Winter), Vol. 15, No. 1, 30-52.

Kerr, S. T. (1997) *Why Vygotsky? The Role of Theoretical Psychology in Russian Education Reform*. Presented at the Annual Meeting of the American Association for the Advancement of Slavic Studies. Available at http://faculty.washington.edu/stkerr/whylsv.html, [accessed on 19th August 2004].

Kilgore, D. W. (1999) 'Understanding learning in social movements: a theory of collective learning', *International Journal of Lifelong Education*, Vol. 18, No. 3, (May-June), 191-202.

Killing King Abacus (2000) 'The Continuing Appeal of Nationalism among Anarchists: A Review of Hakim Bey's *Millenium*', No. 1. Available from http://www.geocities.com/kk_abacus/bey.html, [accessed on 9th June 2004].

King, J. J. (2004) 'The Packet Gang: Openness and its Discontents', *Mute: Culture and Politics after the Net*, (Winter/Spring), No. 27, 80-87. Also available from www.metamute.com, [accessed on 19th September 2004].

Kinginger, C. (2002) 'Defining the Zone of Proximal Development in US Foreign Language Education', *Applied Linguistics*, Vol. 23, No. 2, 240-261.

Klages, M. (2001) *Mikhail Bakhtin*. Also available at http://www.colorado.edu/English/ENGL2012Klages/bakhtin.html, [accessed on 27th February 2001].

Knabb, K. (Ed.) (1989) *Situationist International Anthology*. (Berkeley: The Bureau of Public Secrets).

Knabb, K. (1999) *May 1968 Graffiti*. Also available at http://www.bopsecrets.org/CF/graffiti.htm, [accessed on 3rd August 2004].

Klein, N. (2002) *No Logo: No Space, No Choice, No Jobs*. (Picador).

Korsch, K. (1971) *Three Essays on Marxism*. (London: Pluto).

Kovel, J. (1991) *History and Spirit*. (Boston: Beacon Press).

Kozanoglu, C. (1999) 'Beyond Edirne: Football and the National Identity Crisis in Turkey', pp. 117-125, in G. Armstrong and R. Giulianotti (Eds.), *Football Cultures and Identities*. (London: Macmillan Press Ltd).

Kozulin, A. (1991) 'Life as authoring: The humanistic tradition in Russian psychology', *New Ideas in Psychology*, Vol. 9, No. 3, 335-351.

Kramsch, C. (2000) 'Global and local identities in the contact zone', pp. 131-146, in C. Gnutzmann (Ed.), *Teaching and Learning English as a Global Language: Native and Non-Native Perspectives*. (Tubingen: Stauffenburg Verlag).

Kuutti, K. (1996) 'Activity theory as a potential framework for human-computer interaction research', pp. 17-44, in B. A. Nardi (Ed.), *Context and Consciousness*. (Cambridge, MA: MIT Press).

Kuzmics, H. (1991) 'Embarrassment and Civilization: On some similarities and differences in the work of Goffman and Elias', *Theory, Culture and Society*, Vol. 8, 1-30.

Lachmann, R. (1988-89) 'Bakhtin and Carnival', *Cultural Critique*, Vol. 11, 115-154.

Lafargue, P. (1883/2000) *The Right to be Lazy and Other Studies*. Also available at http://www.marxists.org/archive/lafargue/1883/lazy/, [accessed on 19th August 2004].

Lamont, M. and Aksartova, S. (2002) 'Ordinary Cosmopolitanism: Strategies for Bridging Racial Boundaries among Working-Class Men', *Theory, Culture & Society*, Vol. 19, No. 4, 1-25.

Larsen, D. (2001) '*South Park's* Solar Anus, or, Rabelais Returns: Cultures of Consumption and the Contemporary Aesthetics of Obesity', *Theory, Culture & Society*, Vol. 18, No. 4, 65-82.

Lave, J. (1991) 'Situating learning in communities of practice', pp. 41-62, in L. B. Resnick, J. Levine and S. D. Teasley (Eds.), *Perspectives in socially shared cognition*. (Washington DC: American Psychological Association).

Lave, J. and Wenger, E. (1991) *Situated learning: Legitimate peripheral participation*. (New York: Cambridge University Press).

Le Bon, G. (1895) *The crowd: A study of the popular mind*. (London: Ernest Benn).

Leiman, M. (2001) 'Dialogic Sequence Analysis and the Zone of Proximal Development as

Conceptual Enhancements to the Assimilation Model: the case of Jan revisited',
Psychotherapy Research Vol. 11, No. 3, 311-330.

Lenin, V. I. (1975) *'Left-Wing' Communism: An Infantile Disorder.* (Peking: Foreign Languages Press).

Leontiev (Leontyev), A. N. (1977) 'Activity and consciousness', pp. 180-202, in *Philosophy in the USSR: Problems of Dialectical Materialism.* (Moscow: Progress Publishers).

Leontiev (Leontyev), A. N. (1981) *Problems of the Development of the Mind.* (Trans.) M. Kopylova. (Moscow: Progress Publishers).

Lektorsky, V. A. (1999) 'Historical Change of the Notion of Activity: Philosophical Presuppositions', pp. 100-113, in S. Chaiklin *et al.* (Eds.), *Activity Theory and Social Practice.* (Aarhus: Aarhus University Press).

Lewontin, R. C. (1998) 'The maturing of capitalist agriculture; farmer as proletarian', *Monthly Review,* (July-August), Vol. 50, No. 3, 72-84.

Libertarian Organisation & Structure (LOS) (1987) *The Future in the Present: No. 1. Critical Anarchy.* (Newcastle-upon-Tyne: Tyneside Free Press).

Lightfoot, C. and Valsiner, J. (1992) 'Parental belief systems under the influence: social guidance of the construction of personal cultures', pp. 393-414, in I. Sigel, A. McGillicuddy-DeLisi and J. Goodnow (Eds.), *Parental belief systems: The psychological consequences for children.* (Hillsdale, NJ: Erlbaum).

Lindblom, J. and **Ziemke, T.** (2003) 'Social Situatedness of Natural and Artificial Intelligence: Vygotsky and Beyond', *Adaptive Behavior,* Vol. 11, No. 2, 79-96.

Linebaugh, P. (1986) *The Incomplete, True, Authentic and Wonderful History of MAY DAY.* Available at http://www.midnightnotes.org/May Day/, [accessed on 20th April 2003].

Linebaugh, P. (1991) *The London Hanged: class and civil society in the 18[h] century.* (London: The Penguin Press).

Linebaugh, P. and **Rediker, M.** (2001) *The Many-Headed Hydra: Sailors, Slaves, Commoners, and the Hidden History of the Revolutionary Atlantic.* (Beacon Press).

Linqvist, G. (2003) 'Vygotsky's theory of creativity', *Creativity Research Journal,* Vol. 15, Nos. 2 and 3, 245-251.

Liverpool, H. (1993) *Rituals of Power & Rebellion: The Carnival Tradition in Trinidad & Tobago 1763-1962.* (Chicago, Jamaica, London, Republic of Trinidad & Tobago: Frontline Distribution Int'l Inc.).

Lobe, J. (2004) *Leo Strauss' Philosophy of Deception.* Also available at http://www.alternet.org/story/15935/, [accessed on 20th August 2004].

Lock, A. J. (2000) 'Phylogenetic Time and Symbol Creation: Where Do Zopeds Come From?', *Culture & Psychology,* Vol. 6, No. 2, 105-129.

Lovell, A. (1982) 'Epic Theatre and Counter-Cinema's Principles', *Jump Cut,* No. 27.

Lukács, G. (1990) *History and Class Consciousness.* (London: Merlin Press).

Luria, A. R. (1987) 'Afterword to the Russian edition', pp. 359-373, in L. Vygotsky, (1987) *The collected works of L. S. Vygotsky, Vol. 1.* (New York: Plenum).

Lyon, A. and **Conway, M.** (1995) 'Who's Sandra Harding? Where's she Standing?', *JAC: A Journal of Composition Theory,* Vol. 15, No. 3, 1-6.

McCafferty, S. G. (2002) 'Gesture and Creating Zones of Proximal Development for Second Learning Languages', *The Modern Language Journal,* Vol. 86, No. 2, 192-203.

McGinty, P. (1978) *Interpretation and Dionysus: Method in the Study of a God.* (The Hague: Mouton).

McGuire, M. (1980) 'Metakinesic behaviour- Some theoretical considerations', pp. 125-137, in W. von Raffler-Engel (Ed.), *Aspects of nonverbal communication.* (Bath, UK: Pitman Press).

McKay, A. (2001) '*Kicking the Buddha's Head:* India, Tibet and Footballing Colonialism', *Soccer & Society,* Vol. 2, No. 2, (Summer), 1-14.

McLaughlin, K. (2003) 'Identities: Should we survive or surpass them?', *Journal of Critical Psychology, Counselling and Psychotherapy,* Vol. 3, No. 1, spring, 48-58.

McLuhan, M. (1964) *Understanding Media: the extension of the man.* (New York: McGraw Hill).

McNeill, D. (1999) 'Triangulating the growth point- arriving at consciousness', pp. 77-91, in L. S. Messing and R. Campbell (Eds.), *Gestures, Speech, and Sign.* (Oxford: Oxford University Press).

McPherson, S. (1998) 'Dashi Matsuri: Festival as Ritual and Iconographic Public Spheres', *Iconomia: studies in visual culture.* Available at http://www.humnet.ucla.edu/humnet/arthist/icono/McPherson/dashi.htm, [accessed on 27th July 2004].

Mac Ginty, R. (2004) 'Looting in the context of violent conflict: a conceptualisation and typology', *Third World Quarterly,* Vol. 25, No. 5, 857-870.

Mahabir, J. A. I. (2002) 'Rhythm and Class Struggle: The Calypsoes of David Rudder', *Jouvert,* Vol. 6, No. 3, 1-28.

Maiers, W. and **Tolman C. W.** (1996) 'Critical Psychology as Subject-Science', Chapter 7, pp. 105-115, in I. Parker and R. Spears (Eds.), *Psychology and Society: Radical Theory and Practice.* (London, Chicago, IL: Pluto Press).

Malinowski, B. (1960) 'The problem of meaning in primitive languages', in C. K. Ogden and I. A. Richards, (Eds.), *The Meaning of Meaning.* (London: Routledge and Kegan Paul).

Marcuse, H. (1964) *One-Dimensional Man.* Also available at *http://www.marxists.org/reference/archive/marcuse/works/one-dimensional-man/,* [accessed on 20th August 2004].

Marti, P., Pucci, F. and **Rizzo, A.** (2001) 'External Aids for Social Memory', *Information, Communication & Society,* Vol. 4, No. 2, 261-273.

Martin, L. M. W., Nelson, K. and **Tobach, E.** (1995a) *Sociocultural Psychology: Theory and practice of doing and knowing.* (Cambridge, New York, Melbourne: Cambridge University Press).

Martin, L. M. W., Nelson, K. and **Tobach, E.** (1995b) 'Introduction', pp. 1-17, in L. M. Martin, K. Nelson and E. Tobach (Eds.), *Sociocultural Psychology: Theory and practice of doing and knowing.* (Cambridge, New York, Melbourne: Cambridge University Press).

Martin- Baró, I. (1994) *Writings for a Liberation Psychology.* Translated by A. Aron and S. Crone. (Cambridge, MA: Harvard University Press).

Marx, K. (1844/1984) 'Excerpts from James Mill's elements of Political Economy', pp. 259-278, in *Early Writings.* (Middlesex and London: Penguin Books and New Left Review).

Marx, K. (1844/1964) *The economic and philosophical manuscripts of 1844.* D. J. Struik (Ed.). M. Milligan (trans.). (New York: International Publishers).

Marx, K. (1844/1984) 'Economic and Philosophical Manuscripts', pp. 279-400, in *Early Writings.* (Middlesex and London: Penguin Books and New Left Review).

Marx, K. (1845/1984) 'Concerning Feuerbach', pp. 421-423, in *Early Writings.* (Middlesex and London: Penguin Books and New Left Review).

Marx, K. (1846-47/1978) *The Poverty of Philosophy.* (Peking: Foreign Language Press).

Marx, K. (1847-48/1986) *The Communist Manifesto.* (Middlesex: Penguin Books).

Marx, K. (1852/2000) Hej-dahom-e Brumer-e Lou-ee Bonapart (Farsi), [The Eighteenth Brumaire of Louis Bonaparte]. (Translator) Bagher Parham. (Tehran: Nashr Ketab).

Marx, K. (1857/1974) *Grundrisse.* (Middlesex: Penguin Books).

Marx, K. (1867/1979) *Capital: Volume 1.* (Middlesex and London: Penguin Books and New Left Review).

Marx, K. (1871/1974) 'The Civil War in France', in *Political Writings, Volume 3.* (Harmondsworth, Middlesex: Penguin).

Marx, K. (1984) *Early Writings.* Introduction by Lucio Colletti. (Middlesex, England: Penguin Books).

Mattick, P. (1937) 'The barricades must be torn down'. Originally appeared in *International Communist Correspondence*, Chicago, Nos. 7-8, (August). Also available at http://www.marxists.org/archive/mattick-paul/1937/spain.htm, [accessed on 14th May 2004].

Mattick, P. (1938) 'The Masses and the Vanguard'. Originally appeared in *Living Marxism*, Vol. 4, No. 4, (August). Also available at http://www.marxists.org/archive/mattick-paul/1938/mass-vanguard.htm, [accessed on 13th May 2004].

Mattick, P. (1978) *Anti-Bolshevik Communism.* (London: Merlin Press).

Mattick, P. (1983) *Marxism: Last refuge of the Bourgeoisie?* (New York and London: Sharp Inc. and Merlin).

May, T. (1998) 'Reflexivity in the age of reconstructive social science', *International Journal of Social Research Methodology*, Vol. 1, No. 1, 7-24.

Melancholic Troglodytes (1998) 'Thus Stammered Zarathushtra', No. 2, 13-16. (Available form Meltrogs, c/o 56a Infoshop, 56a Crampton Street, Walworth, London SE17 3AE).

Melancholic Troglodytes (1999) 'Base-Structure-Superstructure & the Weimar Cinema', No. 2$^{1/2}$, 45-65. (Available form Meltrogs, c/o 56a Infoshop, 56a Crampton Street, Walworth, London SE17 3AE).

Melancholic Troglodytes (2001a) *The Glorious Proletarian Siege of Oxford Street: A Revisionist Misinterpretation of the May Day 2001 Debacle.* (Available form Meltrogs, c/o 56a Infoshop, 56a Crampton Street, Walworth, London SE17 3AE).

Melancholic Troglodytes (2001b) *The Afghan Crisis and the Transformation of Bourgeois Law.* Also available at http://web.onetel.net.uk/~davewalton/recent/Global/afghantwo.html, [accessed on 23rd August 2003].

Melancholic Troglodytes (2001c) *Mindful Thuggery and the Spectacularisation of Drama.* (Available form Meltrogs, c/o 56a Infoshop, 56a Crampton Street, Walworth, London SE17 3AE).

Melancholic Troglodytes (2001d) 'Feminism Reinvigorated?', *Psychology and the Class Struggle*, No. 4, 20-25. (Available form Meltrogs, c/o 56a Infoshop, 56a Crampton Street, Walworth, London SE17 3AE).

Melancholic Troglodytes (2002) *Zapping the Zanj.* Also available at http://www.geocities.com/CapitolHill/Senate/7672/zanj.html, [accessed on 3rd August 2004].

Melancholic Troglodytes (Eds.) (2003a) 'Anti-Capitalism (Special Issue)', *Annual Review of Critical Psychology*, No. 3. (Manchester: Manchester Metropolitan University).

Melancholic Troglodytes (2003b) *Hydro-Jihad: water conflict and the class struggle.* Also available at http://web.onetel.net.uk/~davewalton/recent/Global/hydro-jihad.html, [accessed on 11th October 2003].

Melancholic Troglodytes (2006) *Disrespecting Multifundamentalism.* Available at http://www.metamute.org/?q=en/disrespecting-multifundamentalism, [accessed 5th June 2006].

Mentinis, M. (2006) *Zapatistas: The Chiapas Revolt and What It Means for Radical Politics.* (London and Ann Arbor, MI: Pluto Press).

Merkell, U. (2000) 'The Hidden Social and Political History of the German Football Association (DFB), 1900-50', *Soccer and Society,* Vol. 1, No. 2, 167-186.

Mey, J. (1985) *Whose Language: A Study in Linguistic Pragmatics.* (Amsterdam: John Benjamins).

Midnight Notes Collective (1992) *Midnight Oil: Work, Energy, War, 1973-1992.* (Brooklyn: Autonomedia).

Min, E. (2001) 'Bakhtinian Perspectives for the Study of Intercultural Communication', *Journal of Intercultural Studies,* Vol. 22, No. 1, (April), 5-18.

Mitropoulos, A. (2006) 'Under the beach, the barbed wire', pp. 34-42, in Mute, 2006, *Dis-Integrating Multiculturalism,* Vol. II, No. 2, (London: Mute publishing Ltd).

Moghaddam, F. M. (1997) 'The Haji-Baba of Georgetown', pp. 191-201, in Michael Harris Bond (Ed.), *Working at the Interface of Cultures: Eighteen Lives in Social Science.* (London: Routledge).

Moorish Orthodox Radio Crusade Collective (1992) *Radio Sermonettes.* (New York City: The Libertarian Book Club).

Morris, P. (Ed.) (1994) *The Bakhtin Reader: selected writings of Bakhtin, Medvedev, Voloshinov.* (London, NY, Melbourne, Auckland: Edward Arnold).

Morrow, R. A. and **Brown, D. D.** (1994) 'Deconstructing the conventional discourse of methodology: quantitative versus qualitative methods', pp. 199-225, in *Critical Theory and Methodology.* (London: Sage).

Morson, G. (1994) *Narrative and freedom: The shadows of time.* (New Haven: Yale University Press).

Morss, J. R. (1996) *Growing Critical: Alternatives to developmental psychology.* (London and New York: Routledge).

Morton, B. X. (2003) 'Swing Time for Hitler', *The Nation,* September 15. Also available at http://web.isp.cz/jcrane/Swing.html, [accessed 21st July 2004].

Murasov, J. (2001) *The Body in the Sphere of Literacy: Bakhtin, Artaud and Post-Soviet Performance Art.* Available at http://www.artmargins.com/content/feature/murasov.html, [accessed on 1st October 2001].

Mute (2005) *Precarious Reader,* Vol. II, No. 0. (London: Mute publishing Ltd). Also available from www.metamte.org website.

Mute (2006) *Dis-Integrating Multiculturalism,* Vol. II, No. 2, (London: Mute publishing Ltd). Also available from www.metamte.org website.

Nader, L. (1993) 'Paradigm busting and vertical linkage', *Contemporary Sociology,* Vol. 33, 6-7.

Nardi, B. (1996) *Context and Consciousness: Activity theory and human-computer interaction.* (Cambridge, MA: MIT Press).

Nauright, J. (1999) 'Bhola Lethu: Football in Urban South Africa', in G. Armstrong and R.

Giulianotti (Eds.), *Football Cultures and Identities.* (London: Macmillan Press Ltd).

Nead, L. (1997) 'From alleys to courts: Obscenity and the mapping of mid-Victorian London', *New Formations,* No. 37, 33- 46.

Negri, T. (1988) *Revolution Retrieved: Selected Writings on Marx, Keynes, Capitalist Crisis and New Social Subjects 1967-83.* (London: Red Notes).

Negri, T. (1989) *The Politics of Subversion: A Manifesto for the Twenty-First Century.* (Cambridge: Polity Press).

Negri, T. (1992) 'Interpretation of the Class Situation Today: Methodological Aspects' in W. Bonefeld, R. Gunn and K. Psychopedis (Eds.), *Open Marxism,* Vol. 2, 69-105.

Negrin, L. (1993) 'On the Museum's Ruins: A Critical Approach', *Theory, Culture and Society,* Vol. 10, 97-125. (London, Newbury Park and New Delhi: Sage).

Newman, F. and Holzman, L. (1993a) *Lev Vygotsky: revolutionary scientist.* (London and New York: Routledge).

Newman, F. and Holzman, L. (1993b) *Don't Explain: A Study of Social Therapy as a Vygotskian-Wittgensteinian Synthesis.* Manuscript submitted for publication.

Nicholl, T. (1998) *Vygotsky.* Also available at http://www.massey.ac.nz/~alock/virtual/trishvyg.htm, [accessed on 19th August 2004].

Neilson, B. and Rossiter, N. (2006) 'Towards a Political Anthropology of New Institutional Forms', *ephemera: theory & politics in organization,* Vol. 6, No. 4, 393-410. Available at www.ephemeraweb.org, [accessed on 14th August 2007].

Nietzsche, F. (1872/1994) *The Birth of Tragedy: Out of the Spirit of Music.* (London, New York, Victoria, Toronto: Penguin).

Nietzsche, F. (1883/1969) *Thus Spoke Zarathustra.* (London, New York, Victoria, Toronto: Penguin).

Nikander, P. (1995) 'The return to the text: the critical potential of discursive social psychology', *Nordiske Ukkast,* Vol. 2, 3-15.

Nissen, M., Axel, E. and Jensen, T. B. (1999) 'The Abstract Zone of Proximal Conditions', *Theory & Psychology,* Vol. 9, No. 3, 417-426.

Nogawa, H. and Maeda, H. (1999) 'The Japanese Dream: Soccer Culture Towards the New Millennium', pp. 223-233, in G. Armstrong and R. Giulianotti (Eds.), *Football Culture and Identities.* (London: Macmillan Press Ltd).

Nyikos, M. and Hashimoto, R. (1997) 'Constructivist Theory Applied to Collaborative Learning in Teacher Education: In Search of ZPD', *The Modern Language Journal,* Vol. 81, No. 4. Special Issue: Interaction, Collaboration, and Cooperation: Learning Languages and Preparing Language Teachers (Winter), 506-517.

Olson, D. R. (1995) 'Writing and the mind', pp. 95-123, in J. V. Wertsch, P. del Rio, and A. Alvarez (Eds.), *Sociocultural studies of mind.* (Cambridge, New York, Melbourne: Cambridge University Press).

Osherow, N. (1981) 'Making sense of the nonsensical: An analysis of Jonestown', chapter 6. In E. Aronson (Ed.), *Readings about the Social Animal.* (San Francisco and Oxford: W. H. Freeman and Company).

Palinorc, F. (2003) 'Review Essay: Changing the World!', pp. 182-194, *Annual Review of Critical Psychology,* No. 3. (Manchester: Manchester Metropolitan University).

Pancer, S. M. (1997) 'Social Psychology: The Crisis Continues', pp. 150-165, in D. Fox and I. Prilleltensky (Eds.), *Critical Psychology: An Introduction.* (London, Thousand Oaks, New

Delhi: Sage Publications).

Pannekoek, A. (1920) 'The New Blanquism'. Originally appeared in *Der Kommunist* (Bremen), No. 27, 1920. Also available at http://www.geocities.com/CapitolHill/Lobby/2379/tnb.htm, [accessed on 16th August 2007].

Pannekoek, A. (1933) 'Destruction as a means of struggle'. First published in *Persdienst van de Groep van Internationale Communisten* 1933, No. 7. Available at http://www.geocities.com/~johngray/destruct.htm, [accessed on 8th May 2004].

Pannekoek, A. (1944-47) *Workers' Councils*. (London: Echanges et Mouvement).

Pannekoek, A. (1952) 'Letter on Workers' Councils'. Originally appeared at *Kurasje Council Communist Archive*. Also available at http://www.marxists.org/archive/pannekoe/works/1952-letter.htm, [accessed on 7th May 2004].

Parker, I. (1992) 'Discovering discourses, tackling texts', pp. 3-22, in *Discourse Dynamics: Critical Analysis for Social and Individual Psychology*. (London: Routledge).

Parker, I. (2005) *Qualitative Research: Introducing Radical Research*. (Buckingham: Open University Press).

Parker, I. (2007) *Revolution in Psychology: Alienation to Emancipation*. (London, Ann Arbor, MI: Pluto).

Parker, I. and Burman, E. (1993) 'Against Discursive Imperialism, Empiricism and Constructionism: Thirty two problems with discourse analysis', in E. Burman and I. Parker (Eds.), *Discourse Analytic Research: Repertoires and Readings of Texts in Action*. (London and New York: Routledge). Also available at www.discourseunit.com.

Parker, I. and Spears, R. (1996) *Psychology and Society: Radical Theory and Practice*. (London, Chicago, IL: Pluto Press).

Parker, I. and the Bolton Discourse Network (1999) *Critical Textwork: An Introduction to varieties of Discourse and Analysis*. (Buckingham: Open University Press).

Parrington, J. (1997) 'In perspective: Valentin Voloshinov', *International Socialism*, Vol. 75, 117-150.

Partington, J. S. (2003) 'H. G. Wells's eugenic thinking of the 1930s and 1940s', *Utopian Studies*, (Winter), Vol. 4, No. 1, 74-83.

Pea, R. D. (1993) 'Practices of distributed intelligence and deigns for education', in G. Salomon (Ed.), *Distributed Cognitions: psychological and educational considerations*. (Cambridge: Cambridge University Press).

Pea, R. D. (1994) 'Seeing what we build together: Distributed multimedia learning environments for transformative communications', *The Journal of Learning Sciences*, Vol. 3, No. 3, 285-299.

Pechey, G. (1989) 'On the borders of Bakhtin: dialogisation, decolonisation', pp 39-67, in K. Hirschkop and D. Shepherd (Eds.), *Bakhtin and Cultural Theory*. (Manchester: Manchester University Press).

Peck, J. and Tickell, A. (2002) 'Neoliberalizing Space', *Antipode*, Vol. 34, No. 3, 380-404.

Perlman, F. (1983) *Against His-story, Against Leviathan!* (Detroit: Black and Red).

Piatelli, D. and Leckenby, D. (2003) *Sandra Harding*. Also available at http://www.bc.edu/schools/cas/sociology/vss/harding/, [accessed on 9th August 2004].

Pines, M. (2002) 'The Coherency of Group Analysis', *Group Analysis*, Vol. 35, No. 1, 13-26.

Poddiakov, A. N. (2001) 'Counteraction as a Crucial Factor of Learning, Education and

Development: Opposition to Help', *Forum: Qualitative Social Research*, Vol. 2, No. 3, (September), 1-14.

Poll Tax Riot: 10 hours that shook Trafalgar Square. (1990) (Available from Acab Press, BM 8884, London WC1N 3XX).

Popovic, A. (1999) *The Revolt of African Slaves in Iraq in the 3rd/9th Century.* (Princeton: Markus Wiener Publishers).

Rappaport, J. (1984) 'Studies in empowerment: Introduction to the issue', *Prevention in Human Services*, No. 5, 1-7.

Ratner, C. (1971) 'Principles of Dialectical Psychology', *Telos*, No. 9, (Fall), 83-109.

Ratner, C. (1991) *Vygotsky's Sociohistorical Psychology and its Contemporary Applications.* (New York and London: Plenum Press).

Ratner, C. (1994) 'The Unconscious: A Perspective from Sociohistorical Psychology', *Journal of Mind and Behavior*, No. 15, 323-342.

Ratner, C. (1997) 'In Defense of Activity Theory', *Culture and Psychology*, Vol. 3, 211-223. Available at http://www.humboldt1.com/~cr2/reply.htm, [accessed on 2 April 2004].

Ratner, C. (1999) 'Three Approaches to Cultural Psychology: A Critique', *Cultural Dynamics*, No. 11, 7-31.

Ratner, C. (2000) 'A cultural-psychological analysis of emotions', *Culture and Psychology*, Vol. 6, No. 1, 5-39.

Ravenscroft, N. and **Matteucci, X.** (2003) 'The Festival as Carnivalesque: Social Governance and Control at Pamplona's San Fermin Fiesta', *Tourism, Culture & Communication*, Vol. 4, 1-15.

Rawick, G. (1969) 'Working Class Self-activity', *Radical America*, Vol. 3, No. 2.

Rediker, M. (2004) *Villains of All Nations: Atlantic Pirates in the Golden Age.* (London and New York: Verso).

Reflections on May Day 2000. (2000) 'Churchill, the Cenotaph and May Day 2000', pp. 10-13. (One-off magazine available form PO Box 2474, London N8 0HW).

Reicher, S. (1996) '*The battle of Westminster.* Developing the social identity model of crowd behaviour in order to explain the initiation and development of collective conflict', *European Journal of Social Psychology*, Vol. 26, 115-134.

Reicher, S. (2001) 'The Psychology of Crowd Dynamics', pp. 182-208, in M. A. Hogg and S. Tindale (Eds.), *Blackwell Handbook of Social Psychology: Group Processes* (Oxford: Blackwell).

Reicher, S. and **Potter, J.** (1985) 'Psychology Theory as Intergroup Perspective: A Comparative analysis of *Scientific* and *Lay* Accounts of Crowd Events', *Human Relations*, Vol. 38, No. 2, 167-189.

Rejali, D. M. (1994) *Torture and Modernity: Self, Society, and State in Modern Iran.* (Boulder, San Francisco, Oxford: Westview).

Riegel, K. F. (1976) 'The dialectics of human development', *American Psychologists*, No. 31, 689-700.

Riesel, R. (1969) 'Preliminaries on the Councils and Councilist Organization', pp. 270-282, in K. Knabb (Ed.), *Situationist International Anthology*, (Berkley: Bureau of Public Secrets, 1981).

Rey, F. L. G. (1999) 'Personality, Subject and Human Development: The Subjective Character of Human Activity', 253-275, in S. Chaiklin *et al.* (Eds.), *Activity Theory and Social Practice.* (Aarhus, Oxford, Oakville: Aarhus University Press).

Roberts, J. M. (2004) 'From Populist to Political Dialogue in the Public Sphere: A Bakhtinian approach to understanding a place for radical utterances in London, 1684-1812', *Cultural Studies*, Vol. 18, No. 6, 884-910.

Rogoff, B. (1995) 'Observing sociocultural activity on three planes: Participatory appropriation, guided participation, apprenticeship', pp. 139-164, in A. Alvarez, P. del Rio and J. V. Wertsch (Eds.), *Perspectives on sociocultural research.* (Cambridge: Cambridge University Press).

Rogoff, B., Radziszewska, B. and Masiello, T. (1995) 'Analysis of developmental processes in sociocultural activity', pp. 125-149, in L. Martin, K. Nelson and E. Tobach (Eds.), *Sociocultural Psychology: Theory and practice of doing and knowing.* (Cambridge, New York, Melbourne: Cambridge University Press).

Rose, N. (1985) *The Psychological Complex: Psychology, Politics and Society in England 1869-1939.* (London, Boston, Melbourne and Henley: Routledge & Kegan Paul).

Rose, S., Kamin, L. J. and Lewontin, R. C. (1984) *Not in Our Genes: Biology, Ideology and Human Nature.* (Pelican Books).

Rosenberg, S. W. (1988) 'The Structure of Political Thinking', *American Journal of Political Science*, Vol. 32, No. 3, (August), 539-566.

Rosenberg, W. G. and Koenker, D. P. (1987) 'The Limits of Formal Protest: Worker Activism and Social Polarization in Petrograd and Moscow, March to October, 1917', *The American Historical Review,* Vol. 92, No. 2, (April), 296-326.

Rosenfeld, M. J. (1997) 'Celebration, politics, selective looting and riots: a micro level study of the Bulls riot of 1992 in Chicago', *Social Problems*, Vol. 44, No. 4, (November), 483-492.

Ross, E. A. (1919) 'The Crowd', pp. 43-62, in *Social Psychology: An outline and source book.* (New York: Macmillan Co.). Also available at http://spartan.ac.brocku.ca/~lward/Ross/Ross_1919/Ross_1919_03.html, [accessed on 18th August 2004].

Roth, M. (1997) 'Carnival, creativity, and the sublimation of drunkenness', *Mosaic (Winnipeg),* Vol. 30, No. 2, (June), 1-18.

Rothbart, R. (1980) 'The Limits of Mattick's Economics: Economic Law and Class Struggle'. Originally appeared in *Solidarity for Social Revolution,* 11 (January - February 1980): supplement 1-8; see: 1, 2, 4, 7n2. Also available at http://www.geocities.com/cordobakaf/rothbart.html, [accessed on 14th May 2004].

Routledge, P. (2004) 'Convergence of Commons: Process Geographies of People's Global Action', *The Commoner,* No. 8. Also available at http://www.thecommoner.org.uk/08routledge.pdf, [accessed on 6th August 2004].

Rubin, I. I. (1982) *Essays on Marx's Theory of Value.* (Montreal: Black Rose Books).

Ryan, M. (1989) *Marxism and Deconstruction: A Critical Articulation,* (Baltimore and London: The John Hopkins University Press).

Ryder, M. (1998) *Spinning Webs of Significance: Considering anonymous communities in activity systems.* Originally presented at the International society for Cultural Research and Activity Theory in Aarhus, Denmark, June 7-11. Also available at http://carbon.cudenver.edu/~mryder/iscrat_99.html, [accessed 15th September 2004].

Saburi, H. (1996) Varzesh Dar Islām (Farsi), [Sport in Islam]. (Qom: Office for Islamic Propagation, Seminary of Qom, Publication Centre).

Sadr, H. R. (2001) Rouzi, rouzegāri footbāl (Farsi) [Once upon a time football], (Tehran: Avizhe Publishing).

Sandywell, B. (1998) 'The shock of the old: Mikhail Bakhtin's contributions to the theory of time and alterity', pp. 196-213, in Bell and Gardiner (Eds.), *Bakhtin and the Human Sciences*. (London: Sage Publications).

Sans Titre (2002) *Open Letter to the People's Global Action*. Available at http://www.pgaconference.org/_postconference_/pp_sanstitre.htm, [accessed on 6th June 2004].

Saussure, Ferdinand de (1959) *Course in general linguistics*. (New York: Philosophical Library).

Sawchuk, P. H., Gawron, Z. and Taylor J. (2002) 'E-Learning and Union Mobilization', *Journal of Distance Education*, Vol. 17, No. 3, 80-96.

Schmitt, R. L. and Leonard II, W. M. (1986) 'Immortalizing the Self through Sport', *American Journal of Sociology*, Volume 91, No. 5, (March), 1088-1111.

Schneider, M. (1974) 'Neurosis and Class Struggle: Toward a Pathology of Capitalist Commodity Production', *New German Critique*, Vol. 0, No. 3, 109-126.

Scribner, S. (1984) 'Studying working intelligence', pp. 9-40, in B. Rogoff and J. Lave (Eds.), *Everyday cognition: Its development in social context*. (Cambridge: Cambridge University Press).

Scribner, S. (1985) 'Vygotsky's uses of history', pp. 119-145, in J. Wertsch (Ed.), *Culture, communication and cognition: Vygotskian perspectives*. (Cambridge: Cambridge University Press).

Seeger, F. (2001) 'The Complementarity of Theory and Praxis in the Cultural-Historical Approach: From Self-Application to Self-Regulation', pp. 35-55, in S. Chaiklin (Ed.), *The Theory and Practice of Cultural-Historical Psychology*. (Aarhus, Oxford, Oakville: Aarhus University Press).

Sellman, J. C. (1999) 'Social movements and symbolism of public demonstrations: the 1874 Women's Crusade and German resistance in Richmond, Indiana', *Journal of Social History*, Vol. 32, No. 3, (spring), 557- 588.

Sève, L. (1978) *Man in Marxist Theory and the Psychology of Personality*. (Hassocks: The Harvest Press).

Shakespeare, W. (1967) *Merchant of Venice*. (Harmondsworth, Middlesex: Penguin Books).

Shakespeare, W. (1968) *Tempest*. (Harmondsworth, Middlesex: Penguin Books).

Shakespeare, W. (1988) *Othello*. (Harmondsworth, Middlesex: Penguin Books).

Shakespeare, W. (1989) *Hamlet: Prince of Denmark*. (Cambridge, New York, Melbourne: Cambridge University Press).

Sherzer, J. (1987) 'A discourse-centered approach to language and culture', *American Anthropologist*, No. 89, 295-309.

Shipway, M. (1987a) 'Council Communism', pp. 104-126, in M. Rubel and J. Crump (Eds.), *Non-Market Socialism in the Nineteenth and Twentieth Centuries*. (London: Macmillan Press).

Shipway, M. (1987b) 'Situationism', pp. 151-172, in M. Rubel and J. Crump (Eds.), *Non-Market Socialism in the Nineteenth and Twentieth Centuries*. (London: Macmillan Press).

Shotter, J. (1993) *Conversational realities: Constructing life through language*. (London: Sage).

Shotter, J. (1995) *Talk of Saying, Showing, Gesturing, and Feeling in Wittgenstein and Vygotsky*. Department of Communication, University of New Hampshire, Durham. Available at http://www.massey.ac.nz/~alock/virtual/wittvyg.htm, [accessed on 18th August 2004].

Shotter, J. (1996) *Vico, Wittgenstein, and Bakhtin: 'Practical trust' in Dialogical Communities*. Draft paper for the conference: democracy and Trust, Georgetown University, Nov 7-9. Also available at http://www.massey.ac.nz/~alock/virtual/js.htm, [accessed on 19th august 2004].

Shotter, J. (1997) *The Social Construction of Our 'Inner' Lives.* To appear in the *Journal of Constructivist Psychology.* Also available at http://www.massey.ac.nz/~alock/virtual/inner.htm, [accessed on 26th October 2000].

Shotter, J. (in press) *Life inside the dialogically structured mind: Bakhtin's and Vološinov's account of the mind as out in the world between us.* To appear in J. Rowan and M. Cooper (Eds.), *The Plural Self: Polypsychic Perspectives* (London: Sage Publications). Also available at www.massey.ac.nz/~ALock/virtual/rowan.htm, [accessed on 5th August 2001].

Shotter, J. and Billig, M. (1998) 'A Bakhtinian Psychology: from Out of the Heads of Individuals and into the Dialogues Between Them', pp. 13-29, in M. Bell and M. Gardiner (Eds.), *Bakhtin and the Human Sciences: No Last Words.* (London: Sage Publications).

Shukaitis, S. and Graeber, D. (Eds.) (2007) *Constituent Imagination: Militant Investigations, Collective Theorization.* (Oakland, Edinburgh, West Virginia: AK Press).

Sigel, L. E. (1993) 'The centrality of a distancing model for the development of representational competence', pp. 141-160, in R. R. Cocking and K. A. Renninger (Eds.), *The Development and Meaning of Psychological Distances.* (Hillsdale, NJ: Lawrence Erlbaum).

Sina (1999) *The most comprehensive history of Iranian soccer.* Available at http://www.iransportspress.com/main/frontpg/history.htm, [accessed on 18th August 2004].

Singleton, A. (2003) *Saddam's Private Army: How Rajavi Changed Iran's Mojahedin from Armed Revolutionaries to an Armed Cult.* (UK: Iran-Interlink).

Slater, H. (2001) 'Occasional Documents: Toward Situation', *Variant*, 14, (winter). Available at http://www.variant.randomstate.org/14texts/Variant_Forum.html, [accessed on 25th June 2007].

Slater, H. (2004) 'Proposteral Organisations', *Mute: Culture and Politics after the Net*, No. 28, 88-90.

Sohn-Rethel, A. (1978) *Intellectual and Manual Labor: A Critique of Epistemology.* (London and Basingstoke: Macmillan Press Ltd.).

Sohn-Rethel, A. (1987) *The Economy and Class Structure of German Fascism.* (London: Free Association Books).

Solomon, M. (1979) *Marxism and Art: Essays Classic and Contemporary.* (Harvester Press).

Sontag, S. (1990) *Aids and its metaphors.* (New York: Farrar, Straus & Giroux).

Speaker, Jr., R. B. (1999) *Reflections on Vygotsky.* Also available at http://ed.uno.edu/Faculty/RSpeaker/Epistemologies/Vygotsky.html, [accessed on 3rd March 2004].

Speer, P. W. (2000) 'Intrapersonal and Interactional Empowerment: Implication for Theory', *Journal of Community Psychology*, Vol. 28, No. 1, 51-61.

Spender, D. (1980) *Man Made Language.* (London: Routledge and Kegan Paul).

Stables, A. (2003) *Institutions as Inscriptions; Inscription as Empowerment: developing voices in discursive space.* Paper presented at the International Conference of Critical Psychology. (Bath: University of Bath).

Stalder, F. (2003) *One-size-doesn't-fit-all. Particulars of the Volunteer Open Source Development Methodology.* Available at http://openflows.org/article.pl?sid=03/10/25/172242, [accessed on 2nd May 2004].

Stallybrass, P. (1990) 'Marx and Heterogeneity: Thinking the Lumpenproletariat', *Representations,* Vol. 0, No. 31. Special Issue: The Margins of Identity in Nineteenth-Century England, (summer), 69-95.

Stallybrass P. and **White, A.** (1986) *The Politics and Poetics of Transgression.* (New York: Cornell University Press).

Stam, R. (1992) *Subversive Pleasures: Bakhtin, Cultural Criticism, and Film.* (Baltimore and London: The John Hopkins University Press).

Steinem, G. (1995) *Outrageous Acts and Everyday Rebellions.* (New York: Owl Books).

Stetsenko, A. P. (1999) 'Social Interaction, Cultural Tools and the Zone of Proximal Development: In Search of a Synthesis', pp. 235-252, in S. Chaiklin *et al.* (Eds.), *Activity Theory and Social Practice.* (Aarhus, Oxford, Oakville: Aarhus University Press).

Stetsenko, A. and **Arievitch, I. M.** (2004) 'The Self in Cultural-Historical Activity Theory: Reclaiming the Unity of Social and Individual Dimensions of Human Development', *Theory & Psychology,* Vol. 14, No. 4, 475-503.

Stewart, S. (1986) 'Shouts on the Street; Bakhtin's Anti-Linguistics', pp. 41-57, in, G. S. Morson (Ed.), *Bakhtin: Essays and Dialogues on His Work.* (Chicago: The University of Chicago Press).

Stokes, J. (1994) 'The unconscious at work in groups and teams: contributions from the work of Wilfred Bion', in A. Obholzer and V. Roberts (Eds.), *The unconscious at work.* (London: Routledge).

Stone, C. A. (1998) 'The Metaphor of Scaffolding: Its Utility for the Field of Learning Disabilities', *Journal of Learning Disabilities,* Vol. 31, No. 4, (July), 334-364.

Stott, C. and **Drury, J.** (2000) 'Crowds, context and identity: Dynamic categorization processes in the *poll tax riot*', *Human Relations,* Vol. 53, No. 2, 247-273.

Strickland, G. and **Holzman, L.** (1989) 'Developing Poor and Minority Children as Leaders with the Barbara Taylor School Educational Model', *Journal of Negro Education,* Vol. 58, No. 3, Shaping the Urban Future: People and Places, Problems and Potentials, 383-398.

Subbotsky, E. (1996) 'Vygotsky's distinction between lower and higher mental functions and recent studies on infant cognitive development', *Journal of Russian and East European Psychology,* Vol. 34. No. 2, 61–66.

Sullivan, L. L. (2005) 'Activism, Affect and Abuse: Emotional Contexts and Consequences of the ESF 2004 Organising Process', *ephemera: theory & politics in organization,* Vol. 5, No. 2, 344-369. Available at www.ephemeraweb.org, [accessed on 14th August 2005].

Summers-Effler, E. (2002) 'The Micro Potential for Social Change: Emotions, Consciousness, and Social Movement Formation', *Sociological Theory,* Vol. 20, No. 1, (March), 41-60.

Super, C. M. and **Harkness, S.** (1986) 'The developmental niche: A conceptualization at the interface of child and culture', *International Journal of Behavioral Development,* No. 9, 545-569.

Taussig, M. T. (1980) *The Devil and Commodity Fetishism in South America.* (Chapel Hill: The University of North California Press).

The London Mayday Collective (2001) *Mayday Monopoly: Game Guide.* (London). Also available at www.maydaymonopoly.net.

Thompson, E. P. (1975) *Whigs and Hunters: The Origin of the Black Act.* (London: Allen Lane).

Thompson, S. and **Hoggett, P.** (2001) 'The emotional dynamics of deliberative democracy', *Policy & Politics,* Vol. 29, No. 3, 351-364.

Thrall (2001) *Anarchism as a Scapegoat of the 21ˢᵗ century: violence, anarchism and anti-globalisation protests.* At www.thrall.orcon.net.nz/21scapegoat.html, [accessed on 14ᵗʰ July 2005].

Tilly, C. (2003) *The Politics of Collective Violence.* (Cambridge: Cambridge University Press).

Tilly, C. (2004) *Social Movements, 1978-2004.* (Boulder, London: Paradigm Press).

Tokarev, S. (1989) *History of Religion.* (Moscow: Progress Publishers).

Tolman, C. W. (1994) *Psychology, Society, and Subjectivity: An Introduction to German Critical Psychology.* (London and New York: Routledge).

Tolman, C. W. (2001) 'The Origins of Activity as a Category in the Philosophies of Kant, Fichte, Hegel and Marx', pp. 84-92, in S. Chaiklin (Ed.), *The Theory and Practice of Cultural-Historical Psychology.* (Aarhus: Aarhus University Press).

Tomba, M. (2007) 'Differentials of Surplus-Value in the Contemporary Forms of Exploitation', *The Commoner,* No. 12, (spring/summer). Available at http://www.commoner.org.uk/12tomba.pdf, [accessed on 18ᵗʰ August 2007].

Tompsett, F. (2000) '1606 and all that: the Virginian conquest', *Race & Class,* Vol. 41, 29-41.

Tormey, S. (2005) 'From Utopian Worlds to Utopian Spaces: Reflections on the Contemporary Radical Imaginary and the Social Forum Process', *ephemera: theory & politics in organization,* Vol. 5, No. 2, 394-408. Available at www.ephemeraweb.org, [accessed on 14ᵗʰ August 2005].

Traverso, E. (2002) 'Bohemia, Exile and Revolution: Notes on Marx, Benjamin and Trotsky', *Historical Materialism,* Vol. 10, No. 1, 123-153.

Tronti, M (1964) 'Lenin in England', now in Red Notes (Eds.), *Working Class Autonomy and the Crisis.* (London: Red Notes/CSE Books).

Trotter, A. (1995) 'Introduction', pp. 7-18, in J. Camatte, *This world We Must Leave and Other Essays.* (New York: Autonomedia).

Trotsky, L. (1947) *Stalin.* (London: Hollis & Carter).

Tudge, J. R. H. (1992) 'Processes and consequences of peer collaboration: A Vygotskian analysis', *Child Development,* Vol. 63, 1364-1379.

Turner, T. (1999) 'Activism, Activity and the New Culture Politics: An Anthropological Perspective', pp. 114-135, in S. Chaiklin *et al.* (Eds.), *Activity Theory and Social Practice.* (Aarhus, Oxford, Oakville: Aarhus University Press).

Tzuriel, D. and **Kaufman, R.** (1999) 'Mediated Learning and Cognitive Modifiability: Dynamic Assessment of Young Ethiopian Immigrant Children to Israel', *Journal of Cross-Cultural Psychology,* Vol. 30, No. 3, (May), 359-380.

Useem, B. (1985) 'Disorganization and the New Mexico Prison Riot of 1980', *American Sociological Review,* Vol. 50, No. 5, (October), 677-688.

Valsiner, J. (1994) 'Vygotskian dynamics of development: Commentary', *Human Development,* No. 37, 366-369.

van der Veer, R (2001) 'The Idea of Units of Analysis: Vygotsky's Contribution', pp. 93-106, in S. Chaiklin (Ed.), *The Theory and Practice of Cultural-Historical Psychology.* (Aarhus: Aarhus University Press).

van der Linden, M. (1997) 'Socialisme ou Barbarie: A French Revolutionary Group (1949-65)', *Left History,* 5.1. Also available at http://www.geocities.com/CapitolHill/Lobby/2379/s_ou_b.htm, [accessed on 19ᵗʰ September 2004].

van der Veer, R. and Valsiner, J. (1994a) *Understanding Vygotsky: A Quest for Synthesis*. (Oxford, UK and Cambridge, USA: Blackwell).

van der Veer, R. and Valsiner, J. (1994b) *The Vygotsky Reader*. (Oxford: Blackwell).

van Elteren, M. (1992) 'Karl Korsch and Lewinian social psychology: failure of a project', *History of Human Sciences*, Vol. 5, No. 2, 33-61.

van Geert, P. (1994) 'Vygotskian dynamics of development', *Human Development*, No. 37, 346-365.

van Geert, P. (1998) 'A dynamic systems model of basic development mechanisms: Piaget, Vygotsky and beyond', *Psychological Review*, Vol. 105, No. 4, 634-677.

Vercellone, C. (2005) *From Formal Subsumption to 'General Intellect': Elements for a Marxist Reading of the Thesis of Cognitive Capitalism*. Paper presented at the 'Towards a Cosmopolitan Marxism' conference organised jointly by Historical Materialism, Socialist Register and the Isaac and Tamara Deutscher Memorial Prize Committee. Held between 4-6 November 2005 at the University of London, School of Oriental and African Studies (SOAS), London, UK.

Veresov, N. N. (1996) *The Problem of Consciousness in Vygotsky's Approach*. At http://www.marxists.org/subject/psychology/works/veresov/consciousness.htm, [accessed on 8th August 2003].

Vološinov, V. N. (1973) *Marxism and the Philosophy of Language*. (Cambridge, Massachusetts and London: England: Harvard University).

Vološinov, V. N. (1987) *Freudianism: a Critical Sketch*. (Bloomington, IN, and Indianapolis: Indiana University Press).

Vygotsky, L. S. (1927/1987) *The Historical Meaning of the Crisis in Psychology: A Methodological Investigation*, chapter 7. Also available from http://www.marxists.org/archive/vygotsky/works/crisis/index.htm, [accessed on 19th August 2005].

Vygotsky, L. S. (1930/1971) *The psychology of art*. (Cambridge, MA: MIT Press).

Vygotsky, L. S. (1978) *Mind in Society: The Development of Higher Psychological Processes*. (Cambridge, Massachusetts, London, England: Harvard University Press).

Vygotsky, L. S. (1987a) *The collected works of L. S. Vygotsky, Vol. 1*. (New York: Plenum).

Vygotsky, L. S. (1987b) *Thought and Language*. Translation A. Kozulin. (Cambridge, MA: MIT Press).

Vygotsky, L. S. (1987c) 'Thinking and Speech', in R. Rieber and A. Carton (Eds.), *The Collected Works of L. S. Vygotsky. Volume I: Problems of General Psychology*. Including the volume 'Thinking and Speech', translation N. Minick, pp. 43–287, (New York: Plenum Press).

Vygotsky, L. S. (1989) 'Concrete human psychology', *Soviet Psychology*, Vol. 27, No. 2, 53-77.

Vygotsky, L. S. (1997a) 'The socialist alteration of man', pp. 175-184, in R. W. Rieber and J. Wollock (Eds.), *The Collected Works of L. S. Vygotsky: Volume 3*. (New York and London: Plenum Press).

Vygotsky, L. S. (1997b) 'Thought in schizophrenia', pp. 313-326, in R. W. Rieber and J. Wollock (Eds.), *The Collected Works of L. S. Vygotsky: Volume 3*. (New York and London: Plenum Press).

Vygotsky, L. S. (1997c) 'Fascism in psychoneurology', pp. 327-337, in R. W. Rieber and J. Wollock (Eds.), *The Collected Works of L. S. Vygotsky: Volume 3*. (New York and London: Plenum Press).

Vygotsky, L. S. (1999) 'Consciousness as a problem in the psychology of behaviour', pp. 251-281, in N. Veresov, *Undiscovered Vygotsky: Etudes on the pre-history of cultural-historical psychology (European Studies in the History of Science and Ideas. Vol. 8)*. (Peter Lang Publishing).

Wall, A. and **Thomson, C.** (1993) 'Cleaning Up Bakhtin's Carnival Act', *Diacritics,* Vol. 23, No. 2, 47-70.

Wardekker, W. L. (n.d.) *Critical and Vygotskian theories of education: a comparison.* Available at http://psych.hanover.edu/vygotsky/wardekkr.html, [accessed on 18th August 2004].

Waterman, P. (1990) 'Communicating Labour Internationalism: A Review of Relevant Literature and Resources', *Communications: European Journal of Communications,* Vol. 15, Nos. 1 and 2, 85-103.

Wells, G. (1999) 'The Zone of Proximal Development and its Implications for Learning and Teaching', chapter 10, in *Dialogic inquiry: Towards a sociocultural practice and theory of education.* (New York: Cambridge University Press).

Wells, G. (2002) 'The Role of Dialogue in Activity Theory', *Mind, Culture, and Activity,* Vol. 9, No. 1, 43-66.

Wells, H. G. (1905/2003) *The Modern Utopia.* Also available at http://www.marxists.org/reference/archive/hgwells/1905/modern-utopia/, [accessed on 19th August 2005].

Wells, H. G. (1928) *The Open Conspiracy: Blue Prints for a World Revolution.* Available at http://www.mega.nu:8080/ampp/hgwells/hg_cont.htm, [accessed on 12th August 2005].

Wells, H. G. (1931/2002) *What Are We To Do With Our Lives?* Also available at http://gutenberg.net.au/ebooks02/0201081h.html, [accessed on 7th August 2004].

Wells, H. G. (1933/2002) *The Shape of Things to Come: The Ultimate Revolution.* (House of Stratus).

Wells, H. G. (1939/2001) *The Holy Terror.* (House of Stratus).

Wertsch, J. V. (1980) *Semiotic mechanisms in joining cognitive activity.* Paper presented at the US-USSR Conference on the Theory of Activity. (Moscow: Institute of Psychology, USSR Academy of Sciences).

Wertsch, J. V. (1991) *Voices of the Mind: A Sociocultural Approach to Mediated Action.* (London, Sydney, Singapore: Harvester Wheatsheaf).

Wertsch, J. V., del Rio, P. and **Alvarez, A.** (1995) 'Sociocultural studies: history, action, and mediation', pp. 1-34, in J. V. Wertsch, P. del Rio, A. Alvarez (Eds.), *Sociocultural studies of mind.* (Cambridge, New York, Melbourne: Cambridge University Press).

Wertsch, J. V., del Rio, P. and **Alvarez, A.** (1995) *Sociocultural studies of mind.* (Cambridge, New York, Melbourne: Cambridge University Press).

Wertsch, J. V. and **Tulviste, P.** (1996) 'L. S. Vygotsky and contemporary developmental psychology', pp. 53-74, in H. Daniels (Ed.) *An Introduction to Vygotsky.* (London and New York: Routledge).

West, C. (2001) 'Play/Therapy: A Vygotskian Perspective', *Journal of Systematic Therapies,* Vol. 20, No. 3, 60-67.

West Essex Zapatista (2005) *Why is organising on a 'Europe-wide' basis such a bad idea?* 17th May 2005. Also available at http://chinabone.lth.bclub.org.uk/~saul/docs/drafts/why_is_organising_europe_bad.txt, [accessed on 20th August 2005].

Whitebook, J. (1998) 'Omnipotence and finitude', *Radical Philosophy*, No. 90, (July/August), 5-8.

Whitman, W. (1855/1986) *Leaves of Grass.* (Harmondsworth, Middlesex: Penguin Books).

Wiegers, Y. (1998) 'Male Bodybuilding: The Social Construction of a Masculine Identity', *Journal of Popular Culture*, Vol. 32, No. 2, (Fall), 147-161.

Wikipedia (2004) *Leo Strauss.* Available at http://en.wikipedia.org/wiki/Leo_Strauss, [accessed on 20th August 2004].

Wildcat (1992) *Outside and Against Unions.* This pamphlet is also available at http://www.geocities.com/CapitolHill/Lobby/3909/oatu/, [accessed on 24th October 2004].

Williams, R. (1973) 'Base and superstructure in Marxist cultural theory', *New Left Review,* No. 82, (Nov-Dec).

Williams, R. (1978) *Marxism and Literature.* (Oxford: Oxford University Press).

Willis, C. (1989) 'Upsetting the public: carnival, hysteria and women's texts', pp. 130-151, in Hirschkop and Shepherd (Eds.), *Bakhtin and cultural theory.* (Manchester: Manchester University Press).

Witheford, N. (1994) 'Autonomist Marxism and the Information Society', *Capital & Class,* No. 52, (Spring), 85-125.

Wolmark, J. (1995) 'Cyborg bodies and problems of representation', pp. 13-20, in E. Burman, A. J. Gordo-Lopez, R. Macauley and I. Parker (Eds.), *Cyberpsychology: Conference, Interventions and Reflections.* (Manchester: Discourse Unit, Manchester Metropolitan University).

Wood, D., Bruner, J., and **Ross, G.** (1976) 'The role of tutoring in problem solving', *Journal of Child Psychology and Child Psychiatry*, Vol. 17, 89-100.

Woofitt, R. (1993) 'Analyzing Account', in N. Gilbert (Ed.), *Researching Social Life.* (London: Sage).

Wright, S. (2002) *Storming Heaven: Class composition and struggle in Italian Autonomist Marxism.* (London, Sterling, Virginia: Pluto Press).

Wright, S. (2005) *A Party of Autonomy?* Also available at http://libcom.org/library/party-autonomy-steve-wright, [accessed on 14th August 2007].

Wright, T. (1875) *A History of Caricature and Grotesque in Literature and Art.* (London: Chatto).

Xenos, N. (2004) *Leo Strauss and the Rhetoric of the War on Terror.* Also available at http://www.logosjournal.com/xenos.htm, [accessed on 20th August 2004].

Zarembka, P. (2002) 'Primitive Accumulation in Marxism, Historical or Trans-historical Separation from Means of Production?', *The Commoner,* Debate 01. Available at http://www.thecommoner.org.uk/debzarembka01.pdf, [accessed on 5th August 2004].

Zarembka, P. (2003) 'Lenin as Economist of Production: A Ricardian Step Backwards', *Science and Society*, Vol. 67, No. 3, 276-302.

Zerzan, J. (1988) *Elements of Refusal.* (Seattle: Left Bank Books).

Zinchenko, P. I. (1983-84) 'The problem of voluntary memory', *Soviet Psychology*, Vol. 22, 55-111.

Zinchenko, V. P. (1985) 'Vygotsky's ideas about units for the analysis of mind', pp. 94-118, in J. V. Wertsch (Ed.), *Culture, communication, and cognition: Vygotskian perspectives.* (New York: Cambridge University Press).

Zinchenko, V. P. (1995) 'Cultural-historical psychology and the psychological theory of activity: retrospect and prospect', pp. 37-55, in J. W. Wertsch, P. del Rio, and A. Alvarez (Eds.), *Sociocultural studies of mind.* (Cambridge, New York, Melbourne: Cambridge University

Press).

Zinchenko, V. P. (2001) 'External and Internal: Another Comment on the Issue', pp. 135-147, in S. Chaiklin (Ed.), *The Theory and Practice of Cultural-Historical Psychology.* (Aarhus, Oxford, Oakville: Aarhus University Press).

Zinn, H. (2003) *A People's History of the United States: 1492-present.* (New York: Perennial Classics).

Žižek, S. (2001) 'Can Lenin Tell Us About Freedom Today?', *Rethinking Marxism*, Vol. 13, No. 2, (Summer). Available at http://www.egs.edu/faculty/zizek/zizek-can-lenin-tell-us-about-freedom-today.html, [accessed on 7th August 2004].

Zwerin, M. (2000) *Swing under the Nazis: Jazz as a Metaphor for Freedom.* (New York: Cooper Square Press).

Zwick, D. and **Andrews, D. L.** (1999) 'The Suburban Soccer Field: Sport and America's Culture of Privilege', pp. 211-222, in G. Armstrong and R. Giulianotti (Eds.), *Football Culture and Identities.* (London: Macmillan Press Ltd).

NEWSPAPERS AND BULLETIN BOARDS

BBC News. (31 March 1990) 'Violence flares in poll tax demonstration'. Available at http://news.bbc.co.uk/onthisday/hi/dates/stories/march/31/newsid_2530000/2530763.stm, [accessed on 18th April 2004].

BBC News. (26 November 1999) 'Online activists plan global protest'. Available at http://news.bbc.co.uk/1/hi/uk/537587.stm, [accessed on 15th July 2007].

Ourmayday website. (2003) 'Mayday 2003'. Available at http://www.riseup.net/ourmayday/mayday/index03.html, [accessed on 29th September 2004].

The Guardian. (3 May 2000) Michael White. 'MPs condemn May demo *thuggery*'. Available at http://www.guardian.co.uk/m2k/article/0,2763,216627,00.html, [accessed on 26th October 2004].

The Guardian. (3 May 2000) Staff and agencies. 'Hague links May Day riots to mayoral race'. Available at http://www.guardian.co.uk/parl/Story/0,2763,216814,00.html, [accessed on 26th October 2004].

The Guardian. (27 May 2000) J. Vidal and N. Hopkins. 'I'm no mastermind, says protester'. Available at http://www.guardian.co.uk/uk_news/story/0,,319042,00.html, [accessed on 26th October 2004].

The Guardian. (8 April 2001) 'Police chiefs will lose jobs if they fail to block May Day anarchy'. Available at http://observer.guardian.co.uk/uk_news/story/0,,470192,00.html, [accessed on 26th October 2004].

The Guardian. (1 May 2001) S. Left, S. Jeffery, J. Perrone and agencies. 'Violence erupts in Central London'. Available at http://www.guardian.co.uk/mayday/story/0,7369,481319,00.html, [accessed on 24th October 2004].

The Guardian. (7 May 2001) 'Why Wombles won't speak to journalists'. Available at http://www.guardian.co.uk/mayday/story/0,7369,486883,00.html, [accessed on 24th October 2004].

The Guardian. (1 May 2002) Sarah Left. 'Nothing to lose but their chains'. Available at http://www.guardian.co.uk/mayday/story/0,7369,708306,00.html, [accessed on 24th October 2004].